The International Law Foundations of Palestinian Nationality

Graduate Institute of International and Development Studies

VOLUME 7

The titles published in this series are listed at the end of this volume.

The International Law Foundations of Palestinian Nationality

A Legal Examination of Nationality in Palestine under Britain's Rule

By

Mutaz M. Qafisheh

MARTINUS NIJHOFF PUBLISHERS

LEIDEN • BOSTON
2008

This book is printed on acid-free paper.

Library of Congress Cataloging-in-Publication Data

Qafisheh, Mutaz M.
The international law foundations of Palestinian nationality : a legal examination of nationality in Palestine under Britain's rule / by Mutaz M. Qafisheh.
p. cm. — (Graduate Institute of International Studies (Series); v. 7)
Includes bibliographical references and index.
ISBN 978-90-04-16984-5 (hardback : alk. paper) 1.
Citizenship—Palestine—History. I. Title. II. Series.

K3224.Q34 2008
342.569408'3—dc22

2008027613

ISSN 1572-5618
ISBN 978 90 04 16984 5

PRINTED IN THE NETHERLANDS

To the memory of my father

CONTENTS

PREFACE

At the sixtieth anniversary of the Palestinians' *nakba* (catastrophe), 2008 turns six decades of Palestine nationality's denial. This denial is in no means theoretical. It affects the life and legal status of each individual who or whose parents or grandparents was once linked to Palestinian nationality before 15 May 1948. The denial takes different forms, depending on the legal status of the individual in the territory where she or he ended up. This book is trying to explain how various statuses of 'Palestinians' and ex-Palestinians were 'legally' made up, back during the British Empire's control over Palestine from December 1917 to May 1948.

My original intention was to conduct a comprehensive study on Palestinian nationality in international law, since Palestine has practically acquired a nationality after the Britain occupation of Jerusalem in December 1917 until the present. I desired to crystallize the initial research that I undertook in the late nineties of the last century on a number of aspects on Palestinian nationality, which was put together in a book, *Nationality and Domicile in Palestine*, published by the International Studies Institute of Birzeit University in 2000. However, after passing the 2005 winter at the League of Nations Archives in Geneva reading first-hand documents, I noticed the need for a work that sets out the international law ground of Palestinian nationality as had been constructed under Britain. I then realized that covering all the legal aspects of Palestinian nationality would lead to multi-volume book and require endless research, and thus decided to confine this study to the British period.

By focusing on the past, this study projects towards the future. At the end of British rule in Palestine, Palestinian nationality had become well established in accordance with both domestic and international law. Hence, the genesis of that nationality lies in this nearly thirty-year period, as the status of Palestinians has never been settled since. Any legal consideration, being academic or legislative policy, relating to the future status of the individuals who once held Palestinian nationality should commence from the point at which the British rule over Palestine was terminated. The book offers a legal basis for the future settlement of the *de facto* statuses of former Palestinians that emerged in the sixty years following the Mandate's termination: Israeli citizens, inhabitants of the occupied Palestinian territory and Palestine refugees. Nationality, as officially formulated under Britain, had created an acquired juridical status that cannot be altered without international law standards.

Throughout the writing process in Switzerland, France, Lebanon and Palestine, a number of friends as well as colleagues and family members have supported me.

I must thank, first and for most, the professors whose advice has shaped the substantive outcome of the book. Vera Gowlland, the supervisor of this work that was originally a Ph.D. thesis prepared at the Geneva Graduate Institute of International Studies, guided me by her sharp international law and relations vision that motivated me since the beginning to the end. Andea Bianchi's particular remarks on the use of case law in such a work tackling the status of individuals have greatly enriched the book's reasoning. Guy Goodwin-Gill of Oxford, as my external supervisor, gave me scientific insights and drew my attention to the relevance of the project to the question of refugees. John Quigley of Ohio State University read the manuscript and provided detailed comments that improved a number of technical aspects of the work. The experience and wisdom of Georges Abi-Saab methodologically directed me, during our brief discussions, to the significance of nationality under British rule.

Other professors' cooperation should be acknowledged. I am indebted to John Strawson of the University of East London for reading an early version of the manuscript, providing useful comments and references, and to Anis F. Kasim, former editor of the *Palestine Yearbook of International Law*, for handing me rare-to-find materials. I similarly admit the help of Amin Dawwas, Ghassan Framand, Sari Hanafi, Roger Heacock, Michael Karayanni, Camille Mansour, Feras Milhem, Abbas Shiblak and Andreas Zimmermann.

My friend Audrey Ryan did an excellent job in reviewing the final manuscript, correcting the English. Claudie Barrat, Lance Bartholomeusz, Helene Butter, Amanda Dimaria and Melissa George have revised early parts of the manuscript and provided valuable feedback. Last, but not least, I should like to express my sincere appreciation to Ellen Girmscheid of Brill for her careful consideration and extremely professional efforts as well as her patience in preparing the book for publication. My gratitude is due to Bernhardine Pejovic of the League of Nations Archives, Irina Gerassimova and Salvatore Leggio at the United Nations Library in Geneva and Saad Amer of Montesquieu Library at Birzeit University's Institute of Law. I very much appreciated the kind assistance of Isabelle Gerardi, Daniele Avanthay and Slobodan Djajic of the Graduate Institute. I will never forget the moral support of Frej Fenniche, Ingrid Jaradat and Samira Trad.

Without my family, this book would not have come out. The patience of my wife, Claudie, during the hard years of writing and her persistence encouragement was crucial for the completion of this work. My mother, Wedad, and her confidence have inspired me along the way. My parents-in-law, Françoise and Michel, are to be likewise greeted.

The final version, needless to say, is mine and I assume the sole responsibility for any error that might be found, including in translations from Arabic and French into English.

Mutaz M. Qafisheh
Jerusalem, May 2008

FOREWORD

The question of Palestinian nationality is a complex issue, legally, historically and politically. Surprisingly, it has hitherto attracted very little scholarly attention, by contrast with the seemingly more immediate questions of self-determination, Statehood, return and compensation, or with the current challenges to international law posed by the Israeli 'Wall' and the continuing settlement and sub-division of Palestinian land. Nevertheless, the uncertainty attaching to the precise status of Palestinians today affects their protection and rights, both in the Middle East and in the many countries throughout the world in which they have settled or sought refuge; clearly, their status is bound up with their future.

For these reasons alone, Dr Qafisheh's monograph is extremely valuable. It provides an essential and coherent context to contemporary questions and, above all, a well-researched historical background to the development of Palestinian nationality, particularly during the British mandate. Within this crucial political context, Dr Qafisheh examines the legal status of Palestine through and to the end of the mandate, and so reveals the juridical roots of Palestinian citizenship. His review of the literature enables him to fill in a number of gaps and to show, in his words, that although there was no Palestinian State before 1948, Palestinian citizenship was internationally recognized and Palestinians were never regarded or treated as stateless.

The citizenship issue, of course, is inseparable from that of self-determination and the identification of the Palestinian people in international law. The significance, in juridical terms, of a people's relationship in fact to territory has already been accepted in other contexts. Dr Qafisheh's argument for an existing and complete Palestinian nationality may be resisted by, among others, the architects of political solutions, but his comprehensive, well-researched and persuasive thesis will prove of immense value in delineating the present and future status of Palestinians in the Occupied Territories and elsewhere.

Dr Qafisheh is to be congratulated on bringing the question of Palestinian citizenship into the foreground, and his work will be essential reading for everyone concerned with this key legal issue and its part in a future lasting solution.

Guy S. Goodwin-Gill
Senior Research Fellow & Professor of International Refugee Law
All Souls College
Oxford
May 2008

I

INTRODUCTION

1. *Nationality: a definition*

The definition of the concept of 'nationality' has been subject to numerous studies. Thus, it is of little benefit to replicate such scholarship here. For the purpose of this book, however, it is merely sufficient to define and understand the term 'nationality' as the legal link between an individual and a sovereign, which has an international legal personality and is normally (but not exclusively)[1] an independent state. This link makes an individual citizen of that sovereign; any person who does not possess that sovereign's nationality is therefore a foreigner.[2]

1 On a recent survey regarding the nationality of various political entities, especially non-independent states, see Andrew Grossman, "Nationality and the Unrecognized State", *The International and Comparative Law Quarterly*, Vol. 50, 2001, pp. 849–867.

2 This statement stems, to a large extent, from the definition of nationality by the International Court of Justice (ICJ) in the *Nottebohm* case: "[N]ationality is a legal bond having as its basis a social fact of attachment, a genuine connection of existence, interests and sentiments, together with the existence of reciprocal rights and duties" (*Liechtenstein v. Guatemala*, Judgment, Second Phase, 6 April 1955—ICJ Reports, 1955, p. 23). On the concept of 'nationality', in its legal sense, see, *inter alia*, W.W. Willoughby, "Citizenship and Allegiance in Constitutional and International Law", *The American Journal of International Law*, Vol. 1, 1907, pp. 914–929; Robert Redslob, "Le principe des nationalités", in *Recueil des cours*, Académie de droit international (The Hague), 1931–III, Librairie du Recueil Sirey, Paris, Vol. 37, 1932, Vol. 37, pp. 1–82; L. Oppenheim, *International Law*, Longmans, London/New York/Toronto, 5th ed. (by H. Lauterpacht), 1937, Vol. I, pp. 511–513; J. Mervyn Jones, *British Nationality Law and Practice*, Oxford University Press, Oxford, 1947, pp. 1–26; P. Weis, *Nationality and Statelessness in International Law*, Stevens & Sons Limited, London, 1956, pp. 1–13, 31–35; Ian Brownlie, "The Relations of Nationality in Public International Law", *The British Year Book of International Law*, 1963, pp. 284–289; Majid Alhalawani, *Private International Law*, Literature and Science Press, Damascus, 1965 (Arabic), Vol. I, pp. 84–110; Jose Francisco Rezek, "Le Droit international de nationalité", in *Recueil des cours: Collected Courses of the Hague Academy of International Law*, Martinus Nijhoff, Dordrecht/Boston/London, Vol. 203, 1987–III, pp. 344–345; Ruth Donner, *The Regulation of Nationality in International Law*, Transnational Publishers, New York,

Throughout this study, 'nationality' and 'citizenship' are treated as synonymous.[3] And the following terms will be used as synonyms: 'citizen', 'national' and 'subject', unless otherwise indicated. Although certain states distinguish between various classes of citizens based mainly on the individual's capacity to enjoy civil and political rights, such a distinction is irrelevant from the viewpoint of international law.[4]

The link of 'nationality', in its legal sense, aims to establish rights and duties between an individual and a state. The law recognizes this link and places it over other considerations such as race, common origin, language or religion. Such considerations, either separately or jointly, might constitute 'race', 'identity' or the 'political' relationship between a 'person' (albeit not necessarily a 'citizen') and a 'nation' (albeit not necessarily a 'state').[5] While these considerations are often

---

1994, pp. 1–120; Yaffa Zilbershats, "Reconsidering the Concept of Citizenship", *Texas International Law Journal*, Vol. 36, 2001, pp. 689–734.

3 On discussion relating to the definition of nationality in Palestine under the British rule, see below pp. 59–60, 77.

4 See Weis, *op. cit.*, pp. 6–7.

5 See in this respect, among others, René Johannet, *Le principe des nationalités*, Nouvelle librairie nationale, Paris, 1918; W.B. Pillsbury, *The Psychology of Nationality and Internationalism*, D. Appleton and Company, New York/London, 1919; John Oakesmith, *Race and Nationality: An Inquiry into the Origin and Growth of Patriotism*, Frederick A. Stokes Company, New York, 1919; Sydney Herbert, *Nationality and its Problems*, Methuen & Co., London, 1920; Bernard Joseph, *Nationality: Its Nature and Problems*, George Allen & Unwin Ltd., London, 1929; Robert Redslob, "The Problem of Nationalities", *Problems of Peace and War*, Vol. 17, 1932, pp. 21–34; Frederick Hertz, *Nationality in History and Politics: A Psychology and Sociology of National Sentiment and Nationalism*, Routledge & Kegan Paul Ltd., London, 1951; Boyd C. Shafer, *Le Nationalisme: Mythe et Réalité*, Payot, Paris, 1964; S. James Anaya, "The Capacity of International Law to Advance Ethnic or Nationality Rights Claims", *Human Rights Quarterly*, Vol. 13, 1991, pp. 403–411; Gidon Gottlieb, "Nations without States", *Foreign Affairs*, Vol. 73, 1994, pp. 100–112; André Liebich, ed., *Citizenship East and West*, K. Paul International, London/New York, 1995; Rodney Bruce Hall, *National Collective Identity: Social Constructs and International Systems*, Columbia University Press, New York, 1999; Hegen Schulze, *States, Nations and Nationalism from the Middle Ages to the Present*, Blackwell Publishers, Cambridge/Oxford, 1996; Jacqueline Bhabha, "'Get Back to Where You Once Belonged': Identity, Citizenship and Exclusion in Europe", *Human Rights Quarterly*, Vol. 20, 1998, pp. 592–627; Vincent P. Pecora, ed., *Nations and Identities: Classic Readings*, Blackwell Publishers, Malden/Oxford, 2001, pp. 147–155; Georgios Varouxakis, *Mill on Nationality*, Routledge, London/New York, 2002; Thomas Janoski and Brian Gran, "Political Citizenship", in Engin N. Isin and Bryn S. Turner, eds., *Handbook of Citizenship Studies*, SAGE, London/Thousand Oaks/New Delhi, 2002, pp. 13–52; Anthony Woodiwiss, "Economic Citizenship: Variations and the Threat of Globalization", in *ibid.*, pp. 53–68; Maurice Poche, "Social Citizenship: Grounds of Social Change", in *ibid.*, pp. 69–86; Carsten Holbraad, *Internationalism and Nationalism in European Political Thought*, Palgrave Macmillan, New York, 2003; Martine Spensky, *Citoyenneté(s): perspectives internationales*, Presses Universitaires Blaise Pascal, Clermont-Ferrand, 2003. Concerning Palestinian 'nationality' from 'non-legal' perspectives, see, for example, Elihu Grant, *The People of Palestine*, J.B. Lippincott Company, Philadelphia/London, 1921; Y. Porath, *The Emerging of the Palestinian-Arab National Movement: 1918–1929*, Frank Cass, London, 1974; Baruch Kimmerling and

deemed by scholars to constitute 'nationality', such a definition and understanding of the term belong to such schools of thought as those of the political or social sciences or ethnology, rather than deriving from a rigorous legal assessment. Hence, such considerations are beyond the scope of this juridical study.

2. *Basic assumption*

This study is based on the assumption that the Palestine Mandate was a valid legal instrument (as it reflected the existing international law prevailing at the time) and, therefore, the legal acts deriving from the Mandate were, in principle, also valid. These acts included, *inter alia*, the legislation enacted by Britain or by the British-run Government of Palestine as well as the decisions of the Palestine courts and the British courts. In addition, the acts undertaken by the League of Nations regarding Palestine had authoritative legal value. Such acts of the Mandatory, its courts as well as of the League of Nations are directly related to Palestinian nationality.

That is not to say, however, that the arguments advanced by some writers on the invalidity of the Palestine Mandate and the actions derived from it[6] are without foundation.[7] Such arguments represent one extreme approach in dealing with

---

Joel S. Migdal, *Palestinians: The Making of A People*, Harvard University Press, Harvard/Cambridge/Massachusetts, 1994; Rashid Khalidi, *Palestinian Identity: the Construction of Modern National Consciousness*, Colombia University Press, New York, 1997; Samih K. Farsoun and Christina E. Zacharia, *Palestine and the Palestinians*, Westview Press, Colorado, 1997; Walid Salim, "Citizenship in Palestine: Problems of Concept and Framework", *Palestinian Politics*, No. 14, 1997; Nadine Picaudou, "Identité-mémoire et construction nationale palestinienne", in Nadine Picaudou, ed., *La Palestine en transition: crise du projet national et construction de l'Etat*, institut national des langues et civilisations orientales, Paris, 2001, pp. 339–361; Xavier Baron, *Les Palestiniens: genèse d'une nation*, Seuil, Paris, 2003.

6 Such arguments were first advanced by W.F. Boustany, *The Palestine Mandate: Invalid and Impracticable*, American Press, Beirut, 1936. Similar views were later developed by Henry Cattan, *Palestine and International Law: The Legal Aspects of the Arab-Israeli Conflict*, Longman, London/New York, 1976, pp. 63–68. See below pp. 128–129.

7 Yet, if one was to undertake a critical juridical analysis, in the light of the recent developments in international humanitarian law, one might reach a bitter conclusion. Put simply, by following the argument on the invalidity of the Palestine Mandate, then Britain would be considered as having been an occupying power in Palestine. As such, Britain would have had no authority to transfer foreign civilians, especially its own citizens, into the territory it occupied or to naturalize them therein. If such an action occurred in the present day, it would be prohibited in international law, particularly under Article 49(6) of the Geneva Convention relative to the Protection of Civilian Persons in Time of War of 12 August 1949 (UNTS, Vol. 75, 1950, p. 287); and Article 8(2)(b)(viii) of the Rome Statute of the International Criminal Court of 17 July 1998 (UNTS, Vol. 2187, 2002, p. 90). The League of Nations, together with its Member States, would probably share the responsibility with Britain on this illicit act. Nevertheless, international law had

the status of Palestine as whole. At the other extreme are the studies (reflecting, to a large extent, the position of certain states) which deny the right of return of Palestinian refugees to their places of habitual residence in Palestine before 1948.[8] This study would try to strike a balance between these two extremes by recognizing the then existing international legal order as represented by the League of Nations and subsequently by the United Nations as well as their juridical organs, i.e. the Permanent Court of International Justice and the International Court of Justice. Each of these bodies has endorsed the validity of the Palestine Mandate, for example, as a legal instrument that formed part of the overall mandate system.[9]

3. *Objectives*

This study attempts to achieve three objectives: academic, juridical and policy.

At the academic level, the study intends to fill the gap in the existing literature with regard to Palestinian nationality. As will be explained shortly, most studies conducted on Palestinian nationality or related issues (such as the status of Palestinian refugees), have given little or no consideration to the question of nationality under British rule. It is true that some readers might regard certain issues discussed herein as moot or to be of limited legal value today (e.g. Ottoman nationality, the capitulation system, the nationality of Palestine-natives who were residing abroad upon the enforcement of the 1925 Palestinian Citizenship Order and the Jewish immigration to, together with the naturalization of Jews in, Palestine). Such issues are, nonetheless, of historical significance and cannot be ignored, as they constitute factual and legal developments that shaped the formation of Palestinian nationality as it stands at the present day.

More importantly, in the juridical field, this study attempts to illustrate the international legal status of Palestinian nationality and how it stood at the end of the mandate. Any serious legal consideration of that nationality should start from the moment at which the Mandate over Palestine was ended. In other words, Palestinian nationality as it existed under the British rule forms the root of the various

---

not been developed to that level at the time of the mandate. Hence, such an analysis (which is beyond the scope of this study) would be difficult, though not impossible.

8 On the relevance between Palestinian nationality and the status of Palestine refugees, see below pp. 13–16.

9 It is sufficient here to generally mention that in the following decision and advisory opinions the Mandate system, in principle, was recognized as a valid legal system: *Mavrommatis Palestine Concessions* (*Greece v. Great Britain*), Permanent Court of International Justice (Objection of the Jurisdiction of the Court), 19 August 1924 (Permanent Court of International Justice, Series A, No. 2, 1924); *International Status of South-West Africa*, International Court of Justice (Advisory Opinion), 11 July 1950 (ICJ Reports, 1950); *Legal Consequences of the Construction of a Wall in the Occupied Palestinian Territory*, International Court of Justice (Advisory Opinion), 9 July 2004 (ICJ Reports, 2004).

statuses in existence today of those persons who were residing in Palestine on or before 14 May 1948: (1) Israel citizens, Jews and Arabs; (2) the inhabitants of the occupied Palestinian territory, i.e. the West Bank, including East Jerusalem, and the Gaza Strip; (3) and Palestinian refugees. Any change in the legal status relating to the nationality of those individuals who once bore Palestinian nationality under the British rule cannot produce more than *de facto* statuses according to international law or, at best, effects within certain domestic jurisdictions. While it is true that Israel had abrogated the nationality legislation which had been in force during the mandate period by the Nationality Law of 1952,[10] and that Jordan granted its nationality to those Palestinians residing in the West Bank in 1949, which was confirmed by the Jordanian Nationality Law in 1954,[11] these statuses did not alter the very existence of Palestinian nationality from the viewpoint of international law, which must ultimately prevail over such unilateral domestic actions by any individual state in cases of conflict. Such Israeli and Jordanian legislative actions (which are the most obvious, but are not the only, examples of domestic law's treatments of ex-Palestinian citizens), from an international law standpoint, were—and to a large extent still are—of limited legal effect; they could only apply within their respective domestic jurisdictions.

Above all, it is to be hoped that this study will provide some guidance to policy makers. This guidance might be useful to both the Palestinian Authority (PA) and to the Palestine Liberation Organization (PLO). The relevance of this study for the PA relates to the substantive provisions of future nationality legislation in the state of Palestine, including: the treatment of previous nationality legislation which had been valid in Palestine; the basis of any new nationality law, *jus sanguinis* and *jus soli*; naturalization by residence; the recovery of Palestinian nationality for those who were displaced and effectively lost their nationality after 1948; and the nationality of women and children. For this reason, certain substantive provisions of both the Ottoman Nationality Law of 1869 and the Palestinian Citizenship Order of 1925 will be discussed in some detail and, where necessary, compared with the nationality legislation of other states. The examination of Palestinian nationality from the perspective of international law may provide the PLO with a sound basis upon which future polices may be formulated. It may prove to be of assistance in negotiations with Israel and in relation to, *inter alia*, the right to return or other solutions to the question of Palestinian refugees; diplomatic protection of Palestinians abroad; the admission of foreigners into the country; and human rights obligations relating to nationality under customary or treaty law. Some of these international issues will be tackled in detail in the coming chapters.

---

10 See *infra* notes 465, 719.
11 See *infra* notes 465, 623 and below p. 15.

4. *Scope*

This study will address the question of Palestinian nationality under the British rule from the viewpoint of public international law as this law applies to individuals. Thus, the study will not examine the nationality in Palestine in the period following the British rule, nor Palestinian nationality in private international law, or the nationality of companies—or the moral person at large.

Notwithstanding its crucial significance in international law, Palestinian nationality under the British rule has never been the subject of a comprehensive study; a gap in determining the legal characteristics of that nationality still exists. Thus, as will become apparent following the forthcoming review of relevant scholarship on the matter, this study can be regarded as an attempt to fill this research gap. As a preliminary step to the study of Palestinian nationality, nationality within the Ottoman Empire (of which Palestine was a constituent part from 1516 until 1917) will be briefly reviewed, with particular focus on Ottoman nationality's influence in Palestine and Palestinian nationality during the period of the British rule.

In the case of Palestine, nationality is relevant to international law because, chiefly, "the status of the inhabitants of Mandated... Territories cannot be a domestic question".[12] The international nature of Palestinian nationality is derived not only from the fact that the "Mandatory does not have sovereignty over territory",[13] but also from the many international factors inherited within that nationality. These factors include: the mandate as an international system, the involvement of the League of Nations; state succession; the recognition of Palestinian nationality by other states; the diplomatic protection afforded to Palestinians abroad; naturalization of foreigners; immigration and return; the effects of multilateral nationality conventions in Palestine; and the ultimate role of the United Nations in defining the nationality in the country. These issues, amongst others, will be discussed in detail later.

More generally, nationality at both the domestic and international levels relates to almost every discipline of law. Nationality is directly linked to refugee law,[14]

---

12 Brownlie, *op. cit.*, p. 315.

13 *Ibid.* Many writers have addressed the question of sovereignty over the mandated-territories, in general, and the sovereignty over Palestine under the mandate, in particular. This question has been properly set forth, with reference to nationality, by James C. Hales, "Some Legal Aspects of the Mandate System: Sovereignty—Nationality—Termination and Transfer", *Problems of Peace and War*, Vol. 23, 1937, pp. 86–95.

14 See below pp. 14–16.

immigration law,[15] diplomatic law,[16] human rights,[17] humanitarian law,[18] law of state succession,[19] criminal law,[20] extradition law,[21] law of the sea,[22] and civil aviation law.[23] Defining the relevance of such legal fields to nationality is not necessary

---

15 Peter J. Spiro, "Dual Nationality and the Meaning of Citizenship", *Immigration and Nationality Law Review*, Vol. 18, 1997, pp. 491–564; Gabrielle M. Buckley, "Immigration and Nationality", *The International Lawyer*, Vol. 32, 1998, pp. 471–487; Robert J. Steinfeld, "Subjectship, Citizenship, and the Long History of Immigration Regulation", *Law and History Review*, Vol. 19, 2001, pp. 645–653.

16 See Chapter VIII, Section 3.

17 That includes 'nationality' itself as a right and the rights derived from nationality—chiefly civil and political, but also economic, social and cultural rights. See D.H. Pingrey, "Citizenship and Rights There-under", *The Central Law Journal*, Vol. 24, 1887, pp. 540–544; William L. Griffin, "The Right to a Single Nationality", *Temple Law Quarterly*, Vol. 40, 1966–1967, pp. 57–65; Myres S. McDougal/Harold D. Lasswell/Lung-chu Chen, "Nationality and Human Rights: The Protection of the Individual in External Arenas", *Yale Law Journal*, Vol. 83, 1973–1974, pp. 900–998; Geoff Budlender, "On Citizenship and Residence Rights: Taking Words Seriously", *South African Journal on Human Rights*, Vol. 5, 1989, pp. 37–59; Lisa C. Stratton, "The Right to Have Rights: Gender Discrimination in Nationality Laws", *Minnesota Law Review*, Vol. 77, 1992–1993, pp. 195–239; William E. Forbath, "Civil Rights and Economic Citizenship: Notes on the Past and Future of the Civil Rights and Labor Movements", *University of Pennsylvania Journal of Labor and Employment Law*, Vol. 2, 1999–2000, pp. 697–718; Mark Strasser, "The Privileges of National Citizenship: On Saenz, Same-Sex Couples, and the Right to Travel", *Rutgers Law Review*, Vol. 52, 1999–2000, pp. 553–588; Linda Bosniak, "Citizenship and Work", *North Carolina Journal of International Law and Commercial Regulation*, Vol. 27, 2001–2002, pp. 497–506. See also references in *infra* note 1093.

18 Job E. Hedges, "Citizenship and the Constitution in Time of War", *The Constitutional Review*, Vol. 1, 1917, pp. 131–140; Arnold D. McNair, "British Nationality and Alien Status in Time of War", *The Law Quarterly Review*, Vol. 35, 1919, pp. 213–232; Willis Smith, "Citizenship and the Bill of Rights in War Time", *Insurance Counsel Journal*, Vol. 9, 1942, pp. 5–11; John Hanna, "Nationality and War Claims", *Columbia Law Review*, Vol. 45, 1945, pp. 301–344; Bartram S. Brown, "Nationality and Internationality in International Humanitarian Law", *Stanford Journal of International Law*, Vol. 34, 1998, pp. 347–406.

19 See below text accompanying notes pp. 69–70, 102–103, 200, 203 and the references thereof.

20 Geoffrey R. Watson, "Offenders Abroad: The Case for Nationality-Based Criminal Jurisdiction", *Yale Journal of International Law*, Vol. 17, 1992, pp. 41–84; Zsuzsanna Deen-Racsmany, "The Nationality of the Offender and the Jurisdiction of the International Criminal Court", *The American Journal of International Law*, Vol. 95, 2001, pp. 606–623.

21 Martin T. Manton, "Extradition of Nationals", *Temple Law Quarterly*, Vol. 12, 1935–1936, pp. 12–24; Michael Plachta, "(Non-)Extradition of Nationals: A Neverending Story", *Emory International Law Review*, Vol. 13, 1999, pp. 77–159.

22 Myres S. McDougal/William T. Burke/Ivan A. Vlasic, "The Maintenance of Public Order at Sea and the Nationality of Ships", *The American Journal of International Law*, Vol. 54, 1960, pp. 25–116; Simon W. Tache, "The Nationality of Ships: The Definitional Controversy and Enforcement of Genuine Link", *International Lawyer*, Vol. 16, 1982, pp. 301–312.

23 Robert Kingsley, "Nationality of Aircraft", *The Journal of Air Law*, Vol. 3, 1932, pp. 50–57; J.G. Gazdik, "Nationality of Aircraft and Nationality of Airlines as Means of

for the purpose of this study. However, two issues which are directly connected to the nationality and to Palestine require some attention. One is the relevance of nationality under the mandate to private international law and, secondly, the nationality of companies.

Notwithstanding its relevance to Palestinian nationality, private international law shall be excluded from the scope of this study. Three reasons might be given for such exclusion. Firstly, several studies have already examined Palestinian nationality for the purpose of private international law under the British rule. Two detailed studies (one prepared shortly after the regularization of Palestinian nationality by Britain and the second at the end of the mandate), might be cited in this connection. In 1926, Frederic Goadby (the then Director of Legal Studies of the Government of Palestine in Jerusalem) wrote a book entitled *International and Inter-Religious Private Law in Palestine*.[24] Goadby was the first-ever author to have had studied nationality in a bid to resolve the conflict of laws regarding personal status matters in Palestine. Another detailed study was undertaken by Edoardo Vitta, *The Conflict of Laws in Matters of Personal Status in Palestine*, in 1947.[25] The significance of Vitta's work stems not only from the fact that it was done at the end of the mandate (and covered aspects which arose after Goadby's), but also from Vitta's consideration of twenty-years' practice in respect to nationality issues arising in private relations involving foreigners before Palestinian courts.[26] The second reason for excluding private international law from the scope of this study is the little or no value of that law in the West Bank and Gaza Strip at present. This in turn is due to the dominant jurisdiction of Israel courts over issues relating to foreigners residing in the occupied territories since 1967; the exclusion of cases involving foreigners from the jurisdiction of Palestinian courts by the Israeli-Palestinian peace agreements of 1994–1995, and due to the automatic applicability of religious laws, which eliminates the possibility of applying private foreign laws before Islamic and Christian personal status courts/tribunals in the West Bank and Gaza Strip. The third,

---

Control in International Air Transportation", *The Journal of Air Law and Commerce*, Vol. 25, 1958, pp. 1–7; Gerald F. FitzGerald, "Nationality and Registration of Aircraft Operated by International Operating Agencies and Article 77 of the Convention on International Civil Aviation, 1944", *The Canadian Yearbook of International Law*, Vol. 5, 1967, pp. 193–216; Z. Joseph Gertler, "Nationality of Airlines: A Hidden Force in the International Air Regulation, Equation", *Journal of Air Law and Commerce*, Vol. 48, 1982–1983, pp. 51–88.

24 Hamadpis Press, Jerusalem. See, in particular, his discussion on Palestinian nationality pp. 22–37. Goadby's work was also translated into Arabic in 1931 (by Hasan Sidqi Dajani and Salah Al-Din Al-Abasi, Biet Al-Maqdis Press, Jerusalem) with a view to be used as a reference in Middle Eastern countries that lacked studies relating to private international law at the time.

25 S. Bursi Ltd., Tel-Aviv. In particular, Vitta discussed Palestinian nationality at pp. 60–98.

26 See *infra* note 702.

and final, reason for not examining private international law issues here is the existence of recent studies on the topic,[27] including one by the present writer.[28]

Notwithstanding, too, the legal significance of the nationality of companies,[29] and the nationality of the moral persons at large,[30] in the West Bank and Gaza Strip at the present time,[31] this study is limited to the nationality of natural persons, or individuals. This exclusion in particular is due, firstly, to the direct reliance of the

---

27 See Amin Raja Dawwas, *Conflict of Laws in Palestine*, Dar Al-Shorok, Amman/Ramallah, 2001 (Arabic). Dawwas' study is a textbook, based on a comparative approach, for the purpose of teaching private international law to undergraduate students at faculties of law in Palestinian universities in the West Bank and Gaza Strip. It does not offer detailed solutions to the conflict of nationalities in personal status matters before Palestinian courts at present. This question would remain anomalous and confusing until the creation of Palestinian state or, at least, once Palestinian courts in the 1967 occupied territories acquire explicit jurisdiction to adjudicate cases relating to private international law involving foreigners. This question cannot be discussed further here.

28 Mutaz Qafisheh, *Nationality and Domicile in Palestine*, International Studies Institute, Birzeit University, Birzeit, 2000 (Arabic), pp. 197–207. (See above p. xi.)

29 Cleveland Cabler, "The Citizenship of Corporations", *American Law Review*, Vol. 56, 1922, pp. 85–107; William Grafton Elliott, Jr., "Some Constitutional Aspects of Corporate Citizenship", *Georgetown Law Journal*, Vol. 16, 1927–1928, pp. 55–72; Maurice Travers, "La nationalité des sociétés commerciales", in *Recueil des cours*, Académie de droit international (The Hague), 1930–III, Librairie du Recueil Sirey, Paris, Vol. 33, 1931, pp. 1–110; Lawrence F. Daly, "Diversity of Citizenship as Applied to Corporations", *The Marquette Law Review*, Vol. 17, 1932–1933, pp. 32–43; Heinrich Kronstein, "The Nationality of International Enterprises", *Colombia Law Review*, Vol. 52, 1952, pp. 983–1002; George M. Esahak, "Diversity Jurisdiction: The Dilemma of Dual Citizenship and Alien Corporations", *Northwestern University Law Review*, Vol. 77, 1982–1983, pp. 565–587; Ron Harnden, "Corporations: Corporate Citizenship—Principal Place of Business", *Washburn Law Journal*, Vol. 11, 1971–1972, pp. 486–490.

30 Nationality of the 'legal', 'juridical', 'juristic' or 'moral' person (which includes companies, associations, ships, aircrafts and the like) is largely connected with private international law. Nationality has been utilized, by courts and then by legislation, as a test to determine the applicable law in cases of conflict. See, for example, E. Hilton Young, "Nationality of a Juristic Person", *Harvard Law Review*, Vol. 22, 1908–1909, pp. 1–26.

31 In the occupied Palestinian territories at the present time, the legislation applicable in the West Bank differs from that of the Gaza Strip. Most legislation in the Gaza Strip was introduced under the British rule before 1948. In the West Bank, most legislation goes back to the Jordanian administration from 1948 to 1967. When the Palestinian Authority was established, it declared (on 20 May 1994) that all legislation applicable in both areas would continue to be valid until being consolidated (Presidential Decree No. 1, Palestine Gazette, No. 1, 20 November 1994, p. 10). This general situation affected the nationality of companies, whereby a company in one area is regarded as a foreign company in the other. According to Article 2 of the Companies Ordinance of 1929 which applies to the Gaza Strip (Laws of Palestine, p. 181), a company is deemed to be foreign if it was created outside Palestine (i.e. outside the Gaza Strip in the present case). While in the West Bank, the company is deemed to be foreign if it was established abroad and its administration centre is also located abroad (see Article 38(1) and Article 40(4) of Companies Law of 1964—Jordan Gazette, No. 1757, 3 May 1964, p. 493). On the registration of the West Bank companies as foreign companies in the Gaza Strip, see, for example: Palestine Gazette, Special Issue No. 3, 21 January 1996, p. 355; Palestine

nationality of moral persons on the nationality of individuals (i.e. nationality of the latter can be extended to the former as a matter of existence) and, secondly, because the nationality of companies in Palestine during the Palestinian Authority period has already been examined in a separate study by the present author.[32]

5. *Gap in existing studies*

A. *Early studies*

While writers have considered the issue of Palestinian nationality under the British rule as part of other studies, with only a few exceptions, that consideration has tended to be brief.

One year after the enactment of the 1925 Palestinian Citizenship Order,[33] two writers studied the question of Palestinian nationality. The first was the aforementioned Goadby's, whose work was used as a textbook for Palestinian students studying law at the School of Legal Studies in Jerusalem. As indicated previously, Goadby's study was not deeply concerned with the significance of nationality in public international law. In his article, *Nationality in Mandated Territories Detached from Turkey*, Norman Bentwich,[34] the then Attorney-General of the British-run Government of Palestine, touched upon the question of Palestinian nationality from a public international law perspective. Bentwich discussed some aspects of Palestinian nationality as an example of nationalities in the mandated-territories under the British and French administration in the Middle East: Iraq, Syria, Lebanon and Palestine. It seems that Bentwich had relied heavily on his official position as a basis for the consideration of the question at hand, as his study lacked primary references to support its arguments. He even failed to refer to some basic facts which existed at the time, not least the involvement of the Jewish Agency for Palestine in the drafting process of the Palestinian Citizenship Order of 1925 and relevant legislation.[35] His study also lacked critical analyses of the said 1925 Order, its context and its motives. Perhaps his official position prevented him from tackling certain sensitive issues in the Order. Yet Bentwich's article has been cited in most studies which addressed Palestinian nationality under the British rule.[36]

Gazette, Special Issue No. 5, 31 August 1996, p. 60. This question was discussed in Qafisheh, *Nationality and Domicile in Palestine, op. cit.*, pp. 137–147, 213–216.

32 Mutaz Qafisheh, *Palestinian Nationality: Nationality of Individuals and Nationality of Companies*, Institute of Law, Birzeit University, Birzeit, 2001 (Arabic, Master's thesis).

33 See below Chapter IV.

34 *The British Year Book of International Law*, 1926, pp. 97–109.

35 See below p. 83.

36 In 1939, the same writer summarized his previous views in a three-page article's "Palestine Nationality and the Mandate" (*Journal of Comparative Legislation and International Law*, Vol. 21, pp. 230–232).

A similar article, P. Lampué's *De la nationalité des habitants des pays à mandat de la Société des Nations*,[37] tackled the issue from a broader theoretical perspective, without detailed consideration for Palestinian nationality.[38]

A number of subsequent works addressed Palestinian nationality from the viewpoint of public international law. Most of these works discussed the question as part of either a comprehensive study on the status of Palestine under the mandate, or under selected issues relating to that mandate. An example of the former included J. Stoyanovsky's *The Mandate for Palestine: A Contribution to the Theory and Practice of International Mandates*, published in 1928.[39] Despite his manifest research efforts and profound legal analysis, Stoyanovsky mixed the legal with the political aspects of nationality.[40] Similar studies were carried out by Maurice Mock[41] and, a shorter one, by Abraham Baumkoller.[42] Under selected issues relating to the international status of Palestine or the mandated territories, at least two studies examined Palestinian nationality. Of these, one writer established his arguments upon ideological and somewhat emotional, rather than legal, grounds.[43] The other outlined Palestinian nationality as being only one of several examples of nationality in the mandated-territories.[44]

Other works on nationality had referred to the question of Palestinian nationality under British rule in order to serve the completion of their general studies. One such work is the book of J. Mervyn Jones, entitled *British Nationality Law and*

37 *Journal du droit international*, Vol. 52, 1925, pp. 54–61.

38 See also Quincy Wright, "Status of the Inhabitants of Mandated Territory", *The American Journal of International Law*, Vol. 18, 1924, pp. 306–315.

39 Longmans, Green and Co., London/New York/Toronto, pp. 263–279.

40 He did not, for example, distinguish between the concept of Palestinian *nationality* (a legal link) and what he called the 'principle of *nationality* of the Jewish people' (a political link). He presented groundless legal arguments relating to what he called 'the historical connection of the Jewish people with Palestine' (pp. 51–68).

41 *Le mandat britannique en Palestine*, Editions Albert Mechelinck, Paris, 1932 (Ph.D. thesis), pp. 175–184.

42 *Le mandat sur la Palestine*, Librairie Arthur Rousseau, Paris, 1931, pp. 179–181.

43 Nathan Feinberg, *Some Problems of the Palestine Mandate*, Tel-Aviv, 1936, pp. 47–64. For example, Feinberg said that "...it is clear and obvious that those who worded and framed the text [of Article 129 of the Treaty of Sèvres of 1920—it will be discussed later in this study] were essentially led by nationalistic ideology, and that by the insertion of this Article in the Treaty, they wanted to uphold a principle which they considered well founded. Palestine was recognized as the national home for the Jewish People, and the automatic acquisition of Palestinian citizenship by all the Jews resident in Palestine...appeared but a logical outcome of this recognition" (p. 52). "*No right to opt for Palestinian citizenship*", he continued in pp. 55–56, "*has been granted to Arabs living outside the boundaries of Palestine*, although the majority of its population was Arab. The Arab majority was intentionally not recognized as a permanent and decisive factor, and *Palestine has*—with total disregard of this majority—*not been considered as an Arab country*....Palestine was to be excluded from the list of States for which Arabs were entitled to opt" (emphasis in original). No evidence or reference was introduced to support these contentions. See also his artificially-grounded conclusions in pp. 61–64.

44 James C. Hales, *op. cit.*, pp. 95–112.

Practice, published in 1947,[45] which addresses Palestinian nationality as part of his consideration of nationality in the British Empire (i.e. in the United Kingdom, British domains, colonies and mandated-territories). His consideration (which interestingly came at the end of the mandate in Palestine) was incomplete, as many substantive issues relating to Palestinian nationality were ignored and even obvious errors were to be found.[46] A second book, which has been described as an "excellent study",[47] is P. Weis's *Nationality and Statelessness in International Law*, which touched upon the question of Palestinian nationality as part of a historical survey on nationality in the mandated and trust-territories.[48] Yet Weis's consideration of Palestinian nationality was by no means complete. For this reason, perhaps, Weis, who was writing in 1956, admitted that the "question of Palestinian nationality, though now obsolete, has been referred to here in some detail as it is mainly with reference to this territory [Palestine] that the problem of nationality in mandated-territories has been elucidated by judicial decisions".[49]

Perhaps the most specialized study to examine the question of Palestinian nationality was Paul Ghali's *Les nationalités détachées de l'Empire ottoman à la suite de la guerre* of 1934.[50] In this study, Ghali had explored the origin of nationalities in the Middle East, and examined the question of Palestinian nationality in a wider international and regional context. He also conducted a comparative analysis on nationality legislation and practices in the various territories which had been detached from the Ottoman Empire in the aftermath of World War I. A similar consideration, but with a more updated characterization of the question at hand, can be found in the article of George M. Abi-Saab, *Nationality and Diplomatic Protection in Mandated and Trust Territories*.[51] Yet, based on an inductive comparison between various territories, Abi-Saab's article had drawn broader conclusions concerning nationality under the mandate, which were not necessarily related to Palestinian nationality in particular.[52] This article focused on contemporary issues relevant at the time of writing.[53]

45 *Op. cit.*, pp. 278–285.
46 See, for example, below p. 142.
47 Brownlie, *op. cit.*, p. 303.
48 *Op. cit.*, pp. 22–28.
49 *Ibid.*, pp. 24–25. *Cf.* Brownlie, *op. cit.*, pp. 315–317.
50 Les Editions Domat-Montchrestien, Paris, pp. 199–229.
51 *Harvard International Law Club Bulletin*, Vol. 3, 1961–1962, pp. 44–76.
52 See, for example, pp. 52–58, where no reference to Palestine, understandably however, was made.
53 Such issues included nationality in South-West Africa (pp. 57–59) and the nationality in the Trusteeship territories (pp. 59–71).

B. *Recent studies*

Most of the studies conducted after the end of the British rule which dealt with issues normally connected with nationality, examined certain *de facto* effects resulting from the abolition of the mandate in the areas which constituted part of Palestine or in relation to those persons who were considered as Palestinians. These studies, broadly speaking, fell under three categories. The first category comprised a set of legal studies which addressed either the nationality of former Palestinians in Israel as part of studying Israel nationality,[54] or the nationality of the inhabitants of the West Bank as part of Jordanian nationality.[55] A second category of studies dealt with the period of Israel's occupation and addressed certain humanitarian questions relating to nationality, such as family reunification,[56] and the deportation of native inhabitants.[57] A third type of studies examined the question of Palestinian refugees. It can be safely said that no study to date has sufficiently relied upon Palestinian nationality under the British rule, as an international legal basis, to support its findings.

Recent studies on Palestinian nationality have either totally ignored the question of nationality under the British rule or mentioned it in very general terms. Even the most credible studies on Palestinian refugees have attached only a minor significance to the question of Palestinian nationality, although this should be the main basis of such legal studies.[58] Perhaps the assumption of such writers has been

---

54 See Louis A. Warsoff, "Citizenship in the State of Israel—A Comment", *New York University Law Review*, Vol. 33, 1958, pp. 857–861; M.D. Gouldman, *Israel Nationality Law*, Institute for Legislative Research and Comparative Law, the Hebrew University, Jerusalem, 1970; Marwan Darweish and Andrew Rigby, *Palestinians in Israel: Nationality and Citizenship*, Department of Peace Studies, University of Bradford, Bradford, 1995; Albert K. Wan, "Israel's Conflicted Existence as a Jewish Democratic State: Striking the Proper Balance under the Citizenship and Entry into Israel Law", *Brooklyn Journal of International Law*, Vol. 29, 2003–2004, pp. 1345–1402.

55 Qafisheh, *Nationality and Domicile in Palestine, op. cit.*, pp. 57–60. The nationality of the inhabitants of the Gaza Strip, on the other hand, was treated as part of the question of Palestinian refugees; most of the residents of the Strip were, and still are, refugees who fled from those areas of Palestine wherein Israel was established in 1948 or which were annexed by Israel during the 1948–1949 wars (*ibid.*, pp. 60–62).

56 Yoram Dinstein, "The Israel Supreme Court and the Law of Belligerent Occupation: Reunification of Families", *Israel Yearbook on Human Rights*, Vol. 18, 1988, pp. 173–188; Ian Brownlie, "The Application of Contemporary Standards of International Law to Cases Involving Separation of Husband and Wife as a Consequence of Administrative Action by the Israeli Authorities in the Occupied Territories", *The Palestine Yearbook of International Law*, Vol. 6, 1990–1991, pp. 113–122.

57 Joost R. Hiltermann, "Israel's Deportation Policy in the Occupied West Bank and Gaza", *The Palestine Yearbook of International Law*, Vol. 3, 1986, pp. 154–185; Yoram Dinstein, "The Israel Supreme Court and the Law of Belligerent Occupation: Deportations", *Israel Yearbook on Human Rights*, Vol. 23, 1993, pp. 1–26.

58 An essential element for defining the term 'refugee', according to Article 1(A)(2) of the Geneva Convention relating to the Status of Refugees of 28 July 1951 (UNTS,

that the question of nationality under the British rule had been solved long ago. Thus, with a few exceptions, writers have tended to focus on the right of return of Palestinian refugees (based on international legal instruments, notably those in the field of human rights), without according much attention to the law of nationality, and least of all, Palestinian nationality under the British rule. The lack of research on Palestinian nationality under the British rule and its significance in international law has led most writers (who examined the status of Palestinian refugees) to build their arguments on a non-legal basis or on solutions created to serve functional or humanitarian exigencies. As a result, unusual conclusions have been reached.

Lex Takkenberg's detailed study, *The Status of Palestinian Refugees in International Law*,[59] provides a typical example. Takkenberg had touched upon the question of Palestinian nationality under the British rule very briefly.[60] He consequently reached ill-founded conclusions such as the following: "as there is no [Palestinian] state, *ipso facto* Palestinian nationality is non-existent as well. Palestinians who have not acquired the nationality of a third state therefore continue to be stateless for the purpose of international law".[61] This assertion was made without due regard to the status of Palestinians under British rule, without making a distinction between the various statuses of Palestinians according to the law of state succession,[62] and without defining "the purpose of international law". Although he admitted the existence of a "*de facto* Palestinian citizenship in respect to the residents of the autonomous areas", Takkenberg insisted that "[f]or the purpose of international law, residents of the self-rule areas who do not possess the nationality of a third state must, therefore, continue to be considered as stateless persons until such time as a Palestinian state has been officially established".[63] Yet he failed to mention the

---

Vol. 189, 1954, p. 150), is the fact that the person in question is "outside the country of his nationality". On the general relevance of nationality to the status of a 'refugee', see James C. Hathaway, *The Law of Refugee Status*, Butterworths, Toronto/Vancouver, 1991, pp. 6–10; Guy S. Goodwin-Gill, *The Refugees in International Law*, Clarendon Press, Oxford, 1996, pp. 4–7, 18–20, 29–31; Pirkko Kourula, *Broadening the Edges: Refugee Definition and International Protection Revised*, Martinus Nijhoff, The Hague/Boston/London, 1997, pp. 35–48, 56–146; Carol A. Batchelor, "Statelessness and the Problem of Resolving Nationality Status", *International Journal of Refugee Law*, Vol. 10, 1998, pp. 156–183.

59 Clarendon Press, Oxford, 1998, pp. 178–183.

60 He did not refer to previous studies on Palestinian nationality which were carried out at the time of the mandate, nor did he cite any primary documents which were of relevance to Palestinian nationality.

61 P. 181. *Cf.* Goodwin-Gill, *op. cit.*, pp. 241–246.

62 It is of a general knowledge that the inhabitants of the territories occupied by Israel in 1967 comprise, broadly speaking, two groups: 'original residents' and 'refugees' who fled from those areas of Palestine in which Israel was established and settled in the West Bank and Gaza, mostly in 'refugee camps'.

63 See pp. 182–183. A somewhat similar position has been expressed by Goodwin-Gill, *op. cit.*, p. 246. However, the latter's view was less definite than that of Takkenberg's. Goodwin-Gill was precise by considering that only a certain group of Palestinians (i.e. "Palestinians who...do not or are not able to return to [1967-occupied] Palestinian

fact that although there was no Palestinian state before 1948, Palestinian nationality was internationally recognized and Palestinian citizens had never been regarded or treated as stateless at the time.[64]

Nonetheless, the existence of a distinct Palestinian nationality during the period of British rule has never been denied by those writers who have addressed the issue of Palestinian refugees. A few studies, particularly those advocating the right of return, have indeed given the question of nationality some legal account; however, they did so without sufficient discussion.[65] Other writers have excluded

---

territory"), for certain international law purposes (e.g. "obtain[ing] protection from the Palestinian authorities"), were refugees or stateless persons. Yet Goodwin-Gill's short discussion on Palestinian nationality under the British rule (pp. 241–243) was not intended to be a comprehensive characterization of that nationality, because that discussion was conducted for the sake of completion of a comprehensive work on refugees, not only the Palestinians, in international law.

64 See, as background, Edward H. Buehrig, *The UN and the Palestinian Refugees: A Study in Nonterritorial Administration*, Indiana University Press, Bloomington/London, 1971; Benny Morris, *The Birth of the Palestinian Refugee Problem, 1947–1949*, Cambridge University Press, Cambridge, 1989 (also Morris' revised version of 2004); Naseer Aruri, ed., *Palestinian Refugees: The Right of Return*, Pluto Press, London/Sterling/Virginia, 2001 (sixteen studies); Mathieu Bouchard, *L'Exode Palestinien: construction d'une représentation occidentale du conflit israélo-arabe*, L'Harmattan, Paris, 2003; Ann M. Lesch and Ian S. Lustick, *Exile and Return: Predicaments of Palestinians and Jews*, University of Pennsylvania Press, Philadelphia, 2005 (fifteen studies).

65 Amongst these studies are Kathleen Lawand, "The Right to Return of Palestinian Refugees in International Law", *International Journal of Refugee Law*, Vol. 8, 1996, pp. 532–568; and John Quigley, "Mass Displacement and the Individual Right of Return", *The British Year Book of International Law*, 1997, pp. 65–125. Nationality is at the centre of Lawland's analysis and it is the basis for the right of Palestinian refugees to return. However, despite her attempt to outline the question at length in her article (pp. 558–565), Lawland did not conduct a review of the characteristics of that nationality. For example, she did not examine any reference or document which discussed nationality under the mandate. Rather, she went beyond that primary question to discuss the right of Palestinians to return to their 'own country', or to the country of their nationality (pp. 557–558). A study on Palestinian nationality at the time could have constituted a supporting factor to the legal arguments of Lawland. That is not say, however, that Lawand's conclusion is inconsistent with the established legal basis relating to Palestinian nationality under the British rule (see pp. 565–568), although one may query how Lawland reached the conclusion (p. 564) that residents of the Gaza Strip were stateless from 1948 until 1967 (a conclusion that runs contrary to her general logic). On the other hand, Quigley has advanced a step forward. He demonstrated, by citing several international cases involving territorial change throughout the twentieth century, that the right to nationality can be extended to national absentees, and by extension to Palestinian refugees (pp. 71, 76, 84, 107–108, 112–114, 116, 118, 120–121). This would apply "even if the national has never set foot in its territory" (p. 67). Yet the previous nationality of Palestinian refugees (i.e. Palestinian nationality under British rule), has not been sufficiently characterised in Quigley's article. Again, it seems that this writer (as with many other scholars), considered the pre-existence of Palestinian nationality before 1948 to be an issue beyond any doubt. To the present writer's knowledge, no serious doubt has been raised with regard to the very existence of Palestinian nationality during the mandate period. However, *cf.* Chapter VIII, Section 1.

the question of Palestinian nationality under the British rule from the scope of their studies,[66] devoted little attention to it,[67] or ignored it at once.[68] However, no writer (including those Israeli authors who questioned the right of Palestinian refugees to return),[69] has denied the existence of Palestinian nationality under the mandate. Thus, it was interestingly observed, "...the unanimous recognition of a proper nationality for their [i.e. Mandated-territories of Class 'A'] inhabitants might throw light upon the status and the rights of the Palestinian Arab refugees acquired under the Mandate".[70]

It was only after the creation of the Palestinian Authority that new studies on Palestinian nationality started to emerge. Some of these studies dealt with the effects of the 1993–1995 Israeli-Palestinian agreements on the status of the inhabitants, while others concentrated on the nationality or citizens' rights in the territories administrated by the PA. Yet other scholars examined both of these areas. However, with a few exceptions, none of these studies have examined in any great detail the period of the British rule in Palestine as being a period in which Palestinian nationality had been legally constituted from the viewpoint of public international

66 Kurt René Radey ("The Palestinian Refugees: The Right to Return in International Law", *The American Journal of International Law*, Vol. 72, 1978, pp. 586–614) discussed the various grounds for refugees to return, but he emphasised that "the question of Palestinian nationality is not dealt with here" (p. 612).

67 See, e.g., Susan M. Akram, "Reinterpreting Palestinian Refugee Rights under International Law", in Aruri, *op. cit.*, pp. 165–194. Akram, rather oddly, said (p. 170) that "under the British Mandate, Palestinians had recognized legal status as either nationals or citizens of Palestine, or *both*" (there is no explanation on how the Palestinians could be 'both', as in the added emphasis, nationals and citizens). This quotation was Akram's only reference to Palestinian nationality before 1948.

68 See, e.g., Yoav Tadmor, "The Palestinian Refugees of 1948: The Right to Compensation and Return", *Temple International & Comparative Law Journal*, Vol. 8, 1994, pp. 403–434). Tadmor has entirely ignored the question of nationality, let alone Palestinian nationality. Furthermore, he neglected to refer to nationality as a pre-requisite for the characterization of a refugee status.

69 See, *inter alia*, Ruth Lapidoth, "The Right of Return in International Law, with Special Reference to the Palestinian Refugees", *Israel Yearbook on Human Rights*, Vol. 16, 1986, pp. 103–125; Eyal Benvenisti and Eyal Zamir, "Private Claims to Property Rights in the Future Israeli-Palestinian Settlement", *The American Journal of International Law*, Vol. 89, 1995, pp. 295–340. Lapidoth said that Palestinian refugees "never were nationals or prominent nationals of Israel" (p. 111; repeated at p. 114). She added that the Palestinians should not return because they are "hostile refugees [who] without doubt violate 'the rights and freedoms of others' in Israel" and would damage the public order of that state (p. 114). She concluded that their return (as stipulated in various United Nations resolutions which Lapidoth herself cited), implied "the destruction of the State of Israel" (p. 120). Benvenisti and Zamir suggested, for instance, that "a just solution to the 1948 refugees problem...does not entail a general right of return" (p. 329). Again, none of these authors argued against the very existence of Palestinian nationality under the British rule.

70 Abi-Saab, *op. cit.*, p. 51. See further Chapter VIII, Section 1.

law. Most of these studies, including one conducted by the present writer,[71] have merely provided an overview of Palestinian nationality and failed to reach the heart of the problem.[72]

An example of such studies is Andreas Zimmermann's *The Nationality of the Inhabitants of the Palestinian Autonomous Territories*, published in 1999.[73] This author attempted to conduct a historical review on Palestinian nationality, from the time of the detachment of Palestine from the Ottoman Empire until the day of writing.[74] He thus offered an overview on the subject. Although he referred to key studies (but not primary documents) relating to Palestinian nationality under the mandate, Zimmermann, ironically, reached an ill-founded conclusion in this regard by stating that Palestinian nationality at the British time was not 'full'.[75] Following the practice of some single states, particularly Israel (and Germany, albeit in a different

71 Mutaz Qafisheh, "La nationalite palestinienne selon les principes du droit local et du droit international", in Nadine Picaudou, ed., *op. cit.*, pp. 39–77.

72 See, *inter alia*, Uri Davis, *Citizenship and the State: A Comparative Study of Citizenship Legislation in Israel, Jordan, Palestine, Syria and Lebanon*, Garnet Publisher and Ithaca Press, London, 1997, pp. 83–113; Jaume Saura Estapa, *Criteria for the Establishment of the Palestinian Citizenship within the Framework of a Palestinian Sovereign State*, Universitat de Barcelona, Barcelona, 1997 (un-published); Mohammed S. Dajani, *The Palestinian Authority and Citizenship in the Palestinian Territories*, Al-Quds University, Jerusalem, 1997 (unpublished). Davis did not make more than a brief presentation, with short comments, of certain documents which had mentioned Palestinian nationality (e.g. the Palestinian Citizenship Order of 1925, United Nations Partition Plan of 1947, Palestinian National Charter of 1968, and Palestinian Authority draft Basic Law of 1995). He did not attach any significance to Palestinian nationality under British law, apart from presenting two provisions of the 1925 Order (p. 83) and the Partition Plan (pp. 87–88). He further personalized parts of his study by, for example, introducing the data of his own Palestinian identity card issued to him by the Palestinian Liberation Organization (pp. 93–94). Davis, lastly, discussed some issues which are entirely irrelevant to the question of Palestinian nationality as part of his conclusion on 'citizenship' in Palestine (pp. 100–107). See also his 'non-legal' recommendations (pp. 202–204). Although he tried to propose pragmatic legal criteria to the conferment of Palestinian nationality, Estapa introduced a somewhat ambiguous presumption: "In 'normal' State successions, the individuals affected by the change of sovereignty possess a certain, single, citizenship that can be referred to by the new State. Since this does not exist in the present case, we need to know…the persons that are 'interested' in this eventual State succession; who are 'Palestinians', or who composes the 'Palestinian people'…" (p. 7). Furthermore, the following statement is both unclear and apparently ill-founded: "It should be made clear that this [Palestinian] 'citizenship' [during the mandate period] was not so, since Palestine was not a sovereign State" (p. 8, note 18). Estapa, lastly, made no reference to any study on nationality under the British rule. Finally, Dijani's study belongs to the non-legal studies referred to in *supra* note 5; it focused on the civil and political rights in the Palestinian Authority-controlled territory.

73 In Amos Shapira and Mala Tabory, eds., *New Political Entities in Public and Private International Law with Special Reference to the Palestinian Entity*, Kluwer Law International, The Hague/Boston/London, 1999, pp. 231–246.

74 See pp. 232–238.

75 On the doubts relating to the full existence of Palestinian nationality, see below pp. 141–142.

context), Zimmermann asserted that the inhabitants of the West Bank and Gaza Strip were and continue to be stateless.[76] As had been the case with Takkenberg,[77] such a conclusion was based on the fact that there was no Palestinian state, without providing further analysis.[78] However, after extensive examples of the granting of nationalities in non-state entities,[79] Zimmermann accurately pointed out: "even entities *sui generis*, that cannot be characterized as States under international law, sometimes have developed ties to natural persons the characteristics of which are quite similar to nationality in the proper sense".[80] He continued: "it seems to be appropriate to consider the permanent inhabitants of the autonomous areas—despite the fact that they do not (yet) possess the nationality of a State—*not to be stateless anymore*. The effects of this 'citizenship' are, however, still limited".[81] After reviewing selected facts which emerged after the 1995 Oslo agreement,[82] he concluded that there is a Palestinian "nationality in *statu nascendi*".[83] Yet these conclusions have been reached without sufficient regard for Palestinian nationality as it existed under the period of British rule. On the effects of both 'citizenship' in the West Bank and Gaza Strip, and the acquisition of another nationality, he stated: "Given the fact that even the former Palestine Mandate citizenship, formally created by the existing Palestinian Citizenship Order which had also entitled a similar right to abode, did not lead to these results, *a fortiori* the same result should apply in the case of the autonomous Palestinian areas".[84] Had a comprehensive study on nationality under the British rule been available to Zimmermann,[85] he perhaps would not have made this analogy.[86]

---

76 See pp. 236–237.

77 Above pp. 14–15.

78 Both Takkenberg and Zimmermann have concurred with C. Bierwirth's conclusion in *Zum Einbürgerungsanspruch in der Bundesrepublik Deutscbland geborener Kinder palästinensischer Eltern* ("Naturalization Claims of Children Born in the FRG [Federal Republic of Germany] of Palestinian Parents"—Takkenberg's translation, p. 178, note 24), ZDWF, Bonn, 1990.

79 See pp. 240–242.

80 P. 242.

81 P. 245; emphasis added.

82 See pp. 243–246.

83 P. 246.

84 *Ibid.*

85 As will be illustrated below (Chapter VII, Section 2), the acquisition of a foreign citizenship was a reason for the loss of Palestinian nationality; and, likewise, the acquisition of Palestinian nationality was a reason for the loss of foreign citizenship in some cases, in accordance with the 1925 Citizenship Order and its amendments.

86 For similar examples, see Anis F. Kassim, "The Palestinians: From Hyphenated to Integrated Citizenship", in Nils A. Butenschon, Uri Davis and Manuel Hassassian, eds., *Citizenship and the State in the Middle East: Approaches and Applications*, Syracuse University Press, 2000, pp. 201–224; Victor Kattan, "The Nationality of Denationalized Palestinians", *Nordic Journal of International Law*, Vol. 74, 2005, pp. 67–102. Kassim conducted an overview on Palestinian nationality during the mandate (pp. 203–204), as part of his consideration to the definition of who the 'Palestinian' is. His study is primarily based on the statuses of individuals, who held Palestinian nationality before 1948,

In all studies, from 1926 until 2006, a considerable number of issues relating to Palestinian nationality under the period of British rule, and its international legal consequences, have not been thoroughly discussed or, in many instances, not even mentioned. Such issues which merit further attention include, *inter alia*, the following: the effects of Ottoman nationality on Palestinian nationality and the relevance of the law of state succession in this respect; the various stages of evolution of that nationality, from 1917 until 1925; the nationality of individuals who were residing in Palestine upon the enactment of the Palestinian Citizenship Order in 1925 (based on the statistics relating to the status of population at the time); the motives of the said Citizenship Order, its drafting process, its origin and legal value; the regional context in which Palestinian nationality had been evolved; the status of Palestine natives residing abroad; naturalization as a key tool to confer Palestinian nationality on immigrants and its direct connection with the overall goal of the mandate; the substantive provisions of the 1925 Citizenship Order in relation to other states; with the exception of one writer,[87] the evaluation of the legal consequences to the judgements of the Palestine Supreme Court in regard to nationality; the international recognition of Palestinian nationality; diplomatic protection of Palestinians abroad; Palestinian passports and identity documents; the relationship between the admission of foreigners into Palestine and nationality; applicability of the international treaties relating to nationality in Palestine; nationality at the end of the British rule as envisaged, in particular, in the United Nations Partition Plan of 29 November 1947, and the legal value and future implications of such a Plan on nationality. Obviously, these issues are directly connected with public international law. Regarding the references, most of the previous studies

in accordance with the laws of their present places of residence rather than according to international law. In this connection, see also Abbas Shiblak, "Residency Status and Civil Rights of Palestinian Refugees in Arab Countries", *Journal of Palestine Studies*, Vol. 25, No. 3, 1996, pp. 36–45. Despite their novel content and attractive research style, no reference to Palestinian nationality has been made in the latter two works. See also Takkenberg, *op. cit.*, pp. 131–171. On the other hand, Kattan devoted his work to the study of Palestinian nationality from the international legal perspective. But he primarily focused, as many writers did, on "Israel's denationalization of the former non-Jewish citizens of the British mandate of Palestine" (p. 70) without attaching significance to the nationality of these 'former' Palestinians in international law. This, among other gaps in Kattan's analysis, might have led him to 'simply' conclude, without apparent regard for the legal repercussions of such a position, that "for the purposes of international law Palestinians have no nationality" (p. 90). He did not say what are the 'purposes of international law', which directed him to think that 'Palestinians', without distinction between their various categories, are 'stateless persons'. "The reason for this", he went on, "is that Palestinians were denationalized by Israel in 1952". While, it is true, the 1952 nationality law applies to inhabitants of the parts of Palestine that became Israel, it did not apply outside Israel, including in the West Bank and Gaza Strip. Moreover, Israel law cannot alter, as Kattan himself observed, a rule of international law, particularly the law of state succession, which obliges the successor state (Israel) to confer *ipso facto* its nationality on citizens of the predecessor state (Palestine).

87 Vitta, *op. cit.*; see *infra* note 702.

relied on a certain set of documents, mainly the League of Nations documents, as well as, albeit to a lesser extent, British government documents and, in a few instances, the legislation of Palestine and case law. No study to date has involved a comprehensive inquiry of the available materials and literature.

For these reasons, a study on Palestinian nationality under the British rule is required.

6. *Sources*

This study is largely based on primary materials. Equal consideration will be given to both international documents and to legal instruments produced in Palestine.

At the international level, these documents incorporate treaties, resolutions and reports of the League of Nations (and, to a lesser extent, United Nations), policy papers of Britain as a Mandatory, the case law of international judicial bodies and decisions of municipal courts, as well as the nationality legislation of other states.

The legislation of Palestine (constitutional instruments, ordinances, regulations and rules) and the decisions of the Palestinian courts (especially the Supreme Court sitting as a High Court of Justice), are widely utilized. Such legislation and court precedents are of international value as they were enacted or decided directly by the British government, by the British-run Government of Palestine or by the Palestinian courts, which were principally managed by British judges and monitored by the (British) Privy Council acting as a court of appeal for the decisions of Palestinian courts. The court's decisions are particularly significant because they were of such considerable value that amounted to the level of legislation. This is due to the fact that the court's judgments, following the English Common Law system,[88] had binding effects, not only upon the case in question, but also upon all other cases, which were decided by any court at the same or lower levels.

Aside from primary materials, secondary academic works are also consulted. These works, books and articles, would be used to provide brief backgrounds on certain historical contexts in Palestine at the time, or to examine the broader legal position, before the consideration of specific substantive points relating to Palestinian nationality. Rather than involving itself in a detailed academic discourse and theoretical argumentation, this study is concerned with functional matters relating to nationality as they were concretely and legally existed in Palestine under the

88 According to Articles 7–9 of the (British) Foreign Jurisdiction Act of 4 August 1890, which was extended to Palestine and other British colonies (Laws of Palestine, p. 3233), Palestinian courts were regarded as British courts. For this reason, decisions of the Supreme Court of Palestine were subject to appeal by the (British) Privy Council, which might then uphold or reject the rulings of the Palestinian Court; see Articles 44 of the Palestine Order-in-Council (Constitution) of 1922 (Laws of Palestine, p. 3303). On the applicability of certain British laws, and the binding effects of the English Courts' judgements in Palestine, see Article 43 of the said Order-in-Council.

British rule or shortly before that rule. This might lead, in some parts of the study, to the lack of discussion on certain general historical or legal matters. But that can be easily substituted by the references listed within relevant parts; to avoid replicating issues that already studied by other writers.

7. *Division*

With this Introduction (Chapter I), the present study consists of twelve chapters.

Chapter II will be devoted to nationality under the Ottoman Empire, as the status of 'Ottoman subject' was required for the automatic acquisition of Palestinian nationality when the latter nationality was first initiated. The Chapter will then review the context in which the Ottoman Nationality Law of 1869 was enacted, particularly the influence of the Capitulation system which was applicable in the Empire at the time, and the substantive provisions of that Law. This will be of benefit in terms of understanding how nationality subsequently evolved in Palestine. The question of Ottoman passports, with brief reference to the Ottoman identity cards, will also be studied; these passports and cards were considered as acceptable evidence for Ottoman status in Palestine. The overall influence of Ottoman nationality on the Palestinian legal system, especially with regard to the treatment of foreigners in Palestinian courts, will lastly be mentioned.

The transitional period between the end of the Ottoman presence in Palestine (1917) and the enactment of Palestinian Citizenship in 1925 will be explored in Chapter III. This period incorporates three stages. The first started on 9 December 1917 when the British forces invaded Palestine and lasted until the adoption of the Palestine Mandate by the League of Nations on 24 July 1922. The second stage commenced from the latter date until the enforcement of the Treaty of Lausanne on 6 August 1924, whereby Palestine was officially detached from the Ottoman Empire. The final stage ran from that date until 1 August 1925, the day on which the Palestinian Citizenship Order (which was enacted on 24 July 1925) came into effect. Before determining the status of nationality in Palestine during these stages, the regional context within which Palestinian nationality developed, namely the evolution of nationality in Palestine's neighboring countries, will be briefly highlighted.

Chapter IV will outline the historical and philosophical background as well as the legal value and the motives of the 1925 Palestinian Citizenship Order. This chapter forms a necessary introduction to the substantive provisions of the Citizenship Order that will themselves be detailed in the subsequent three chapters.

Perhaps the most important part of this study, from a practical viewpoint and that of domestic law, is Chapter V, which will clarify the status of 'natural Palestinians', or those individuals whose Ottoman nationality was automatically replaced by Palestinian nationality upon the enforcement of the 1925 Palestinian Citizenship Order. The status of Ottoman subjects who were habitually residing in Palestine (and who constituted the bulk of the Palestinian population) upon the enforcement of the said Order will be first reviewed. The problematic status of those persons who were born in Palestine but were residing abroad upon the enforcement of the same Order will then be addressed in the light of the applicable law and in accordance with the practice of the British Empire and the British-run Government of Palestine. It might be useful to note, from the outset, that the status of this group of Palestine-natives had never been addressed (except in very general terms) by any of the authors who wrote about Palestinian nationality. This chapter will conclude by touching upon the two legal principles that underlined the acquisition of Palestinian nationality at birth, *jus sanguinis* and *jus soli*.

Chapter VI will discuss the acquisition of Palestinian nationality by naturalization. This chapter has a particular significance as it deals with the issue of naturalization not only in accordance with the 1925 Citizenship Order (which in itself, comparatively speaking, differed little from similar legislation on naturalization in other states); but also as it examines the practical effects of that naturalization by which (in 1946) some 130,000 foreigners, 99% of whom were Jews, had acquired Palestinian nationality. These naturalized Palestinian citizens, along with a larger number of Jewish immigrants as well as Jewish refugees and a smaller number of Palestine-native Jews, constituted the citizens of Israel on 15 May 1948.

Expatriation, or the loss of nationality (mainly in accordance with the 1925 Palestinian Citizenship Order), shall be considered in Chapter VII. By comparing the Order's provisions with the nationality legislation of other states, with special reference to the British law, this chapter will touch upon the loss of Palestinian nationality as a result of naturalization abroad, revocation of nationality as punishment, by marriage of Palestinian women with a foreigner, or by a minors' declaration of alienage.

Chapter VIII will tackle selected external aspects of Palestinian nationality. Although these aspects are many in number, the chapter will address only three external issues according to which Palestinian nationality had become plainly manifest at the international level. These are: the recognition of Palestinian nationality by other states, particularly through the examination of selected decisions of domestic courts; the question of Palestinian passports which were issued by the Government of Palestine and by British consulates abroad; and the protection of Palestinian citizens during their travel or residence outside Palestine.

As a closely connected subject to nationality, Chapter IX will briefly review the admission of foreigners into Palestine. This admission had a direct influence on Palestinian nationality, as the systematic immigration of foreign Jews into Palestine was used as a preliminary step for the naturalization of immigrants with Palestinian nationality. This topic will examine the provisions of various immigration legislation (ordinances, regulations and rules) as well as related British policy and practice. The chapter will conclude by a note on the admission of Palestinian citizens into Palestine and its relevance to the question of deportation.

A somewhat different issue, which might appear to be an unusual topic, is the study on the applicability of international nationality instruments in Palestine, which will be raised in Chapter X. These instruments comprise the Convention on Certain

Questions Relating to the Conflict of Nationality Laws and its Protocols, which were adopted by the first conference on the codification of international law, convened in The Hague in 1930. The chapter will first review those legal procedures which led to the extension of the said instruments into Palestine and, then, examine the substantive influence of these instruments on the Palestinian legal system. The purpose of such a review is to open the debate on the fate of the numerous international treaties that were brought to Palestine and their future effects in the would-be Palestinian state. For this reason, the chapter will conclude with a note evaluating the on-going validity of the said instruments at present.

The legal value of the rules on Palestinian nationality as envisaged in the United Nations proposal for the Partition of Palestine of 29 November 1947 will be studied in Chapter XI. This will be done by evaluating the said rules in the light of the international law of state succession plus the existing facts relating to nationality at the end of the mandate.

In the Conclusion (Chapter XII), the findings of the study will be summed up. Tentative conclusions on the implication of the issues discussed in this study on the future of Palestinian nationality will be finally flagged.

II

NATIONALITY IN PALESTINE UNDER THE OTTOMAN EMPIRE

1. *A short history*

The land of Palestine formed part of the Ottoman/Turkish Empire from 1516. By the end of the sixteenth century, Ottoman rule extended westward in Europe to the borders of Austria and along the southern rim of the Mediterranean Sea into Algeria.[89] During this period, there was no entity called 'Palestine'. Rather, this land fell under the administrative divisions of the Turks. In 1874 towards the end of the Ottoman Empire, Jerusalem and its surrounding towns became a separate district governed directly from Istanbul. This division did not change the international legal status of that Ottoman territory. In the midst of World War I, during which Britain and Turkey were enemies, the territory that became known as Palestine fell under British military occupation on 9 December 1917.[90]

---

89 On the history of the Ottoman Empire, in general, see Lucy M. Garnett, *Turkey of the Ottomans*, Sir Isaac Pitman & Sons Ltd., London, 1911; André Mandelstam, *Le sort de l'Empire Ottoman*, Librairie Payot, Lausanne/Paris, 1917; René Pinon, *L'Europe et l'Empire Ottoman: les aspects actuels de la question d'orient*, Librairie académique, Paris, 1917; William Miller, *The Ottoman Empire and its Successors, 1801–1922*, University Press, Cambridge, 1923; Antoine Hokayem and Marie Claude Bittar, *L'Empire Ottoman: les Arabes et les grandes puissances, 1914–1920*, Les editions universitaires du Liban, Beyrouth, 1981; Efraim Karsh and Inari Karsh, *Empire of the Sand: The Struggle for Mastery in the Middle East, 1789–1923*, Harvard University Press, Cambridge/Massachusetts/London, 1999; Mohammad Harb, *The Ottomans in History and Civilization*, Al-Qalam House, Damascus, 1999 (Arabic).

90 On the history of Palestine under the Ottoman Empire, see, *inter alia*, Vital Cuinet, *Syrie, Liban et Palestine, géographie administrative: statistique, descriptive et raisonnée*, Ernest Leroux, Paris, 1896, pp. 513 ff.; Noël Verney and George Dambmann, *Les puissances étrangères dans le levant en Syrie et en Palestine*, Librairie Guillaumin, Paris, 1900; Ellsworth Huntington, *Palestine and its Transformation*, Houghton Mifflin Company, Boston/New York, 1911; Albert M. Hyamson, *Palestine: The Rebirth of an Ancient People*, Sidgwick & Jackson, London, 1917; Historical Section of the [British] Foreign Office, *Mohammedanism: Turkey in Asia*, H.M. Stationary Office, London, Vol. I, 1920; Stephen S. Wise and Jacob De Haas, *The Great Betrayal*, Stratford Press,

Under Ottoman rule, the inhabitants of Palestine were Ottoman subjects. Those persons known later as 'Palestinians', had no particular legal status under Ottoman rule. As such, a distinct 'Palestinian people' did not exist at that time. The 'Palestinians' constituted a sector of the larger 'Ottoman people'.

To acquire Palestinian nationality at its first inception, one was required to hold the status of 'Ottoman subject', or Ottoman citizen. Upon the entry into force of the Treaty of Lausanne (the international instrument according to which Palestine was legally separated from Turkey) on 24 July 1923,[91] Ottomans who resided in the territory of Palestine became *ipso facto* 'Palestinian citizens'. This was domestically confirmed by the Palestinian Citizenship Order, which was enacted by Britain in 1925.[92] Hence, it is imperative to review Ottoman nationality as it forms the root of Palestinian nationality in accordance with international law.[93]

2. *Ottoman Nationality Law, 1869*

A. *General*

Ottoman nationality was first codified by the Ottoman Nationality Law, enacted on 19 January 1869 (hereinafter: 'the 1869 Law').[94] This Law constituted the only

---

New York, 1930, pp. 11–50; Angelo S. Rappoport, *Histoire de la Palestine des origines jusqu'a nos jours*, Payot, Paris, 1932, pp. 211–226; Norman Bentwich, *Palestine*, Ernest Benn, London, 1934, pp. 31–72; Herbert Sidebotham, *Great Britain and Palestine*, Macmillan and Co., London, 1937, pp. 3–66; Nevill Barbour, *Nisi Dominus: A Survey of the Palestine Controversy*, George G. Harrap, London, 1946, pp. 42–87; Kayyali, *Palestine: A Modern History*, Billing and Sons, London, 1979, pp. 11–41; A.W. Ann Mosely Lesch, *Arab Politics in Palestine: The Frustration of a National Movement*, Cornell University Press, London, 1979; Joan Peters, *From Time Immemorial: The Origins of Arab-Jewish Conflict over Palestine*, Harper & Row, New York, 1984; Charles D. Smith, *Palestine and the Arab Israeli Conflict*, St. Martin's Press, New York, 1992, pp. 10–25; Alexander Scholch, *Palestine in Transformation 1856–1882: Studies in Social, Economic and Political Development*, Institute for Palestine Studies, Washington, D.C., 1993; Samih K. Farsoun and Christina E. Zacharia, *Palestine and the Palestinians*, Westview Press, Colorado, 1997, pp. 67–72. On the legal system under the Ottoman Empire, with particular reference to Palestine, see Feras Milhem, *The Origins and Evolution of the Palestinian Sources of Law*, Vrije Universiteit Brussel, Faculty of Law, Brussels, 2004, pp. 17–51 (Ph.D. thesis—unpublished).

91 See below Chapter III, Section 4.

92 See below Chapter IV.

93 For details on Ottoman nationality, see P. Arminjon, "De la nationalité dans l'Empire ottoman spécialement en Egypte", *Revue générale de droit international public*, Vol. VIII, 1901, pp. 520–567; Pierre Arminjon, *Etrangers et protégés dans l'Empire ottoman*, Librairie Marescq Ainé, Paris, 1903, pp. 81–259 (Mr. Arminjon was a judge in the Egyptian Mixed Courts, which adjudicated cases involving foreigners); Goadby, *op. cit.*, pp. 37–42; Ghali, *op. cit.*, pp. 57–78.

94 For the text of this law, see Collection of Nationality Laws, p. 568.

legislation that governed nationality under the Ottoman Empire. The 1869 Law was the legislative instrument that was governing the nationality of Palestine's inhabitants on the eve of the British occupation of Palestine on 9 December 1917.

The 1869 Ottoman Nationality Law was never expressly repealed in Palestine and therefore it may be viewed as having some legal validity even today. However, most of that Law's substantive provisions were replaced by a number of nationality legislation that was incrementally enforced in the various entities into which the country was divided after 1948. Certain provisions of that Ottoman law will be addressed under relevant topics later in the present study.

Prior to the 1869 Law, nationality was based on the Islamic law that was applicable in the Ottoman Empire and individuals were classified along religious lines.[95] *Ra'aya* (or subjects) in the Islamic state (or *dar al-Islam*) were all the world's Muslims. Persons belonging to religious minorities permanently residing within the Islamic state, notably Christians and Jews, were called *thimmiyyeen* (or protected persons). *Thimmiyyeen* were treated on the same footing as Muslims except in private matters such as marriage, divorce and inheritance. Such matters were governed by each religious group according to its own tradition/religion.

Apart from the Muslims and the *thimiyyeen*, all persons residing outside the Islamic domains (or *dar al-harb*) were deemed to be foreigners. Foreigners, in turn, were divided into two categories, *muharibeen* and *mustamineen. Muharibeen* (literally meaning hostiles or 'alien enemies')[96] included those persons who belonged to countries which were in a state of war with the Muslims. *Mustamineen* (literally meaning secured persons or 'alien friends')[97] encompassed subjects of those states which enjoyed peaceful relations with *dar al-Islam*.

The 1869 Law was considered an evolution in the concept of nationality under the Ottoman Empire and in the history of Islam as a whole. It transformed the idea of citizenship into a secular concept by abandoning religion as the basis for nationality. In classifying all persons as either citizens or foreigners, regardless of their religion, the drafters of the law were inspired by the French legal model.[98] However, the 1869 Law remained true to such previous practices, such as the granting of citizenship to all Muslims and the prohibition of nationality's change. It should be noted that the adoption of the said Nationality Law constituted part of the overall reform process (or *tanzimat*) adopted by the Ottoman Empire in the

95 On the nationality and Islam, in general, see Jean S. Saba, *L'Islam et la nationalité*, Librairie de jurisprudence ancienne et moderne, Paris, 1931 (Ph.D. thesis); Adulkarim Zeedan, *The Status of the Thimiyyeen* [non-Muslim citizens] *and Mustamineen* [foreigners] *in the Islamic State*, Alresala Foundation, Cairo, 1988 (Arabic); Salah Eldeen Jamal Eldeen, *The Legal System of Nationality in the Islamic State*, Dar Alfikr Aljamie, Alexandria, 2004 (Arabic); Haytham Manna, *Citizenship in Arab Islamic History*, Cairo Institute for Human Rights, Cairo (undated); Ghali, *op. cit.*, pp. 36–43.

96 On the concept and status of enemy aliens in Britain, see William Evan Davies, *The English Law Relating to Aliens*, Stevens and Sons, London, 1931, pp. 230–250.

97 On 'alien friend', see *ibid.*, pp. 160–229.

98 Arminjon, *Etrangers et protégés dans l'Empire ottoman, op. cit.*, pp. 72, 91; Arminjon, "De la nationalité dans l'Empire ottoman", *op. cit.*, p. 520; Ghali, *op. cit.*, p. 61.

mid-nineteenth century to modernize its old-fashioned laws and institutions.[99] Hence, it can be generally said, the nationality rules that existed at the end of the Empire were derived from mixed Islamic and European legal traditions.[100]

Due to its weakness at the time, European Powers had increased their pressure on the Ottoman Empire. The European intervention in the internal affairs of the Empire had been initiated on the pretext of protecting religious minorities. That intervention was then systematically extended to the foreigners by excluding them from laws applicable to the Ottoman subjects. Such systematic intervention, which was demonstrable in a set of agreements concluded between Turkey and other Powers (mainly Western), came to be known as the 'capitulation system'.[101]

The capitulation system dated back to the sixteenth century.[102] It was exemplified by the agreement concluded between France and the Ottoman Empire in 1535.[103] This agreement, *inter alia*, gave France the power to extend its protection to the Christian Catholics in Bethlehem and Jerusalem. Under the system, foreigners were exempt from the application of most local Ottoman laws pertaining to civil, commercial, criminal and personal matters. Ottoman courts had no jurisdiction to pronounce upon cases involving foreigners. Instead, consular tribunals were given such jurisdiction. Foreigners enjoyed the freedom to publish, travel, import and

---

99 See, in detail, Ed Engelhardt, *La Turquie et le Tanzimat, ou histoire des réformes dans l'Empire Ottoman depuis 1826 jusqu'a nos jours*, Libraires du Conseil d'Etat, Paris, 1884; Saba, *op. cit.*, pp. 65–87; Milhem, *op. cit.*, pp. 27–49.

100 However, it should be noted that 'nationality', or its application throughout the history of Islam, has never been mentioned in the *Koran* (the holy book that Muslims believe as the words of God) or the *Sunna* (Prophet Mohammad's sayings and conduct). The concept of nationality was rather developed by Islamic scholars based on, *inter alia*, the idea that Muslims constitute one unified *umma* (or nation). See Saba, *op. cit.*, pp. 36–64. And on the sources of law under the Ottoman Empire as applied in Palestine, see, e.g., Ahmad Safwat, *Legislative and Judicial System in Palestine*, Aletimad Press, Egypt, 1918 (Arabic); C.A. Hooper, *The Civil Law of Palestine and Trans-Jordan*, Jerusalem, 1936, Vol. II; Majid Khadduri and Herbert Liebesny, eds., *Law in the Middle East*, The Middle East Institute, Washington, D.C., 1955, Vol. I ("Origin and Development of Islamic Law"); Mohammad Al-Zohayli, *History of the Judiciary in Islam*, Dar Al-Fikr, Beirut/Damascus, 1995 (Arabic), pp. 424–470; Milhem, *op. cit.*, pp. 17–51.

101 *Cf.* Khadduri and Liebesny, *op. cit.*, p. 309.

102 See, in detail, G. Pélissié du Rausas, *Régime des capitulations dans l'Empire ottoman*, Arthur Rousseau, Paris, 1910, Vol. I, pp. 1–128, 197–411; Lucius Ellsworth Thayer, "The Capitulations of the Ottoman Empire and the Question of their Abrogation as it affects the United States", *The American Journal of International Law*, Vol. 17, 1923, pp. 207–233; Frederick Perker Walton, "Egyptian Law: Sources and Judicial Organization", in Elemér Balogh, ed., *Les sources du droit positif... Egypte—Palestine—Chine—Japon*, Hermann Sack Verlag, Birlin, 1929, pp. 13–37; Khadduri and Liebesny, *op. cit.*, pp. 309 ff.; Arminjon, "De la nationalité dans l'Empire ottoman", *op. cit.*, pp. 523–33; Arminjon, *Etrangers et protégés dans l'Empire ottoman, op. cit.*, pp. 5–80; Goadby, *International and Inter-Religious Private Law in Palestine, op. cit.*, pp. 56–88; Saba, *op. cit.*, pp. 24–35.

103 Auguste Benoit, *Etude sur les capitulations entre l'Empire ottoman et la France*, Librairie nouvelle de droit et de jurisprudence, Paris, 1890.

export and were exempt from tax and certain custom duties. In short, the capitulation system constituted, according to the treaties and subsequent practice, "a state within a state"[104] and severely undermined the Empire's sovereignty.

The European Powers were the main beneficiaries of the capitulation. The last capitulation treaties, agreed upon with the Ottoman rulers, involved fifteen states. These states can be enumerated as follows:[105] Britain (1675), Austro-Hungary (1718), Norway (1737), Sweden (also 1737), France (1740), Denmark (1756), Germany (1761), Spain (1782), Russia (1783), Belgium (1838), Portugal (1843), Greece (1855), Netherlands (1860), Italy (1861) and Romania (1906). Two American Powers, namely the United States (1830) and Brazil (1858), were signatories of similar treaties.[106] The capitulation treaties had significantly influenced the substantive provisions of the 1869 Ottoman Nationality Law.

B. *Substance*

In its nine articles, the 1869 Ottoman Nationality Law addressed the main issues that were covered by nationality laws of other states at the time. Although it was not directly referred to within the Law, the capitulation system had significantly shaped Ottoman nationality. The existence of the capitulation explains the rather anomalous rules of the 1869 Law in regard to such issues as naturalization, the changing of nationality and the status of dependants (married women and children).

The 1869 Law adopted the two widely recognized principles that govern the acquisition of nationality by birth: *jus sanguinis* and *jus soli*.[107] Article 1 defined Ottoman citizens as: "Persons born at a time when their parents or only father are of Ottoman nationality". This provision was a manifestation of the *jus sanguinis* principle, according to which children acquire the father's nationality at the time of the child's birth.[108] The Law recognized *jus soli* in two cases. Firstly, it enabled any foreigner born in the Empire to opt for Ottoman nationality within the three years from the date on which he attained his majority (Article 2).[109]

---

104 Thayer, *op. cit.*, p. 207.

105 The date in brackets is the year of the latest capitulation treaty concluded by the Ottoman Empire with the relevant state.

106 *The British Yearbook of International Law*, 1937, p. 79 (note); Thayer, *op. cit.*, pp. 211–212. *Cf. infra* note 201.

107 On these two principles, see below Chapter V, Section 3.

108 Arminjon, *Etrangers et protégés dans l'Empire ottoman, op. cit.*, p. 80.

109 The majority age was not determined by this article. But it was "presumably to be calculated according to the foreign law" (Goadby, *International and Inter-Religious Private Law in Palestine, op. cit.*, p. 38). Arminjon (*Etrangers et protégés dans l'Empire ottoman, op. cit.*, pp. 85–86), believes that the majority age should be fixed according to Ottoman personal status law applicable to foreigners. In this case, the majority age might differ from one foreigner to another based on his or her religion, because the age of majority should be fixed by the religious law. This problem was solved later by the Treaty of Lausanne, then in the Palestinian Citizenship Order of 1925, by fixing the

Secondly, Article 9 regarded every person inhabiting Ottoman territory as an Ottoman citizen, unless the person proves his foreign status.[110] The latter rule implied that a child born in the Empire to unknown or stateless father/parents was to be deemed as an Ottoman citizen.[111]

Naturalization in the Empire was permitted in two cases. By residing in an Ottoman territory for five years or more, Article 3 gave any foreigner the right to apply for the Empire's nationality.[112] In Article 4,[113] the Ottoman Government reserved for itself the right to naturalize any foreigner, even if he did not meet the requirement of five-year residence. Under this rule, "converts to Islam were often admitted to Ottoman Nationality".[114] This practice was influenced by the pre-1869 Law precedent that, as already mentioned, all Muslims of the world being regarded as subjects of the Empire/Islam's domain. Under the same provision, it was reported that during World War I the Empire had granted Ottoman nationality by naturalization to all subjects of the Allied Powers.[115]

The rules of the 1869 Law regarding expatriation (or the changing of one's Ottoman nationality) provoked controversy in the Empire's international relations. Indeed, this was *la raison d'être* of the 1869 Law.[116] Most of those who acquired foreign nationality were Ottoman Christians with a view to benefit from the capitulation immunities and privileges, which were afforded to European or American citizens.[117] Thus, prohibiting expatriation intended "to prevent dishonest naturalization".[118] This question was summarized as follows:

> Owing to the capitulatory régime in Turkey, a peculiar system had developed which enabled many Ottomans to place themselves under the protection of foreign diplomatic nations and thereby escape Ottoman jurisdiction. Under that system many Ottomans...were accepted as *protégés*. The practice became so widespread that finally in some places the number of *protégés* exceeded the number of Turks. In order to correct that situation, the Ottoman Government passed a law in 1860 requiring all *protégés* to leave

---

majority age at eighteen for all nationality purposes. See below Chapter III, Section 4, and p. 85.

110 For the application of this rule in Palestine, see *Hausdorff v. Director of Immigration*, Palestine Court sitting as High Court of Justice, 6 July 1933 (Law Reports of Palestine, p. 822).

111 Arminjon, "De la nationalité dans l'Empire ottoman", *op. cit.*, p. 521.

112 A request to this effect had to be submitted to the Ottoman Ministry of Foreign Affairs.

113 This article is borrowed from Article 9 of the French Civil Code (Arminjon, *Etrangers et protégés dans l'Empire ottoman, op. cit.*, p. 84).

114 Goadby, *International and Inter-Religious Private Law in Palestine, op. cit.*, p. 39.

115 See, for example, *Robinson v. Press and Others*, Supreme Court of Palestine sitting as Court of Appeal, 20 February 1925 (Law Reports of Palestine, p. 27). *Cf. Nahum Razkovsky v. Leonine Razkovsky and Others*, Supreme Court of Palestine sitting as a Court of Appeal, 23 May 1927 (*ibid.*, p. 144).

116 Arminjon, *Etrangers et protégés dans l'Empire ottoman, op. cit.*, pp. 70–71.

117 Rausas, Vol. II, pp. 80–177.

118 Goadby, *International and Inter-Religious Private Law in Palestine, op. cit.*, p. 39.

> the empire within three months, with the provision that if they remained they became subject to Ottoman law. Admitting the justice of the Ottoman law, the various diplomatic missions recognized it under the form of 'Regulations in Regard to foreign Consulates' of 1863.... While the regulations of 1863 ended the abuse of the *protégé* system, they gave rise to a new method of evasion of Ottoman jurisdiction. Former *protégés* in large numbers became naturalized citizens of another country in order to place themselves under the protection of the capitulations. Within a few years the number of 'naturalized' persons in the empire exceeded the number of real foreigners. That abuse was met by the Ottoman law of 1869, which denied the right of expatriation.[119]

Accordingly, Article 5 of the 1869 Law advanced this rule as follows:

> Persons who, being authorized, enter from Ottoman into a foreign nationality are, from the date when they changed their nationality, considered as foreign subjects and treated as such. But if he should enter into a foreign nationality without being authorized by the Imperial Ottoman Government his new nationality shall be considered as null and void, and he shall be considered as an Ottoman subject as before, and in every matter he shall be treated exactly as Ottoman subjects are treated. In any case, the abandonment by an Ottoman subject of his or her nationality depends on an instrument to be granted in virtue of an imperial *irade* [sultan's decree].

The regime created a situation whereby Ottoman citizens could go abroad, acquire foreign nationality, then return to their native land and be exempt from Ottoman laws like other foreigners. The situation was complicated by the fact that, as one writer reported, "some of the returned emigrants acted as agents in fomenting revolutionary activity"[120] against the Empire. Many of them owned property in Ottoman territory for which, as foreigners, they paid no taxes.[121] To appreciate the concerns of the Ottoman rulers, it is worthwhile to note that of an estimated 1.2 million Ottomans who had emigrated to the Americas in the period of 1860–1914 (and apparently acquired foreign nationality), one-third subsequently returned to their native homes.[122] As has been documented, "In the first twenty-four years of the twentieth century, it is estimated that 70,000 naturalized Americans returned to Turkey, and questions regarding their rights have caused endless controversy between the Ottoman and American Governments".[123]

In particular, the Empire exercised its power to deny the return of those Ottomans who had acquired foreign nationality to its territory. On 21 April 1869, the Government declared in a memorandum circulated to foreign offices in Istanbul that a citizen might become a foreigner if he moved to live abroad:

> C'est ainsi qu'il s'est formé en Turquie tout un corps de protégés étrangers dont le nombre dépassait celui des sujets étrangers eux-mêmes. C'étaient tous des sujets ottomans

119 Leland J. Gordon, "The Turkish American Controversy over Nationality", *The American Journal of International Law*, Vol. 25, 1931, p. 659.

120 *Ibid.*, p. 661.

121 *Ibid.*

122 See Kemal H. Karpat, "The Ottoman Emigration to America, 1860–1914", *International Journal of Middle East Studies*, Vol. 17, 1985, p. 185.

123 Gordon, *op. cit.*, p. 658.

> qui tout en ayant domicile permanent dans l'Empire, se soustrayaient à leur autorité légitime. En dehors de protégés, la Sublime Porte s'est trouvée en présence d'un certain nombre de sujets ottoman qui revendiquaient les privilèges et les immunités octroyées par les capitulations en vertu d'une naturalisation des étrangers.[124]

Therefore, an Ottoman citizen who acquired foreign nationality could not benefit from the status of a foreigner within the Empire. Such a person had no right, for instance, to claim diplomatic protection during his sojourn in Turkey.[125] Nor could an ex-Ottoman, unlike other foreigners, own real estate within the Empire according to the *Law concerning the Disposition of Foreign Subjects of Property*, 9 June 1867.[126] The Ottoman Government instructed, on 20 June 1873, that the property of an Ottoman woman should not be transferred to her foreign husband or children by inheritance.[127] Thus, "naturalized Turks are debarred from inheriting from Ottoman subjects".[128] It was further reported on 3 May 1895 that Ottoman consulates in the United States refused to grant visas to certain naturalized Americans from Ottoman origin.[129] Some returnees were even arrested.[130]

States responded variously to the protection of those Ottomans *within* the Empire, who concurrently were nationals of those states. In general, European states were sympathetic to the Ottoman law and therefore developed special regulations concerning naturalized citizens who sought to return to their native land. Belgium, France and the Netherlands refused to naturalize Ottoman subjects without Imperial consent. Germany and Italy protected all naturalized persons on their return to their native countries, with the exception of those from Turkey. Britain and Russia generally refrained from protecting these ex-Turks during their stay in Turkey; a note to this effect was indicated on passports that were granted to naturalized persons.[131] However, the United States insisted on its right to protect naturalized Americans of Ottoman origin in all countries, including during their residence in their native land.[132] This issue caused much controversy in Ottoman-American relations for many years.[133]

---

124 *Mémoire du gouvernement ottoman en date d'avril 1869* (Arminjon, *Etrangers et protégés dans l'Empire ottoman, op. cit.*, p. 338).

125 Arminjon, *Etrangers et protégés dans l'Empire ottoman, op. cit.*, pp. 73–74 (note).

126 Completion of Ottoman Laws, Vol. 3, p. 139, Article 1. The date, as provided in the source, is 6 *Safar* 1284 *Hijri* (see *infra* note 485), which is equivalent to 9 June 1867.

127 See Instructions concerning Inheritance of Foreigner's Wives Who are Nationals of the State; Completion of Ottoman Laws, Vol. 3, p. 141.

128 Digest of International Law, Vol. III, 1906, p. 679 (report dated 21 July 1885).

129 *Ibid.*, p. 680.

130 *Ibid.*, pp. 701–702.

131 *Ibid.*, pp. 685–686, 702–703.

132 For various cases in which the United States exercised or tried to exercise protection to American citizens residing in the Ottoman Empire, see *ibid.*, pp. 679–708.

133 For details, see Gordon, *op. cit.*

Governmental authorization was exceptionally granted when naturalization of Ottomans occurred *outside* the Empire.[134] Such naturalization was given "only upon condition that the applicant shall stipulate either never to return, or, [if] returning, to regard himself as a Turkish subject [i.e. not to benefit from diplomatic protection from the county of naturalization]".[135] Thus, passports delivered to these persons stated that they "will not be allowed to set foot again on Ottoman territory" (Imperial *irede*, 9 October 1896).[136] Many of them, nonetheless, had returned.[137]

Internationally, the prohibition of expatriation had little practical effect *vis-à-vis* other states outside the Empire's jurisdiction. The Ottoman expatriation rule was rejected at the diplomatic and judicial levels.

Diplomatically, from the outset, states have disregarded the Ottoman prohibition of nationality change. For example, shortly after the enactment of the Ottoman Nationality Law, the French Ministry of Foreign Affairs, in a memorandum dated 27 May 1869, protested:

> Attendu que, pour qu'il résultât de la loi nouvelle une atteinte aux droits et privilèges conférés par les capitulations et les usages il faudrait ou que cette loi, en reconnaissant la qualité d'étranger à certains individus, leur enlevât en tout ou en partie les privilèges qui leur sont actuellement attribués, ou bien que, par une disposition rétroactive, elle retirât la qualité d'étranger à ceux qui l'auraient régulièrement obtenue en vertu de la législation antérieure; qu'on devrait également considérer comme une atteinte indirecte aux capitulations toute disposition qui aurait pour effet d'imposer à certaines catégories d'étrangers la nationalité ottoman contrairement à leur volonté;—Considérant qu'aucune disposition de ce genre ne se trouve dans la loi du 19 janvier 1869.

The same memorandum further stated:

> Il y a des personnes qui paraissent croire que la loi aurait un effet rétroactif parce que la Sublime Porte ne veut pas admettre la validité des changement de nationalité opérés abusivement et en dehors des prescriptions des lois mêmes des pays d'adoption de ces nouveaux sujets. Mais les dispositions de la loi ne concernent que les sujets ottomans dont le changement de nationalité se fait légalement. Les autres n'ont été acceptés à aucune époque.[138]

Russia and Greece expressed similar positions.[139] On 11 August 1874, the United States signed a naturalization treaty with Turkey in Istanbul. The treaty provided, *inter alia*, that a naturalized person returning to his native land and residing there for more than two years, without justified reasons set down in the treaty, would lose his acquired American citizenship. The treaty, however, had never been ratified as

---

134 For further details on this problem, see Arminjon, "De la nationalité dans l'Empire ottoman", *op. cit.*, pp. 562–567; Rausas, *op. cit.*, Vol. I, pp. 412–443.

135 Digest of International Law, p. 691; see also pp. 688, 706.

136 *Ibid.*, p. 706.

137 Gordon, *op. cit.*, p. 663.

138 *Ibid.*, pp. 70–72.

139 *Ibid.*, pp. 72–77.

the United States maintained its opposition to the expatriation rule within the1869 Ottoman Nationality Law.[140]

At the judicial level, foreign courts and international tribunals considered the naturalization of Ottoman citizens abroad to be valid. In one typical case before the Franco-Turkish Mixed Arbitral Tribunal (created under the 1923 Treaty of Lausanne) the claimant was originally an Ottoman and subsequently became a French citizen by naturalization without Ottoman Government's authorization. Turkey contended that the claimant was still a Turkish citizen as the 1869 Law did not recognize his naturalization without the Government's permission. In rejecting the defense of the Turkish Government, the Tribunal, interestingly, held:

> According to the principles of international law, the effects of naturalization granted by one State ought to be recognised not only by the authorities of that State, but also by the judicial and administrative authorities of all other States. In the exceptional case where the laws of a State require previous authorization for the naturalization of their subjects abroad, it is only the authorities of that State who are bound by any effects of the failure to comply with the requirement of such authorization. In the present case, the Turkish authorities were entitled to refuse to recognise the French naturalisation of the claimant. But all other judicial authorities, including the international tribunals, far from being bound in this matter by Turkish municipal legislation, were according to public international law under a duty to recognise the validity of the naturalization and to treat the claimant as a French subject.[141]

An international arbitral tribunal reached a similar conclusion in another case, whereupon it was decided:

> The Turkish law [of 1869] which makes the acquisition of foreign nationality dependant on the permission of the Government is internationally not to be objected to.... This rule, however, only means that the State which he leaves cannot reclaim him from the State the nationality of which he acquires, and that the State of origin shall not be entitled to contest the other State's right to bestow nationality on an immigrant. But the above-mentioned principle does not prevent the State of origin making by its national legislation the loss of its nationality dependant on a special permission of its Government, which means that it may treat the emigrant again as its national as soon as he returns into its territory.[142]

---

140 Digest of International Law, pp. 707–708; Gordon, *op. cit.*, pp. 664–666; Karpat, *op. cit.*, pp. 189–192.

141 *Apostolidis v. Turkish Government*, 23 May 1928 (Annual Digest, 1927–1928, p. 312).

142 *Salem Case, United States v. Egypt*, 8 June 1932 (Annual Digest, 1931–1932, p. 188). For further details on the judicial implementation and practical implication of this provision in Palestine after the Ottoman Empire, see, for instance, *Nadeen Markoff v. Habib George Daoud Homsi & 7 ors., all heirs of George Daoud Homsi*, Supreme Court of Palestine sitting as a Court of Civil Appeal, 20 April 1945 (Annotated Law Reports, 1945, Vol. II, p. 617).

Dual, or multiple,[143] nationality was strictly prohibited under the Ottoman rule.[144] This is understood from the rules prescribed by the 1869 Law, which disallowed citizens from changing their nationality without Government authorization and provided for the forfeit of their nationality, had they not received that authorization. Yet, in practice, the fact that the Ottoman Empire did not recognize nationality changes created persons with dual nationality.[145] In a case before a French court, for example, a person born as an Ottoman citizen but then naturalized with French nationality, "had been French in the eyes of French Courts, while remaining an Ottoman subject in the eyes of the Ottoman authorities".[146]

The revocation of nationality was employed as a sanction against citizens which the Ottoman Government considered as having been disloyal to the Empire.[147] Actions such as the acquisition of foreign nationality or engagement in military service for another state without the Government's permission were considered to be disloyal acts. To this effect, Article 6 of the 1869 Law, in part, provided for the withdrawal of Ottoman nationality from a "person who without authorization from the Imperial Ottoman Government, changes his nationality in a foreign country, or enters into the military service of a foreign government".[148] This article also outlawed the "return into the imperial domains of persons of this category whose nationality has been rejected".

Acquiring nationality by marriage was loosely regulated. Article 7 of the 1869 Ottoman Nationality Law prescribed the following provision: "The woman who, while an Ottoman subject, marries a foreigner may return to her original [Ottoman] nationality if, within three years following the date of her husband's death, she petitioned for it". It is not clear from this provision whether the woman would lose her Ottoman nationality merely by marrying a foreigner; or only if she voluntarily acquired her husband's nationality; or if the husband's state conferred automatically its nationality on the wife upon her marriage.[149]

---

143 In this study, the terms 'dual', 'double', 'plural' and 'multiple' nationality have identical meaning.

144 On dual nationality, in general, see C. Maugham, "Some Cases of Double Nationality", *The Juridical Review*, Vol. 4, 1892, pp. 135–143; Richard W. Flournoy, Jr., "Dual Nationality and Election", *Yale Law Journal*, Vol. 30, 1920–1921, pp. 693–709; Lester B. Orfield, "Legal Effects of Dual Nationality", *The George Washington Law Review*, Vol. 17, 1948–1949, pp. 427–445; Linda Bosniak, "Multiple Nationality and the Post-national Transformation of Citizenship", *Virginia Journal of International Law*, Vol. 42, 2002, pp. 979–1004.

145 Edwin M. Borchard, "Basic Elements of Diplomatic Protection of Citizens Abroad", *The American Journal of International Law*, Vol. 7, 1913, p. 509.

146 *Saad v. Tabet*, Civil Tribunal of the Seine, France, 2 July 1930 (Annual Digest, 1929–1930, p. 233).

147 Arminjon, "De la nationalité dans l'Empire ottoman", *op. cit.*, pp. 224–225.

148 See Digest of International Law, pp. 699–700.

149 On the change of nationality, see below Chapter VII.

Contrary to its logic regarding nationality change,[150] the 1869 Law failed to state whether Government authorization was required for an Ottoman woman to acquire her husband's foreign nationality. Nor does the Law make clear whether the marriage itself would be authorized should the woman decide to marry a foreigner whose country automatically awarded her its nationality.[151] Therefore, it would appear that the acquisition of foreign nationality by an Ottoman woman through marriage was subject to the general rules of naturalization.[152] In other words, the woman was obliged to obtain imperial authorization should she desire to assume her husband's nationality.[153] Should such woman have failed to acquire authorization, she would theoretically have been subject to the same penalties that were applicable to unauthorized naturalized persons; i.e. her naturalization would not have been recognized by the Ottoman authorities.[154]

The Law, furthermore, incorporated no provision relating to a foreign woman who married an Ottoman man. Thus, as in a reverse to the case of an Ottoman woman who married with a foreigner, the status of such a woman was governed by the general rules of naturalization. Namely, a foreign woman who married an Ottoman could become an Ottoman citizen by residing for five years within the Empire; or, without satisfying the five-year residence, at the discretion of the Imperial Government.[155] This notwithstanding, one writer after concluding that "an Ottoman woman lost her nationality by marriage with an alien", argued, "by analogy", that "an alien woman marrying an Ottoman became Ottoman".[156]

The foregoing shows that marriage *per se* had no significant effect on nationality within the Ottoman legal system. Citizens retained their Ottoman status even if they married foreigners. Non-citizens would remain foreigners even if they married Ottomans. This practice created hardships for families when a foreign woman married an Ottoman man under the capitulation system; while the foreign woman could exercise her rights, her Ottoman husband and children could not.[157] Such a practice stood in stark contrast to nationality legislation in most other states at the time, pursuant to which wives could obtain the nationality of their spouse.[158]

---

150 See above pp. 199–204.

151 Arminjon, *Etrangers et protégés dans l'Empire ottoman, op. cit.*, pp. 93–94.

152 See above p. 30.

153 For further discussion on this point, see Arminjon, *Etrangers et protégés dans l'Empire ottoman, op. cit.*, pp. 94–101.

154 See above pp. 30–34.

155 Arminjon, *Etrangers et protégés dans l'Empire ottoman, op. cit.*, pp. 101–107.

156 Goadby, *International and Inter-Religious Private Law in Palestine, op. cit.*, p. 41.

157 *Ibid.*, p. 103.

158 Legislation giving the right to nationality by marriage to women included, among many others, the following states: Bolivia Civil Code of 1830 (Collection of Nationality Laws, p. 46), Article 8; Costa Rica Constitution of 7 December 1871 (*ibid.*, p. 184), Article 6(2); Hungary Law of 20 December 1879 Concerning the Acquisition and Loss of Hungarian Citizenship (*ibid.*, p. 337), Articles 5 and 7; Luxemburg Civil Code of 1807 (*ibid.*, p. 420), Article 12; Portugal Civil Code of 1867 (*ibid.*, p. 490), Article

A foreign husband, on the other hand, was unable to become an Ottoman citizen except through the general rules relating to naturalization. Similar provisions were evident in nationality legislation of other states at the time. Only a few countries (most of which were in Latin America), such as Argentina,[159] Brazil,[160] and Paraguay,[161] gave a foreign man or woman the right to acquire nationality by marrying a citizen (in addition, of course, to the foreign women who married male citizens).[162]

Contrary to the laws of most states, the naturalization of the father had no effect upon his children. A child would remain Ottoman even if his father ceased to be a citizen of the Empire. This was a consequence of the rule of the 1869 Law which forbade citizens from changing their Ottoman nationality. Nor could children automatically assume the status of their father should he become an Ottoman by naturalization.[163] If the child wished to become an Ottoman in this case, he could apply for naturalization upon attaining his majority age.[164] The separate status of children from that of their father created cases of dual nationality.[165] Dual nationality occurred when the law of the state to which the father was naturalized conferred nationality on his Ottoman children, which was the case in the majority of states.[166] On this point, as the case in most of its provisions, the 1869 Law was less advanced than the nationality laws of most states at the time.

18(6); and United States Law of 10 February 1855, as amended in revised statutes, 1878 (*ibid.*, p. 577), Article 1994.

159 Law of 8 October 1869 (Collection of Nationality Laws, p. 10), Article 2, paragraph 2(7) (without additional condition).

160 Constitution of 1891 (Collection of Nationality Laws, p. 48), Article 69(5), (provided that the man "holds real estate in Brazil").

161 Constitution of 25 November 1870 (Collection of Nationality Laws, p. 470), Article 36.

162 See Harmodio Arias, "Nationality and Naturalisation in Latin America from the Point of View of International Law", *Journal of the Society of Comparative Legislation*, Vol. 11, 1910–1911, pp. 126–142.

163 Article 8. See Arminjon, *Etrangers et protégés dans l'Empire ottoman, op. cit.*, pp. 17–133.

164 This provision was taken from Article 12 of the French Civil Code; Goadby, *International and Inter-Religious Private Law in Palestine, op. cit.*, p. 41.

165 This was also the case of Ottoman citizens who acquired foreign nationality without government authorization.

166 Examples of legislation which allowed children to assume the nationality of their father included, *inter alia*, the following: Argentina Law of 8 October 1869, *op. cit.*, Article 3; Brazil Legislative Decree of 7 June 1899 (Collection of Nationality Laws, p. 49), Article 4; Hungary Law of 20 December 1879, *op. cit.*, Article 7; Luxemburg Constitution of 17 October 1868 (Collection of Nationality Laws, p. 419); Paraguay Constitution of 25 November 1870, *op. cit.*, Article 35(2); Spain Civil Law of 1889 (Collection of Nationality Laws, p. 537), Article 18; and United States Law of 14 April 1802 (*ibid.*, p. 567).

3. *Ottoman passports*

Ottoman citizens who desired to travel abroad were required to hold passports.[167] Written in both the Turkish and French languages, the Ottoman passport was employed in the Empire as of 1 August 1844.[168] With the enactment of the *Regulations Relative to the Passports Offices in the Empire* on 17 July 1869, Ottoman passports were regulated, and started to be systematically issued by a specialized governmental department.[169] The passport legislation, which was operative in the final days of the Empire, was the Ottoman Passport Law of 9 June 1911.[170] This law continued to be valid in Palestine after the British control of that ex-Ottoman territory in 1917.

While it was not considered *per se* as a proof of nationality according to Article 18 of the Passport Law, the passport was regarded as a *prima facie* evidence of nationality.[171] For example, "United States passports held by [Ottoman] persons... are recognized by the Turkish authorities as evidence of the fact of naturalization and citizenship".[172] Similarly, foreign citizens who wished to invoke certain privileges accorded to them by the capitulation, or to claim diplomatic protection, were required to present passports as an indication of their nationality.[173] Ottoman passports were also considered one of the key evidences to prove the status of 'Ottoman subject' as a pre-requisite for the *ipso facto* acquisition of the status of 'Palestinian citizen' when Palestinian nationality was formed in 1925.[174]

Article 13 of the Ottoman Passport Law included rules about a type of identity cards called *teskéré*. *Teskérés* were issued to Ottoman citizens for internal use, such as travel, within the Empire. In order to obtain an Ottoman passport, *teskéré* was amongst the required documents.[175] Yet those travelling outside Ottoman territory were permitted to use their *teskérés* in lieu of passports. In fact, the *teskéré* was introduced in the 1830s, continued to operate as a *de facto* passport until well after regular Ottoman passports were issued.[176] "Foreign governments would honor the *teskéré* as long as it was not stamped 'reserved for the interior'".[177] The *teskéré* was also issued from Ottoman passport offices to those foreigners who wished to travel within the Empire.[178] This document of identification was similar, therefore, to the

167 See, in general, Rausas, *op. cit.*, Vol. I, pp. 149–166.
168 *Ibid.*, p. 150.
169 *Ibid.*, pp. 151–152.
170 Completion of Ottoman Laws, Vol. 5, p. 270.
171 On the relationship between the passport and nationality, see below Chapter VIII, Section 2.
172 Digest of International Law, p. 705.
173 See Rausas, *op. cit.*, Vol. I, p. 153.
174 See below Chapter V, Section 1.
175 Ottoman Passport Law, 'Temporary Article'.
176 Karpat, *op. cit.*, p. 187.
177 *Ibid.*
178 See Rausas, *op. cit.*, Vol. I, p. 153.

residence permit.[179] The admission of foreigners to the Empire, and their residence therein, was governed by the *Regulations Relative to the Passports and the Teskérés of Foreign Subjects Residing in the Empire* issued on 7 August 1869.[180]

More regular identity cards were issued in the Empire according to the *Ottoman Population Law* of 27 August 1914.[181] These cards, as required by Articles 3 and 4, incorporated, *inter alia*, the following data: the person's full name; name of the parents, date and place of birth; religion; sect, if any; place of residence; profession; ability to read and write; eligibility for legislative election; military district in which the person belonged; and physical specifications like height, eye and hair colour. Such a card was required, it seems, only by men; the name of the wife, not the husband, was one of the items to be inserted in the card.

It is not clear, from the provisions of the Population Law, whether it was compulsory to obtain such an identity card. But, as stipulated in Article 7, the presentation of the card was required in legal actions such as real estate contracts, legislative election, employment, marriage and applications for passport. It follows that holding such a card became compulsory in practice.

Based upon the Population Law (which was passed just three years before the occupation of Palestine in 1917 by the British army), the Ottoman Government had established an administration (called the 'Population Department') for population affairs whereby detailed records relating to the data registered in the identity cards were maintained.[182] Each Ottoman citizen, whether man or woman, was obliged to register and ensure that their data was current.[183] The Population Department also maintained comprehensive data regarding births,[184] marriages,[185] deaths[186] domicile and address.[187] As a transitional provision, the *teskéré* was accepted in lieu of the new identity card until these cards were to be fully distributed.[188] It is not clear to which extend the Population Department was able to undertake its functions before the British occupation of Palestine. Nor one could find data relating to the number of inhabitants that were registered by, and acquired identity cards from, that Department. One can doubt, however, the ability of the Population Department to register, and issue identity cards, to all inhabitants during the three years between the Department's official establishment in 1914 and the end of the Ottoman rule in Palestine, especially as the Empire was in a state of war during these years.

In order to enter the country, foreigners were obliged, under Article 9 of the Ottoman Passport Law, to acquire an entry visa from an Ottoman consulate abroad.

---

179 *Ibid.*, p. 150.
180 *Ibid.*, pp. 151–152.
181 Completion of Ottoman Laws, Vol. 4, p. 271.
182 See Population Law, Articles 3, 6, 8, 9, 14 and 18.
183 *Ibid.*, Article 13.
184 *Ibid.*, Articles 19–25.
185 *Ibid.*, Articles 26–30.
186 *Ibid.*, Articles 31–36.
187 *Ibid.*, Articles 37–40.
188 *Ibid.*, 'Transitional Article'.

Ironically, Ottoman citizens residing abroad were also required, by the same article, to obtain a visa to return home. But the consequence of failing to obtain a visa differed for foreign and Ottoman citizens. If a foreigner arrived without a passport or a visa, he was obliged under Article 13 of the Passport Law to obtain a passport from his consulate operating in the Empire, and then to pay an amount equivalent to the visa fee as a fine.[189] Otherwise, he would be expelled.[190] Indeed, such expulsion of foreigners had frequently occurred.[191] On the other hand, Ottoman citizens residing abroad who failed to obtain a visa were never expelled, but were obliged to pay twice the regular visa fee. This may imply that the real motive behind requesting an entry visa from Ottoman citizens residing (and normally working) abroad was to get fees, not to acquire permission to enter the Empire. Such was one example of the benefits that the Ottoman Government could gain from "the economic achievements of its subjects residing abroad".[192]

4. *Influence of Ottoman nationality in Palestine*

Shortly before taking part in World War I, the Ottoman Empire unilaterally decided to abolish the capitulation treaties in their entirety.[193] In September 1914, the Ottoman Government notified embassies in Istanbul that the capitulations were to be considered abrogated as of 1 October 1914.[194] The decision was legally justified based upon the international law's doctrine relating to a fundamental change of circumstance as a reason for treaty revocation and due to the fact that the capitulations were merely treaties terminable at will.[195] Capitulatory states denied the legal validity of this abrogation because, as was argued, the capitulation "is not an autonomous institution of the [Ottoman] Empire but a resultant of international treaties, diplomatic agreements, and contractual acts".[196]

In the negotiations between Turkey and the Allies (Britain, France, Japan, Greece, Romania and the Serb-Croat-Slovene State—most of whom were capitulatory Powers)[197] in Lausanne late in 1922, Turkey reaffirmed its position that the capitulations were invalid for various reasons, including the fact that they violated

189 The passport law provided no solution for those foreigners who had no diplomatic or consular representation within the Empire.

190 See Rausas, *op. cit.*, Vol. I, p. 154.

191 See Digest of International Law, pp. 701–705.

192 Karpat, *op. cit.*, p. 189.

193 See *Imperial Irade* [sultan's decree] *concerning the Abolition of the Capitulation* (Completion of Ottoman Laws, Vol. 6, p. 363).

194 Thayer, *op. cit.*, p. 214.

195 *Ibid.*, pp. 224–228.

196 *Ibid.*, p. 224 (Thayer, in this quotation, referred to a reply by a capitulatory government to the Empire's decision to abolish the capitulation system).

197 With regard to Japan, see below pp. 42, 63–64.

its sovereignty.[198] While representatives of the Allies sympathized with Turkey on this matter, they maintained that the capitulations were treaties, which could not be unilaterally terminated.[199] Ultimately, however, Article 28 of the Treaty of Lausanne of 1923 did provide for the "complete abolition of the Capitulations *in Turkey*".[200] For this reason, perhaps, the system continued to be applicable in ex-Ottoman territories, notably, as a typical example, in Egypt where the capitulation was abolished only on 18 May 1937.[201] Palestine was no exception.[202]

Upon the British occupation, the capitulation system was legally suspended and the "status of foreigners in Palestine has been completely altered".[203] To this effect, Article 8 of the Palestine Mandate[204] stated that: "The privileges and immunities of foreigners, including the benefits of consular jurisdiction and protection as formerly enjoyed by capitulation or usage in the Ottoman Empire, shall not be applicable in Palestine...". However, as the capitulation was considered to be "unnecessary under the mandates system which placed Palestine under...a European Power",[205] the same article added that "these privileges and immunities shall, at the expiration of the mandate, be immediately re-established...".[206]

The favourable treatment of certain foreigners was codified in Articles 58 to 67 of the Palestine Order in Council of 1922[207] (known as 'the Constitution of Palestine'). Under the Constitution, foreigners enjoyed judicial privileges before courts in criminal, procedural and personal status matters. These privileges included, for example, the right to trial before a British, instead of Palestinian, judge and to benefit

198 See "Memorandum read by the Turkish Delegate at the Meeting of December 2, 1922, of the Commission on the Regime of Foreigners", in British Government, *Lausanne Conference on Near Eastern Affairs, 1922–1923: Records of the Proceedings and Draft Terms of Peace*, His Majesty's Stationary Office, London, 1923 (hereinafter: 'Lausanne Conference'), pp. 471–480.

199 *Ibid.*, pp. 435–438, 466–470.

200 Emphasis added.

201 See *Convention regarding the Abolition of the Capitulations in Egypt*, Montreux, Switzerland (LN Treaty Series, 1937–1938, Vol. 182, p. 37). This Convention definitively abrogated the capitulation treaties reached previously with the Ottoman Empire, which then included Egypt. The following states signed the Montreux Convention with Egypt: United States, Belgium, Britain, Denmark, Spain, France, Greece, Italy, Norway, Netherlands, Portugal, Sweden. (Germany and Austria, renounced their capitulations treaties with Turkey in 1917 and 1918, respectively—Thayer, *op. cit.*, p. 228; Russia later followed—see Lausanne Conference, *op. cit.*, pp. 473–474.) For a commentary on the Convention with Egypt, see "Abolition of the Capitulation System in Egypt", *The British Year Book of International*, 1938, pp. 161–197.

202 For further details, see Norman Bentwich, "The End of Capitulation System", *The British Year Book of International Law*, 1933, pp. 89–100; Taylor, *op. cit.*, pp. 224–230.

203 J. Stoyanovsky, *op. cit.*, p. 192.

204 See below Chapter III, Section 3.

205 Stoyanovsky, *op. cit.*, p. 192.

206 *Cf.* Mandate for Syria and Lebanon, *infra* note 322, Article 5. See also Paul Pic, *Syrie et Palestine: mandats français et anglais dans le Proche-Orient*, Librairie Ancienne Edouard Champion, Paris, 1924, pp. 110–117.

207 Laws of Palestine, p. 3303.

from consular representation.[208] To this end, Article 59 of the Constitution defined the term 'foreigner' as "any person who is a national or subject of a European or American State or of Japan". Hence, this "definition is clearly intended to include all foreigners (with the addition of Japan) who previously enjoyed privileges under the capitulations".[209] And these "privileges are enjoyed whatever the religion of the person may be".[210]

These constitutional privileges showed the continued influence of the capitulation system, albeit in a new context.[211] This context arose from the fact that the mandate was adopted by member states of the League of Nations who had interest to preserve the privileges enjoyed under the capitulation. Japan, as a key allied Power to the victors in World War I, also benefited from these privileges because it was one of those states who had established the new world order under the League.

However, by this time most of the legislation enacted by the British-run administration had altered the substantive provisions of the capitulation treaties. Indeed, legislation relating to civil,[212] commercial,[213] and criminal[214] matters had become applicable to Palestinians and foreigners alike. Hence, there remained no practical justification for the on-going applicability of the capitulation regime.

Yet two sets of legislation relating to foreigners continued to be relevant.

The first concerned personal status issues as regulated by the Constitution and by more specific legislation such as the Succession Ordinance of 1923.[215] The necessity of having special rules on personal status for foreigners stemmed from the absence of a general law governing personal status matters in existence in Palestine. Such matters were governed by religious rules and limited to members of each religion. Foreigners, whose status was previously detrained by capitulation treaties, were not subject to such religious rules applicable to Palestinians.

The second set of special rules applicable to foreigners incorporated matters which normally governed the status of foreigners and were recognized under international law and/or under the laws of most states. Such matters included, *inter alia*,

---

208 See *Regulations Made under Article 67 of the Palestine Order-in-Council, 1922, concerning the Powers of Consuls in matters of Personal Status of Nationals of their State*, 15 November 1922 (Legislation of Palestine, Vol. II, p. 66).

209 Goadby, *International and Inter-Religious Private Law in Palestine, op. cit.*, p. 81.

210 *Ibid.*

211 Ghali, *op. cit.*, p. 265.

212 See, for example, Landlords and Tenants (Ejection and Rent Restriction) Ordinance, 1934 (Palestine Gazette, No. 432, Supplement 1, 5 April 1934, p. 207); Civil Wrongs Ordinance, 1944 (Palestine Gazette, No. 1380, Supplement 1, 28 December 1944, p. 149).

213 See, for instance, Companies Ordinance, 1929, *op. cit.*; Bankruptcy Ordinance, 1936 (Palestine Gazette, No. 566, Supplement 1, 24 January 1936, p. 31). However, the former Ordinance contained special rules (Articles 248–250) relating to foreign companies, such as registration and eligibility to own real estate.

214 See, for example, Criminal Procedure (Trial upon Information) Ordinance, 1924 (Laws of Palestine, p. 515); Criminal Code Ordinance, 1936 (Palestine Gazette, No. 652, Supplement 1, 14 January 1936, p. 399).

215 See below p. 65.

immigration, travel and residence, consular and diplomatic laws,[216] extradition and the exchange of judicial documents.[217] A number of these issues were governed by treaties.[218] Other legislation limited certain rights to Palestinian citizens only, such as political rights, notably the eligibility to participate in legislative election,[219] and the ability to occupy certain professions, such as medical practice.[220] Addressing these issues is, of course, beyond the scope of the present study.[221]

On 29 November 1947, the United Nations Partition Plan[222] envisioned the permanent abolition of the capitulation system in post-mandate Palestine. In this regard, the Plan provided that: "States whose nationals have in the past enjoyed in Palestine the privileges and immunities of foreigners, including the benefits of consular jurisdiction and protection, as formerly enjoyed by capitulation or usage in the Ottoman Empire, are invited to renounce any right pertaining to them to the re-establishment of such privileges and immunities in the proposed Arab and Jewish States and the City of Jerusalem".[223] As the United Nations Partition Plan was never implemented, the application of the capitulation, technically speaking, in the post-mandate entities, including the West Bank and Gaza Strip, may still have relevance and raise certain legal questions even today.

5. *Concluding remarks*

Ottoman nationality was well-established in Palestine as the Ottoman Empire was independent and effectively controlling its territory for hundreds of years. Other states recognized the Empire's independence, concluded treaties and exchanged diplomatic envoys with it. No state denied, in principle, the Empire's supremacy over its extended territory and subjects. In particular, no other state claimed sovereign rights over Palestine. Indeed, the Empire's sovereignty over, and thus Ottoman nationality in, Palestine cannot legally be contested.[224]

---

216 See, for example, Personal Status (Consular Powers) Regulations, 1922 (Laws of Palestine, p. 3356).

217 See, for example, Foreign Jurisdiction Rules, 1928 (Laws of Palestine, p. 2953); Arbitration (Foreign Awards) Ordinance, 1934 (Palestine Gazette, No. 446, Supplement 1, 14 June 1934, p. 245).

218 On examples of such treaties, see below pp. 69–70.

219 See below p. 64.

220 See Medical Parishioners Ordinance, 1935 (Palestine Gazette, No. 547, Supplement 1, 31 September 1935, p. 235). This legislation permitted foreigners who enjoyed permanent residence in Palestine to practice medical profession.

221 A historical-legal study on the position of foreigners in Palestine, since the Ottoman Empire and the present day, is needed for the adoption of a new policy in the future Palestinian state.

222 See below Chapter XI.

223 Part IV.

224 On the link between sovereignty and nationality, see below pp. 46, 81.

The Ottoman Nationality Law of 1869 was enacted for political ends, that is, to reduce the influence of the capitulation system. In law, however, nationality was conferred without discrimination on the basis of race or religion.[225]

Regardless of its motives, the said Nationality Law was the sole legislative instrument which governed the inhabitants' nationality after the separation of Palestine from Turkey. That Ottoman Law continued in operation until 1925, when Britain enacted the Palestinian Citizenship Order. The relevance of Ottoman nationality in Palestine from 1917 through 1925 will be examined next.

225 This was not the case in Palestine at the end of the British rule, where race and religion became essential grounds for the acquisition of nationality. See below Chapter XI, Section 1.

III

PALESTINIAN NATIONALITY IN TRANSITION, 1917–1925

1. *Regional context*

From the beginning of the British occupation in 1917 until the enactment of the Palestinian Citizenship Order in Council in 1925,[226] the nationality of Palestine's inhabitants remained in transition.[227] While the Palestine Mandate (adopted in 1922) and the Treaty of Lausanne (enforced in 1924) recognized a distinct nationality for Palestine's inhabitants on the international plane, Palestinian nationality lacked comprehensive domestic regulation at that time. These eight years constituted the first transitional period in the history of Palestinian nationality.[228]

---

226 Although it will be addressed in detail in the next chapter, the 1925 Palestinian Citizenship Order is also mentioned in the present chapter exceptionally in order to illustrate certain points.

227 With focus on the period under discussion, see, *inter alia*, Herbert Sidebotham, *England and Palestine, Essays towards the Restoration of the Jewish State*, Constable and Company Ltd., 1918; Historical Section of the [British] Foreign Office, *Syria and Palestine*, H.M. Stationary Office, London, 1920 (in *Mohammedanism: Turkey in Asia*, Vol. I, *op. cit.*); Frederec Goadby, *Introduction to the Study of Law: a Handbook for the use of Law Students in Egypt and Palestine*, William Clowes and Sones Limited, London/Beccles, 1921; Norman Bentwich, "Mandated Territories: Palestine and Mesopotamia (Iraq)", *The British Year Book of International Law*, 1921–1922, pp. 49–50; W.D. McCrackan, *The New Palestine*, Jonathan Cape, London, 1922; Mark Carter Mills, "The Mandatory System", *The American Journal of International Law*, Vol. 17, 1923, pp. 50–62; W. Basil Worsfold, *Palestine of the Mandate*, T. Fisher Unwin Ltd., London, 1925; Paltiel Novik, *La situation de la Palestine en droit international*, Jouve & Editeurs, Paris, 1927; Department of State, *Mandate for Palestine*, Government Printing Office, Washington, 1927; Doreen Ingrams, *Palestine Papers, 1917–1922: Seeds of Conflict*, Cox & Wyman, London, 1972; Bernard Wasserstein, *The British in Palestine: The Mandatory Government and the Arab-Jewish Conflict, 1917–1929*, Royal Historical Society, London, 1978; Pic, *op. cit.*, pp. 49 ff.; Stoyanovsky, *op. cit.*, pp. 1–87; Rappoport, *op. cit.*, pp. 227–239; Baumkoller, *op. cit.*; Mock, *op. cit.*, pp. 22–100.

228 In fact, Palestinian nationality, including in the period of 1925–1948, has remained, in the absence of an independent Palestinian state, in transition until the present day. Thus, addressing that nationality during this period is useful to understand Palestinian

In international law, when a former state ceases to exist and new states are being established, "the population follows the change of sovereignty in matters of nationality".[229] As a rule, therefore, citizens of the former state should automatically acquire the nationality of the successor state in which they were habitually residing. Following its separation from the Ottoman Empire, Palestine found itself surrounded by recently emerged countries. Hence, it is useful to examine the boundaries of Palestine in order to define the piece of land on which Palestinian nationality was established. The determination of the borders will also serve as illustration of the new nationalities of the inhabitants in the neighbouring countries who were, until then, Ottoman citizens. Such a determination will thus clarify, by exclusion, those who bore Palestinian nationality.

Upon its detachment from the Ottoman Empire, the territory of Palestine and its inhabitants became distinct from its neighbouring countries. This separation had started as a matter of fact between Palestine and the newly-created Arab 'states': Trans-Jordan, Egypt, Syria and Lebanon.[230] Soon thereafter, Palestine's frontiers acquired permanent recognition through bilateral agreements held with the representatives of neighbouring states.[231] In addition, following the international legal framework established by the Treaty of Lausanne,[232] each of the four countries mentioned above and their respective populations developed a distinct nationality of their own through domestic legislation.[233] The nationalities of each of these countries have since then become well-established.

The eastern border of Palestine with Trans-Jordan was of particular importance.[234] The Palestine Mandate was originally incorporated the territory of Trans-Jordan

---

nationality in other transitional situations in subsequent periods of Palestine's history. For historical background on the transition in Palestine, in a wider context, see Scholch, *op. cit.*

229 Brownlie, *op. cit.*, p. 220. See also Borchard, "Basic Elements of Diplomatic Protection of Citizens Abroad", *op. cit.*, p. 504.

230 See, in general, René Vanlande, *Le chambardement oriental, Turquie—Liban—Syrie—Palestine—Transjordanie—Irak*, J. Peyronnet & Cie, Paris, 1932.

231 See, in detail, Patricia Toye, ed., *Palestine Boundaries 1833–1947*, University of Durham, Durham, 1989 (in particular the first chapter thereof written by J.C. Hurewitz, "Introduction: boundaries of mandated Palestine", Vol. I, pp. xi–xxxii); Stoyanovsky, *op. cit.*, pp. 202–210; Scholch, *op. cit.*, pp. 9–17; Mock, *op. cit.*, pp. 213–224.

232 See below Chapter III, Section 4.

233 The nationality legislation of Egypt and Trans-Jordan, which will be discussed presently, were enacted in 1926 and 1928, respectively. They are mentioned here because of the international context in which they were enacted, particularly the Treaty of Lausanne. Similar legislation was passed in other neighbouring countries around this time. See, in detail, Ghali, *op. cit.*

234 For a historical review on Trans-Jordan and its status, see Samuel Ficheleff, *Le statut international de la Palestine orientale (la Transjordanie)*, Librairie Lipschutz, Paris, 1932; Eugene L. Rogan, *Frontiers of the State in the Late Ottoman Empire, Transjordan, 1850–1921*, Cambridge University Press, Cambridge, 1999; Hooper, *op. cit.*; Mock, *op. cit.*, pp. 326–330.

within the scope of 'Palestine'.[235] Article 25 of the Mandate accorded Britain the power, "with consent of the Council of the League of Nations, to postpone or withhold [the] application of such provisions of this mandate as... [it] may consider inapplicable to the existing local conditions". Subsequently, on 16 September 1922, the Council of the League of Nations passed a resolution by which it approved a proposal submitted by Britain to exclude Trans-Jordan from the scope of Palestine's territory;[236] and, ultimately, the borders between Palestine and Trans-Jordan were fixed as suggested by Britain.[237]

The aforesaid resolution of the Council of the League of Nations confirmed previous practice and paved the way for the future settlement of Palestine's eastern border. Trans-Jordan was earlier excluded from the territory of Palestine by Article 86 of the Palestine Order in Council (Constitution) of 1922, which stated: "This Order in Council shall not apply to such parts of the territory comprised in Palestine to the east of the Jordan [River] and the Dead Sea".

On 20 February 1928, Britain reached an agreement with the Amir of Trans-Jordan,[238] by which the former recognized the existing autonomous government of Trans-Jordan while maintaining the territory under its supervision in a form of mandate. Hence, the unilaterally-drawn border of Palestine with Trans-Jordan was confirmed.[239] Finally, on 22 March 1946, after reaching a treaty of alliance with Britain, Trans-Jordan declared its independence as a separate state.[240] As a result, the lengthiest section of Palestine's borders had been settled.

Trans-Jordan developed a distinct nationality for its own population from that of Palestine. To begin with, on 16 September 1922, it was decided that Article 7 of

---

235 However, Britain continued to treat Trans-Jordan as part of Palestine for international relations purposes. For example, the British Government included Trans-Jordan within its annual reports submitted to the Council of the League of Nations, pursuant to Article 24 of the Palestine Mandate, regarding its administration of Palestine. A number of these reports will be cited hereinafter.

236 League of Nations, *Official Journal*, Geneva, November 1922, p. 1188. The purpose of this resolution was to exclude Trans-Jordan from the scope of the Jewish national home in Palestine. It is for this reason the provisions of the Palestine Mandate relevant to the national home ceased to apply for Trans-Jordan (these provisions are: recitals 2 and 3 of the preamble, parts of Article 2, Articles 4 and 6, second sentence of Article 7, parts of Article 11, Articles 13, 14, 22 and 23).

237 See *Memorandum by Lord Balfour*, League of Nations Document No. C.66.M.396.1922. VI, 16 September 1922—League of Nations, *Official Journal*, November 1922, pp. 1390–1391.

238 *Agreement between the United Kingdom and Trans-Jordan*, signed at Jerusalem, His Majesty's Stationary Office, London, 1928 (see also Toye, *op. cit.*, Vol. 3, p. 809), Article 2.

239 Norman Bentwich, "The Mandate for Trans-Jordan", *The British Year Book of International Law*, 1929, pp. 212–213.

240 *Treaty of Alliance between His Majesty in respect of the United Kingdom and His Highness the Amir of Transjordan*, London (UN Treaty Series, Vol. 6, 1947, p. 143). This treaty came into force on 17 June 1946 upon the exchange of the instruments of ratification at Amman, Trans-Jordan.

the Palestine Mandate (relating to Palestinian nationality) would not be applicable to Trans-Jordan.[241] The nationality of Trans-Jordan's inhabitants was then expressly excluded from the scope of Palestinian nationality by the Palestinian Citizenship Order of 24 July 1925. Article 21 of that Order read:

> For the purpose of this Order: (1) The expression 'Palestine' includes the territories to which the mandate for Palestine applies, except such parts of the territory comprised in Palestine to the East of the Jordan and the Dead Sea as were defined by Order of the High Commissioner dated 1st September 1922.[242]

Trans-Jordan eventually enacted its own nationality law on 1 May 1928.[243] Article 1 of this law conferred Trans-Jordanian nationality on all Ottoman subjects resident in the territory of Trans-Jordan retroactively as of 6 August 1924. Trans-Jordanian nationality constituted a distinct nationality from that of Palestine not only in law,[244] but also in practice throughout the mandate. Trans-Jordanians, for example, were required to obtain official permission to be admitted into Palestine.[245]

This particular relationship between Palestinian and Trans-Jordanian nationalities arose in a case before the Supreme Court of Palestine, which served as a High Court of Justice, on 14 December 1945. In *Jawdat Badawi Sha'ban v. Commissioner for Migration and Statistics*,[246] Mr. Sha'ban, who was a Palestinian citizen and had acquired Trans-Jordanian nationality by naturalization, argued that "Trans-Jordan is a territory and not a state... in any case it is not a foreign state [in relation to Palestine]". By refusing this argument, the Court, in a decision that summarized the status of Palestine *vis-à-vis* Trans-Jordan, in general, and the question of nationality, in particular, held:

> Now, Trans-Jordan has a government entirely independent of Palestine—the laws of Palestine are not applicable in Trans-Jordan nor are their laws applicable here. Moreover, although the High Commissioner for Palestine is also High Commissioner for Trans-Jordan, Trans-Jordan has an entirely independent government under the rule of an Amir and apart from certain reserved matters the High Commissioner cannot interfere with the government of Trans-Jordan.... Trans-Jordan comes within the meaning of the word 'state' as used in Article 15 [of the 1925 Palestinian Citizenship Order].... Trans-Jordan nationality is recognised and we know that Trans-Jordan can, as in this

241 As only the second sentence of Article 7 of the Palestine Mandate (see *supra* note 236), by which Britain was requested to grant Palestinian nationality to immigrant Jews, ceased to apply to Trans-Jordan; Britain was still under a duty to enact nationality law in Palestine, which should also include Trans-Jordan, according to the first sentence of Article 7. In practice, however, Britain did not enact a nationality law for Trans-Jordan and reserved this task for the Trans-Jordanian government.

242 See *Order defining Boundaries of Territory to which the Palestine Order-in-Council does not apply*, 1 September 1922 (Legislation of Palestine, Vol. II, p. 405).

243 *Trans-Jordan Nationality Law of 1928* (Laws Concerning Nationality, p. 274).

244 See Permanent Mandates Commission, *Minutes of the Fifteenth Session*, League of Nations, Geneva, 1929—hereinafter: 'Mandates Commission Minutes 1929', pp. 100–101. For details, see Ghali, *op. cit.*, pp. 221–226.

245 See below pp. 161–162.

246 Annotated Law Reports, 1946, Vol. I, p. 116.

case, grant a person naturalisation, *i.e.* grant an alien or foreigner Trans-Jordan nationality which is a separate nationality and distinct from that of Palestine citizenship.... Palestinians and Trans-Jordanians are foreigners and therefore Trans-Jordan must be regarded as a foreign state in relation to Palestine.

With regard to the northern borders of Palestine, Britain and France (the then occupying Power, and later the Mandatory, of Syria and Lebanon) signed an agreement which settled key aspects relating to the Palestinian-Syrian borders (Paris, 23 December 1920).[247] Three years later, the British High Commissioner for Palestine and the French High Commissioner for Syria and Lebanon reached, at Jerusalem on 16 December 1923, another agreement to regulate additional aspects of the said borders.[248] On 2 February 1926, the latter agreement was replaced by the *Bon Voisinage Agreement to Regulate Certain Administrative Matters in Connection with the Frontier between Palestine and Syria.*[249]

Both Syria and Lebanon regulated their own nationalities on 30 August 1924. Enacted by the French High Commissioner, the two nationalities were formulated by separate Ordinances *(arrêtés): the Ordinance Concerning Turkish Subjects Established in Syria*[250] and *the Ordinance Concerning Turkish Subjects Established in Greater Lebanon.*[251] The Syrian and Lebanese nationalities were further confirmed

247 *Franco-British Convention on Certain Points Connected with the Mandates for Syria and the Lebanon, Palestine* [including Trans-Jordan] *and Mesopotamia* [i.e. Iraq]; LN Treaty Series, 1924, Vol. 22, p. 355.

248 Legislation of Palestine, Vol. II, p. 512.

249 Palestine Gazette, 2 February 1926, p. 69. Legislation enacted in Palestine from 1935 until 1948 were published in the Official Gazette of the Government of Palestine, known as 'The Palestine Gazette'. Legislation enacted under British rule from 1918 until 1934 were compiled by Mr. Robert Harry Drayton in four volumes. Drayton, the then British official served as the Solicitor-General of the Government of Palestine, was appointed as the Legal Draftsman to the Government in 1931. He was assigned to collect and edit all legislation enacted in the country (see "Revised Edition of the Laws Ordinance of 1934"—Laws of Palestine, p. 290). In fact, the Government decided to compel the Palestinian legislation upon a request from the League of Nations (Permanent Mandates Commission, *Minutes of the Twenty Third Session*, League of Nations, Geneva, 1933, p. 106). In 1935, the British Government informed the League that the English version of the revised edition of Palestine laws was ready but waiting for the translation into Arabic and Hebrew texts to be published simultaneously with the English version—the three official languages of Palestine. The said Government was expected to submit copies to the League in 1936 (British Government, *Report to the Council of the League of Nations on the Administration of Palestine and Trans-Jordan*, 1935, p. 83). Unless otherwise indicated, the present study, for practical reasons, will follow the page numbers of the legislation as published in the Arabic version of both the Laws of Palestine and the Palestine Gazette (1918–1947—the 1948 legislation are available in English only). But when the text of certain article or provision is cited, the English-original text/wording will be provided.

250 Collection of Nationality Laws, p. 303.

251 *Ibid.*, p. 299.

and elaborated by two separate 'Orders' issued on 19 January 1925.[252] Both the Syrians and Lebanese were subsequently treated as foreigners in Palestine.[253]

The southern-western border of Palestine with Egypt dates back to the late nineteenth century. Originally, this border was drawn up on a *de facto* basis, as the Ottoman Empire recognized Egypt's autonomy.[254] Formally, however, two border agreements between the Ottoman Empire and Egypt were reached in 1906. The first came in the form of an Exchange of Notes between Britain [which was controlling Egypt since 1882] and Turkey relative to the Maintenance of the *Status Quo* in the Sinai Peninsula, signed in Constantinople on 14 May.[255] The second, more detailed, was the *Agreement between Egypt and Turkey for the fixing of an Administrative Line between the Vilayet* [province] *of Hejaz and the Governorate* [district] *of Jerusalem and the Sinai Peninsula*, signed in Rafah, on 1 October.[256] The separation of Egypt from Turkey, as of 5 November 1914, was ultimately recognized by Articles 17 and 19 of the Treaty of Lausanne.

On 26 May 1926, Egypt regulated its own nationality by a Decree-Law.[257] This legislation stipulated that Egyptian nationality had been originally established in November 1914, when Britain had declared itself to be a protectorate over Egypt, with retroactive effect. On 19 February 1929, a detailed Decree-Law concerning Egyptian Nationality was enacted, which confirmed, in Article 1, that Ottoman nationals who on 5 November 1914 had their habitual residence in Egypt were Egyptian citizens.[258]

In conclusion, nationalities in the neighbouring countries of Palestine were clearly distinguishable from Palestinian nationality shortly after the collapse of the Ottoman Empire. Palestinian citizens were treated as foreigners in these countries, while citizens of these neighbouring countries were likewise considered as foreigners in Palestine. This situation in both law and practice was to continue, as will be illustrated in the coming chapters, throughout the Palestine Mandate period.[259] This

252 *Ibid.*, p. 301 (Order No. 16/S, Syria) and p. 298 (Order No. 15/S, Lebanon).
253 See, for instance, *Nahas v. Kotia and Another*, Supreme Court of Palestine sitting as a Court of Appeal, 31 October 1938 (Law Reports of Palestine (Baker), 1938, p. 518).
254 See, in general, Mahmoud H. Alfariq, *The Egyptian Constitutional Law and the Development of the Egyptian State*, The Great Commercial Printer, Cairo, 1924 (Arabic), Vol. I, pp. 25–110.
255 Consolidated Treaty Series, Vol. 201, 1906, p. 190.
256 *Ibid.*, Vol. 203, 1906, p. 19.
257 "Décret-Loi sur la nationalité égyptienne" (Ghali, *op. cit.*, p. 343).
258 Collection of Nationality Laws, p. 225.
259 For further details on the British rule in Palestine, see Fannie Fern Andrews, *The Holy Land under Mandate*, The Riverside Press, Borton/New York, 1931; Norman Bentwich, *England in Palestine*, the Mayflower Press, London, 1932; M.J. Landa, *Palestine as It Is*, Edward Goldston Ltd., London, 1932; Steuart Erskine, *Palestine of the Arabs*, George G. Harrap & Co. Ltd., London/Bombay/Sydney, 1935; Gert Winsch, *Le régime Anglais en Palestine*, M. Müller & fils, Berlin, 1939; Benjamin Akzin, "The Palestine Mandate in Practice", *Iowa Law Review*, Vol. 25, 1939–1940, pp. 32–77; William B. Ziff, *The Rape of Palestine*, Argus Books Inc., New York, 1946; Esco Foundation for Palestine, Inc., *Palestine: A Study of Jewish, Arab, and British Politics*, Yale University

general conclusion remains valid notwithstanding the special treatment accorded to citizens from neighbouring countries in Palestine, such as the visa exemption, which was either based on bilateral agreements or in accordance with Palestinian law.[260]

From the point of view of international law, Palestinian nationality underwent three developmental stages during this transitional period. The first began with the British occupation on 9 December 1917 and continued until the adoption of the Palestine Mandate on 24 July 1922. The second stage ran from the latter date until the ratification of the Treaty of Lausanne on 6 August 1924. The last, and the shortest, stage lasted from the ratification of the aforementioned treaty until the enforcement of the Palestinian Citizenship Order on 1 August 1925.

2. *Nationality in Palestine under the British occupation, 1917–1922*

A. *The occupation*

During this period, Palestine was first placed under military rule and then under a civil administration. From 9 December 1917 until the adoption of the Palestine Mandate on 24 July 1922 by the League of Nations, the international legal status of the country remained undetermined. As a result, the nationality of Palestine's inhabitants, similar to those in other ex-Ottoman territories at the time, remained "quite anomalous".

The British occupation did not alter the international status of Palestine as occupied Turkish territory. Meanwhile, the Allied Powers gathered in San Remo, Italy, to discuss a settlement with Turkey and to determine the future of Iraq along with Palestine and Syria. On 25 April 1920, these Powers decided that Ottoman Arabic-speaking territories would not be restored to Turkey.[261] Instead, France was allotted the mandate for Syria (including Lebanon) and Britain was allotted the mandates for Iraq and Palestine (including Trans-Jordan). Shortly after the San Remo Conference, Britain declared unilateral mandate over Palestine on 1 July 1920.

Press, New Haven/London/Oxford, 1947; Albert M. Hyamson, *Palestine under Mandate, 1920–1948*, Methuem & Co., London, 1950; Mahmoud K. Khela, *Palestine and the British Mandate, 1922–1939*, Institute for Palestine Studies, Beirut, 1974 (Arabic); Naomi Shepherd, *Ploughing Sand: British Rule in Palestine, 1917–1948*, John Murray, London, 1999; Tom Segev, *One Palestine Complete: Jews and Arabs under the British Mandate*, Little, Brown and Co., London, 2001. See also the references of *supra* note 227 and of *infra* notes 1095 and 1148.

260 On examples relating to the special treatment of the entry into Palestine by Trans-Jordanians, Syrians and Lebanese, see below pp. 161–162.

261 See Baumkoller, *op. cit.*, pp. 67–72; Mock, *op. cit.*, pp. 47–48; Helmreich, *op. cit.*, pp. 291–313; Ingrams, *op. cit.*, pp. 88–93.

It also established a civil administration to replace the military government which had ruled the country since December 1917.[262]

As the unilaterally declared mandate had no legal effect, Palestine remained (at least nominally) an Ottoman territory. Britain itself accepted this international legal position.[263] In May 1922, before the adoption of the Palestine Mandate, the Legal Secretary of the British-run Government of Palestine wrote:

> The principles enunciated in the Mandate await the beginning of realisation when the Council of the League of Nations shall at last have given its decision. And it is only when that step has been taken that the sovereign powers of the Mandatory can be effective, and the '*damnosa hereditas*' from the Ottoman Empire, which has to a large extent clogged the reforming activity of the provisional administration, can be finally discarded.... The Mandatory, in the same way as a protecting Power, will be entrusted with the control of the foreign relations of the Mandated State, and will have the right to afford diplomatic and consular protection to citizens of Palestine outside its territorial limits. Palestine will have a separate Government and form a separate national unity with its particular citizenship.[264]

As a consequence, Palestine's inhabitants continued to be Ottoman citizens in accordance with the 1869 Ottoman Nationality Law. The on-going effect of that Law was part of the general application of Ottoman laws in Palestine. Apart from the military laws executed by military courts, civil courts dealt with "all civil matters according to the Ottoman law".[265] The Palestinian Citizenship Order of 1925, in its first article, considered the inhabitants of Palestine as Ottoman citizens and granted them Palestinian nationality.[266] Thus, the inhabitants of Palestine in this period were, in virtue of local and international law, Ottoman citizens. In practice, however, Ottoman nationality had become ineffective.

The validity of Ottoman nationality in Palestine might be compared with the on-going effect of that nationality in Palestine's neighbouring countries. In Egypt, while the 1869 Ottoman Law was officially applicable, inhabitants were considered to be *de facto* Egyptians until November 1914, when Britain declared war against Turkey and its protection over Egypt. To this effect, Article 2 of the *Decree-Law concerning Egyptian Nationality* of 1926[267] defined Egyptian citizens as those Ottoman citizens who were habitually residing in Egypt as of 5 November 1914.[268] Similar situations existed in Syria and Lebanon following the French occupation in

---

262 Herbert Samuel [the High Commissioner for Palestine], *An Interim Report on the Civil Administration of Palestine, 1 July 1920–30 July 1921*, League of Nations, Geneva, 1921; British Government, *Report of the High Commissioner on the Administration of Palestine, 1920–1925*, His Majesty's Stationary Office, London, 1925, pp. 3–59. See also Ingrams, *op. cit.*, pp. 105–120.

263 Bentwich, "The Legal Administration of Palestine", *op. cit.*, pp. 147–148.

264 Bentwich, "Mandate Territories", *op. cit.*, p. 53.

265 *Ibid.*, p. 139.

266 See below Chapter V, Section 1.

267 *Op. cit.*

268 For details, see Ghali, *op. cit.*, pp. 117–168.

1918 until the enactment of Syrian and Lebanese nationality legislation in 1925.[269] Ottoman nationality was also applicable in Iraq since the British occupation in 1918 until 9 October 1924, when the Iraq Nationality Law[270] (Article 1) awarded Ottoman subjects residing in the country with Iraq citizenship.[271]

The validity of Ottoman nationality in Palestine at the time can be explained by the general international law rule that occupation or conquest does not provide any title to the occupying power over the occupied territory. This is also in line with international humanitarian law; Article 43 of both The Hague *Regulations Respecting the Laws and Customs of War on Land* of 1899,[272] and The Hague *Regulations Concerning the Laws and Customs of Land Warfare* of 1907,[273] oblige the occupant to respect "the laws in force in the country".

This position was identical with the British policy towards other colonies. As one senior British judicial official observed, the rule of Common Law is that "the laws of a conquered or ceded Colony remain in force until they are altered".[274] With regard to nationality in particular, the British Empire did claim sovereignty over certain territories in which the French Civil Code, including its nationality rules, were in force. This was the case, for example, in Quebec and Mauritius: where the said Code referred to *France* and *français*, these terms had been interpreted to mean (*mutatis mutandis*) *Québec* and *québécois* or *Mauritius* and *Maurice*, as the case might be.[275] By analogy, one could conclude that where 'Ottoman Empire' and 'Ottoman subject' were mentioned in the 1869 Law, these terms could be interpreted and replaced by 'Palestine' and 'Palestinian citizen', respectively.

B. De facto *Palestinian nationality*

Although the inhabitants of Palestine remained Ottoman citizens according to international law, in practice they started to be gradually regarded as Palestinians.

As an Occupying Power, Britain became responsible for the international relations of Palestine and for protecting its inhabitants abroad.[276] Britain, as such, found itself

269 See more in *ibid.*, pp. 231–258.
270 Collection of Nationality Laws, p. 348.
271 Ghali, *op. cit.*, pp. 170–190.
272 *Annex to Convention with respect to the Laws and Customs of War on Land*, The Hague, 29 July 1899 (in *The American Journal of International Law*, Vol. I (supplement), 1907, p. 129).
273 *Annex to Convention Regarding the Laws and Customs of Land Warfare*, The Hague, 18 October 1907 (in *The American Journal of International Law*, Vol. 2 (supplement), 1908, p. 90).
274 Francis Piggott, *Nationality including Naturalization and English Law on the High Seas and beyond the Realm*, William Clowes and Sons, London, 1907, Part I, p. 208. (Mr. Piggott was the British Chief Justice of Hong Kong.)
275 *Ibid.*, pp. 209, 216–217.
276 On the protection of the Palestinians abroad, see below Chapter VIII, Section 3.

obliged to take certain measures to regulate the inhabitants' nationality.[277] To this end, the Government of Palestine, which was the authority established by Britain to administrate the country, took the following actions: it issued provisional nationality certificates to Ottoman residents in Palestine; granted Palestinian passports and travel documents; extended diplomatic protection to those inhabitants residing and travelling abroad; and made a clear distinction between citizens and foreigners regarding the admission into Palestine, residence and political rights. The terms 'Palestinian' or 'Palestinian citizen' were regularly employed.

Endorsing the actual separation of the territory from Turkey, the British-run Government of Palestine issued provisional certificates of Palestinian nationality.[278] Serving as preliminary indication of Palestinian nationality, these certificates were "recognised by foreign countries and allow[ed] the holders to receive protection and assistance from a British Consular Officers".[279] To qualify for a Palestinian nationality certificate, the applicant had to meet three conditions: (1) that either he (women had to follow their fathers or husbands), or his father, had been born in Palestine; (2) that he had expressed his intention to opt for Palestinian nationality as soon as the law of Palestine's nationality was passed; and (3) that he intended to reside permanently in Palestine.[280]

Since the beginning of the occupation, the inhabitants of Palestine were free to leave the country by using travel documents (*laissez-passer*) issued to them by the British military authorities, apparently without detailed legislative regulation.[281] An early *Proclamation* issued by the British military in Palestine on 30 March 1918,[282] in its Article 10, prescribed: "No person shall attempt to enter or leave Occupied Enemy Territory [i.e. Palestine] without complying with the passport regulations for the time being in force". Such passport regulations were, apparently, the Ottoman Passport Law and regulations, elaborated earlier in this study,[283] in addition to the said regulations themselves. "At this time" (the winter of 1918–1919 onwards), therefore, "no one was allowed to cross to the east side of the Jordan, unless provided with a military pass".[284]

A preliminary system of Palestinian passports and travel documents was introduced in August 1920 by the *Palestine Passport Regulations*.[285] While the passport was granted to Ottoman citizens residing in Palestine, a form of emergency *laissez-passer* was given to foreigners who were un-represented in the country by

277 British Government, *Report on Palestine Administration 1922*, His Majesty Stationary Office, London, 1923, p. 53.

278 *Ibid.*

279 *Ibid.*

280 *Ibid.*

281 See Palestine Passports Regulations 1920 (Legislation of Palestine, Vol. I, p. 635), the preamble and Article 1(2).

282 Legislation of Palestine, Vol. I, p. 599.

283 See above Chapter II, Section 3.

284 McCrackan, *op. cit.*, p. 220.

285 *Op. cit.*

foreign consuls and unable to obtain other forms of travel documentation.[286] The issuance of passports and travel documents was motivated by security considerations. Palestinians and foreigners had to obtain, in addition to either a passport or travel document, a permit to leave Palestine.[287] While not always granted, such a permit was nominally obtainable from the Department of Immigration and Travel or from the police office of the district in which the person resided.[288] The *laissez-passer* was considered valid only for the journey for which it was issued.[289] The Passport Regulations employed the term 'inhabitant of Palestine' rather than 'Palestinian citizen'. For example, Article 2 of this legislation stated: "Pending the enactment of a Law of Nationality for the inhabitants of Palestine, an inhabitant of Palestine who is not a foreign subject, may obtain a *laissez-passer* in lieu of a passport".[290]

Palestinian passports and travel documents were used abroad to claim diplomatic protection provided by British consuls. In a case before the Anglo-Turkish Mixed Tribunals on 14 December 1927, which offers an example that reflects a general practice at the time, "the claimant produced [*inter alia*] a *laissez passer*, dated 16 March 1920, and issued by the British military authorities in occupation of Egypt, which described him as '*sujet palestinien, protégé britannique*'".[291] Thus, the inhabitants of Palestine were regarded by other states as being both Palestinian citizens and British protected persons.[292]

By issuing passports to the inhabitants of Palestine and extending international protection to them, Britain dealt with Palestine like the case with other British controlled territories (e.g. protectorates, colonies and mandated areas).[293] This British practice applied to Palestine during this period and continued throughout the mandate until 14 May 1948, as it will be further elaborated later.[294]

Locally, the Government of Palestine made a distinction between the status of Ottoman citizens and the foreigners residing in the country. It developed, for instance, special rules relating to the treatment of foreigners before Palestinian courts. In June 1918, the senior British judicial officer issued Rules of Court which defined the term 'foreign subjects' as "subjects of any European or American state... but does not include [British] protected persons".[295] Though formulated for the purpose of the Rules, this definition was later endorsed by the Constitution of Palestine, in

286 Report on Palestine Administration 1922, *op. cit.*, p. 53.
287 Palestine Passport Regulations, Article 1(1).
288 *Ibid.*, Article 4.
289 *Ibid.*, Article 5(2).
290 See also Articles 1, 3, 4, 6 and 9.
291 *N.N. Berouti v. Turkish Government* (Annual Digest, 1927–1928, p. 310).
292 For a similar conclusion, though in broader context, see Oppenheim, *op. cit.*, pp. 514–515.
293 For a historical review on the nationality in the British colonies, see Piggott, *op. cit.*, pp. 205–226.
294 Chapter VIII, Section 2.
295 Philip Marshal Brown, "British Justice in Palestine", *The American Journal of International Law*, Vol. 12, 1918, pp. 830–831.

1922.[296] In order to be distinguished from Ottoman subjects residing in Palestine, foreign citizens continued to register themselves at their respective consulates.[297]

Foreign citizens who desired to enter Palestine were obliged to obtain a visa, either from the Government of Palestine or from British consulates abroad.[298] Unlike the previous Ottoman practice which obliged citizens to obtain a visa in order to return to the Ottoman Empire,[299] such a visa was no longer required of those Palestinians who wished to return home.

The entry of Palestinians and foreigners into Palestine was systematically regulated by the Immigration Ordinance of 26 August 1920.[300] This Ordinance gave the Government the authority to regulate the entry of persons into Palestine "according to the conditions and needs of the country".[301] Specifically, the Ordinance: (1) established the position of Immigration Director;[302] (2) prescribed the conditions for admission into Palestine;[303] (3) authorized the inspection of entering persons;[304] (4) obliged such persons to register at police offices;[305] and (5) waived the immigration rules for certain foreigners.[306]

Various terms were used to describe the actual existence of Palestinian nationality. The Immigration Ordinance directly employed the term 'citizen of Palestine'. For instance, the Ordinance permitted the deportation of any person "who has not become a citizen of Palestine".[307] The same Ordinance also employed the term 'permanent residents' of Palestine.[308] In practice, which complies with the new realities on the ground, the Government used the term 'Palestinian' to describe the inhabitants of Palestine in a number of forms, including 'Palestinian officials', 'Palestinian magistrates', 'Palestinian members [of a court]', 'Palestinian Public Prosecutor', 'young Palestinians', 'British and Palestinian'.[309]

Palestinian nationality existed despite a lack of comprehensive legislative regulation. Similar practical existence in the absence of domestic law on Palestinian nationality arose in Egypt after its separation from the Ottoman Empire in 1914. By the time at which the Law-Decree concerning Egyptian Nationality was enacted

---

296 See above pp. 41–42.

297 For example, Bernard Razkovsky, a French citizen who had been residing in Palestine since 1895, on 9 February 1922, "renewed his inscription at the French Consulate in Jaffa" (*Nahum Razkovsky v. Leonine Razkovsky and Others, op. cit.*).

298 Palestine Passport Regulations 1920, Article 3; Immigration Ordinance 1920, Article 15.

299 See above p. 40.

300 Legislation of Palestine, Vol. I, p. 637.

301 Article 1.

302 Article 2.

303 Article 5.

304 Article 6.

305 Article 7.

306 Article 10. (Article 9 set out sanctions to be imposed following the violation of immigration rules.)

307 Article 8.

308 Article 5.

309 Samuel, *op. cit.*, various sections.

in 1926,[310] the Ottoman Nationality Law of 1869 was practically ineffective. Most jurists were of the opinion that Egyptian nationality came into existence following the separation of Egypt from the Empire. Others, however, believed that Egypt's inhabitants remained Ottomans in effect, until the said Law-Decree was passed.[311]

With respect to nationality status in such situations, it had been concluded:

> A [Mandatory or Occupying] State promises diplomatic protection within the boundaries of certain Oriental countries to certain natives.... Such protected natives are... called '*de facto* subjects' of the protecting State. Their position is quite anomalous; it is based on custom and treaties, and no special rules of the Law of Nations [i.e. international law] itself are in existence concerning them. *Every State which takes such de facto subjects under its protection can act according to its discretion*, and there is no doubt that as soon as these Oriental States have reached a level of civilization equal to that of the Western States [sic], the whole institution of *de facto* subjects will disappear.[312]

This British practice was in line with the overall British policy towards Palestine at the time. Such policy was included in a statement presented to the British Parliament by the Secretary of State for the Colonies on 23 June 1922 (commonly known as 'the White Paper').[313] Among other things, the White Paper declared:

> [I]t is contemplated that the status of all citizens of Palestine in the eyes of the law shall be Palestinian, and it has never been intended that they, or any section of them, should possess any other juridical status.[314]

The foregoing discussion shows that Palestinian nationality was effectively established or, at the least, had begun to emerge. This *de facto* nationality was created at the domestic level in accordance with both the law applicable to Palestine and British practice. At the same time, Palestine's inhabitants remained *de jure* (i.e.

---

310 See above p. 50.

311 For these views, see Shams Eddin Alwakil, *Nationality and Status of Foreigners*, Munshaat Al-Maaref, Alexandria, 1966 (Arabic), pp. 70–71; Ghali, *op. cit.*, pp. 117–168. See also Abi-Saab, *op. cit.*, pp. 73–74 (footnote): "Egypt... in the period from 1880 to 1914, was nominally a part of the Ottoman Empire, but had a separate government.... The inhabitants were called 'Egyptiens sujets local'".

312 Oppenheim, *op. cit.*, pp. 514–515. Nonetheless, it is not clear whether or not Oppenheim (in the added emphasis) was describing the practice of the European states in the Orient or advising on how to treat peoples under the '*de facto* subjection'. In fact, the British behaviour in regard to Palestinian nationality, at this stage, was to a large extent in line with Oppenheim's statement.

313 See *British Policy in Palestine*, in British Government, *Correspondence with the Palestine Arab Delegation and the Zionist Organization*, His Majesty's Stationary Office, London, 1922 (reprinted in 1929), pp. 17–21. This policy document is also known as 'Churchill White Paper'.

314 *Ibid.*, p. 18. See also British Government, *Mandate for Palestine: Letter from the Secretary to the Cabinet to the Secretary-General of the League of Nations of July 1, 1922, enclosing a Note in reply to Cardinal Gasparri's letter of May 15, 1922, addressed to the Secretary-General of the League of Nations presented to Parliament by Command of His Majesty*, His Majesty Stationary Office, London, 1922, p. 4.

according to public international law), Ottoman citizens,[315] however nominal this status was.

3. *Nationality after the Palestine Mandate, 1922–1924*

A. *Framework*

"In the period between the creation of the Mandates system and the ratification of the Treaty of Lausanne",[316] as a very much similar situation in the pre-mandate period in Palestine, "the inhabitants of these [mandated] territories were theoretically still Ottoman subjects.... This was obviously an anomalous situation that could not be easily characterized in law".[317] This section, however, shall try to characterise such a situation based on the existing international and domestic legal instruments relating to Palestine and by reviewing relevant practices at the time.

This stage commenced on 24 July 1922 with the adoption of the Palestine Mandate by the Council of the League of Nations.[318] It ended when Britain ratified the Treaty of Lausanne on 6 August 1924. Two important points are worth noting here. Firstly, although the Mandate of Palestine had been declared by Britain in 1920, it only legally entered into force on 29 September 1923,[319] together with the Mandate for Syria.[320] But the present discussion is concerned with the mentioned date of the adoption of the Mandate only; by this date Palestine was recognized as a separate political entity at the international level. Secondly, notwithstanding that the Palestine Mandate, including its nationality article, continued to be applicable until 1948, this section is limited to the developments of Palestinian nationality during this transitional stage, which lasted for a bit over two years.

The Mandate system was established after World War I, by Article 22 of the Covenant of the League of Nations, to deal with ex-Turkish and German territories. In practice, mandates were classified as A, B or C based on what was considered to be a country's readiness for self-rule. All the five occupied Arab territories (Iraq, Palestine, Trans-Jordan, Syria and Lebanon) were placed in class A, implying the ability of these territories to govern themselves and that the period of the mandate was to be relatively short. Regarding Palestine, the Council of the League of Nations

---

315 *N.N. Berouti v. Turkish Government, op. cit.*

316 Abi-Saab, *op. cit.*, p. 48.

317 *Ibid.*

318 For the text of the Palestine Mandate, see League of Nations, *Official Journal*, August 1922, p. 1007.

319 "Note by the Secretary-General", League of Nations, *Official Journal*, October 1923, p. 1217.

320 Council of the League of Nations, *Minutes of Twenty-First Meeting*, 28 September 1929 (League of Nations, *Official Journal*, October 1923, p. 1349).

which convened in London, confirmed the Mandate on 24 July 1922. Thus, Britain acquired an international legal basis for its presence in that territory.

In a special article of the Palestine Mandate, which did not exist in other mandates,[321] the framework for Palestinian nationality was drawn up.[322] Thus, Article 7 of the Mandate reads:

> The Administration of Palestine shall be responsible for enacting a nationality law. There shall be included in this law provisions framed so as to facilitate the acquisition of Palestinian citizenship by Jews who take up their permanent residence in Palestine.

Obviously, as a matter of law, the objective of regulating Palestinian nationality as enshrined in Article 7 of the Mandate was to confer that nationality on immigrant Jews.[323] This came as a logical consequence to the overall goal of the Palestine Mandate; i.e. to establish a national home for the 'Jewish people' in Palestine.[324]

Using 'nationality' and 'citizenship' in this article implied that both terms were synonymous.[325] It also demonstrated that the definition of nationality was considered to presume the existence of a legal relationship between the individuals and Palestine as a mandated territory, or as a state. In other words, Palestinian nationality, at least in the way in which it was 'framed', was not based upon racial, religious or other political considerations. Indeed, "la citoyenneté palestinienne n'est pas une nationalité juive";[326] nor, equally, was such 'citoyenneté' deemed to be "une nationalité arabe".[327] Therefore, "under Article 7 of the Mandate, the intention to

---

321 Stoyanovsky, *op. cit.*, pp. 149–150.

322 For the text of all mandates, see *The American Journal of International Law*, Vol. 17, 1923 (supplement), pp. 138–194. The following mandates were confirmed by the Council of the League of Nations in Geneva on 17 December 1920: Britain's Mandate over the German possessions in the Pacific Ocean situated South of the Equator with the exception of German Samoa and Nauru, Japan's Mandate over former German possessions in the Pacific Ocean lying north of the Equator, Britain's Mandate for Nauru, Britain's Mandate for German Samoa, and Britain on behalf of South Africa's Mandate for German South-West Africa. The following mandates, in addition to the Palestine Mandate, were confirmed by the said Council at London on 22 July 1922: Britain's Mandate for Cameroons, France's Mandate for Cameroons, Belgium's Mandate for East Africa, Britain's Mandate for East Africa, France's Mandate for Syria and the Lebanon, Britain's Mandate for Togoland, and France's Mandate for Togoland. Britain's Mandate for Iraq was the first mandate instrument to be concluded on 23 August 1921 (reproduced in Boustany, *op. cit.*, p. 143).

323 For other objectives, or motivations, of the nationality law (i.e. the 1925 Palestinian Citizenship Order), see below Chapter IV, Section 3.

324 Ghali, *op. cit.*, p. 104. More generally, see Adel Aljader, *Impact of the British Mandate Laws in Establishing the Jewish National Home in Palestine*, Centre of Palestine Studies, Baghdad University, Baghdad (Arabic—undated), pp. 93–182.

325 Ghali, *op. cit.*, p. 209. *Cf.* Stoyanovsky, *op. cit.*, pp. 51–61.

326 Ghali, *op. cit.*, p. 217. See also Moch, *op. cit.*, pp. 178–181.

327 Ghali, *op. cit.*, p. 210. See also the White Paper of 1922, *op. cit.*, p. 19.

take up permanent residence in Palestine is a *sine qua non* in the case of those Jews whose acquisition of Palestinian citizenship is to be facilitated".[328]

The origin of Article 7 of the Palestine Mandate dated back to 10 August 1920, when the (draft) Treaty of Sèvres[329] was signed between Turkey and the Allies. As Turkey refused to ratify it, the Treaty of Sèvres never came into force. Instead, the draft was replaced by the Treaty of Lausanne, signed in 1923.

With respect to nationality in Palestine, Article 129 of the Treaty of Sèvres stipulated:

> Jews of other than Turkish nationality who are habitually resident, on the coming into force of the present Treaty, within the boundaries of Palestine, as determined in accordance with Article 95 [of the Treaty of Sèvres][330] will *ipso facto* become citizens of Palestine to the exclusion of any other nationality.

Neither of these two articles was adopted in the definitive Treaty of Lausanne. The content of this article was apparently disregarded for humanitarian reasons. The article intended to impose "Palestinian citizenship on foreign Jews habitually resident in Palestine. But objection was taken to that clause as derogating from the principle that a person should not be deprived of his nationality against his will".[331] And "in the end the clause was not included in the definitive treaty".[332]

In fact, an amended version of this article was incorporated into Article 35 of the *Draft Final Act* of the Treaty of Lausanne and presented to the Turkish delegation at the Lausanne Conference.[333] Article 35 reads:

> Jews of other than Turkish nationality who are habitually resident in Palestine on the coming into force of the present Treaty will have the right to become citizens of Palestine by making a declaration in such form and under such conditions as may be prescribed by law.

---

328 *Palevitch v. Chief Immigration Officer*, Supreme Court of Palestine sitting as a High Court of Justice, 28 February 1929 (Law Reports of Palestine, p. 353).

329 *Op. cit.*

330 Article 95 stated: "The High Contracting Parties agree to entrust, by application of the provisions of Article 22, the administration of Palestine, within such boundaries as may be determined by the Principal Allied Powers, to a Mandatory to be selected by the said Powers. The Mandatory will be responsible for putting into effect the declaration originally made on November 2, 1917, by the British Government, and adopted by the other Allied Powers, in favour of the establishment in Palestine of a national home for the Jewish people, it being clearly understood that nothing shall be done which may prejudice the civil and religious rights of existing non-Jewish communities in Palestine, or the rights and political status enjoyed by Jews in any other country…".

331 Norman Bentwich, "The Mandate for Palestine", *The British Year Book of International Law*, 1929, p. 140.

332 Bentwich, "Nationality in Mandated Territories Detached from Turkey", *op. cit.*, p. 102.

333 Lausanne Conference, *op. cit.*, p. 684.

The sub-commission appointed to discuss the question of nationalities at the Lausanne Conference, concluded its work on 26 January 1923, and after extensive discussion on the draft, chose in the final instance not to adopt the above article.[334]

Practically, there was no need to retain this article on Palestinian nationality in the Treaty of Lausanne because, when this treaty was finalized in 1923, the substance of both Article 129 of the draft Treaty of Sèvres and Article 35 of the draft Treaty of Lausanne, had been already incorporated some months previously, albeit in different form, in Article 7 of the Palestine Mandate in 1922.[335]

In a broader international legal context, the "Nationality law... showed that the Palestinians formed a nation, and that Palestine was a State, though provisionally under guardianship".[336] The inclusion of Palestinian nationality in the text of the Palestine Mandate was the first step towards an international recognition of the Palestinian people as distinct from the Ottomans and other peoples. Indeed, Palestinian nationality, like any other nationality, constituted the legal bond which connected individuals to collectively form a people as an element of a state.[337]

With regard to the nationality of the inhabitants of the mandated territories, in general, the Council of the League of Nations adopted the following resolution on 23 April 1923:

> (1) The status of the native inhabitants of a Mandated territory is distinct from that of the nationals of the Mandatory Power, and cannot be identified therewith by any process having general application.
> (2) The native inhabitants of a Mandated territory are not invested with the nationality of the Mandatory Power by means of the protection extended to them.
> (3) It is not inconsistent with (1) and (2) above that individual inhabitants of the Mandated territory should voluntarily obtain naturalization from the Mandatory Power in accordance with arrangements which it is open to such Power to make, with this object, under its own law....[338]

334 See "Final Report presented by M. Montagna, President of the Sub-Commission on Nationalities and Antiquities in Turkey, to the President of the Second Commission, his Excellency Marquis Garroni" (in *ibid.*, p. 532).

335 Other differences between the nationality provisions of the Treaty of Sèvres and the Treaty of Lausanne were the provisions relating to the status of Bulgaria, Cyprus, Greece, Egypt and Hejaz. See Ghali, *op. cit.*, pp. 106–108.

336 Permanent Mandates Commission, *Minutes of the Thirty-Second (Extraordinary) Session Devoted to Palestine*, League of Nations, Geneva, 1937, pp. 86–87.

337 On the people element of the state, in general, see Ian Brownlie, *Principles of Public International Law*, Clarendon Press, Oxford, 1977, pp. 537–543; Malcolm N. Shaw, *International Law*, Grotius Publications Limited, Cambridge, 1991, pp. 178–181; Nguyen Quoc Dinh, Patrick Daillier, Alain Pellet, *Droit international public*, LGDJ, Paris, 1992, pp. 395–398; Peter Malanczuk, *Akehurst's Modern Introduction to International Law*, Poutledge, London/New York, 1997, pp. 76–77; Georges J. Perrin, *Droit international public: sources, sujets, caractéristiques*, Schulthess Polygraphischer Verlag, Zurich, 1999, pp. 613–624; Joe Verhoeven, *Droit international public*, Larcier, Bruxelles, 2000, pp. 278–295; Oppenheim, *op. cit.*, pp. 510–523.

338 League of Nations, *Official Journal*, June 1923, p. 604. For background on this resolution, see Council of the League of Nations, *Minutes of the Sixty Meeting*, 20 April 1923 (*ibid.*, pp. 567–572, 658–659).

Although this resolution related to the mandate of types B and C, it covered, given its general nature, all types of mandate, including type A,[339] as was the case of Palestine.[340] While the nationality question was ambiguous in other mandated territories,[341] it had already been settled in the ex-Turkish territories (type A), by Article 123 of the Treaty of Sèvres, back in 1920;[342] and, more generally, in Article 22 of the Covenant of the League of Nations which recognized a separate national character of the inhabitants of such territories.[343] Hence, there was no reason to include the question of nationality for the inhabitants of type A mandated areas within this resolution.[344] Indeed, it was widely believed that this League's resolution "embodies the correct doctrine" for all mandated territories.[345]

B. *Domestic application*

Despite the absence of specific legislation on nationality at this stage, Palestinian nationality had already begun to be well-defined by the highest-ranked legislation of Palestine. Besides Article 7 of the Mandate, a definition of Palestinian nationality can be found in two key Orders—Palestine Order in Council (Constitution) and Legislative Election Order—and other lower-level legislation. A clear distinction between Palestinian citizens and foreigners had also been established. Certain practices of the Palestine government and courts, together with some international supporting factors, gave effect to these instruments.

---

339 On the various types of the mandate, see Norman Bentwich, "Le système des mandates", in *Recueil des course*, Académie de droit international (The Hague), 1929–IV, Librairie Hachette, Paris, Vol. 29, 1930, pp. 111–186; Norman Bentwich, *The Mandates System*, Longmans, Green and Co., London/New York/Toronto, 1930; Hales, *op. cit.*, pp. 85–126.

340 *Cf.* Wright, *op. cit.*, p. 314: "The League's decisions [like the said resolution] with reference to the status of territory and inhabitants under mandate have been negative in character"; and Abi-Saab, *op. cit.*, p. 56: "This resolution decided the question in part only.... It made it abundantly clear that the inhabitants of the Mandated territories did not acquire the nationality of the Mandatory. But on the other hand it did not pass on their national status, and left it as ambiguous as before".

341 Stoyanovsky, *op. cit.*, p. 263.

342 The said article runs as follows: "Turkish subjects habitually resident in territory which in accordance with the provisions of the present Treaty is detached from Turkey will become *ipso facto*, in the conditions laid down by the local law, nationals of the State to which such territory is transferred".

343 See, for instance, Wright, *op. cit.*, p. 314; Lampué, *op. cit.*, p. 60; Mock, *op. cit.*, p. 176; Abi-Saab, *op. cit.*, p. 46. See also D.P. O'Connell, "Nationality in C Class Mandates", *The British Year Book of International Law*, Vol. 31, 1954, pp. 458–641.

344 For details, see Marquis Alberto (Special Rapporteur appointed by the League's Mandates Commission), *Report Submitted to the Council on the Question of Nationality of the Inhabitants of B and C Mandated Areas* (League of Nations, *Official Journal*, June 1922, pp. 589–608).

345 Weis, *op. cit.*, p. 23. See also Oppenheim, *op. cit.*, p. 194; Ghali, *op. cit.*, p. 202.

Seventeen days after the adoption of the Mandate, Britain issued the Palestine Order in Council on 10 August 1922. The Order intended to execute, through domestic legislation, the international obligations laid down in the Mandate.

The Palestine Order in Council was, both substantively and administratively, regarded as a constitution. The Order stipulated the legislative, judicial and executive authorities of the country. In its official Arabic version, the Palestine Order in Council was called *dustour*, which literally means 'constitution'. Courts of Palestine dealt with the Order as a constitution. In several cases before the Palestine Supreme Court, it was confirmed that the said Order in Council had a constitutional value to the extent that all lower-level legislation should comply with it and all authorities had to adhere to its provisions, including the High Commissioner.[346] Thus, hereinafter the Order in Council of 1922 will be referred to as: 'the Constitution of Palestine' or 'the Constitution'. Furthermore, the text of the Palestine Mandate itself had been part of the constitutional structure of the country. Article 18 of the Constitution provided: "No law shall be enacted in contrary to the Palestine Mandate in any aspect".[347]

The Constitution provided a functional definition of the term 'foreigner'. Article 59, paragraph 1, defined a 'foreigner' as "any person who is a national or subject of a European or American State or of Japan, but shall not include: (i) Native inhabitants of a territory protected by or administered under a mandate granted to a European State, (ii) Ottoman subjects, (iii) Persons who have lost Ottoman nationality and have not acquired any other nationality". This definition confirmed that the inhabitants of Palestine were still Ottoman citizens but protected by a European state (i.e. Britain).[348] Referring to 'foreigners' and 'Palestinian citizens', Article 65 of the Constitution additionally stated: "Nothing...shall be construed to prevent foreigners from consenting to such matters being tried by the Courts...having jurisdiction in like matters affecting Palestinian citizens".

Clearly, such constitutional provisions failed to define who exactly the 'Palestinians' were. In Articles 58 to 67 of the Constitution, the definition of 'foreigner' intended to accord, as already noted, 'Western' and Japanese citizens certain privileges before Palestinian courts, such as consular assistance in criminal proceedings. These special articles came as a consequence of the on-going effects of the capitulation system which had been applicable in the Ottoman Empire in the previous centuries and

346 In *Attorney-General v. Abraham Altshuler* (Supreme Court of Palestine, May 1928—Annual Digest, 1927–1928, p. 56), for instance, the Court considered certain Regulations enacted by the High Commissioner to be invalid according to, *inter alia*, "Article 17 of the Palestine Order in Council". See also *Rozenblatt v. Register of Land*, Supreme Court of Palestine sitting as a High Court of Justice, 9 June 1947 (Annual Digest, 1947, p. 29). This case confirmed, *inter alia*, certain regulations enacted by the High Commissioner in accordance with the Palestine Constitution.

347 *Attorney General v. Abraham Altshuler, op. cit.* The constitutional structure of Palestine was further governed by the Royal Instructions dated 14 August 1922 (Legislation of Palestine, Vol. II, p. 529). For details, see Goadby, "Palestinian Law: Sources and Judicial Organization", *op. cit.*, pp. 41–52; Melhim, *op. cit.*, pp. 63–64.

348 Ghali, *op. cit.*, pp. 226–227.

which had favoured the Western states and Japan.[349] The privileged provisions were also accorded to citizens of European states and Japan because these states were Members of the League of Nations and that their citizens enjoyed certain rights in accordance with the Palestine Mandate that enacted by the League itself;[350] concerning American citizens, Britain reached an agreement with the United States, which was not a member of the League, according Americans similar rights and placing them on the same footing as those citizens who belonged to member-states of the League.[351]

The day on which the Constitution was enacted (10 August 1922), Britain introduced the Palestine Legislative Council Election Order in Council.[352] Whereas the Constitution had defined the term 'foreigner', the Election Order defined the term 'Palestinian citizens'. Article 2 stipulated that "the following persons shall be deemed to be Palestinian citizens... Turkish subjects habitually resident in the territory of Palestine at the date of commencement of this Order".[353] Although it was provided for the purpose of the legislative election,[354] this definition had in fact established the future status of those individuals who would henceforth be regarded as Palestinian nationals ("Turkish subjects habitually resident in Palestine"). Thus, as some rightly observed, this definition constituted a practical amendment to the Ottoman Nationality Law of 1869.[355]

In addition to the Constitution and the Legislative Election Order, other domestically-enacted legislation set out different rights and duties for Palestinians and

---

349 See above Chapter II, Section 4.

350 It should be noted that the definition of 'foreigner' had been altered after the enactment of the Palestinian Citizenship Order in 1925 (see below Chapter IV) as it defined who constituted a Palestinian citizen. To be sure, Article 59 of the Constitution was specifically modified by Article 2(*d*) of the Palestine (Amendment) Order-in-Council of 1935 (Palestine Gazette, No. 496, 28 February 1935, p. 263). 'Foreigner', herein, was defined in a simple manner to include all persons who were not Palestinian citizens. *Cf. Nahas v. Kotia and Another* (1938), *op. cit.*

351 See *Anglo-American Convention on Palestine*, London, 3 December 1924 (Legislation of Palestine, Vol. I, p. 527), Article 2. For a background on this Convention, see D.P. O'Connell, *State Succession in Municipal Law and International Law*, Cambridge University Press, London, 1967, Vol. II, pp. 297–298.

352 Laws of Palestine, p. 3386. In addition to this Order in Council, the Palestinian Legislative Council was regulated by Articles 17–34 of the Constitution. However, the legislative election, which only partially took place in 1922, was ultimately cancelled. Thus, the amended Palestine Order in Council 1923 (see Laws of Palestine, p. 3332) suspended the application of the articles of the 1922 Constitution related to the Council. Consequently, the Executive, represented by the British Government and the High Commissioner, had exercised the legislative function throughout the mandate period. That legislative function was based on Article 1 of the Palestine Mandate, Article 89 of the Constitution, and Article 3 of the Palestine (Amendment) Order in Council 1923.

353 For details, see Feinberg, *op. cit.*, pp. 65–94.

354 The paragraph that provided the aforesaid definition started as: "For the purposes of this Order... the following persons shall be deemed to be Palestinian citizens". *Cf.* Vitta, *op. cit.*, p. 77.

355 Ghali, *op. cit.*, p. 232.

for foreigners. Such legislation included, *inter alia*, the *Regulations made under Article 67 of the Palestine Order in Council on the Powers of Consuls in matters of Personal Status of Nationals of their State* of 15 November 1922;[356] and the *Succession Ordinance* of 8 March 1923.[357] The latter Ordinance distinguished between foreigners and Palestinians in regard to the jurisdiction of civil courts in cases of succession upon death. It directly employed the term 'Palestinian citizen' in Articles 3 and 4. The same Ordinance used the term 'foreigner' as defined in the Constitution of Palestine.[358] Such regulations and ordinances had been operative besides the existing legislation on immigration and passport-related matters.[359]

A distinction between Palestinians and foreigners had further been drawn up at the international level. A typical example can be found in the *Mavrommatis Palestine Concessions* case before the Permanent Court of International Justice on 19 August 1924.[360] This case arose from the alleged refusal of the Government of Palestine to recognize the rights acquired by Mr. Mavrommatis, a Greek citizen, under contracts and agreements he concluded with the Ottoman authorities with respect to concessions for certain public works to be constructed in Palestine (Jordan Valley, Jerusalem and Jaffa). Greece, on behalf of Mavrommatis, filed a claim on 13 May 1924 at the Permanent Court of International Justice against the Government of Palestine, which was represented at the Court by Britain, for its alleged failure to fulfil its contractual obligations with the Greek citizen.[361]

Although the Palestine Mandate authorized Britain to pass a law on Palestinian nationality, the enactment of such a law was delayed for three years. This late enactment was questioned at the international level. In 1922, the Permanent Mandate Commission of the League of Nations asked Britain, *inter alia*, whether it had enacted a nationality law. The Commission also enquired as to whether that law had been framed in such a way as to facilitate the acquisition of Palestinian citizenship by Jews, whose permanent residence in Palestine was in accordance with Article 7 of the Mandate.[362] In its annual report submitted to the Council of the League in 1923, Britain replied to the question by stating that: "An Order in

---

356 Legislation of Palestine, Vol. II, p. 66.

357 *Ibid.*, Vol. I, p. 350.

358 Article 2(*m*) read: "'Foreigner' means any person who is a foreigner with the meaning of Article 59 of the Palestine Order-in-Council".

359 See above p. 56.

360 Objection of the Jurisdiction of the Court (Permanent Court of International Justice, *Collection of Judgements*, Series A, No. 2, 1924, p. 7). On the role of the Permanent Court with regard to Palestine, as set out in Article 26 of the Mandate, see Stoyanovsky, *op. cit.*, pp. 325–334.

361 For detailed analysis, see Edwin M. Borchard, "The Mavrommatis Concessions Cases", *The American Journal of International Law*, Vol. 19, 1925, pp. 728–738.

362 League of Nations, *Mandate for Palestine: Questionnaire Intended to Assist the Preparations of the Annual Reports of the Mandatory Powers*, League of Nations Doc. No. C.553.M.335.1922.VI, 23 August 1922, p. 3.

Council concerning Palestinian Nationality is now under consideration".[363] And before defining who the 'Palestinians' were, Article 2 of the Palestinian Legislative Council Election Order in Council of 1922 began by stating: "For the purpose of this Order, *until the enactment of the Palestinian Citizenship Order*, the following persons shall be considered Palestinians…".[364] Thus, draft legislation on Palestinian nationality was ready at the time. Yet it seems that Britain preferred to wait until it had first acquired a full legal basis for its presence in the country by concluding a peace agreement with Turkey, the legitimate sovereign over Palestine.

As in the previous stage, the 1869 Ottoman Nationality Law remained the domestic basis for the nationality of Palestine's inhabitants. The application of that law was similar to other Ottoman legislation in effect at this time. The on-going application of the Ottoman legislation was confirmed in general terms by the Constitution which, in its Article 46, pronounced: "The jurisdiction of the Civil Courts shall be exercised in conformity with the Ottoman Law…". Palestinian courts reaffirmed that the Ottoman laws are applicable in the country, in accordance with the aforesaid article.[365] However, as Britain had been recently authorized by the Palestine Mandate to enact a Palestinian nationality law, the 1869 Ottoman Nationality Law could be then, however implicitly, duly amended or repealed.

The British-run Government of Palestine naturalized certain groups of foreign residents in the country to enable them to participate in the legislative election in accordance with the Palestine Legislative Council Election Order in Council of 1922.[366] These residents, "mostly immigrants Jews who had come to settle in the national home",[367] entered Palestine in the period of 1920–1922.[368] "A Proclamation was made on September 1st [1922],[369] providing that any person of other than Ottoman nationality, habitually resident in Palestine on that date, might within two months apply for Palestinian Citizenship".[370] As a result, "19,293 Provisional Certificates of Citizenship were granted in respect of 37,997 persons, wives and minor

---

363 British Government, *First Annual Report to the League of Nations on the Palestine Administration*, Colonial Office, London, June 1924, p. 9.

364 Emphasis added.

365 See, for example, *'Ata Naser Eddin and Others v. President and Members of the Supreme Moslem Council*, Supreme Court of Palestine sitting as a High Court of Justice, 7 May 1932 (Law Reports of Palestine, p. 710); *The Palestine Mercantile Bank v. Jecob Freyman and Ritan Belkind*, Supreme Court of Palestine sitting as a Court of Appeal, 4 March 1938 (Supreme Court Judgements, 1938, Vol. I, 1938, p. 148); *London Society for Promoting Christianity among the Jews v. Orr and Others*, Supreme Court of Palestine sitting as a Court of Civil Appeal, 13 May 1947 (Annual Digest, 1947, p. 33).

366 *Op. cit.*

367 Bentwich, "Nationality in the Mandated Territories", *op. cit.*, p. 104.

368 Report on Palestine Administration 1922, *op. cit.*, p. 5.

369 The date of 1 September 1922 was the day on which the Legislative Council Election Order in Council was simultaneously published in the Palestine Gazette and came into force (see Article 21 of the same Order; also Laws of Palestine, p. 3394—footnote).

370 Report on Palestine Administration 1922, *op. cit.*, p. 53.

children being included on certificates issued to heads of families".[371] In addition, naturalization was granted "exceptionally to ex-Russian nationals, who...had been permanently resident in this country and were forced to assume Ottoman nationality during [the First World] War".[372] All these persons were deemed, at this stage, as Palestinian citizens only for the purpose of the legislative election and were not considered to be full citizens. Three years later, however, these persons would be ultimately granted Palestinian nationality by naturalization under a special proviso of the 1925 Palestine Citizenship Order.[373]

Palestinian courts recognized the provisional Palestinian nationality. In a case before the Supreme Court of Palestine regarding the extradition of two persons resident in Jerusalem, it was stated:

> The accused persons in Palestine were alleged to have been Ottoman subjects. They had applied and obtained provisional certificates of special [Palestinian] citizenship, which were issued by the Government [of Palestine] prior to the enactment of the Palestine Citizenship Order in Council.[374]

In sum, during this period, the *de facto* existence of Palestinian nationality not only continued but was further strengthened by the adoption of the Palestine Mandate and the enactment of a number of key legislation. The status of Palestinian nationality had yet to be *de jure* acknowledged from the international law standpoint. This was because the peace treaty between Turkey and the Allies, including Britain, according to which Palestine would be officially and definitively separated from the Ottoman Empire had been still awaiting the entry into force.

4. *Palestinian nationality after the Treaty of Lausanne, 1924–1925*

The Treaty of Peace, which was agreed upon by the Allied Powers and Turkey, officially ended World War I and was signed in Lausanne on 24 July 1923 (hereinafter referred to as 'the Treaty of Lausanne' or 'the Treaty').[375] It came into

371 *Ibid.* See also Permanent Mandates Commission, *Minutes of the Fifth Session (Extraordinary)*, Geneva, 1924 (hereinafter: 'Mandates Commission Minutes 1924'). At this session, the High Commissioner for Palestine, Mr. Herbert Samuel, was present. Samuel, in replying to a question raised by the Commission's Chairman, said that "almost the whole Jewish population [in Palestine] had announced their intention of accepting Palestinian nationality.... The number of persons affected...was about 38,000. This figure...for the most part consisted of Jews" (p. 81).

372 Bentwich, "Nationality in the Mandated Territories", *op. cit.*, p. 104.

373 See below p. 126.

374 *Attorney-General v. Goralschwili and Another* (Annual Digest, 1925–1926, p. 47). While no date for this judgement was provided, an application for appeal from the judgement was granted on 24 February 1925 (*ibid.*, p. 48).

375 The Treaty was signed between Britain, France, Italy, Japan, Greece, Romania and the Serb-Croat-Slovene State (the Allies), on the one hand, and Turkey, on the other. Greece ratified the Treaty on 11 February 1924; Turkey on 31 March 1924; Britain, Italy and

force for Britain (which by then was the Mandatory for Palestine, Trans-Jordan and Iraq), on 6 August 1924. Setting out the legal status of the territories detached from Turkey, the Treaty had the effect of law in Palestine, as it was extended to this country by domestic Ordinance, from 6 August 1924.[376]

The status of Palestine and the nationality of its inhabitants were finally settled by the Treaty of Lausanne from the international law perspective. In a report submitted to the League of Nations, the British Government rightly pointed out: "The ratification of the Treaty of Lausanne in Aug., 1924, finally regularised the international status of Palestine".[377] And, thereafter, "Palestine could, at last, obtain a separate nationality".[378] Most of the post-World War I peace treaties embodied nationality provisions; the Treaty of Lausanne was no exception.[379]

The Treaty of Lausanne addressed the nationality of the inhabitants in the territories detached from Turkey in Articles 30–36. These articles replaced, with certain modifications, Articles 123–131 of the draft Treaty of Sèvres of 1920.[380]

Drawing up the framework of nationality, Article 30 of the Treaty of Lausanne stated:

> Turkish subjects habitually resident in territory which in accordance with the provisions of the present Treaty is detached from Turkey will become *ipso facto*, in the conditions laid down by the local law, nationals of the State to which such territory is transferred.

To qualify for Palestinian nationality in virtue of this Article, the individual had to meet two conditions. He or she should first be a Turkish citizen, or subject.[381] Secondly, such a person had to be habitually resident ('*établis*', or established, in the authentic French version) in Palestine as of 6 August 1924, the day on which the Treaty of Lausanne came into being.[382] In other words, residents in Palestine who had no Ottoman nationality (i.e. foreign citizens or stateless persons) had no right to become Palestinian citizens. Similarly, Ottoman citizens residing outside Palestine on the above date were not deemed to be Palestinians. An exception to

---

Japan on 6 August 1924; France on 30 August 1924. See *Treaty of Peace with Turkey and other Instruments Signed at Lausanne on 24 July, 1923*, His Majesty's Stationary Office, London, 1923; see also LN Treaty Series, Vol. 28, 1924, p. 13.

376 See Treaty of Peace (Turkey) Ordinance, 1925, 1 September 1925 (Legislation of Palestine, Vol. I, p. 576).

377 British Government, *Report on the Administration under Mandate of Palestine and Trans-jordan*, 1924 (hereinafter: 'Report on the Administration of Palestine 1924'), p. 6.

378 Bentwich, *England in Palestine*, *op. cit.*, p. 106.

379 See, in general, William O'Sullivan Molony, *Nationality and the Peace Treaties*, George Allen & Unwin Ltd., London, 1934. See also below pp. 69–70.

380 See, in detail, Ghali, *op. cit.*, pp. 95–114. In general, see Paul C. Helmreich, *From Paris to Sèvres: The Partition of the Ottoman Empire at the Peace Conference of 1919–1920*, Ohio State University Press, Columbus, 1974.

381 In the original French text, 'subjects' read as 'ressortissants'.

382 See Stoyanovsky, *op. cit.*, pp. 265–269.

the latter provision applied to those individuals who were born in Palestine and fell under Article 34 of the Treaty which will be elaborated later.[383]

Article 30 is of great importance, even if it mainly constituted a mere declaration of existing international law and the standard practice of states. This was in spite of the fact that there was no definite rule in the law of state succession under which nationals of the predecessor state could acquire *ipso facto* the nationality of the successor.[384] "As a rule, however, States have conferred their nationality on the former nationals of the predecessor State...".[385]

In practice, almost all peace treaties concluded between the Allies and other states at the end of World War I embodied similar nationality provisions to those of the Treaty of Lausanne.[386] These treaties included:[387] the Treaty with Germany,[388]

---

383 See below Chapter V, Section 2.

384 See, in detail, C. Fred Fraser, "Transfer of Sovereignty and Non-Recognition as Affecting Nationality", *Alberta Law Quarterly*, Vol. 4, 1940–1942, pp. 138–155; F.A. Mann, "The Effect of Changes of Sovereignty upon Nationality", *The Modern Law Review*, Vol. 5, 1941–1942, pp. 218–224; Yasuaki Onuma, "Nationality and Territorial Change: In Search of the State of the Law", *The Yale Journal of World Public Order*, Vol. 8, 1981–1982, pp. 1–35; C. Luella Gettys, "The Effects of Change of Sovereignty on Nationality", *The American Journal of International Law*, Vol. 21, 1992, pp. 268–278; Jeffrey L. Blackman, "State Succession and Statelessness: The Emerging Right to an Effective Nationality under International Law", *Michigan Journal of International Law*, Vol. 19, 1998, pp. 1160–1161; Constantin P. Economides, "Les effets de la succession d'Etats sur la nationalité des personnes physiques", *Revue Générale de Droit International Public*, Vol. 103, 1999, pp. 583–589; Weis, *op. cit.*, pp. 140–164; Brownlie, "The Relations of Nationality...", *op. cit.*, pp. 319–326; O'Connel, *op. cit.*, Vol. I, pp. 497–542.

385 Weis, *op. cit.*, p. 149.

386 In 1929, the University of Harvard conducted comprehensive research on nationality laws of various states. The research also proposed articles relating to future codification of international law on nationality. See *The American Journal of International Law*, Vol. 23, Special Number, 1929 (hereinafter: 'Harvard Research on Nationality'), p. 61). In the second part of Article 18, the Harvard Research on Nationality provided: "When a part of the territory of a state...becomes the territory of a new state, the nationals of the first state who continue their habitual residence in such territory lose the nationality of that state and become nationals of the successor state, in the absence of treaty provisions to the contrary...". It is interesting to note that seventy years later, the International Law Commission (ILC) adopted a similar provision: "Persons concerned having their habitual residence in the territory affected by the succession of States are presumed to acquire the nationality of the successor State on the date of such succession" (Article 5). ILC, *Draft Articles on Nationality of Natural Persons in Relation to the Succession of States*, 1999 (ILC, *Yearbook*, United Nations, New York/Geneva, 2003, Vol. II, Part Two, pp. 21–23)—hereinafter: 'ILC Articles on Nationality and State Succession'. The draft articles were endorsed by the United Nations General Assembly Resolution 55/153 of 30 January 2001.

387 See Laws Concerning Nationality, pp. 586–591. On the history of the peace treaties concluded at the end of World War I, in general, see F.S. Marston, *The Peace Conference of 1919: Organization and Procedure*, Oxford University Press, London/New York/Toronto, 1944; Hankey, *The Supreme Control at the Paris Peace Conference 1919*, George Allen and Unwin Ltd., London, 1963.

388 Versailles, France, 28 June 1919, Article 278.

the Treaty with Poland,[389] the Treaty with Romania,[390] and the Treaty with the Serb-Croat-Slovene State,[391] amongst other treaties.[392] Henceforth, the inhabitants of Palestine, as the successors to this territory, acquired Palestinian nationality even, arguably, if there was no treaty with Turkey.[393]

'Palestine' was not mentioned in the Treaty of Lausanne, let alone Palestinian nationality. However, there was no need to mention these terms because the Treaty provided generic provisions applicable to all territories detached from Turkey, including Palestine. This 1923 Treaty differed from the draft Treaty of Sèvres (1920), which introduced a separate regime for each ex-Turkish territory, with special reference to Palestinian nationality in Article 129.[394] Instead, a similar clause to the latter article was embodied, as already detailed,[395] in Article 7 of the Palestine Mandate. Therefore, with regard to Palestinian nationality, the Mandate and the Treaty of Lausanne complemented each other.

Palestinian nationality was regulated by the Treaty of Lausanne in a similar way to how the nationalities of other mandated-territories in the Middle East were regulated. The Iraq Nationality Law of 1924[396] defined Iraqi citizens as those Ottoman subjects who were habitually resident in Iraq on 6 August 1924.[397] Equally, the Trans-Jordan Nationality Law of 1928[398] considered all Ottoman citizens habitually resident in Trans-Jordan on 6 August 1924 to be Trans-Jordanian citizens.[399] In Syria and Lebanon under the French mandate, inhabitants residing on 30 August 1924 (the day on which the Treaty of Lausanne was ratified by France) were deemed to be Syrian or Lebanese citizens.[400] With regard to Egypt,[401] the Treaty entered

389 Versailles, France, 28 June 1919, Articles 4 and 6.
390 Paris, France, 9 December 1919, Articles 4–6.
391 St. Germain-en-Laye, France, 10 September 1919, Articles 4–6.
392 The Treaty with Austria (St. Germain-en-Laye, France, 10 September 1919), Articles 64–65 and Article 230; the Treaty with Czechoslovakia (St. Germain-en-Laye, France, 10 September 1919), Articles 4–6; the Treaty with Bulgaria (Neuilly-sur-Seine, France, 27 November 1919), Articles 51–52; and the Treaty with Hungary (Trianon, France, 4 June 1920), Articles 56–57 and Article 213.
393 For details on the nationality in peace treaties, see O'Connell, *State Succession..., op. cit.*, Vol. II, pp. 529–536.
394 See above p. 60.
395 See above pp. 59–60.
396 *Op. cit.*
397 For details, see Bentwich, "Nationality in Mandated Territories", *op. cit.*, pp. 108–109; Ghali, *op. cit.*, pp. 170–191.
398 *Op. cit.*
399 For details, see Ghali, *op. cit.*, pp. 199–229.
400 See above pp. 49–50. For details, see Ghahi, *op. cit.*, pp. 231–258; Alhalawani, *op. cit.*, pp. 157–159.
401 See above p. 50.

into force retroactively on 5 November 1914 and the Ottoman inhabitants of Egypt were considered Egyptians from that date.[402]

The courts in the respective states had confirmed such provisions. In the judgement of a case before an international tribunal in Egypt (which could be said to be relevant for all mandated territories detached from Turkey in accordance with the Treaty of Lausanne), it was held:

> Syria and the Lebanon, being countries placed under an 'A' Mandate, are, in accordance with the Covenant of the League of Nations, to be deemed to be independent States and persons of public international law, and the inhabitants have acquired the nationality of those States. Syrians and Lebanese must, therefore, be considered in Egypt as foreigners on the same basis as the subjects of countries which had been detached from the Turkish Empire prior to the Great War.[403]

Also, Article 30 of the Treaty of Lausanne stipulated that the new nationality should be acquired in accordance with "the conditions laid down by the local law". The local law, or legislation,[404] in Palestine was at the time the Ottoman Nationality Law of 1869.[405] Hence, the Treaty could be considered to have been complementary to the provisions of the said Ottoman law. In case of conflict, the Treaty was to prevail over the local law, as it provided a generic reference. And any future nationality legislation in Palestine was to comply with the nationality rules laid down in the Treaty.

The Treaty incorporated additional provisions that usually emerge in cases of state succession. These provisions related to the individual's right to opt for another nationality; the status of natives residing abroad; and the nationality of women and children.

An individual's right to choose his or her nationality in times of state succession was recognized in two cases. Firstly, those who acquired Palestinian nationality were entitled to retain their Turkish nationality.[406] Secondly, persons who differed in race from the majority of the Arab Palestine's inhabitants were empowered to opt for the nationality of a state where the majority of its inhabitants had belonged to their race (e.g. Armenians or Persians resident in Palestine were allowed to opt for

402 In this connection, Article 17 of the Treaty of Lausanne declared: "The renunciation by Turkey of all rights and titles over Egypt...will take effect as from the 5th November, 1914".

403 *Antoine Bey Sabbagh v. Mohamed Pacha Ahmed and Others*, Mixed Court of Mansura, Egypt, 15 November 1927 (Annual Digest, 1927–1928, pp. 44–45).

404 The term 'local law' derived from 'législation locale' as appeared in the French text.

405 The Ottoman Nationality Law of 1869 was invoked and executed in cases before Palestinian courts. One example was *Robinson v. Press and Others, op. cit.*, which came before the Supreme Court of Palestine on 20 February 1925.

406 In this respect, Article 31 reads: "Persons over eighteen years of age, losing their Turkish nationality and obtaining *ipso facto* a new nationality under Article 30 [in the present case, Palestinian nationality], shall be entitled within a period of two years from the coming into force of the present Treaty to opt for Turkish nationality". On the right of option as applied in Palestine, see below pp. 94–95.

the nationalities of Armenia and Iran, respectively).[407] Either way,[408] such persons were expected to transfer their place of residence to the state whose nationality they sought to claim.[409]

The Treaty of Lausanne gave those persons who were born in Palestine and residing abroad the right to opt for Palestinian nationality. This option had no automatic effect. Rather, it required an application by the person concerned, within two years after the enforcement of the Treaty, and the approval of the Government of Palestine. To this effect, Article 34 of the Treaty runs as follows:

> Subject to any agreements which it may be necessary to conclude between the Governments exercising authority in the countries detached from Turkey and the Governments of the countries where the persons concerned are resident, Turkish nationals of over eighteen years of age who are natives of a territory detached from Turkey under the present Treaty, and who on its coming into force are habitually resident abroad, may opt for the nationality of the territory of which they are natives, if they belong by race to the majority of the population of that territory, and subject to the consent of the Government exercising authority therein. This right of option must be exercised within two years from the coming into force of the present Treaty.

The application of this article, as translated into Article 2 of the Palestinian Citizenship Order of 1925, created hardships for thousands of Palestinian natives who were resident abroad. This issue will be addressed in detail later.[410]

Lastly, the Treaty of Lausanne regulated the nationality of women and children in such a way as to ensure their dependency on their husbands and parents, respectively. In this connection, Article 36 stipulated that "...the status of a married woman will be governed by that of her husband, and the status of children under eighteen years of age by that of their parents". Therefore, a foreign woman would *ipso facto* acquire Palestinian nationality if her husband was considered to be a Palestinian citizen.[411]

---

407 Article 32 states: "Persons over eighteen years of age, habitually resident in territory detached from Turkey in accordance with the present Treaty, and differing in race from the majority of the population of such territory shall, within two years from the coming into force of the present Treaty, be entitled to opt for the nationality of one of the States in which the majority of the population is of the same race as the person exercising the right to opt, subject to the consent of that State".

408 In fact, there were little or no practical implications from these provisions in relation to Palestine.

409 This provision was regulated in Article 33 as follows: "Persons who have exercised the right to opt in accordance with the provisions of Articles 31 and 32 must, within the succeeding twelve months, transfer their place of residence to the State for which they have opted. They will be entitled to retain their immovable property in the territory of the other State where they had their place of residence before exercising their right to opt. They may carry with them movable property of every description. No export or import duties may be imposed upon them in connection with the removal of such property".

410 Chapter V, Section 2.

411 *Cf.* below pp. 187–190.

The Treaty confirmed the previous practice whereby the inhabitants of Palestine were effectively regarded as Palestinians. To be sure, as it would soon become apparent, most of the nationality rules of the Treaty were later embodied in the 1925 Palestinian Citizenship Order and became part of the country's legal system.

The Treaty of Lausanne, including its nationality rules, remained legally binding and effectively applicable throughout the mandate period (until 14 May 1948).[412] For instance, the '*Bon Voisinage* Agreement' between Syria and Palestine of 1926,[413] in Article 10, stipulated that the nationality of inhabitants living near the Syrian and Lebanese borders could be determined, should any conflict arise, in accordance with Articles 30–36 of the Treaty of Lausanne. The Treaty was additionally invoked several times in judicial proceedings before Palestinian courts on issues relating to conflict of laws. Examples included, *inter alia*, a case before the Palestine Land Court of Jaffa in November 1937[414] and another before the Supreme Court of Palestine sitting as a Court of Civil Appeal in March 1947.[415] In both cases, a conflict arose with the Government of Palestine over private land bought by the heirs of the Ottoman Sultan Abdul Hamid.[416] At the international level, the Treaty was first invoked before the Permanent Court of International Justice in *Mavrommatis Palestine Concessions*.[417] The nationality provisions of the Treaty were also invoked before the courts in England[418] and Egypt.[419]

In conclusion, Palestinian nationality was first founded on 6 August 1924, "and treaty nationality in Palestine runs from that date".[420] The Treaty of Lausanne had transformed the *de facto* status of, and practice relating to, Palestinian nationality into *de jure* existence from an international law angle.[421] Indeed, "The coming into force of the Treaty of Peace enabled Laws of Nationality to be issued by the three Governments [Iraq, Palestine and Syria], and the change of subjection which has

---

412 Most legislation enacted during the Mandate period in Palestine is still valid at present. Thus, it is arguable that the Treaty of Lausanne *per se* still has current significance. At any rate, as most of its nationality provisions were integrated within the 1925 Palestinian Citizenship Order, the Treaty is still valid.

413 *Op. cit.*

414 *Heirs of the Prince Mohamed Selim v. The Government of Palestine*, Palestine Land Court of Jaffa, October and November 1937 (Annual Digest, 1935–1937, p. 123).

415 *Amine Namika Sultan v. Attorney-General*, 31 March 1947 (Annual Digest, 1947, pp. 36–40).

416 See Norman Bentwich, "State Succession and Act of State in the Palestine Courts", *The British Year Book of International Law*, 1946, pp. 330–333. See also *Nadeen Markoff v. Habib George Daoud Homsi…, op. cit.*

417 Permanent Court of International Justice, *op. cit.*, p. 11.

418 *The King v. Ketter*, England, Court of Criminal Appeal, 21 February 1939 (Annual Digest, 1938–1940, p. 46).

419 *Saikaly v. Saikaly*, 15 December 1925 (Annual Digest, 1925–1926, p. 48).

420 Survey of Palestine, Vol. I, p. 206.

421 For other perspectives, see, for example, Mohammad K. Al-Azhari, "The Palestinian Concept of Self-Determination between the End of the Ottoman Rule and the British Mandate", *Journal of Arab Affairs*, No. 40, December 1984, pp. 130–159 (published in Arabic by the League of Arab States, Tunis).

occurred *de facto* to be transformed into a changed *de jure*".[422] Meanwhile, the Ottoman Empire ceased to exist and was now limited to the boundaries of the 'Republic of Turkey'.[423] Hence, no legal ground was left to consider Palestine's inhabitants as Turkish or Ottoman citizens.

Likewise, on 6 August 1924, for the first time ever, international law certified the birth of the 'Palestinian people' as distinct from all neighbouring peoples.

As the Treaty of Lausanne did not regulate the specific details of nationality, this task was to be carried out within the demesne of domestic law. The Treaty did, however (by its very nature as public international law instrument), impose limitation on the content of the nationality legislation which would be enacted.[424] This legislation, along with its connection with the Treaty, will be discussed next.

422 Bentwich, "Nationality in Mandated Territories", *op. cit.*, p. 97.
423 See Articles 2–3 of the Treaty of Lausanne.
424 Johns, *British Nationality Law and Practice, op. cit.*, p. 279; Ghali, *op. cit.*, p. 112; Abi-Saab, *op. cit.*, p. 56.

IV

PALESTINIAN CITIZENSHIP ORDER 1925

1. *Background*

The "Palestinian Citizenship Order 1925",[425] as it is officially called,[426] was enacted by Britain on 24 July 1925.[427] Pursuant to its Article 26, the Citizenship Order came into force on 1 August 1925.[428] It was amended in 1931 and several times thereafter.[429] By 1939,[430] significant provisions of the 1925 Citizenship Order had been altered. An additional two amendments were passed in 1940[431] and 1942.[432] The original Order and its amendments were reproduced in 1944 in a single instrument called the *Consolidated Palestinian Citizenship Orders, 1925–1941*.[433] The 1925 Citizenship Order constituted the 'nationality law' of Palestine, which was referred to in Article 7 of the Palestine Mandate.[434]

The text of the 1925 Order, as ultimately embodied in the 1941 amendment, is particularly significant for the following reasons: (1) it was the final nationality text applicable in Palestine at the end of the mandate; (2) it affected nationality laws enacted in Israel in 1952 and in Jordan (which then included the West Bank), in 1954; (3) it was effectively applicable in the Gaza Strip under the Egyptian administration from 1948 to 1967; (4) it is still valid in all the Palestinian Authority areas at the present day; and (5) the Palestinian legislator would have

425 Legislation of Palestine, Vol. I, p. 37; and Laws of Palestine, p. 3404.
426 Article 27 stated: "This Order shall be known as the Palestinian Citizenship Order 1925".
427 It is may be relevant to note that the date of 24 July 1925 marks the second anniversary of the Treaty of Lausanne which was signed on 24 July 1923.
428 "This Order shall come into force on the 1st day of August 1925."
429 Laws of Palestine, p. 3414.
430 Palestine Gazette, No. 917, Supplement 2, 31 August 1939, p. 845.
431 Palestine Gazette, No. 1076, Supplement 2, 16 February 1941, p. 242.
432 Palestine Gazette, No. 1210, Supplement 2, 16 July 1942, p. 1530.
433 Palestine Gazette, No. 1351, Supplement 2, 10 August 1944, p. 912.
434 See above p. 59.

no choice but to review that text in the drafting process of nationality legislation in the future Palestinian state.

Among all the mandates adopted by the League of Nations, as indicated earlier,[435] the Palestinian Citizenship Order was the only 'nationality law' provided within a mandate text. It was also the only nationality law enacted by Britain, in all the territories assigned to it as a Mandatory. As described in Chapter III above, in the British mandated territories of Iraq and Trans-Jordan, the nationality laws were enacted by the local authorities in 1924 and 1928, respectively. In the remaining British mandated territories (Cameroon, Togoland and Tanganyika), no nationality legislation was passed[436] and the inhabitants were simply considered to be British protected persons.[437] In other mandated territories linked to Britain, special naturalization legislation was extended from the Mandatory to the inhabitants of the territory (e.g. the extension of the nationality of the Union of South Africa to Southwest Africa/Namibia). Otherwise the inhabitants were merely considered as British protected persons, without nationality legislation; this was the case in Nauru Island under the joint mandate of Britain, Australia and New Zealand.[438]

With regard to the terminology, it was argued that the Order favoured the term 'citizenship' over 'nationality', as it constituted a "fundamental difference which exists in many Oriental countries between allegiance to the state, which is

---

435 See above p. 59.

436 In such situations, the general principle drawn by the League of Nations resolution of 23 April 1923 regarding the nationality of the inhabitants of the mandated territories (see above pp. 61–62) would apply.

437 Jones, *British Nationality Law and Practice, op. cit.*, p. 286.

438 *Ibid.*, pp. 271, 273, 286–287. It might be relevant to mention that the inhabitants of British domains (Australia, Canada, Ireland—until 1922—Newfoundland, New Zealand, South Africa) were treated as British subjects within their respective territories in accordance with nationality legislation enacted locally in each domain (which constituted a virtually re-enactment of the British Nationality Acts). For further details on the legislation of these domains, at the time, see Collection of Nationality Laws, pp. 73–130, 137–144. In British colonies (e.g. Hong Kong, Fiji, Jamaica, Nigeria), and in British India, nationality laws (generally speaking) were adopted locally. Nationality in each colony basically granted its bearers the right of residence and political rights. On the international plane, inhabitants of British domains, colonies and mandated-territories were recognized as British protected persons based on custom and the principles of the English Common Law system widespread over the British Empire. Discussing the question of nationality in the British domains and colonies is, of course, beyond the scope of this study. For further details in this regard, see E.F.W. Gey van Pittius, "Dominion Nationality", *Journal of Comparative Legislation and International Law*, Vol. 13, 1931, pp. 199–202; Piggott, *op. cit.*, pp. 205–226; Jones, *British Nationality Law and Practice*, *op. cit.*, pp. 268–277; Weis, *op. cit.*, pp. 17–22. For subsequent development on the question of British and Commonwealth nationality, see, e.g., Mervyn Jones, "British Nationality Act, 1948", *The British Year Book of International Law*, 1948, pp. 158–197; J.F. Josling, *Naturalisation and other Methods of Acquiring British Nationality*, the Solicitors' Law Stationary Society, Ltd., London, 1949; Clive Parry, *British Nationality, including Citizenship of the United Kingdom and Colonies and the Status of Aliens*, Stevens & Sons Limited, London, 1951.

citizenship, and membership of a nationality within the state, which is a matter of race or religion".[439] But, while it is true that the Citizenship Order used the term 'citizenship' in most of its articles, the term 'nationality' was also utilized for the same purpose.[440] Employing both terms was consistent with Article 7 of the Palestine Mandate, which used the two terms synonymously. Moreover, as it has been evident in several cases, Palestinian courts did not make a clear distinction between both terms.[441] In law and practice of Palestine, therefore, 'nationality' and 'citizenship' were designed to have the same meaning, however interesting the theoretical discussion on this matter might be.[442]

Concerning the form, the Palestinian Citizenship Order was problematic. Unlike the British nationality law from which the Order was chiefly derived, the Order followed no logic in terms of the sequence of its rules. For example, Part III (Articles 7–11), which was devoted exclusively to the question of naturalization, failed to incorporate all naturalization matters.[443] Again, unlike the British nationality law, there was no specific part which dealt with the status of married women and children, or with the question of expatriation. Rather, these matters were considered in various articles in the beginning, the middle and the end of the Citizenship Order, with some repetition.[444]

---

439 Bentwich, "Nationality in the Mandate Territories", *op. cit.*, p. 102. For a detailed reply to this contention, see Ghali, *op. cit.*, pp. 208–212. Amongst other issues, Ghali demonstrated that political difference between 'nationality' and 'citizenship' does exist in Western countries as well. In another reply, Abi-Saab said (*op. cit.*, p. 73, note 114): "He [Bentwich] obviously confuses the sociological meaning of nationality with its legal meaning". For general consideration, however recent might be, see Patrick Weil and Randall Hansen, eds., *Nationalité et Citoyenneté en Europe*, Editions la Découverte, Paris, 1999. See also the references in *supra* notes 2 and 5.

440 The following articles of the Citizenship Order used the term 'nationality': 1, 2, 3, 4, 11, 14, 16 (used 'national') and 19. All these articles, in addition to other nine articles of the Order, used the terms 'citizenship' and 'citizen'.

441 See, e.g., *Sara Mandelberg Rogalsky v. Director of Medical Services*, Supreme Court of Palestine sitting as a High Court of Justice, 25 March 1938 (Law Reports of Palestine (Baker), 1938, p. 230); *Arieh Leopold Zwillinger v. Blanka Schuster*, Supreme Court of Palestine sitting as a Court of Civil Appeal, 8 May 1941 (Supreme Court Judgements, 1941, Vol. I, p. 173); *Jawdat Badawi Sha'ban v. Commissioner for Migration, op. cit.*; and *Palevitch v. Chief Immigration Officer, op. cit.*

442 See above Chapter I, Section 1.

443 Other naturalization provisions can be found in both Articles 5 and 20. The latter article, which dealt with the inclusion of a child in a naturalization certificate, followed Article 19, which authorised the High Commissioner to make regulations to implement the Palestinian Citizenship Order. (Logically, in terms of the sequence, the delegation of legislative powers should follow the substantive issues, including the fact that the Order itself delegated additional powers to the High Commissioner in Articles 23, 24 and 25.)

444 Article 6, for example, stated that the status of married women and children will be governed by that of their husbands or fathers for the purpose of Parts I and II. Again, Article 12(1) considered the wife of a Palestinian man as a Palestinian and the wife of an alien as an alien. Moreover, no titles for the Order's articles were provided; the British Nationality Act of 1914 included such titles.

One finds other drafting errors. The 1925 Order used different dates for similar purposes: e.g., using 'one year' in Article 14(2) but 'twelve months' in Article 9(1). As just noted, the Order employed various terms for the same meanings, such as 'national', 'subject' and 'citizen'; and 'nationality' and 'citizenship'.[445] Such drafting problems affected the clarity of the Order and created difficulties of interpretation for both the administration and the judicial bodies.[446]

To give effect to the Citizenship Order, the Government of Palestine enacted a number of regulations,[447] the most significant (as it set comprehensive procedures to execute the original Citizenship Order) of which were the Palestinian Citizenship Regulations of 1925.[448] Based on Article 19 of the Citizenship Order,[449] these Regulations lay down instructions relating to, *inter alia*, the following matters: the application form for naturalization; the form required for the naturalization certificate; declarations concerning: nationality option, alienage, the acquisition, resumption or retention of nationality; and fees to be paid in respect of any declaration or grant under the Order, as well as other procedural matters.[450] Indeed, such regulations had considerable administrative, more than judicial, value.[451]

Divided into four parts, the Citizenship Order comprised twenty-seven articles in total. Part I, which was composed of Articles 1 and 2, dealt with the natural change from Ottoman to Palestinian nationality as set out in the Treaty of Lausanne in 1923. This part applied to original inhabitants residing in Palestine, and gave the right of opting nationality to Palestine's natives residing abroad. Part II,

---

445 *Cf.* above Chapter I, Section 1.

446 These drafting problems might explain certain confusions which arose in cases relating to the dates fixed for some purposes (see below pp. 90–91, 96) and the meaning of 'residence' in Palestine (see below pp. 89–90, 98–103).

447 These Palestinian Citizenship Regulations were as follows (the numbers of the reference, dates and page numbers in this note refer to Supplement 2 of the Palestine Gazette): Regulations (No. 2) of 1934 (No. 472, 18 October 1934, p. 1277); Regulations (No. 3) of 1934 (No. 474, 1 November 1934, p. 1331); Regulations of 1935 (No. 487, 17 January 1935, p. 39); Regulations of 1936 (No. 598, 28 May 1936, p. 500); Regulations of 1939 (No. 960, 2 November 1939, p. 1448); (Amendment) Regulations of 1942 (No. 1176, 12 March 1942, p. 557); Regulations of 1942 (No. 1196, 21 May 1942, p. 1010); (Naturalization of Alien Women) Regulations of 1942 (No. 1198, 4 June 1942, p. 1128); (Amendment) Regulations of 1942 (No. 1202, 18 June 1942, p. 1328); (Amendment) Regulations (No. 2) of 1942 (No. 1236, 3 December 1942, p. 2309); (Amendment) Regulations of 1944 (No. 1354, 24 August 1944, p. 861); (His Majesty's Forces) (Amendment) Regulations of 1945 (No. 1419, 21 June 1945, p. 881); (His Majesty's Forces) (Amendment No. 2) Regulations of 1945 (No. 1437, 6 September 1945, p. 984); (Amendment) Regulations of 1947 (No. 1602, 7 August 1947, p. 1464); (Amendment No.2) Regulations of 1947 (No. 1609, 4 September 1947, p. 1655).

448 Laws of Palestine, p. 3417.

449 *Cf.* British Nationality Act of 1914, Articles 19–24.

450 Goadby, *International and Inter-Religious Private Law in Palestine, op. cit.*, p. 37.

451 For details in British law, see Jones, *British Nationality Law and Practice, op. cit.*, pp. 214–218.

comprising Articles 3 to 6, addressed the acquisition of nationality by birth, declaration and registration for legislative election and a general rule on the status of married women and minor children. Part III, which incorporated Articles 7 to 11, was devoted to the acquisition of Palestinian nationality by naturalization. Part IV (Articles 12 to 27) included various matters, such as: the nationality of married women and children, expatriation, declaration of alienage and the delegation of powers to the High Commissioner to make regulations, definitions, penalties, transitional provisions and other matters.

For the sake of clarity in terms of evaluating the Palestinian Citizenship Order of 1925, it may be useful to divide the Order, for the purpose of this study, into three parts: the natural acquisition of nationality, naturalization, and expatriation. Thus, Chapter IV of this study will tackle the question of the natural acquisition of nationality which covers: the change from Ottoman nationality to Palestinian nationality for residents of Palestine; the acquisition of nationality by Palestine's natives residing abroad; and the general principles underlying the acquisition of Palestinian nationality at birth. Chapter V will discuss naturalization in Palestine including its ordinary aspects and its actual effects, which went beyond the obvious rules of the Order. And Chapter VI will be dedicated to examining the question of expatriation, or the loss of Palestinian nationality.

2. *Legal value*

As a sign of its legal significance, the Palestinian Citizenship Order of 1925 was enacted by an Order in Council, introduced by the King of the British Empire and not by the Government of Palestine. This fact made the Order superior over all the locally-enacted legislation and gave it a supreme constitutional value. Yet it was argued before an English court, in *The King v. Ketter*,[452] that the Order was "of no force or validity as having been made by the mandatory power and not by the administration in Palestine who were the responsible authority under Article 7 of the Mandate". This argument, however, had been easily dismissed because the obligations under the Mandate were assigned to Britain.

Thus, in practice, both the British Government and the High Commissioner for Palestine represented one Power: the Mandatory. Indeed, Article 1 of the Mandate gave "the Mandatory full powers of legislation and of administration" in Palestine. Article 24 of the Citizenship Order authorised the High Commissioner to amend or to repeal the Order or to add to its provisions, within two years after entering into force, as he might deem necessary to carry out the Order's purposes.

---

452 *Op. cit.*

The Palestinian Citizenship Order was enacted under the Foreign Jurisdiction Act of 4 August 1890,[453] which was applicable at the time in the British colonies.[454] This Act was also applicable in Palestine, wherein Britain had given itself general legislative jurisdiction as it had similarly done in other colonies. In *Sheriff Es Shanti v. Attorney General for Palestine*,[455] the Supreme Court of Palestine sitting as a High Court of Justice held that, as the Orders in Council owed their existence to the Foreign Jurisdiction Act, Britain thereby assumed jurisdiction in countries that were outside its domains.[456] Hence, "Orders in Council made under the Foreign Jurisdiction Act are, in legal sense, Supreme, and unchanged". Such Orders had the same authority to that of the Acts of the British Parliament, which prevailed, as noted earlier, over all locally-enacted laws.[457]

Accordingly, the Citizenship Order formed one of the fundamental pieces of legislation mounted to the level of a constitution. Thus, by virtue of the Palestine Order in Council of 1922,[458] the hierarchy of legislation was as follows (from the highest to the lowest): (1) 'orders-in-council'; (2) 'ordinances' (which constituted the ordinary 'laws'[459] issued by the High Commissioner); (3) secondary legislation, such as 'regulations', 'rules', 'proclamations', which were made by the High Commissioner, or British officials authorised by him, based on specific Order(s) or ordinance(s) or certain provision in a previous Order or ordinance.

The foregoing paragraph shows the great importance which Britain attached to the issue of nationality in Palestine.[460] This importance stemmed from the high degree of interest which the international community (as represented by the League of Nations), accorded to Palestinian nationality in Article 7 of the Mandate.[461]

---

453 *Op. cit.*

454 See the preamble of the Citizenship Order.

455 12 March 1937 (Annual Digest, 1935–1937, p. 110).

456 According to Article 16 of the Act itself.

457 For the same result, see *Sheinfeld v. Officer Commanding No. 3 Court Martial and Holding Centre*..., Supreme Court of Palestine sitting as a High Court of Justice, 16 February 1945 (Annotated Law Reports, 1945, Vol. I, p. 413). For a similar conclusion arrived at by the English courts, see *The King v. Ketter*, *op. cit.* See also Ghali, *op. cit.*, pp. 212–213 (note); Melim, *op. cit.*, pp. 55–56.

458 See the following Articles of the Palestine Order in Council: 3, 5, 17, 24, 26, 49, 64, 73 and 74.

459 The official Arabic translation of the 'ordinance' was *qanoun*, meaning 'law'.

460 In his consideration of the question of nationality outside the United Kingdom, Jones (in *British Nationality Law and Practice* of 1947, *op. cit.*) divided his research into three parts: Part III on 'Dominion and Colonial Local Naturalization' (pp. 269–277), Part IV on 'Palestinian Citizenship' (pp. 278–285), and Part V on 'Other British Territories' (pp. 286–287).

461 Article 17 of the Palestine Constitution stipulated that "no Ordinance shall be passed which shall be in any way repugnant to or inconsistent with the provisions of the Mandate". This means that the Mandate was part of the constitutional structure of Palestine. See above p. 63.

Also, as nationality is inherently connected with sovereignty, it would seem that Britain wished to retain absolute sovereign power by defining the terms of Palestine's nationality. This position was part of a wider policy towards colonies whereby, as one writer put it, "colonies can have no power of legislation with reference to nationality. They cannot alter the [English] common law rule, nor can they extend or curtail nationality by statute, even though such legislation professed to be limited in its effect to the Colony in which it was passed".[462] Therefore, although it was placed under a special regime in the form of the Mandate, Palestine was practically regarded by the British Empire as a colony for the purpose of determining the nationality characteristics.[463]

The legal and practical effects of the Citizenship Order and its amendments lasted until 1948. But the on-going effects of the Order continued long after the mandate period had passed, as it was never totally repealed, locally or by Britain.[464] More generally, most Palestinian legislation which had been enacted during the period of British rule, continued to be valid in the Gaza Strip during the Egyptian administration (1948–1967) and the subsequent Israel occupation (1967–1994). As a result, this British-made legislation is still, legally speaking, in force today in the Palestinian Authority areas of the Gaza Strip. To a lesser extent, some legislation from the time of British rule, including parts of the Citizenship Order, remains

462 Piggott, *op. cit.*, p. 219. *Cf.* Jones, *British Nationality Law and Practice, op. cit.*, pp. 286–287.

463 As alluded to above, Palestine was regarded as a colony for other purposes as it was covered by the Foreign Jurisdiction Act, 1890. See above p. 80.

464 Two days before ending its mandate over Palestine, Britain enacted an Order in Council that revoked a number of key legislation of Palestine. See *The Palestine (Revocations) Order in Council, 1948*, No. 1004, adopted by the British Parliament on 12 May 1948 and came into operation on 14 May 1948 (British Government, *Statutory Instruments Other Than Those of a Local, Personal or Temporary Character for the Year 1948*, His Majesty Stationary Office, London, 1949, Vol. I, p. 1350). This Order revoked a number of orders in council; the Palestinian Citizenship Order was not among these revoked orders. Yet the Israel Nationality Law of 1 April 1952 (Laws Concerning Nationality, p. 263) repealed the Palestinian Citizenship Orders. Article 18 of this law provided: "*(a)* The Palestinian Citizenship Orders, 1925–1942, are repealed with effect from the day of the establishment of the State. *(b)* Any reference in any provision of law to Palestinian citizenship or Palestinian citizens shall henceforth be read as a reference to Israel nationality or Israel nationals". This repeal, however, does not affect the validity of the Citizenship Orders in the territories of Palestine located outside the area that became Israel. *Cf.* Gouldman, *op. cit.*, pp. 16–17. In addition, this domestic law has no power over the international law of state succession, which obliges Israel to accord its nationality to all Palestinian citizens residing in the territory of Palestine that fell under Israeli sovereignty, including those citizens who left, or were forced to leave, their villages and towns during the 1947–1949 war. See Chapter XII (the Conclusion) of this study.

valid in the West Bank today.[465] Hence, the legal evaluation of that Order in this study is not only of historical value but is also of current legal significance.

However, certain rules of the Citizenship Order were, by their very nature, transitional provisions which expired once they exceeded the fixed date of their validity. These provisions included the natural change from Ottoman to Palestinian nationality;[466] the nationality option;[467] and the naturalization of certain foreigners who were residing in Palestine before the Order took effect.[468] A similar fate should theoretically have faced the legislation enacted in order to grant Palestinian nationality by naturalization to those persons who were serving in the British army at the time.[469] Such provisions and legislation had achieved their objective and were not expected to have effects in the future. Yet the naturalization rules within the Order in spite of having long since achieved their intended practical purpose (which was to naturalize foreign Jews in Palestine),[470] can be considered today to be still applicable due to their general terms. All these issues will be examined in some detail later in this study.

Certain specific terms employed in the Order were obviously not applicable once the Mandate had concluded. These terms included references to the High Commissioner,[471] the Government of Palestine,[472] and the British Government (which included the King, British consular or diplomatic missions, and Secretaries of State).[473] Of course, it was the responsibility of the government exercising its authority in those territories detached from the mandated-Palestine to replace such entities with other governmental bodies such as a Council of Ministers, a Minister of Interior or Head of State.[474]

---

465 The Jordan Nationality Law of 1954 (Jordan Official Gazette, No. 1171, 16 February 1954, p. 105) did not directly repeal the Palestinian Citizenship Order of 1925. In general terms, Article 22 of the said law provided: "This Law shall repeal all Ottoman, Jordanian or Palestinian legislation in force before publishing this Law in the Official Gazette *to the extent that the provisions of these legislation contradict with the provisions of this Law*" (emphasis added).

466 Article 1, Clause (1).

467 Article 1, Clauses (2) and (3), Articles 2 and 4.

468 Article 5.

469 See below pp. 127–128.

470 See below Chapter VI.

471 References to the High Commissioner are made, often several times, in the following Articles of the Citizenship Order: 4, 5, 7, 8, 9, 10, 11, 12, 17, 21, 23 and 24.

472 See Articles 2, 10 and the Schedule attached to the Order (Oath of Allegiance).

473 See Articles 10, 18, 24 and 25.

474 This had already occurred in the two nationality laws which succeeded the Palestinian Citizenship Order after 1948. Israel, in its nationality law of 1952 (*op. cit.*), vested the governmental decisions relating to nationality in the Minister of Interior, Minister of Defence, a district court and/or Minister of Justice. Jordan, in its nationality law of 1954 (*op. cit.*), vested such decisions in the King, Council of Ministers, the Government, Minister of Interior and/or the Prime Minister.

3. *Motives*

Three motivations were behind the enactment of the Palestinian Citizenship Order of 1925. Internationally, the Order was based on the 1922 Palestine Mandate and the 1923 Treaty of Lausanne. Domestically, it responded to certain practical needs relating to the status of the local inhabitants of Palestine. Substantively, the Order's provisions were taken principally from British law and adapted to suit the Palestinian context.

Reflecting the international status of Palestine, the Order directly executed Article 7 of the Mandate. According to this article, the 'nationality law' had two objectives: (1) to regularize the status of the inhabitants of Palestine; and (2) to facilitate the acquisition of Palestinian nationality by immigrant Jews who would reside therein. The former objective was realized by the ordinary rules of the Order, which were similar to legislation of other states, as will be explained later. To achieve the latter objective, the British government admitted that representatives of the Zionist movement were consulted in "the Draft Palestine Citizenship Order in Council";[475] thus naturalization of Jews was facilitated through the provisions of the Order.[476] At the same time, Britain found itself bound to regulate the inhabitants' nationality, pursuant to the international law of state succession, as laid down in Articles 30–36 of the Treaty of Lausanne.[477]

As the nationality legislation of a semi-independent country, the Order embodied provisions which responded to the practical needs of Palestine.[478] As in other states, it was imperative to regulate conditions governing the acquisition of nationality (through birth, naturalization and marriage), instances of its loss, as well as cases where dual nationality and statelessness arose from that regulation. The regulation of nationality became a necessity in order to afford the inhabitants of Palestine a specific legal system and to resolve a variety of legal matters inherently connected with the national status of any individual. These matters included, *inter alia*: defining those eligible to exercise civil and political rights in the country (e.g. for participation in legislative election and the holding of public office); determining the individuals who could obtain a Palestinian passport; extending diplomatic protection to citizens abroad; organizing the admission, rejection or expulsion of foreigners; and resolving conflict of laws regarding the personal status of Palestinians abroad and foreigners within Palestine.

Apart from the provisions which were directly taken from the Treaty of Lausanne, most of the 1925 Palestinian Citizenship Order's rules were derived from the British Nationality and Status of Aliens Act of 7 August 1914,[479] as amended

---

475 Report on the Administration of Palestine 1924, *op. cit.*, p. 42.

476 See below Chapter VI, Section 2.

477 See above Chapter III, Section 4.

478 "It [the Citizenship Order] contains certain features of more than local interest" (Bentwich, "Nationality in Mandated Territories", *op. cit.*, p. 102).

479 For the text of the Act, see *Supplement to The American Journal of International Law*, Vol. 9, 1915, p. 413. It should be noted that the British Nationality Act was introduced

in 1918 and 1922 (hereinafter referred to as the 'British Nationality Act, 1914').[480] Shortly after the enactment of the Palestinian Order, Britain declared:

> Principal provisions of that [British] law were reproduced in the Palestine law of nationality which was based on the English nationality law.[481]

Hence, the Palestinian Citizenship Order was interpreted and applied in light of the aforementioned British Act. Such interpretation and application of the English law in Palestine was commonplace in cases of legislative gap. In this connection, Article 46 of the 1922 Palestine Constitution, in part, reads:[482]

> The jurisdiction of the Civil Courts [of Palestine] shall be exercised... in conformity with the substance of the common law, and the doctrines of equity in force in England.[483]

The Citizenship Order introduced a number of new rules, which had not existed previously in Palestine. These rules constituted either a modification to certain provisions within the Ottoman Nationality Law of 1869 or entirely new provisions. The former included issues relating to naturalization, expatriation, repatriation and the nationality of married women and children. These issues shall be discussed in greater detail in the upcoming chapters. Additional new rules were lesser in number but significant in value. These included the age of majority and the change of calendar year. Article 21 of the Citizenship Order defined a child, for all nationality purposes, as follows:

> The age of majority shall be taken to be eighteen years calculated according to the Gregorian calendar.

---

shortly after the outbreak of World War I with a view to distinguishing between nationals, enemy nationals and neutrals. To this end, the Act intended to avoid, as much as possible, the occurrence of cases of dual nationality. See Richard W. Flournoy, "The New British Imperial Law of Nationality", *The American Journal of International Law*, Vol. 9, 1915, pp. 870–882, particularly pp. 877, 879; W.E. Wilkinson, "British Nationality", *International Law Notes*, Vol. 2, 1917, pp. 101–103. Prior to the 1914 Act, British nationality was based on the Common Law system applicable throughout the British Empire (United Kingdom, British domains, colonies and Protectorates). See, for example, W.H. Hastings Kelke, "Nationality and the Common Law", *The Law Magazine and Review & Quarterly Review of Jurisprudence and Quarterly Digest of All Reported Cases*, Vol. 8, 1882–1883, pp. 297–313; Edward Louis de Hart, "The English Law of Nationality and Naturalisation", *Journal of the Society of Comparative Legislation*, Vol. 2, 1900, pp. 11–26.

480 For the amended Acts, see Collection of Nationality Laws, p. 61.

481 Permanent Mandates Commission, *Minutes of the Ninth Session*, League of Nations, Geneva, 1926, p. 172. See also Goadby, *International and Inter-Religious Private Law in Palestine, op. cit.*, p. 23.

482 For cases relating to the application of English law in Palestine, in general, see *supra* note 365. For detailed review on the applicability of the Common Law at nearly the end of the mandate, see *Eliezer Zabrovsky v. The General Officer Commanding Palestine and Another*, England: Privy Council sitting as a Court of Appeal from the Supreme Court of Palestine, 4 December 1946 (Annotated Law Reports, 1947, Vol. I, p. 277).

483 Where relevant in this study, reference will be made to those provisions of the 1925 Palestinian Citizenship Order which were influenced by British law.

This definition of the child reformed the application of the relevant provisions in the 1869 Ottoman Nationality Law, wherein no definition of the child was given, thus leaving the question open to conflicting interpretations.[484] The definition is also consistent with the nationality articles of the Treaty of Lausanne. The reference to the 'Gregorian calendar', which was used almost everywhere in the world, apparently intended to remove the possibility of following the *Hijri*[485] calendar that had been employed under the Ottoman Empire for centuries.

484 See *supra* note 109.

485 The *Hijri* year, which is based on lunar cycles, is the Islamic calendar. It started in the moon year in which Prophet Mohammed immigrated from Makkah to Madinah, in Arabia, on 16 July 622. The *Hijri* year is shorter than the Gregorian year by about 11 days.

V

NATURAL PALESTINIAN CITIZENS

1. *From Ottoman subjects into Palestinian citizens*

> Turkish subjects habitually resident in the territory of Palestine upon the 1st day of August, 1925, shall become Palestinian citizens.

This is what Article 1, Clause (1), of the 1925 Palestinian Citizenship Order *declared* with regard to those persons who formed, according to domestic law, the first 'Palestinians'.[486] As already concluded in Chapter III above, the 'Palestinian people' had been defined according to international law on 6 August 1924, the date at which the Treaty of Lausanne was enforced. Hence, the just quoted clause was a mere declaration of pre-existing international law.

This clause refers to the automatic, or *ipso facto*, acquisition of Palestinian citizenship by those persons resident in Palestine who had replaced their former Turkish, or Ottoman, nationality. Although the term '*ipso facto*' is not literally employed, it should be easily understood as the clause is a direct application of Article 30 of the Treaty of Lausanne, 1923, which stated that "Turkish subjects habitually resident in territory which... is detached from Turkey will become *ipso facto*... nationals...".[487] Thus, Turkish individuals who were covered by this clause became Palestinians by the operation of law without further action.

To qualify for Palestinian nationality in accordance with the above-quoted clause, the person was required to be: (1) a Turkish subject, or citizen; and (2) habitually resident in Palestine. The legal meaning of 'Turkish' and 'habitually resident' cannot be defined in the abstract, especially as court rulings had already interpreted both terms, as reflected in the Treaty of Lausanne, in other areas outside Palestine.

---

486 At the end of the mandate, Palestinian nationality was well-defined. Therefore, the question of a natural change from Turkish to Palestinian nationality, through this Clause, had in fact already been settled.

487 On Article 30 of the Treaty of Lausanne, see above pp. 68–69.

Accordingly, the person was required to be first, and foremost, a Turkish citizen.

The status of a Turkish subject was drawn from the facts surrounding the birth or naturalization of such a person in accordance with the Ottoman Nationality Law of 1869.[488] To this effect, the Government of Palestine established procedures whereby specific evidence was required to prove Ottoman nationality. These procedures were set forth in a document entitled "Instructions to Immigration Officers",[489] under the heading of "Evidence of Ottoman Nationality", which was sent by the said Government to both its immigration officials and to British consulates abroad. According to these Instructions, evidence of Ottoman nationality included, *inter alia*, the possession of an Ottoman passport or birth certificate which indicated clearly that the person was born an Ottoman subject, or the possession of a naturalization certificate demonstrating that the individual had acquired Ottoman nationality.

The status of an Ottoman subject had to have been well-established. This status could, therefore, only be based on original Ottoman nationality which had been acquired by birth or through naturalization by the Ottoman Empire. It follows that, for example, those who acquired provisional Palestinian nationality in order to participate in the legislative election in 1922 would not be regarded as Palestinian citizens under Article 1, Clause (1), of the Citizenship Order (though they were considered under another article, as will be explained later).[490] Likewise, stateless persons who might have claimed Ottoman nationality under Article 9 of the 1869 Ottoman Nationality Law[491] were not considered as Palestinian citizens. To this effect, the Supreme Court of Palestine held:

> Art. 1 of the Palestinian Citizenship Order-in-Council, 1925, applies only to Turkish subjects, that is, to those who have acquired Ottoman nationality by birth or naturalisation and not to those who by Art. 9 of the Ottoman Naturalisation Law [sic] [i.e. the 1869 Nationality Law] are deemed to be Ottoman subjects and are to be treated as such until their foreign status has been regularly established.[492]

A foreigner, regardless of his or her length of residence in Palestine before 1925, had no right to acquire Palestinian nationality under Article 1, Clause (1), of the

488 See above Chapter II, Section 2.

489 Immigration and Travel Section, *Instructions to Immigration Officers and Deputy and Assistant Superintendents of Police*, Government of Palestine, January 1930 (hereinafter: 'Instructions to Immigration Officers'), p. 41, Appendix X. Marked as 'confidential', this document was communicated to the Permanent Mandates Commission of the League of Nations in 1932 (see "Letter from the Chief Secretary of the Government of Palestine, Jerusalem, to the Secretary-General of the League of Nations", Geneva, 29 February 1932; registered at the League under No. 35668, 9 March 1932—the letter is un-published). This document is a vital source of data relating to Palestinian nationality as it shows the practical or administrative aspects of this nationality. The document, therefore, will be frequently cited.

490 See below p. 126.

491 See above p. 30.

492 *Hausdorff v. Director of Immigration, op. cit.*

Order. In a case before a special Palestinian tribunal on 28 May 1946,[493] one of the parties, Ms. Elena Cattan, who had been residing in Palestine for 36 years, since 1910, was nevertheless considered as a foreigner (she was a Russian citizen). In its reasoning, the tribunal said: "There was no evidence we could accept adduced that she was a Turkish subject on the 1st day of August 1925". Ms. Cattan, the tribunal concluded, "does not become a Palestinian citizen under that article".

The second pre-requisite for one to be automatically considered as Palestinian citizen was a proof that the person was 'habitually resident' in Palestine.

The expression 'habitually resident' of Article 1, Clause 1, of the Citizenship Order, which is derived from Article 30 of the Treaty of Lausanne, was the translation of the term 'établis' in the French authoritative version of the Treaty. The term had been already interpreted by the Permanent Court of International Justice when Article 2 of the *Convention concerning the Exchange of Greek and Turkish Populations* (signed at Lausanne on 30 January 1923,[494] which formed, in turn, part of the Treaty peace of Lausanne of 24 July 1923 that applied to Palestine),[495] brought for an advisory opinion (*Exchange of Greek and Turkish Populations*)[496] on 21 February 1925. The term 'établis' of Article 2 of the Convention was translated into 'established' in the English text and, as such, can be extended to mean 'habitually resident' as it appeared in Article 30 of the Treaty.[497] The international Court concluded that the term 'établis' or 'established' "embraces two essential factors: residence and stability, i.e. an intention to continue the residence in particular place for an extended period".[498] It "refers to a situation of fact constituted... by residence of a lasting nature".[499]

A different interpretation of the expression 'habitual resident' was given by the Supreme Court of Palestine on 16 December 1927 in *Kattaneh v. Chief Immigration Officer*.[500] The Court gave a *de facto* meaning to the expression; a person was considered as 'habitual resident' in the place where he was actually, or physically, present on a particular date even if that presence was temporary.[501] As will be noted

493 *Elena Cattan, widow of Issa Ya'coub Cattan v. Saliba Ya'coub Cattan & 4 Others and Mania alias Mary, wife of Elias Ayoub v. Saliba Ya'coub Cattan & 4 Others* (two connected cases), Special Tribunal constituted under Article 55 of the Palestine Order in Council—*ad hoc* tribunal trying personal status matters involving foreigners (Annotated Law Reports, 1946, Vol. II, p. 747).

494 LN Treaty Series, Vol. 32, 1925, p. 76.

495 See Article 19 of the Convention.

496 Permanent Court of International Justice, Series B, No. 10 (1925).

497 See *ibid.*, pp. 17–23.

498 Permanent Court of International Justice, Series B, No. 10 (1925), p. 18.

499 *Ibid.*, p. 26.

500 Law Reports of Palestine, p. 215. The Supreme Court of Palestine was sitting as a High Court of Justice. The facts of this case are introduced later in this study within another context; see below pp. 98–99.

501 See also Stoyanovsky, *op. cit.*, pp. 265–268, who apparently agrees with this *de facto* meaning: "Turkish subjects who for one reason or another left Palestine before August 1, 1925... became stateless" (p. 269). In contradiction to this statement, however, Stoyanovsky (*ibid.*) alleged that "Turkish subject had actually to be resident in Palestine

shortly,[502] the Palestinian Court reached its decision based on its own interpretation of the Treaty of Lausanne and by referring to a precedent held by the British Privy Council. This interpretation chiefly affected those Palestine-born Ottomans residing abroad upon the enforcement of the 1925 Citizenship Order.

In practice, the Government established similar procedures to prove residence in Palestine to those which had been followed in order to prove Ottoman nationality. Sample evidence included, for instance, the ownership of a house in the country.[503]

1 August 1925 was fixed as the date for the automatic acquisition of Palestinian nationality by Article 1, Clause (1), of the Citizenship Order. This was the day on which the same Order came into force according to its Article 26. In this regard, it was noticed that the "insertion of a fixed date upon which Turkish nationals had to be 'habitually resident' in Palestine in order to be able to acquire or to claim Palestinian citizenship…constitute[d] an additional condition for the acquisition of that citizenship".[504] That is, fixing 1 August 1925 is unnecessary addition to the stipulation of Article 30 of the Treaty of Lausanne that mentioned no date and made it understandable that the commencement of the new nationality legislation is on the date of the Treaty's enforcement through ratification by the signatory states.

In other territories detached from Turkey, the date of nationality change was fixed as the day on which the Treaty came into force. Article 3 of the Iraq Nationality Law of 1924,[505] as well as Article 1 of the Trans-Jordan Nationality Law of 1928,[506] fixed 6 August 1924 (the day on which the Treaty of Lausanne was ratified by Britain), as the day the habitual Ottoman residents of Iraq and Trans-Jordan would acquire Iraqi and Trans-Jordanian nationalities, respectively. Likewise, Article 1 of the nationality legislation of Syria[507] and Lebanon,[508] both enacted in 1924 by the French High Commissioner, fixed 30 August 1924 (the day on which the same Treaty of Lausanne was ratified by France), as the day for the commencement of the Syrian and Lebanese nationalities.

---

on the above date, 'habitually' being added merely for the purpose of preventing the acquisition of such citizenship by those who only happened to be in Palestine on August 1, 1925, or might have come there with the sole intention of acquiring Palestinian citizenship". If one is of the opinion that residence means actual presence in a place at certain date, all residents in that place at the same date, in the absence of legislative exception, should be treated equally.

502 See below pp. 99–100.

503 See Instructions to Immigration Officers, *op. cit.*, p. 42, Appendix XI ('Evidence of Radiance in Palestine').

504 Stoyanovsky, *op. cit.*, pp. 268–269.

505 *Op. cit.*

506 This article is identical with Article 1, Clause (1), of the Palestinian Citizenship Order except that the effective date of the acquisition of Trans-Jordanian's nationality was 6 August 1924.

507 Ordinance Concerning Turkish Subjects Established in Syria, *op. cit.* The preamble of this Ordinance referred to Articles 30–36 of the Treaty of Lausanne.

508 Ordinance Concerning Turkish Subjects Established in Lebanon, *op. cit.* The preamble of this Ordinance referred to the same articles of the said Treaty.

However, it may well be said that Article 30 of the Treaty of Lausanne speaks of the acquisition of nationality based on "conditions laid down by the local law". This therefore allowed for the authorities in "the State to which such territory is transferred", to fix at its discretion the date on which nationality could be activated. In any case, it is a well-established fact that 1 August 1925 was the date of the automatic change from Ottoman to Palestinian nationality. The validity of this date had been repeatedly confirmed by Palestinian courts.[509] Yet the Citizenship Order oddly contemplated another date (6 August 1924), as the date on which those persons who were born in Palestine and then resided abroad, had acquired Palestinian nationality.[510]

On 23 July 1931, the Palestinian Citizenship Order of 1925 was amended.[511] Article 1(1) of this amendment considered those Ottoman subjects habitually resident in Palestine on 6 August 1924, and those residing abroad on 1 August 1925, as Palestinian citizens, providing that they had not acquired another nationality. This amendment covered only those who were resident in Palestine on 6 August 1924, not those persons who were residing abroad on this date; no reference was made to those Palestine-born residing abroad on 6 August 1924. The amendment therefore only altered the date of Article 1 of the Citizenship Order (i.e. 1 August 1925) regarding the automatic acquisition of nationality by a particular group of Palestine's inhabitants. It seems that the purpose of this amendment was to comply with Article 30 of the Treaty of Lausanne.

At this historical juncture of Palestinian nationality, it might be relevant to review some facts relating to the population of Palestine and their nationality. This will define those individuals who constituted 'Palestinians' and thereby enjoyed the first-ever Palestinian nationality at the domestic level as from 1 August 1925 in accordance with Article 1, Clause (1), of the Citizenship Order.

It should be noted, from the outset, that this study is concerned with the legal aspects of nationality and does not, as such, intend to provide statistical data. Available statistics will be nevertheless consulted in order to illustrate or support certain legal conclusions. The reference to Turkish subjects of Jewish religion, who then became Palestinian citizens, is of a particular significance since the main objective of the 1925 Citizenship Order was designed with a view of conferring Palestinian nationality on foreign Jews who immigrated to Palestine.[512]

It should be further noted that only the official figures relating to the population as provided by the Government of Palestine will be relied upon here. These figures were derived either by census, conducted in 1922 and again in 1931, or based

---

509 See, for example, *Nabiha Salim Zahwa v. 1. Attorney General, 2. Inspector General of Police and Prisons*, Supreme Court of Palestine sitting as a High Court of Justice, 27 March 1944 (Annotated Law Reports, 1944, Vol. I, p. 347); *Yohannanoff v. Commissioner for Migration and Statistics*, Palestine Supreme Court sitting as a High Court of Justice, 27 March 1947 (Annual Digest, 1947, p. 108).

510 See below p. 96.

511 See Palestinian Citizenship (Amendment) Order, 1931 (Laws of Palestine, p. 3414).

512 See above Chapter IV, Section 3.

on the rates of annual increases in population. Such statistics were also subject to international monitoring by the Permanent Mandates Commission of the League of Nations through the annual reports submitted by Britain on its administration of Palestine, under Article 24 of the Mandate. The publications of the Government's Department of Statistics in the years 1932–1946, which offer similar official figures, will be occasionally consulted as well. Data relating to immigration and to the population of Palestine was carefully compiled by the aforementioned Government in 1946, in a two-volume document entitled "A Survey of Palestine".[513] Other semi-formal sources (notably reports of the Jewish Agency on the immigration of Jews into, and their settlement in, Palestine), will be only cited for the purpose of comparison or clarification.[514]

Exactly one month prior to the enforcement of the Palestinian Citizenship Order in 1925, the British-run Government of Palestine estimated that the total population of the country was 847,238 individuals.[515] This figure incorporated Ottoman citizens and foreigners who had registered as immigrants, i.e. permanent residents. Unfortunately, there was no available data relating to the population's nationality.

In effect, the population of Palestine was officially classified along religious lines throughout the mandate period. In 1946, the said Government explained the reason behind this religious classification:

> The classification by religious communities, viz. Moslems, Jews, Christians and others, had been adhered to throughout the [mandate] period. It is a classification socially necessary by reason of the complete jurisdiction enjoyed by religious communities in matters of the personal status of their members. In the current life of Palestine, however, the further distinction between 'Arabs', 'Jews' and 'Others', which may be described as racial or national, has been found to be necessary.[516]

Most Muslim and Christian residents in Palestine were Arabic-speakers and commonly known as 'Arabs'. They overwhelmingly possessed Ottoman nationality. 'Jews', including some Arabic-speakers, were chiefly immigrants from various European countries who had resided in Palestine from the mid-nineteenth century.[517] A number of Jews, notably those who belonged to the Allied states, were Ottoman subjects upon whom naturalization was imposed by the Ottoman Government during World War I in Palestine and elsewhere in the Empire.[518]

In the absence of data on the inhabitants' nationality at the time of the enactment of the 1925 Palestinian Citizenship Order, one might reach fairly accurate figures on Ottoman subjects by deducting the available number of foreigners from the overall population. The total number of foreigners who registered as immigrants

---

513 *Op. cit.*, pp. 140–164 ('Population') and pp. 165–224 ('Immigration').

514 The aforementioned method and sources will be used not only in this chapter, but also wherever relevant in this study.

515 Survey of Palestine, Vol. I, p. 141.

516 *Ibid.*, p. 140.

517 *Ibid.*, p. 144.

518 See, for example, *Robinson v. Press and Others*, *op. cit.*; *Nahum Razkovsky v. Leonine Razkovsky and Others*, *op. cit.* See also above p. 67.

in Palestine from 1920 to 1925 was 79,368 persons, of all religions.[519] Another number of foreign residents should be also subtracted from the general total of Palestine's population mentioned above; that number is the 37,997 individuals who acquired provisional Palestinian naturalization certificates in September 1922 for the purpose of voting in the legislative election.[520] The remaining number of Palestine's inhabitants constituted Ottoman subjects.

The result of this calculation indicates the total number of Ottoman subjects, from all religions, residing in Palestine in 1925 as being:

847,238 – (79,368 + 37,997) = 729,873 persons.

These 729,873 persons formed the bulk of inhabitants in Palestine who acquired Palestinian nationality by the natural change from the previous Ottoman nationality according to Article 1, Clause (1), of the Palestinian Citizenship Order 1925.

As to the Arab and Jewish Ottomans of Palestine,[521] another calculation is required.

The number of 'Arabs' of the total population in mid-1925 was 717,006 inhabitants (641,494 Muslims and 75,512 Christians).[522] In addition, there were 8,507 persons classified as 'Others'.[523] These 'Others' were mainly Druzes, Bahais and Samiries who were overwhelmingly Arabic-speakers and residing in Palestine as Ottoman subjects.[524] Hence, 'Others' were in fact 'Arabs'. The number of immigrant Arabs who entered and registered in Palestine from 1920 to 1925 was 2,783 persons (mostly Christians).[525]

Thus, the net number of Arabs who were Ottomans, and then acquired Palestinian nationality by natural change, was as follows:

(717,006 + 8,507) – 2,783 = 722,730 'Palestinian Arabs'[526] (or nearly 99%).

On the other hand, the number of Jews within the total population of Palestine, during this period, stood at 121,725 persons.[527] Of these, there were 76,585 foreigners:

---

519 Survey of Palestine, Vol. I, p. 185. This figure is calculated based on the number of immigrants to Palestine from 1920 to 1925.

520 See above pp. 66–67.

521 The division of Palestinian citizens into 'Arabs' and 'Jews' generated significant legal consequences relating to nationality, particularly towards the end of the mandate. See below Chapter XI, Section 1.

522 See Survey of Palestine, Vol. I, p. 144.

523 *Ibid.*, p. 141.

524 The 'Others' class is separately mentioned here only because it was classified as such by the British officials who dominated the Government of Palestine and for the sake of coherence. It seems that there were no immigrants registered from 'Others' class at the period under consideration.

525 See Survey of Palestine, Vol. I, p. 185.

526 On the legal significance of the term 'Palestinian Arabs', see note 529 and below p. 196.

527 See Survey of Palestine, Vol. I, p. 144.

37,997 individuals who acquired provisional Palestinian naturalization certificates in 1922, as just mentioned, and 76,585 registered immigrants who entered Palestine from 1920 to 1925.[528]

Thus, the net number of Jews who were Ottomans and then became Palestinian citizens by natural change was as follows:

121,725 – (37,997 + 76,585) = 7,143 'Palestinian Jews'[529] (or about 1%).

Finally, the Palestinian Citizenship Order of 1925 imported other complementary provisions from the Treaty of Lausanne. Article 1, Clause (2), of the Order gave any person who automatically became a Palestinian citizen the right to opt for Turkish nationality. Similarly, Article 1, Clause (3), enabled any person who became a Palestinian but differed in race from the majority of the population of Palestine, the right to opt for the nationality of the state in which the majority of its population was of his race. The right of option in these two cases had to be exercised within two years as from 6 August 1924. In such cases, if the person opted for another nationality, he would have lost his Palestinian nationality and would have been obliged to transfer his place of residence to the state of his option.

These two optional cases were formulated, again in Article 1 of the Citizenship Order, as follows:

> (2) Any person over eighteen years of age who, by virtue of this Article, becomes a Palestinian citizen may, within a period of two years from the 6th day of August, 1924, by declaration made as hereinafter provided, state his option for Turkish nationality, and subject to the provisions of this Article shall cease to be a Palestinian citizen:
>
> Provided that such person shall not for the purposes of this Order be deemed to have ceased to be a Palestinian citizen unless and until he has obtained a certificate from such officer as may be prescribed by Regulation under this Order that he has transferred his place of residence from Palestine.
>
> (3) Any person over eighteen years of age who by virtue of Clause (1) of this Article becomes a Palestinian citizen and differs in race from the majority of the population of Palestine may, in the like manner and subject to the same conditions, opt for the nationality of one of the States in which the majority of the population is of the same race as the person exercising the right to opt subject to the consent of that State, and he shall thereupon cease to be a Palestinian citizen.

528 *Ibid.*, p. 185.

529 On the utilization of the term 'Palestinian Jews', see, for instance, *Pessia Nuchim Leibovna Schwalboim v. Hirsh (Zvi) Schwalboim*, Supreme Court of Palestine sitting as a Court of Appeal, 31 January 1940 (Supreme Court Judgements, 1940, Vol. I, p. 38); *Eliyahu Bichovsky v. Nitsa Lambi-Bichovsky*, Supreme Court of Palestine sitting as a Court of Appeal, 15 May 1940 (Supreme Court Judgements, 1940, Vol. I, p. 184). In these cases, the Court, though in particular juridical context related to personal status, used the expressions 'Palestinian Jew' and 'Palestinian Arabs'. The expression: "Jews of Palestinian nationality" was used, for example, by the Supreme Court of Palestine in *Arieh Leopold Zwillinger v. Blanka Schuster, op. cit.* See further below pp. 196–197.

These clauses were derived, with administrative adaptation, from Articles 31, 32 and 33 of the said Treaty.[530] Procedures to renounce Palestinian nationality in such cases were established by Regulation 5 of the 1925 Palestinian Citizenship Regulations and the third form attached thereof.[531] These provisions were short-lived and came to an end on 5 August 1926, after the lapse of two years from the day on which the Treaty was enforced (that time was, in effect, a little less than one year due to the late enactment of the Palestinian Citizenship Order).

In conclusion, the bulk of Ottoman citizens residing in Palestine on 1 August 1925 comprised the first generation of the 'Palestinian people' in accordance with local Palestinian law. These totalled, as demonstrated above, 729,873 Palestinian citizens. Internationally, the 'Palestinian people' legally emerged, as already illustrated,[532] upon the enforcement of the Treaty of Lausanne on 6 August 1924.

2. *Original inhabitants of Palestine residing abroad*

A. *The law*

Unlike Ottoman subjects residing in Palestine, the nationality of Palestine's natives residing abroad raised serious legal and humanitarian concerns. The debate in relation to the nationality of this group continued until the end of the mandate period. The formidable developments which occurred after the end of the mandate, particularly the problem of Palestinian refugees during and after the 1948 war, had overshadowed the significance of this issue despite its on-going legal relevance. The various important issues connected with the question of Palestine in international law and other disciplines prompted a number of writers to examine the nationality of this group in some detail. The present study, however, does not intend to explore all the aspects of this group's nationality, but will examine this issue as it stood prior to 15 May 1948, from a legal perspective.

The problem arose from the wording of Article 2 of the 1925 Palestinian Citizenship Order, which read as follows:

> Persons of over eighteen years of age who were born within Palestine and acquired on birth or subsequently and still possess Turkish nationality and on the 1st day of August 1925, are habitually resident abroad, may acquire Palestinian citizenship by opting in such manner as may be prescribed by Regulation under this Order, subject to the consent of the Government of Palestine which may be granted or withheld in its absolute discretion:
>
> Provided that without prejudice to the foregoing provisions the consent of the Government of Palestine may be refused unless an agreement on the subject has been concluded between the said Government and the Government of the country where the

---

530 See above Chapter III, Section 4.

531 Laws of Palestine, p. 2417.

532 See above pp. 73–74.

> person concerned is resident and shall be refused if the person desiring to opt possesses another nationality in addition to the Turkish nationality.
> This right of option must be exercised within two years of the coming into force of this Order.

According to this version of Article 2 of the 1925 Citizenship Order, the right of individuals of this group to opt for Palestinian nationality had to be exercised within two years, from the date on which the Order entered into force (i.e. between 1 August 1925 and 31 July 1927). This indeed is the logic the Order used in its Article 1, Clause (1), which fixed the 1st August 1925 as the starting date of Palestinian nationality for those Turkish subjects residing in Palestine. However, on 12 November 1925, the High Commissioner for Palestine decided by a Proclamation gazetted on 16 November 1925 that the right of option should start retroactively from 6 August 1924.[533] Thus, the time limit to opt for Palestinian nationality was terminated on 5 August 1926, one year after the enactment of the Order. The starting date to exercise the right of option was apparently designed to meet the requirements of Article 34 of the Treaty of Lausanne.

Substantively, however, in formulating Article 2 of the Citizenship Order, the drafters narrowly interpreted Article 34 of the Treaty of Lausanne. A critical case before the Supreme Court of Palestine, regrettably, confirmed this narrow interpretation. In its dealings with this group, the Government of Palestine strictly implemented Article 2 and, in so doing, denied thousands of persons born in Palestine the right to acquire Palestinian nationality solely because they happened to have been outside Palestine on the given date.

Article 34 of the Treaty of Lausanne gave "natives of a territory detached from Turkey" (including Palestine) the right to "opt for the nationality of the territory of which they are natives". Article 2 of the 1925 Order, which rather than being related to Article 34 of the Treaty, as it should had been, replaced the phrase '*native* of Palestine' as appeared in the Treaty, with '*born* within Palestine'. This limitation thereby deprived the descendants of those born in Palestine, whose birth had occurred in a foreign country, from the right to opt for Palestinian nationality, even if their parents were born as Ottoman subjects and such descendants themselves possessed Ottoman nationality.[534] This ran contrary to the *jus sanguinis* principle of the 1925 Order, whereby children follow the nationality of their father regardless of their place of birth.[535]

---

533 Issued in accordance with Article 24 of the Citizenship Order, which gave the High Commissioner for Palestine the power to amend the Order, this Proclamation provided: "The last sentence of Article 2 of the Palestinian Citizenship Order, 1925 shall be amended so as to read as follows:—'This right of option must be exercised within two years from the 6th day of August, 1924'" (Report on the Administration of Palestine 1925, *op. cit.*, p. 162).

534 Besides, the birth in Palestine might occur, at least theoretically, to Ottoman subjects who had no link to that country (e.g. Palestine-born children of travellers, business people or Turkish officials who were serving therein).

535 See bellow Chapter V, Section 3.

Furthermore, the interpretation of 'native' as meaning 'born' was less favourable than that of the authoritative French version of Article 34 of the Treaty of Lausanne, which speaks of persons or '*originaires*' of Palestine[536] (i.e. of Palestinian origin). This official meaning is broader than the mere fact of being born in Palestine. When deliberating upon draft Article 34, during the Lausanne Conference, the authors of the Treaty referred to "the juridical status of persons *belonging to* territories detached from Turkey... but residing outside these territories".[537] Thus, it was duly noted:

> Article 34 seems to be the counterpart of Article 30 [of the Treaty of Lausanne]; while the latter deals with the case of Turkish nationals habitually resident in territory detached from Turkey, the former is concerned with those who habitually reside abroad but belong to such territory, where they have previously acquired Turkish nationality by birth or otherwise. It is hard to see why the factor of birth should be brought in by the Citizenship Order in the case of Article 34 when it is certainly excluded from that of Article 30, which makes no distinction between Turkish nationals whether born within Turkey or without.[538]

Article 2 of the Citizenship Order abandoned the notion of the two-year period afforded by Article 34 of the Treaty of Lausanne to opt for nationality when the Treaty came into force on 6 August 1924. The right of option was practically given after the enforcement of the Order one year later on 1 August 1925. In effect, it was only possible to exercise the right of option when the amendment of the Order was gazetted on 16 November 1925. Hence, in effect, persons concerned had less than nine months, i.e. from the latter date until 5 August 1926 (two years after the enforcement of the Treaty) to opt for Palestinian nationality.

Article 4 of the Citizenship Order added more conditions which served to make the acquisition of Palestinian nationality by persons of this group, even more difficult:

> (1) Any person over eighteen years of age, who, within two years from the date at which this Order comes into force, by declaration made as hereinafter provided, states his desire to become a Palestinian citizen and satisfies the authority before whom the declaration is made that he fulfils the following conditions, namely:—
> (*a*) that the declarant was born within Palestine and acquired on birth or subsequently and still possesses Turkish nationality: and
> (*b*) that the declarant shall have been resident within Palestine for not less than six months immediately prior to the date of making such declaration: and
> (*c*) that the declarant has not, while resident in any country other than Palestine, acquired any foreign nationality:
> may, subject to the approval of the High Commissioner, acquire Palestinian citizenship, and the High Commissioner may grant to such a person a certificate of Palestinian citizenship.

536 *Cf.* Stoyanovsky, *op. cit.*, p. 273.
537 Lausanne Conference, *op. cit.*, p. 533. Emphasis added.
538 Stoyanovsky, *op. cit.*, pp. 273–274.

> (2) A person by whom a declaration has been made, and to whom a certificate of Palestine citizenship has been granted in accordance with the provisions of this Article shall be deemed to be a Palestinian citizen from the date of such certificate.

It is hard to see why if a person belongs to this group could not acquire Palestinian nationality except if he resides in Palestine for at least six months. This residence condition, described as an 'obvious paradox',[539] constituted unnecessary added-stipulation which did not exist in Article 34 of the Treaty of Lausanne.[540]

From the judicial stand-point, which in turn gave effect to legislative provisions, the problem of those residing abroad lay in the interpretation of the expression 'habitually resident abroad'. This expression had been interpreted by the Supreme Court of Palestine sitting as a High Court of Justice, on 16 December 1927, in *Kattaneh v. Chief Immigration Officer*.[541]

The petitioner in this case, Mr. Antoine Francis Kattaneh, who had been born in Palestine as an Ottoman subject was then residing in Lebanon. He had applied for a Palestinian passport, on the assumption that he was a Palestinian citizen, but his application refused by the Government of Palestine. The Government decision was upheld by the Supreme Court on 1 July 1927 at the jurisdiction phase, which is of little relevance here; the decision on the merits of the case (i.e. whether Mr. Kattaneh was eligible for Palestinian nationality), was postponed.[542] The relevant facts of this case, as set out in the judgment of 16 December 1927, are as follows:

> The Petitioner in this case was born in Jerusalem in 1865. He resided there until 1884, when he went for two years to the United States in the employment of Messrs. Thomas Cook & Son. He returned to Jerusalem in 1886 and resided there in the same employment until the year 1889. Between 1889 and 1896 he was similarly employed in Jerusalem save for short periods ranging from 6 months to 12 months, when he worked for this firm in London, Lucerne and Cairo. In 1896 he was sent by Messrs. Cook, as their Manager, to Beyrout, Syria, a post which he has held ever since, coming to Palestine for two or three months every year for his holidays.

In denying the right of Mr. Kattaneh to acquire Palestinian nationality, the Court stated:

> [I]f, in fact, a person who had lived abroad for many years, but nevertheless, as in the case of the Petitioner, retained the *animus revertendi* [i.e. intention to return] to Palestine was 'habitually resident' in the territory under Art. 1 of the [Citizenship] Order…, it appears to us that it would reduce Art. 2 of the Order…to mere surplusage. Under Art. 2 persons of Turkish Nationality over 18 years of age, who were born within Palestine

539 *Ibid.*, p. 274.

540 In addition of being an unnecessary stipulation, the actual placement of Article 4 within the Citizenship Order does not follow a logical form. If it was deemed to have been related to Article 2, which regulated the status of those residing abroad, it should have followed that Article. Instead, it came after Article 3, which related to the principles governing nationality (*jus sanguinis* and *jus soli*) as it will be seen shortly.

541 *Op. cit.*

542 *Kattaneh v. Controller of Permits* (Law Reports of Palestine, p. 152).

> and are habitually resident abroad, may acquire Palestinian citizenship with the consent of the Government of Palestine, but if the Petitioner's contention as to the meaning of Art. 1 is correct, persons conforming with all these conditions, so long as they have the *animus revertendi*, automatically become Palestinian citizens without requiring the consent of the Government. We have to interpret the Order...so as to give a sensible meaning to all parts of it, and the only way in which to interpret these two Articles when read together appears to us to be by attaching the meaning assigned to them by the Respondent [i.e. the Government's Chief Immigration Officer].

The British-run Palestinian Court thus concluded that if the person had been actually (or physically) present in a place, for any reason, he would be considered to have been 'habitually resident' in that place of residence for the purpose of the acquisition of Palestinian nationality.

Although the Court, in the early stages of this decision, had stated that it was "concerned only with the interpretation of the words 'habitually resident' in Art. 1 of the Palestinian Citizenship Order, 1925", the real consequence of this decision (as then extended to Article 34 of the Treaty of Lausanne and Article 2 of the Citizenship Order), affected the right of all Palestine's natives who were residing abroad to acquire Palestinian nationality.[543] This is because Mr. Kattaneh, who lost this case, was born in Palestine as an Ottoman but had been residing outside the country (in Lebanon) on 6 August 1924.

As mentioned earlier,[544] the Palestine Supreme Court based its judgement in *Kattaneh v. Chief Immigration Officer* upon its own interpretation of the Treaty of Lausanne and upon another judicial precedent held by the British Privy Council.

In its interpretation to the Treaty of Lausanne, the Court referred to the official French version of the term 'habitually resident' (i.e. '*établis*'). The Court interpreted 'habitually resident' of Article 30 of the Treaty (Article 1, Clause (1), of the 1925 Palestinian Citizenship Order) as 'ordinary resident' which was found also in Article 21 of the same Treaty. Both Articles 30 and 21 used the word '*établis*' in the French text, but used 'habitually resident' and 'ordinarily resident', respectively, in the translated-English text. The same meaning was also extended to Article 34 of the Treaty (Article 2 of the Order). It is not clear, however, why the Court ignored the self-evident meaning of the French term *établis*, i.e. 'established' (which embraces "residence and stability", as the Permanent International Court of Justice stated), and instead favoured the non-official English term, 'ordinarily resident', which adds nothing further in meaning to the term 'habitually resident'.

The British-run Palestinian Court also based the above meaning of the term 'habitual resident' on the case *Gout and Another v. Cimitian*,[545] ruled by the British Privy Council on 17 November 1921. In this case, the Privy Council decided

543 See above pp. 68–69.

544 See above pp. 89–90.

545 Reported at Frederick Pollock, ed., *The Law Reports of the Incorporated Council of Law Reporting* (House of Lords, Judicial Committee of the Privy Council and Peerage Cases), W. Speaight & Sons, London, Vol. I, 1922, p. 105.

that the plaintiff who was residing in Cyprus (having come to the island originally for health purpose), was "... 'ordinarily resident' and 'actually present' in Cyprus on November 5, 1914 [the date at which Cyprus was annexed by Britain, through Order in Council, and Ottoman subjects residing therein became British nationals], and has consequently made out his case that he is a British subject".[546]

However, it is surprising to view the British judges who were serving in the Palestinian Court ignoring the fact upon which the Privy Council had based its decision; namely that Mr. Cimitian's residence in Cyprus, unlike Mr. Kattaneh's temporary/employment residence in Beirut, was of a lasting nature. One may better understand the meaning of the required residence (i.e. residence of a lasting nature) from the following statement of the Privy Council before concluding that Mr. Cimitian was a British subject:

> The plaintiff was no doubt present in Cyprus on November 5, 1914, as required by the Order in Council; he had been there with his family for several months, and although he went there originally because he was ill, and wanted the change of air, *he had stayed on and brought his family to live with him after he had recovered*, and he continued to live there for nearly a year after the annexation, carrying on business there, *and took no steps... to retain his Ottoman nationality. Under these circumstances*... he is a British subject.[547]

Thus, the Palestine Supreme Court equated the term 'ordinarily resident' as used by the Privy Council in *Cimitian* case with the term 'ordinarily resident' as it had appeared in Article 21 of the Treaty of Lausanne. It then extended this interpretation to the term 'habitually resident' as it had appeared in Articles 30 and 34 of the Treaty (since the terms of Articles 21, 30 and 34 have similar French origin). And, finally, it extended this interpretation to Articles 1 and 2 of the Palestinian Citizenship Order.

These two reasons show that the Palestine Court's decision in *Kattaneh* case, after careful investigation, was groundless. This Court's interpretation of the expression 'ordinary resident' also contradicted, as explained earlier, the interpretation adopted by an advisory opinion of the Permanent Court of International Justice.[548]

Moreover, it was possible for the British-run Palestinian Court to simultaneously retain the significance of both Articles 1 and 2 of the Citizenship Order without losing the relevance of Article 2. That is to say that there could be two separate statuses for those born in Palestine and were residing abroad. The first group comprised those born in Palestine who held temporary residence abroad; this group would be subject to Article 1, similar to those who were physically present in Palestine, because their temporary residence abroad was not considered as 'habitual residence abroad' in any sense (such as tourists, visitors to relatives or friends, traders, students). The second group incorporated those who were born in Palestine and were resident abroad in residence of a lasting nature; this group could

546 *Ibid.*, p. 110.
547 *Ibid.* (emphasis added).
548 See above p. 89.

be indeed the subject of Article 2 because the permanent residence abroad might imply the lack of the resident's interest to retain Palestinian nationality, especially after giving them the two-year time for opting for that nationality.[549]

Indeed, available statistical data suggests that at least one-third of those Ottomans who emigrated from Syria, including Palestine, to the Americas in the period of 1860–1914 actually returned to their homeland.[550] And "most of them were determined to return... after accumulating some money".[551] Even "those who could not or did not wish to return to their original homes maintained ties with the Old World, since most had relatives that had remained behind".[552] It was understood that "in fact, a large proportion of them never acquired citizenship in the New World".[553] Likewise, it was generally known by those who lived in Palestine that most of Palestine's students who attended universities in Cairo or in Beirut (cities in which a number of Palestine's inhabitants used to pursue their higher studies at the time), ultimately returned to their home-towns.

As just noted, there were in fact two categories of Palestine-born persons residing abroad: (1) temporary residents abroad, who should fall under Article 1 of the Citizenship Order and had acquired *ipso facto* Palestinian nationality because they were habitually resident in Palestine; and (2) habitual residents abroad, who were supposed to fall under Article 2 of the Order and had the right therefore to opt for Palestinian nationality. Hence, both Articles 1 and 2 of the Citizenship Order could be (but that was not unfortunately the case, as it was seen) executed in parallel without contradiction. Individuals of the latter group, who opted not to apply for Palestinian nationality, were presumably not interested in attaining Palestinian citizenship and therefore understandably lost their Palestinian status.

However, again, it is not understandable why those who were not present in Palestine on 6 August 1924, because they were temporarily travelling abroad for reasons of business, study or tourism were deprived of Palestinian nationality and citizenship rights such as the right of return to their homes and families.

It should be further noted that the Supreme Court of Palestine sitting as a High Court of Justice gave a different meaning to the term 'residence' on 8 April 1941. In *Arnold Gronner v. Director, Department of Immigration*,[554] the Court held:

---

549 Writing in 1926, Bentwich ("Nationality in Mandated Territories", *op. cit.*, p. 99), is of the opinion that 'habitual residence' as cited in Article 34 of the Treaty of Lausanne (i.e. Article 2 of the Palestinian Citizenship Order) meant 'permanently resident'. He said: "Put concretely, the article enabled a Turkish subject who had been a native of Palestine, Syria, or Iraq, but was then permanently resident in the United States or some other foreign country, to acquire Palestinian, Syrian or Iraq nationality".

550 See Karpat, *op. cit.*, pp. 175–209. Karpat based his work on the Ottoman archives as well as on official population statistics in the United States, Brazil, Argentina and other Latin American countries.

551 *Ibid.*, pp. 178–179.

552 *Ibid.*, p. 185.

553 *Ibid.*, p. 193.

554 Supreme Court Judgements, 1941, Vol. I, p. 130.

> Temporary residence for purposes of travel, or health or business cannot be termed residence [for immigration and nationality purposes].

It is also relevant to refer to the situation of those Ottoman citizens who were natives of other territories detached from Turkey and were residing abroad. In general, such persons were given more legal guarantees to retain the nationality of their native country than those guarantees of Article 2 of the Palestinian Citizenship Order.

This was the case in the British-mandated territories of Iraq and Trans-Jordan. Article 7 of the Iraq Nationality Law[555] of 9 October 1924 gave any 'native' who was residing abroad, even if he/she had not been born in the country, the right to opt for Iraqi nationality. Almost two years were given to such individuals to declare their intention to acquire Iraqi nationality as of 6 August 1924, not just nine months as had been the case with Palestinian nationality. The most flexible legislation among Palestine's neighbouring countries in regard to the question of option was the Trans-Jordan Nationality Law of 1928, which gave any Ottoman born in Trans-Jordan before 6 August 1926 regardless of his place of residence and without a deadline the right to become a Trans-Jordanian citizen (Article 5).

Similarly, Article 5 of both nationality legislation in Syria[556] and Lebanon[557] gave the Syrian and Lebanese 'natives' who had Ottoman nationality and had been residing abroad, within two-year period, the right to opt for the nationality of their native territory. These natives were further given the choice to declare their desire to opt for Syrian or Lebanese nationalities before the diplomatic or consular agents of France in the state where such persons were habitually resident.

No residence condition applied in Iraq, Syria, Lebanon or Trans-Jordan with regard to exercising the right of option by natives residing abroad, whereas residence of at least six months was required by Article 4 of the Palestinian Citizenship Order.

Indeed, the strict rules of Article 2 of the 1925 Palestinian Citizenship Order did not exist in any other nationality legislation of Palestine's neighbouring countries, in spite of the fact that all such legislation were derived, including the question of option, from the same source—namely Article 34 of the Treaty of Lausanne.

Lastly, from the perspective of international law at the time of the enactment of the Palestinian Citizenship Order of 1925, the view was that the right of option was essentially an "international law in development".[558] Moreover, it was believed that such a right "cannot be implicitly presumed in the absence of treaty provisions".[559] In state practice relating to territorial succession, most of the multilateral peace treaties concluded in the early twentieth century had recognized the right of option for citizens residing abroad. In particular, almost all peace treaties which had ended

555 *Op. cit.*

556 *Op. cit.*

557 *Op. cit.*

558 Weis, *op. cit.*, p. 163 referring to the conclusion of a two-volume study of Josef L. Kunz, *Dei Voelkerrechtliche Option*, Breslau, 1925–1928, p. 90.

559 Weis, *op. cit.*, p. 163.

World War I, involved an article whereby all persons born in the territory affected by succession, who had not acquired the nationality of another state, became automatically citizens of the state of their birth, wherever their residence might be. Article 65 of the Treaty with Austria,[560] for instance, stated:

> All persons born in Austrian territory who are not born nationals of another State shall *ipso facto* become Austrian nationals.

A similarly identical article, *mutatis mutandis*, was to be found in an additional six treaties concluded in the similar contexts.[561]

In the present case, the option was provided by the Treaty of Lausanne, which was less favourable to persons born in Palestine and residing abroad than similar treaties. Article 2 of the British-enacted Palestinian Citizenship Order imposed more restrictions on the nationality of these persons. The British-run Palestinian judiciary added even stricter conditions than the Treaty and the Order.[562]

In the absence of an international judicial body to determine the definitive meaning of residence outside Palestine, the nationality of Palestine's natives residing abroad would continue to be a matter of interpretation. In this situation, the decision of the Supreme Court of Palestine in *Kattaneh v. Chief Immigration Officer* had closed the door in the face of those affected, with regard to their right to recourse to the Palestinian judiciary. As a result, the persons in question had become stateless: having on the one hand lost their Turkish nationality by virtue of Article 30 of the 1923 Treaty of Lausanne and, on the other, not being admitted to Palestinian nationality according to the 1925 Citizenship Order.[563]

B. *The practice*

Palestine's inhabitants travelled abroad as part of the overall Ottoman's travel and emigration outside the Ottoman Empire. As was and still is the case across

---

560 *Op. cit.*

561 Treaty with Bulgaria, Article 52; Treaty with Czechoslovakia, Article 6; Treaty with Hungary, Article 57; Treaty with Poland, Article 6; Treaty with Romania, Article 6; and Treaty with the Serb-Croat-Slovene State, Article 6. All these treaties are mentioned above pp. 69–70.

562 For details on the option of nationality in international law, see, e.g., Weis, *op. cit.*, pp. 159–164. In the British practice, see Piggott, *op. cit.*, pp. 87–89; Johns, *British Nationality Law and Practice, op. cit.*, pp. 43–51. It might be relevant, for the sake of illustration, to refer to the ILC Articles on Nationality and State Succession, *op. cit.*, with regard to those inhabitants residing outside the territory affected by change of sovereignty. Article 8 reads: "1. A successor State does not have the obligation to attribute its nationality to persons concerned if they have their habitual residence in another State and also have the nationality of that or any other State. 2. A successor State shall not attribute its nationality to persons concerned who have their habitual residence in another State against the will of the persons concerned unless they would otherwise become stateless".

563 For the same conclusion, see Stoyanovsky, *op. cit.*, p. 269.

the globe, people travelled as traders, students and for pleasure. In the nineteenth century and early twentieth century, the difficult economic conditions in the Ottoman Empire and the frequent wars motivated citizens to seek job opportunities in Europe and, more significantly, in the New World—namely, the Americas.

It is not possible to determine accurately the total number of Palestinian natives who were residing abroad on 6 August 1924, as precise statistics are lacking. In any case, the purpose of this legal study does not require such statistics. However, available data suggests that the total number of emigrants from the then Greater Syria, including Lebanon and Palestine, to both North and South America in the period of 1860–1914 amounted to about 600,000 persons.[564] A French consular report published in 1907 mentioned that emigrants from Palestine to the United States totalled 4,000 persons in ten years.[565] Half of these emigrants from Palestine brought their families over afterwards.[566] Yet most of Palestine's immigrants targeted Latin America, notably Argentina, Brazil, Chile, Honduras, Mexico and El Salvador.[567] In 1927, it was estimated that the number of Palestine's natives in Europe and the Americas constituted 25,000.[568] By 1936, it was reported that this figure had risen to 40,000.[569]

For most of Palestine's natives residing abroad, the nine-month period afforded to them to apply for Palestinian nationality under Article 2 of the Palestinian Citizenship Order of 1925, was inadequate.[570] For example, representatives of these natives residing in Mexico complained, through a letter sent to the British Secretary of Foreign Affairs dated 9 September 1929, that:

> [The 1925 Citizenship Order] did not become known to Palestinians resident abroad because the Palestinian Government would not authorize advertisements in foreign countries to bring the instructions to their notice.[571]

---

564 Karpat, *op. cit.*, p. 185.

565 *Ibid.*, p. 180.

566 *Ibid.*

567 For details, see Adnan A. Musallam, *Folded Pages from Local Palestinian History in the 20th Century*, WIAM/Palestinian Resolution Centre, Bethlehem, 2002 (Arabic), pp. 37–56.

568 Committee of the Defenders of the Rights of Palestine Arab Emigrants in Palestinian Naturalization, *Memorandum submitted to the High Commissioner for Palestine* (League of Nations Document No. 60395, 29 July 1927—un-published, available in the League's archives, located at the United Nations Office, in Geneva), paragraph 5.

569 Palestine Royal Commission, *Report presented by the Secretary of State for the Colonies by Command of His Britannic Majesty*, His Majesty Stationary Office, London, July 1937, *Summary of Report*, p. 21. This Commission was known, following the name of its Chairman, Mr. Earl Peel, as 'Peel Commission'. Based on Peel's Report, Britain decided to divide Palestine into two states: an Arab state and a Jewish state. See bellow Chapter XI.

570 *Ibid.*, p. 329.

571 "Letter from Centro Social Palestino in Mexico to the British Minister of Foreign Affairs", with a cover letter to the League of Nations, 9 September 1929 (un-published—a copy is available in the League archives in Geneva), p. 2.

Even when all conditions to acquire nationality were fulfilled, the Government of Palestine "in its absolute discretion", as Article 2 of the Citizenship Order put it, could choose ultimately whether to grant or withhold Palestinian nationality. In practice, the Government had refused most of the applications: out of nine thousand applications submitted from 1925 until 1936, "not more than 100 were accepted".[572]

Similarly, the British consulates outside Palestine had rejected applications for Palestinian nationality. In this connection, it was reported:

> The British Consuls in Europe and America have asked... Palestinian emigrants to make application for the maintenance of their Palestinian nationality. Applications were duly submitted, and the Palestinian residents abroad in the belief of having complied with the law, awaited the issue of the proper nationality certificates. They were greatly surprised to learn from their Consuls that the Palestine Government had refused its approval, on the plea that the applicants did not reside in Palestine the required [i.e. six-month] period.[573]

These individuals, like any stateless persons, had endured difficult conditions in their countries of residence. They were unable to travel in the absence of Palestinian passports. No diplomatic protection, which was essential in the revolutionary countries of Latin America, in particular, was afforded to them. Many were subjected to deportation from those countries which refused admission to stateless persons at that time, such as Chile and Mexico.[574] In certain countries, such as Panama, previous Turkish citizens, as well as other foreigners, were explicitly deprived from seeking naturalization.[575] In July 1927, the authorities in El Salvador requested foreigners to present documents to prove their nationality as one of the conditions to conduct business, which jeopardized the livelihoods of Palestine's natives residing in that revolutionarily country.[576]

Palestine's natives were also excluded from obtaining visas even to visit their relatives, or to look after their property, in Palestine. Those who applied for visas "received advice of rejection of their application... thus making it physically impossible for them... [to] travel to Palestine".[577] In justifying its refusal to grant Palestinian nationality, the British Government asserted that the intention of such natives was solely to receive diplomatic protection from the British authorities,

---

572 Palestine Royal Commission, *op. cit.*, p. 331.

573 See Committee of the Defenders of the Rights of Palestine Arab Emigrants in Palestinian Naturalization, *op. cit.*, paragraph 1.

574 *Ibid.*, paragraph 7.

575 "Chinese, Turks, Syrians [including Palestine's natives at the time] and North-Africans of Turkish nationality are excluded [from naturalization]"; Panama Law of 22 August 1916 (Collection of Nationality Laws, p. 459), Article 167. This article was confirmed by the Law of 9 November 1926 (*ibid.*, p. 468), Article 1: "Chinese, Turks, Syrians, Japanese, Indo-Orientals, Indo-Aryans, Dravidians, and any other aliens whose immigration is prohibited are not included [in the naturalization provisions]".

576 Musallam, *op. cit.*, p. 49.

577 Letter from Centro Social Palestino in Mexico to the British Minister of Foreign Affairs, *op. cit.*, p. 3.

not to return home.[578] Ironically, however, special facilities were granted to foreign Jewish students abroad to obtain Palestinian nationality without requesting such students to be present in Palestine.[579]

On several occasions, both those persons who were not permitted to return, as well as their families in Palestine, protested to the Palestine and British Governments.[580] When their efforts failed, they petitioned the Permanent Mandates Commission of the League of Nations. In 1927, for instance, eleven Arab natives of Palestine then residing in Honduras, El Salvador and Mexico complained (on 23 April, 10 June, and 19 September, respectively) that they had applied, through the British consular authorities in these countries, for Palestinian nationality and their applications were refused. The following passage, extracted from a report prepared by the League's Permanent Mandates Commission, illustrates the situation at hand:

> The applicants maintained that they were all born in Palestine and that they had not during their absence changed their nationality. Those residents in Honduras added that they still owned land in Palestine, and that, although their engagement in commerce had hitherto prevented their return to Palestine, they expected to return home at some future date. The residents of El Salvador complained that they have been refused passports to visit or return to Palestine. The petitioners of Mexico, represented by the Palestinian Association in Mexico which had membership of more than 3000 Palestinians, asked to be informed by what it meant that native born Palestinians could acquire citizenship in their native land. All the petitioners protested against the decision of the Government of Palestine that rejected their applications for Palestinian citizenship. The claimants argued that under Article 34 of the Treaty of Lausanne, the right of natives of any of the territories detached from Turkey habitually resident abroad to acquire the nationality of that territory was made subject to the consent of the Government exercising authority therein. The British Government maintained that it would entertain options for Palestinian citizenship only for those who maintained a substantial connection with Palestine. This principle was embodied in a rule according to which Turkish nationals, natives of Palestine but resident abroad, could acquire Palestinian citizenship only if they had emigrated from Palestine during or after the year 1920, or if, having emigrated before 1920, they had since returned to Palestine and resided there for not less than six months. This latter condition is explained by the undesirability of creating a class of persons permanently resident abroad who are entitled to British protection.[581]

---

578 Permanent Mandates Commission, "Petition from M.M. Sikaffy and other Arabs living in Honduras and from the 'Sociedad Frateznidad Palestina' of San Salvador: Observations from the British Government", League of Nations Document No. C.P.M. 656, Geneva, 28 October 1927 (document marked 'confidential'—un-published, available at the League archives).

579 Report on the Administration of Palestine 1932, *op. cit.*, p. 43. See below pp. 126–127.

580 See, for example, Committee of the Defenders of the Rights of Palestine Arab Emigrants in Palestinian Naturalization, *op. cit.* (letter sent to the Government of Palestine); Letter from Centro Social Palestino in Mexico to the British Minister of Foreign Affairs, *op. cit.* (sent to the British Government and copied to the Permanent Mandates Commission of the League of Nations).

581 "Petitions from Certain Turkish Subjects of Palestinian Origin, now living some in Honduras, others in Salvador and others in Mexico, dated April 23rd, June 10th, and September 19th, 1927" (Permanent Mandates Commission, *Minutes of the Twelfth Session*, League of Nations, Geneva, 1927, pp. 128–129, 194–195).

The Mandates Commission expressed hope, based on the principle of equity, that the British Government would show a 'liberal spirit' in dealing with these persons. The Commission, however, did not take any practical measures or make further recommendations.[582]

A small number of persons born in Palestine and residing abroad had acquired Palestinian nationality by other means, such as naturalization. For example, out of 4,713 persons naturalized in 1928, only 78 were persons who had been born in Palestine and then resided abroad; the rest were foreign Jews.[583] In 1937, exactly 64 individuals from this category were able to acquire Palestinian nationality, while 21,542 Jews from Poland, Germany and Russia, were naturalized.[584] And in the following year, just 92 persons acquired nationality by this method, whereas 17,988 immigrant Jews were became Palestinian citizens during that year.[585]

A recommendation on how to resolve the nationality problem of these persons was presented to the British Government by the Royal Commission in 1936, which had visited Palestine to investigate the causes of the disturbances of that year and to propose a solution.[586] Among other recommendations, the Commission suggested:

> At least those who are able to establish an unbroken personal connection with Palestine and who are prepared to give a definite formal assurance of their intention to return, should be admitted to Palestinian citizenship.[587]

In 1938, Britain informed the League of Nations that consideration had been given to the recommendation of the Palestine Royal Commission to grant Palestinian nationality to those natives of Palestine then residing abroad.[588]

Accordingly, on 31 August 1939, an amendment to the Palestinian Citizenship Order of 1925 was introduced to allow these persons to return to Palestine and to obtain Palestinian nationality within two years.[589] On 2 November 1939, special regulations were enacted to that effect.[590] The Government of Palestine then advised the inhabitants, by public notice gazetted on 21 November 1939, to inform their relatives and friends abroad to apply for Palestinian nationality through this newly-opened channel.[591]

---

582 *Ibid.*

583 British Government, *Report to the Council of the League of Nations on the Administration of Palestine and Trans-Jordan*, 1928, pp. 93–94.

584 British Government, *Report to the Council of the League of Nations on the Administration of Palestine and Trans-Jordan*, 1937, p. 84.

585 Report on the Administration of Palestine 1938, *op. cit.*, p. 89.

586 Report of Palestine Royal Commission, *op. cit.*, p. 331. See also Report on the Administration of Palestine 1937, *op. cit.*, p. 85.

587 Palestine Royal Commission, *op. cit., Summary of Report*, p. 21.

588 See Report on the Administration of Palestine 1938, *op. cit.*, p. 90.

589 Palestinian Citizenship (Amendment) Order of 1939, Article 1.

590 Palestinian Citizenship Regulations of 1939.

591 See *Notice relating to Palestinian Citizenship Order*, 1939 (Palestine Gazette, No. 960, Supplement 2, p. 1451).

On 11 June 1942, another amendment to the Palestinian Citizenship Order (gazetted on 16 July) was passed, extending the time limit to apply for nationality from two to six years.[592] This Order gave those natives of Palestine residing abroad the right to apply for Palestinian nationality, providing they could establish an unbroken personal connection with the country.

This granting of nationality at this time coincided with a shift in British policy towards Palestine. The policy change was evident in the position taken by the Palestine Royal Commission, for example, and the subsequent policy statement released on 1 May 1939 (commonly known as the 'White Paper'),[593] which attempted to strike a balance between Arab and Jewish demands, including the question of emigration and immigration.

In practice, alas, it proved that only a very limited number of persons were able to opt for Palestinian nationality. In 1946, it was reported that only 465 persons who had been born in Palestine and were residing abroad succeeded in acquiring Palestinian nationality since 1925, while the cases of 87 others remained under consideration.[594] This situation as stood in and after 1939 can be explained by two factors. Firstly, the language of Article 1 of the 1939 amendment gave the Government of Palestine absolute discretion to accept or refuse the application of these persons and that Government insisted that applicants prove an un-broken connection with Palestine, which was apparently a difficult task to be performed from abroad. Secondly, the period during World War II,[595] and the years immediately following (1939–1948), led to the imposition of severe restrictions on entry and immigration into Palestine.[596]

---

592 See Palestinian Citizenship Order (Amendment) of 1942, Article 1.

593 See *Statement of Policy Presented by the Secretary of State for the Colonies to Parliament by Command of His Majesty*, 1 May 1939, His Majesty's Stationery Office, London, 1939. It is to be noted that this White Paper is different from the White Paper of 1922; see above p. 57.

594 Survey of Palestine, Vol. I, p. 206.

595 See on the conditions in Palestine during World War II, for example, Esco Foundation for Palestine, *op. cit.*, Vol. II, pp. 956–1076.

596 See, e.g., Defence (Entry Prohibition) (Amendment) Regulations, 1940 (Palestine Gazette, No. 1062, Supplement 2, 9 October 1940, p. 2017); Defence (Entry Prohibition) Regulations, 1940 (Palestine Gazette, No. 1052, Supplement 2, 18 October 1940, p. 1709). During the war, the state of emergency was declared in Palestine and the Palestinian borders were closed. Entering or leaving the country required special permit and arrangements. Most of those entered were illegal Jewish immigrants form Europe. See below pp. 127, 168–172.

In consequence, nationality of this group and their descendants remained unresolved until now.[597] It can be said, in short, that this group of Palestine's natives constituted the first wave of Palestinian refugees.[598]

3. *Natural-born Palestinians*

In international law, nationality at birth is accorded based on two principles: *jus sanguinis* and *jus soli*.[599] According to *jus sanguinis*, as a general rule, the person follows his or her father's nationality at the time of birth. By *jus soli*, nationality is granted to persons born within the state territory regardless of the father's nationality. The Palestinian Citizenship Order of 1925 adopted the two principles.

A person born to a Palestinian father acquires the father's nationality, wherever the birth may occur, either within or outside of Palestine. To this effect, Article 3 of the Citizenship Order considered the following persons as Palestinian citizens:

(*a*) Any person born in lawful matrimony within Palestine whose father at the time of such a person's birth was a Palestinian citizen.
(*b*) Any person born in lawful matrimony out of Palestine whose father was a Palestinian citizen at the time of that person's birth, and was either born within Palestine or had obtained a certificate of naturalisation, or who had acquired Palestinian citizenship under Article 1 or Article 5 of this Order.

These provisions are a clear manifestation of the *jus sanguinis* principle. In this respect, the Citizenship Order was similar to the Ottoman Nationality Law of 1869.[600] It was also in line with Article 1, paragraph (1,b), of the 1914 British Nationality Act, although the Act was based chiefly on *jus soli*.

---

597 The nationality of these persons is beyond the scope of this study. Their current status today and the possibility to include them within the scope of Palestinian refugees deserve a separate legal study.

598 The second wave of Palestinian refugees was created during 1947–1949 and afterwards until the June 1967 war; the third wave came in and after the latter war.

599 For further details, see, *inter alia*, George D. Collins, "Citizenship by Birth", *American Law Review*, Vol. 29, 1895, pp. 385–394; Henry C. Ide, "Citizenship by Birth—Another View", *American Law Review*, Vol. 30, 1896, pp. 241–252 (appraisal to the previous article); Richard Kleen, "De l'application du jus soli en matière de nationalité", *Revue générale de droit international public*, Vol. III, 1896, pp. 429–434; D.O. McGovney, "French Nationality Laws Imposing Nationality at Birth", *The American Journal of International Law*, Vol. 5, 1911, pp. 325–354; Richard W. Flournoy, Jr., "International Problems in Respect to Nationality by Birth", *Proceedings of the American Society of International Law*, Vol. 20, 1926, pp. 59–66; James Brown Scott, "Nationality: *Jus Soli* or *Jus Sanguinis*", *The American Journal of International Law*, Vol. 24, 1930, pp. 58–64; Durward V. Sandifer, "A Comparative Study of Laws Relating to Nationality at Birth and to Loss of Nationality", *The American Journal of International Law*, Vol. 29, 1935, pp. 249–261; Oppenheim, *op. cit.*, pp. 517–519; Weis, *op. cit.*, pp. 97–98; Brownlie, "The Relations of Nationality…", *op. cit.*, pp. 302–306.

600 Ghali, *op. cit.*, p. 62. See also p. 29.

Obviously, the following phrase of Article 3, Clause (b)—just quoted—of the Citizenship Order is redundant: "either [the father] born within Palestine or had obtained a certificate of naturalisation, or who had acquired Palestinian citizenship under Article 1 or Article 5 of this Order". The first part of the same clause logically includes all the cases referred to in this phrase; simply, when the father is a Palestinian, his children would be Palestinians too. It seems that the phrase intended to clarify that children of a Palestinian father would be Palestinians, regardless of the way by which the father had become Palestinian citizen.[601]

It is not clear, however, why the said phrase excluded those born to a father who had become Palestinian citizen under Article 2 of the 1925 Citizenship Order.[602] This indicates that the Order's drafters had not seriously contemplated the possibility of facilitating the acquisition of Palestinian nationality by Palestine-natives whose residence was abroad. It appears to be the case that children of such persons were presumed to be naturalized Palestinians and, therefore, included under the same phrase implicitly.

The 1925 Citizenship Order partially recognized the *jus soli* principle. In defining Palestinian citizens by birth, Article 3, Clause (c), of the Order provided:

> Any person born whether in or out of lawful matrimony within Palestine who does not by his birth or by subsequent legitimation acquire the nationality of any other State or whose nationality is unknown.

This clause regarded as Palestinians those children born to: (1) a stateless father; (2) an unknown father; or (3) unknown parents, i.e. a foundling child. It follows that the Order did not confer Palestinian nationality by the mere fact of birth in Palestine. Thus, the Order adopted the *jus soli* principle in the "exceptional case[s] of persons who otherwise would have been stateless".[603] This exceptional adoption of the principle was similar to the position of the 1869 Ottoman Nationality Law.[604]

A child born to a foreign father was considered to be a foreigner even if his mother was a Palestinian citizen because, as Article 6 of the Citizenship Order put it exclusively, "minor children shall follow the nationality of their father". It might be relevant here to note, however, that Article 36 of the Treaty of Lausanne stated that the status of children would be governed by "that of their *parents*";[605] it did not say that children's status would follow that of their 'father' only. But the status of a married woman, according to the same article, was governed by "that of her

601 The quoted phrase refers to four means by which the father might have acquired Palestinian nationality: (1) by being a naturally-born citizen; (2) by having held Ottoman nationality and made the automatic change; (3) through naturalization; or (4) through a declaration made under Article 5 of the 1925 Citizenship Order which concerned those who had become Palestinians with the purpose of voting for the 1922 legislative election.

602 On Article 2 of the Palestinian Citizenship Order of 1925, see above Chapter V, Section 2.

603 Stoyanovsky, *op. cit.*, p. 275.

604 See above pp. 29–30.

605 Emphasis added.

husband" (i.e. both women and children are dependant on the husband/father in so far as their nationality was concerned). In this respect, the Palestinian Citizenship Order made clearer reference to the woman/mother, albeit less favourably, than that of the Treaty. In *Yohannanoff v. Commissioner for Migration and Statistics*,[606] despite the fact that the petitioner had been born in Jerusalem to a Palestinian mother, the Supreme Court of Palestine held that "a minor can have no other nationality than that of its father" (who was, in this instance, a Russian citizen).

By establishing itself upon *jus sanguinis*, the 1925 Palestinian Citizenship Order departed from the basic principle of the British law, which grants nationality to any person born on British soil. Article 1(1) of the 1914 British Nationality Act deemed "any person born within His Majesty's dominions and allegiances" as a natural-born British subject. More generally, the Order differed from the English Common Law system, which is based mainly upon *jus soli*.[607] It is obvious, then, that conflict was likely to arise between the Palestinian law and the nationality laws of *jus soli* countries. Put concretely, a child born to a Palestinian father in New York, for example, where *jus soli* applied, would be considered a Palestinian citizen based on the Citizenship Order while, at the same time, the child would be deemed an American national according to the United States law.

The position of the Palestinian Citizenship Order, which had adopted the two internationally recognized principles of nationality, was similar to the situation in many countries of the world. In a research conducted in 1929 by the Harvard Law School, it was concluded:

> From an examination of the nationality laws of the various States it appears that seventeen are based solely on *jus sanguinis*, two equally upon *jus sanguinis* and *jus soli*, twenty-five principally upon *jus sanguinis* but partly upon *jus soli*, and twenty-six principally upon *jus soli* and partly upon *jus sanguinis*. The nationality law of no country is based solely upon *jus soli*. A combination of the two systems is found in the laws of most countries.[608]

606 *Op. cit.*
607 See, e.g., Piggott, *op. cit.*, pp. 41–56; Davies, *op. cit.*, pp. 253–260; Jones, *British Nationality Law and Practice*, *op. cit.*, pp. 123–157.
608 Harvard Research on Nationality (1929), *op. cit.*, p. 29.

VI

NATURALIZATION

1. *Technical aspects*

Naturalization in Palestine, as prescribed in the Palestinian Citizenship Order of 1925, was formulated in a way similar to the nationality laws of other states.[609] The naturalization provisions of the Order followed, to a large extent, the British Nationality Act, 1914 (which, in turn, was taken chiefly from the British Naturalization Act, 1870).[610] In Part III, Articles 7 to 11, of the Citizenship Order regulated the technical, or legal, aspects of naturalization in some detail. It stipulated the requirements for naturalization, its procedures, the rights and obligations of naturalized person, the status of minor children of such person and the effects of naturalization. On the other hand, naturalization by marriage was addressed, *inter alia*, in Part IV, Articles 12 to 13, of the Citizenship Order.[611]

609 On the naturalization, in general, see Alexander Porter Morse, "Citizenship by Naturalization", *American Law Register*, Vol. 18, 1879, pp. 665–675; Edwin M. Borchard, *The Protection of Citizens Abroad or the Law of International Claims*, the Banks Law Publishing, New York, 1919, pp. 528–592; H.J. Randall, "Nationality and Naturalization: A Study in the Relativity of Law", *The Law Quarterly Review*, Vol. 40, 1924, pp. 18–30; Green H. Hackworth, "Naturalization and Loss of Nationality", *Proceedings of the American Society of International Law*, Vol. 19, 1925, pp. 59–68; Henry B. Hazard, "International Problems in Respect to Nationality by Naturalization and of Married Women", *Proceedings of the American Society of International Law*, Vol. 20, 1926, pp. 67–88; Oppenheim, *op. cit.*, pp. 524–525; Weis, *op. cit.*, pp. 98–119; Brownlie, "The Relations of Nationality…", *op. cit.*, pp. 309–310; Donner, *op. cit.*, pp. 31–36, 53–55.

610 In particular, Article 2 of the British Nationality Act, 1914. See, e.g., Davies, *op. cit.*, pp. 274–295. For background on naturalization in Britain, see Piggott, *op. cit.*, pp. 98–129; Jones, *British Nationality Law and Practice*, *op. cit.*, pp. 85–107. A copy of the 1870 Naturalization Act was reproduced in *ibid.*, p. 303.

611 It is to be noted that naturalization, in its broader sense, was subject to another two articles of the Palestinian Citizenship Order: Article 2 (naturalization of persons who were born in Palestine but were residing abroad—see above Chapter V, Section 2); and

Naturalization in Palestine, like in any other nationality, had significant effects on the status of naturalized individuals. Upon receiving a naturalization certificate,[612] a foreigner became an ordinary Palestinian citizen, similar to the native/original citizens (Citizenship Order 1925, Article 8).[613] This was consistent with the definition of a 'Palestinian citizen' as provided in Article 21(2) of the 1925 Order: "a person who is by birth or becomes by naturalization or otherwise a Palestinian citizen". Thus, a naturalized person was entitled to all the political, civil and other rights, powers and privileges to which a native Palestinian citizen was entitled. Similarly, a naturalized person became subject to all those obligations, duties and liabilities that applied to Palestinians.[614]

The principle of equality between original and naturalized Palestinians had been reaffirmed by the Supreme Court of Palestine in *Sara Mandelberg Rogalsky v. Director of Medical Services*.[615] In this case, the Court held, *inter alia*, that "the whole object of Article 8 of the Palestinian Citizenship Order was to ensure that there should be the same law for all Palestinian citizens no matter in what way this nationality was acquired". It further stated that "Section 4 of the Medical Practitioners Ordinance [of 1928, as amended in 1935],[616] inasmuch as it discriminates between the rights of a Palestinian citizen by birth and other Palestinians, including Palestinians by naturalization is *ultra vires* Section [or Article] 8 of the said Order". Yet, for certain purposes, rights of naturalized persons differed from those of natives. Article 10 of the Citizenship Order, for instance, allowed the Government of Palestine to revoke the nationality of naturalized, but not native, Palestinian citizens.[617]

The Palestinian Citizenship Order stipulated the requirements for naturalization in general terms that would apply to any person without distinction based on religion, race or national origin. To this effect, Article 7, Clause (1), of the Order reads:

> The High Commissioner may grant a certificate of naturalisation as a Palestinian citizen to any person who makes application therefor [sic] and who satisfies him:—
> (*a*) That he has resided in Palestine for a period not less than two years out of the three years immediately preceding the date of his application:

Article 5 (naturalization of those who registered for the 1922 legislative election—see above pp. 64, 66–67, 126).

612 On various types of naturalization certificates, see the Palestinian Citizenship Regulations of 1925, Articles 10–12 and Annex 1, Forms 5, 6, 9, 10 and 11 thereof. See also the Palestinian Citizenship (Amendment) Regulations 1947, Form 9 (amended naturalization certificate).

613 Article 8 is similar to Article 3(1) of the British Nationality Act, 1914.

614 See, in general, Thomas R. Marshall, "The Privileges, Duties and Obligations of Citizenship", *Boston University Law Review*, Vol. 4, 1924, pp. 221–234; John O. Hendry, "Duties and Obligations of Citizenship", *Royal Law Journal*, Vol. 6, 1924–1925, pp. 24–31.

615 *Op. cit.*

616 *Op. cit.*

617 See below Chapter VII, Section 3.

(*b*) That he is of good character and has an adequate knowledge of either the English, the Arabic or the Hebrew language:
(*c*) That he intends, if his application is granted, to reside in Palestine.

Accordingly, in order to qualify for Palestinian nationality by naturalization, the applicant was expected to fulfil four conditions (item (*b*) quoted above includes two conditions: good character and language literacy). Each of these four conditions will now be examined in some detail.

The required two-year residence for the purpose of naturalization must, firstly, be "interpreted as meaning lawfully resided in Palestine". This was concluded by the Supreme Court of Palestine sitting as a High Court of Justice in *Fernand Nandor Weiss v. Assistant Commissioner for Migration, Haifa and others*, on 30 June 1944.[618] In this case, the petitioner applied for naturalization based on the fact that he had resided in Palestine for more than three years,[619] as required by Article 7(1)(a) of the Citizenship Order. His application was rejected as his residence in Palestine had proven to have been illegal—he had entered the country as a traveller and overstayed without obtaining official permission. Illegal residence marred the reputation of the person and negated his or her chances of naturalization. Thus, it was held in 1942 that as a woman "was in Palestine illegally before her marriage, she therefore did not become a Palestinian citizen on marriage to a Palestinian".[620]

Residence in Palestine was expected to be permanent. A particular meaning of 'residence' for the purpose of naturalization was adopted by the Supreme Court of Palestine in *Arnold Gronner v. Director, Department of Immigration* on 8 April 1941.[621] The facts of this case, as set out in the judgment, were as follows:

> The Petitioner [Mr. Gronner] was in Palestine for two months in 1938—he again arrived in this country on the 14th February, 1939, on a three months' temporary visa which was extended for another month, and on the 28th July, 1939, he received permission to remain permanently in Palestine and has remained here ever since. In January 1941, he applied for a naturalisation certificate, which was refused. The Petitioner contends that he has 'resided' in Palestine since the 14th February, 1939, *i.e.* for two full years in the last three years, whilst the Director of Immigration says that the qualifying residence for naturalisation under Article 7(1)(a) only begins to run from the date of registration as an immigrant, in this case the 12th July, 1939, when Petitioner received permission to remain permanently in Palestine.

Disregarding temporary stay as a basis for naturalization, the same case added:

618 Annotated Law Reports, 1944, Vol. II, p. 604.
619 From 22 May 1939 to 27 March 1944.
620 *Albert Schutz v. Commissioner for Migration and Statistics*, Supreme Court of Palestine sitting as a High Court of Justice, 13 May 1942 (Supreme Court Judgements, 1942, p. 273).
621 *Op. cit.*

> [C]asual or temporary residence is not included within the scope of Article 7(1)(a) [of the Palestinian Citizenship Order]. Temporary residence for purposes of travel, or health or business cannot be termed residence for the purpose of being naturalized.[622]

It is to be noted that the two-year residence was comparatively short. According to Article 2(1)(a) of the British Nationality Act, 1914 (the counterpart of Article 7(1)(*a*) of the Palestinian Order), the residence's requirement for naturalization was five consecutive years. Similarly, residence for the purpose of naturalization in all Palestine's neighbouring countries, with the exception of Trans-Jordan,[623] ranged between three years to ten years.[624] The two-year residence in this case also altered the five-year residence's requirement for naturalization enshrined in Article 3 of the Ottoman Nationality Law of 1869.[625] Although there is no general rule of international law governing the length of residence, most nationality laws of other states tend to require more than two-year of residence from those seeking naturalization, and most often they required five-year residence.[626] As will be elaborated shortly,

---

622 The last sentence of this extract is already quoted above (see pp. 101–102). *Cf.* the meaning of residence for the purpose of automatic acquisition of Palestinian nationality, above pp. 89–90.

623 Whereby the required residence for naturalization was also two years (Nationality Law of 1928, *op. cit.*, Article 7). This can be explained by two factors: Trans-Jordanian nationality law was inspired by the Palestinian Citizenship Order of 1925. Trans-Jordan with its small population intended to attract as much persons as possible to its nationality. The latter factor, among others, might explain the interest to grant *en masse* Trans-Jordanian nationality to the Palestinians residing in the Jordan River's west bank and to Palestinian refugees who fled to the territory of Trans-Jordan in 1948–1949. See Additional Law of 13 January 1949 of the [Trans-Jordan] Nationality Law, Article 2 (Laws Concerning Nationality, p. 277). See also Jordanian Nationality Law of 4 February 1954, *op. cit.*, Article 3(2), which confirmed Article 2 of the said 1949 law.

624 In Egypt, ten years' residence was required (Decree Law concerning Egyptian Nationality of 1927—Collection of Nationality Laws, *op. cit.*, p. 225, Article 8); in Syria and Lebanon, the requirement was five years (Syria Order of 19 January 1925, *ibid.*, p. 298, Article 3; Lebanon Order of 19 January 1925, *ibid.*, p. 301, Article 3); in Iraq and Hejaz, three years' residence was required (Iraq Law of 9 October 1924, *op. cit.*, Article 10; Hejaz Law of 24 September 1926—Collection of Nationality Laws, p. 331, Article 3).

625 See above p. 30.

626 Examples of states which require five-year residence include (page numbers referred to in this note are taken from: Collection of Nationality Laws): Albania Civil Code of 1 April 1929, Article 7(2), p. 5; Belgium Law of 15 May 1922, Article 13(2), p. 29; Finland Law of 20 February 1920, Article 1(2), p. 237; Italy Law of 13 June 1912, Article 4(2), p. 363; Hungary Law of 20 December 1879, *op. cit.*, Article 8(3); Japan Law of March 1899, as revised on 1 December 1924, Article 7(1), p. 382; Norway Law of 8 August 1924, Article 5(2), p. 453; Sweden Law of 23 May 1924, Article 5(2), p. 545. Ten-year residence is required in Poland Law of 20 January 1920, Article 8(2), p. 479; Romania Law of 23 February 1924, Article 7(3), p. 497; Yugoslavia Law of 21 September 1928, Article 12(5), p. 389. Four-year residence is required by Afghanistan Code of August 1921, Article 86(2), p. 3; Panama Law of 22 August 1916, *op. cit.*, Article 156(a). Some states required no specific number of years, others required one year, two or three years.

residence was reduced into two years in order to facilitate the naturalization of immigrant Jews in Palestine.[627]

Moreover, under Article 7(5) of the Citizenship Order, the High Commissioner could "in any special case, if he thinks fit, grant a certificate of naturalisation although the two years' residence has not been within the three years immediately preceding the date of application". This opened the possibility to accept interrupted residence (or even no residence at all) as a basis for naturalization. This ran contrary to the British law which required continuance of residence in Britain "for not less than one year immediately preceding the application, and previous residence...for a period of four years within the last eight years before the application".[628] Again in *Arnold Gronner v. Director, Department of Immigration*,[629] whereas the applicant for naturalization did not meet the two-year residence, the Court advised that "under Article 7(5) [of] the Order in Council the High Commissioner can make exception to the general rule in cases of hardship. The Petitioner might possibly try this course, as if his statements are true, there would appear to be certain circumstances meriting consideration".[630]

The Citizenship Order did not specify the exact meaning of 'good character',[631] in its second requirement for naturalization in Palestine. Thus, it would be useful to refer to the expression in the British law.[632] In Britain, the applicant was required to submit four testimonials from four British citizens who were householders of standing in Britain, as demonstrable proof of good character.[633] In the nationality laws of other states, in what appears to be equivalent to 'good character',[634] the person applying for naturalization was required to have: a good 'reputation' or demonstrated good 'behaviour' or 'conduct';[635] proof that he had not been convicted

627 Goadby, *International and Inter-Religious Private Law in Palestine*, p. 33). See also below Chapter VI, Section 2.

628 Nationality and Status of Aliens Act, 1914, as amended in 1922, Article 2(2). See Jones, *British Nationality Law and Practice, op. cit.*, pp. 110, 160.

629 *Op. cit.*

630 *Cf. Fatmeh bint Mahmoud As'ad Ammar v. Assistant Inspector General C. I. D. of Jerusalem*, Supreme Court of Palestine sitting as a High Court of Justice, 11 April 1946 (Annotated Law Reports, 1946, Vol. I, p. 442).

631 See, in general, Albert S. Persichetti, "Good Moral Character as a Requirement for Naturalization", *Temple Law Quarterly*, Vol. 22, 1948–1949, pp. 182–194; Harold F. Bonacquist, Jr. and Philip A. Mittleman, "The Evaluation of Good Moral Character in Naturalization Proceedings", *Albany Law Review*, Vol. 38, 1973–1974, pp. 895–920.

632 Nationality and Status of Aliens Act, 1914, as amended in 1922, Article 2(1)(*b*).

633 Jones, *British Nationality Law and Practice, op. cit.*, pp. 159–160.

634 Being of a 'good character' was cited as a pre-requisite for naturalization within the legislation of other states such as: the Iraq Law of 9 October 1924, *op. cit.*, Article 10(ii); Hungary Law of 20 December 1879, *op. cit.*, Article 8(44); Japan Law of March 1899, as revised on 1 December 1924, *op. cit.*, Article 7(3).

635 See, e.g., Finland Law of 20 February 1920, *op. cit.*, Article 1(1); Romania Law of 23 February 1923, *op. cit.*, Article 7(5); Norway Law of 8 August 1924, *op. cit.*, Article 5(3); Yugoslavia Law of 21 September 1928, *op. cit.*, Article 12(5).

of a crime;[636] economic independence: in that his business, profession or country real estate provided sufficient income for himself and his family.[637]

Thirdly, applicants for naturalization were required to have adequate knowledge of English, Arabic or Hebrew. These were the three official languages of Palestine, according to Article 22 of the Palestine Mandate and Article 82 of the Palestine Order in Council (Constitution) of 1922. A regulation was made for the purpose of checking, by a staff member of the Immigration Department, the language ability of those seeking naturalization, with the decision in this regard depending upon the discretion of the said staff member.[638]

Lastly, to qualify for naturalization, the applicant was required to have the intention of physically residing in Palestine henceforth.[639] Otherwise, nationality could be revoked if "the person to whom the [naturalization] certificate is granted has, since the grant [of such certificate], been for a period of not less than three years ordinarily resident out of Palestine".[640]

Upon fulfilling these requirements, a naturalization certificate would be granted. However, such a certificate, it was stated, "shall not take effect until the applicant has taken the oath of allegiance" to the Government of Palestine.[641] The form of the oath, as annexed to the Palestinian Citizenship Order, was as follows:

> I, A.B., Swear by Almighty God that I will be faithful and loyal to the Government of Palestine.

In this regard, the accepted view was that the "oath does not create the bond of allegiance but witnesses or 'attests' it".[642] It emphasized, however, the fact that

---

636 Afghanistan Code of August 1921, *op. cit.*, Article 86(3); Brazil Legislative Decree of 12 November 1902 (Collection of Nationality Laws, p. 50), Article 13; Honduras Law of 4 February 1926 (*ibid.*, p. 334), Article 15.

637 This was one of the most common conditions for naturalization in most states. Examples include the following (all page numbers in this note are taken from: Collection of Nationality Laws): Germany Law of 22 July 1913, Article 8(4), p. 306; Finland Law of 20 February 1920, *op. cit.*, Article 1(3); Hungary Law of 20 December 1879, *op. cit.*, Article 8(5); Japan Law of March 1899, as revised on 1 December 1924, *op. cit.*, Article 7(4); Mexico Law of 28 May 1886, Article 13(3), p. 428; Norway Law of 8 August 1924, *op. cit.*, Article 5(4); Portugal Civil Code of 1867, *op. cit.*, Article 19(1); Sweden Law of 23 May 1924, *op. cit.*, Article 5(4); Romania Law of 23 February 1923, *op. cit.*, Article 7(5).

638 See Palestinian Citizenship Regulations of 1925, *op. cit.*, Article 15.

639 See British Nationality Act, 1914, Article 2(1)(*c*). In Britain, see Piggott, *op. cit.*, p. 100. See also Jones, *British Nationality Law and Practice, op. cit.*, p. 160.

640 Palestinian Citizenship Order of 1925, Article 10(1). See below Chapter VII, Section 3.

641 Palestinian Citizenship Order of 1925, Article 7(2), first sentence. *Cf.* British Nationality Act, 1914, Article 2(4). On the relationship between nationality and allegiance, including the oath of allegiance, in international and comparative law with special reference to British law, see R.S. Fraser, "Nationality and Allegiance", *International Law Notes*, Vol. 4, 1919, pp. 12–34. More generally, see John W. Salmond, "Citizenship and Allegiance", *The Law Quarterly Review*, Vol. 17, 1901, pp. 270–282; Willoughby, *op. cit.*, pp. 914–929.

642 Jones, *British Nationality Law and Practice, op. cit.*, p. 161.

Palestinian nationality carried with it obligations as well as privileges; "hence the provision that naturalization is not effective until the applicant has given solemn and formal proof of his acceptance of these obligations".[643] Thus, applicants could make a solemn affirmation or declaration in lieu of such oath.[644]

Even after fulfilling all such requirements, the High Commissioner reserved an absolute authority to refuse naturalization. In this connection, Article 7(3) stated:

> The grant of a certificate of naturalization shall be in the absolute discretion of the High Commissioner, who may with or without assigning any reason give or withhold the certificate as he thinks most conductive to the public good; and no appeal shall lie from his decision.[645]

This provision illustrates the authoritarian nature of the Palestinian Citizenship Order, which gave the Executive a vast range of powers in granting or refusing the grant of nationality without any supervision, either judicial or administrative. Thirteen of the twenty-seven articles of the Order gave the High Commissioner, or a representative of the Government of Palestine, an absolute authority to grant or refuse the grant of nationality without assigning any reason.[646]

The renunciation of any previous citizenship(s) was not a pre-condition for naturalization,[647] as nothing to this effect was provided in any legislation. In practice, however, the Government of Palestine requested applicants to renounce their existing citizenship(s) before granting naturalization. Applicants, for example, were obliged to submit travel documents in their possession to the Palestinian Immigration Department as part of the naturalization procedures.[648] And to that effect, shortly after the enactment of the 1925 Palestinian Citizenship Order, the British Government informed the League of Nations:[649]

> The British Government had always been firmly opposed to dual nationality. Anyone opting for Palestinian nationality had to renounce his former nationality.... [I]t was the practice of the Palestine Government to inform the consuls of States to which the immigrants belonged whenever Palestinian nationality was granted.[650]

---

643 *Ibid.* See also *Joachim Suchier v. Superintendent of the Detention Camp*, Supreme Court of Palestine sitting as a High Court of Justice, 12 June 1942 (Supreme Court Judgements, 1942, p. 380). Regarding the procedures of the oath or declaration, see Palestinian Citizenship Regulations of 1942, Article 2.

644 Palestinian Citizenship Order of 1925, Article 7(2), second sentence. See also Jones, *British Nationality Law and Practice, op. cit.*, p. 161.

645 *Cf.* British Nationality Act, 1914, Article 2(3).

646 The Articles are as follows: 2, 4(1)(*c*), 5(1), 7(1,3,5), 8, 9(1–2), 10(1–3), 11(1), 12(2), 19, 21, 23 and 24.

647 Goadby, *International and Inter-Religious Private Law in Palestine, op. cit.*, p. 33.

648 See Annex 1, Forms 1 and 2, of the Palestinian Citizenship Regulations, 1925. See also *Instructions to Immigration Officers, op. cit.*, Article 58(vi).

649 Mandates Commission Minutes 1926, *op. cit.*, pp. 171–172. For similar conclusion, see Mandates Commission Minutes 1928, *op. cit.*, p. 52.

650 This was also the case in Britain: "It is the practice of the Home Office when granting a [naturalization] certificate to ensure, as far as possible, that the applicant will not possess dual nationality, and it is therefore usual to require the applicant to obtain release from

The reason for requesting the renunciation of previous citizenship(s) in practice, not in law, was that the withdrawal of such citizenship(s) did not depend on Palestinian law. In 1935, a member of the League of Nations' Permanent Mandates Commission asked "whether, when a person acquired Palestinian nationality, it was a condition that he should forfeit his former nationality in order to avoid double nationality?"[651] Britain replied by saying that "this question depended on the national law of the country from which the person came. It did not depend upon Palestinian law at all".[652] It appears from the aforementioned 1935 question that the ten years of mass naturalization of foreign immigrants in Palestine (which started in 1925) had made the withdrawal of a former nationality impracticable.

Nevertheless, states, at the time, could request the applicant to prove the loss of his former nationality as a pre-condition for naturalization. In such cases, the person would find himself compelled to expatriate himself (or change his previous nationality). Indeed, states developed special procedures for expatriation and this, as it will be shortly seen, was also the case in Palestine.[653] Yet providing evidence of expatriation did not necessarily result in the loss of one's existing citizenship(s).[654]

As a result, a majority of naturalized persons retained former citizenships, along with Palestinian nationality and thereby became dual citizens.[655]

In forcing women to follow their husband's nationality, the Palestinian Citizenship Order of 1925 had chiefly followed the British law. As a rule governing the whole Citizenship Order, "the status of a married woman will be governed by that of her husband".[656] In relation to naturalization, the "wife of a Palestinian citizen shall

---

his alien nationality if possible" (Jones, *British Nationality Law and Practice, op. cit.*, p. 158). Indeed, prior to the enactment of the Palestinian Citizenship Order in 1925, the High Commissioner for Palestine informed the League of Nations, on 29 October 1924, that "the proposed [Palestinian nationality] law was almost identical in this respect with the British law. The previous consent of the Government of the country of origin was not required [for naturalization in Palestine], but the interested party must declare that he renounced his original nationality. Before the [First World] war Russia never allowed Russians to change their nationality, but in spite of this numerous Russians were naturalised in England" (Mandates Commission Minutes 1924, *op. cit.*, p. 82).

651 Permanent Mandates Commission, *Minutes of the Twenty-Seventh Session*, League of Nations, Geneva, 1935, p. 52.

652 *Ibid.* The same view was expressed by Britain nine years earlier (Mandates Commission Minutes 1926, *op. cit.*, p. 171).

653 See below Chapter VII.

654 Yet in the absence of agreements among states, such a person could retain other nationalities and, if he submitted his passport upon naturalization, he could apply for a new passport from his state of origin. Also, the person could hold more passports from different states and yet forfeit only one.

655 This might explain the fact that the majority of Jewish immigrants to Palestine who became then Israel citizens are now dual citizens. See, for instance, Davis, *op. cit.*, p. 44.

656 Palestinian Citizenship Order, Article 6. This article relates to the natural Palestinian citizens as regulated in the first two parts of the Citizenship Order (see above Chapter IV) and it is a direct implementation to Article 36 of the Treaty of Lausanne (see above p. 72).

be deemed to be a Palestinian citizen and the wife of an alien shall be deemed to be an alien".[657] In *Eliyahu Bichovsky v. Nitsa Lambi Bichovsky*,[658] the Palestinian court held that "in order to ascertain if the lady was a Palestinian citizen, one has to enquire if she was the wife *de jure* of a Palestinian citizen". This means that a married woman is obliged *ipso facto* to follow her husband's nationality. But this rule is a step forward when one compares it with the anomalous position of the Ottoman Nationality Law of 1869, whereby women were denied the right to follow their husband's nationality.[659]

In a clear discriminatory provision against women, the Citizenship Order deemed a married woman to be a 'disabled person' for all nationality purposes. The term 'disability', as defined in Article 21(4) of the Order, meant, *inter alia*, "the status of being a married woman". This definition was taken from Article 27(1) of the British Nationality Act, 1914.[660] Thus, a woman was unable on her own account to be naturalized in Palestine.[661] In other words, a foreign married woman could not acquire Palestinian nationality separately from her husband.[662] A woman had the right to apply for naturalization only if she was unmarried, widowed or divorced.[663]

The foregoing consideration meant that a foreign man could not be naturalized, merely by getting married to a Palestinian woman. There is no explicit provision to this effect in the 1925 Citizenship Order. But the overall dependency of a woman on her husband's nationality implied that the man was not entitled to be naturalized based on his wife's nationality. Such a man could be only naturalized, then, according to the general rules of naturalization applicable to other foreigners.[664] In this regard, the Palestinian 'nationality law' and its model, the British law, were in no means progressive when compared to the legislation of other states. Both

657 Palestinian Citizenship Order, Article 12(1). This provision was taken, *mutatis mutandis*, from the first sentence of Article 10 of the British Nationality Act, 1914. For a history on this provision, see Jones, *British Nationality Law and Practice*, *op. cit.*, p. 178. For details on naturalization by marriage in Britain, in general, see *ibid.*, pp. 178–188; Piggott, *op. cit.*, pp. 57–63; Davies, *op. cit.*, pp. 287–295.

658 *Op. cit.* See also *Attorney General v. Rachel Menkes*, Supreme Court of Palestine sitting as a Court of Civil Appeal, 11 January 1943 (Annotated Law Reports, 1943, Vol. I, p. 5); *Sara Mandelberg Rogalsky v. Director of Medical Services*, *op. cit.*; *Nabiha Salim Zahwa v. 1. Attorney General, 2. Inspector General of Police and Prisons*, *op. cit.*

659 See above p. 36.

660 On the nationality of married women with special reference to British law, see Chrystal Macmillan, "Nationality of Married Women: Present Tendencies", *Journal of Comparative Legislation and International Law*, Vol. 7, 1925, pp. 142–154.

661 In this respect, the Palestinian Citizenship Order, Article 9(3), provided that "a certificate of naturalization shall not be granted to any person under disability".

662 Hence, the female person was either a minor girl who followed the nationality of her father or a 'minor woman' who followed the nationality of her husband. A woman was considered to be an adult, for nationality purposes, only if she was single and 18 years of age or above.

663 See Instructions to Immigration Officers, *op. cit.*, Article 87(i).

664 This is also in line with the Ottoman Nationality Law of 1869; see above pp. 115–118.

stood behind the nationality legislation of Argentina,[665] Brazil,[666] China,[667] France,[668] Japan,[669] Latvia,[670] Paraguay,[671] amongst others. In the majority of other states at the time, however, only wives could follow their husbands on matters concerning nationality; Palestine was no exception.

Nonetheless, and more generally, the discriminatory provisions of the 1925-enacted Palestinian Citizenship Order against women were similar to most nationality legislation of other states at that time.[672] By 1939, when Palestine became party to the international instruments on nationality,[673] this disadvantaged status of married women had been somewhat improved.

With respect to minors,[674] the naturalization of a man gave his children the right to become Palestinian citizens, as a rule. This naturalization was not automatic, however. It required an application by the father and approval by the Government of Palestine. But the Government retained an authority, in special cases, to grant naturalization to any minor irrespective of whether or not the naturalization conditions were fulfilled. These rules were laid down in Article 9 of the Palestinian Citizenship Order, which was in line with Article 5 of the British Nationality

---

665 See *supra* note 159.

666 See *supra* note 160.

667 Article 4 of the Law of 5 February 1929 (Collection of Nationality Laws, p. 175). This article recognized the naturalization of a man who married a Chinese woman subject to five-year residence, whereas ten-year residence was required for ordinary foreigners.

668 Law of 10 August 1927 (Collection of Nationality Laws, p. 245), Article 6(2). A man who married a French woman could be naturalized after one year of residence, while other foreigners had to reside in France for three years in order to be eligible for naturalization.

669 See Law of March 1899 as revised in July 1924, *op. cit.*, Article 5(2). A man who married a Japanese woman could have been naturalized if he was 'head of family'.

670 Law of 2 June 1927 (Collection of Nationality Laws, p. 407), Article 7. A man who married a Latvian woman was permitted to be naturalized if he has been a stateless person.

671 See *supra* note 161.

672 See, *inter alia*, Percy L. Edwards, "Should Women Be Admitted to Full Citizenship?" *The Green Bag: An Entertaining Magazine for Lawyers* (Boston), Vol. 7, 1895, pp. 217–222; Cyril D. Hill, "Citizenship of Married Women", *The American Journal of International Law*, Vol. 18, 1924, pp. 720–754; Lucius F. Crane, "The Nationality of Married Women", *Journal of Comparative Legislation and International Law*, Vol. 7, 1925, pp. 53–60; F. Llewellyn-Jones, "The Nationality of Married Women", *Problems of Peace and War*, Vol. 15, 1930, pp. 121–138; Gladys Harrison, "The Nationality of Married Women", *New York University Law Quarterly Review*, Vol. 9, 1931–1932, pp. 445–462; Blanche Crozier, "The Changing Basis of Women's Nationality", *Boston University Law Review*, Vol. 14, 1934, pp. 129–153; Beroe Bicknell, "The Nationality of Married Women", *Problems of Peace and War*, Vol. 20, 1935, pp. 106–122; Waldo Emerson Waltz, *The Nationality of Married Women: A Study of Domestic Policies and International Legislation*, The University of Illinois Press, 1937.

673 See below pp. 187–190.

674 See, in general, Charles O. Monahan, "Nationality of Minors", *Boston University Law Review*, Vol. 14, 1934, pp. 524–581.

Act, 1914.[675] The fact that the naturalization of children was dependent upon their father's nationality represented a departure from Article 8 of the 1869 Ottoman Nationality Law, which denied children to automatically follow the naturalization of their father or parents.[676]

In short, the Palestinian Citizenship Order of 1925 incorporated no peculiar provisions relating to naturalization. Its rules could be found, in one form or another, in the legislation of other states at the time. Yet the particular characteristic of naturalization in Palestine stemmed from the process in which such naturalization had been carried out in practice.

2. *Practical effects*

Mass numbers of foreign Jews acquired Palestinian nationality by naturalization before 1948 with a view to contribute to the establishment of the 'Jewish national home' in Palestine. At the end of the mandate, the total number of persons who acquired Palestinian nationality by naturalization was estimated at 132,616; about 99% of them were Jews.[677]

Under the auspices of the League of Nations and the administration of Britain, this objective had no precedent in world history.[678] As required by the Palestine Mandate, the naturalization provisions of the 1925 Palestinian Citizenship Order were "framed so as to facilitate the acquisition of Palestinian citizenship by Jews who take up their permanent residence in Palestine" (Article 7 of the Mandate).

The Council of the League of Nations took part, systematically, in the question of naturalization of Jews in Palestine. The Council, represented by its Permanent Mandates Commission, had persuaded Britain to speed up its efforts to naturalize immigrant Jews. As early as 23 August 1922, the said Commission inquired whether special nationality provisions were, by using the words of the said Article 7, "framed so as to facilitate the acquisition of Palestinian citizenship by Jews?"[679] In a direct reply to this question, the British Government provided detailed information relating to naturalization. Such information provoked extensive discussion among the members of the Mandates Commission.[680]

The naturalization provisions were the most significant aspect of the Palestinian Citizenship Order, and, again, were an explicit translation of Article 7 of the Palestine

---

675 For naturalization of children in Britain, see Piggott, *op. cit.*, pp. 63–70.

676 See above p. 37.

677 Survey of Palestine, Vol. I, p. 208.

678 The practical implications of naturalization in Palestine, as it shall become shortly apparent, were unique; there was no similar such case in the world, neither in the mandated territories nor elsewhere.

679 League of Nations Document No. C.553.M.335.1922.VI, *op. cit.*, p. 3.

680 See, for example, the following minutes of the Permanent Mandates Commission: 1926, *op. cit.*, p. 171; 1927, *op. cit.*, p. 128; 1929, *op. cit.*, p. 100; 1933, *op. cit.*, p. 106; 1935, *op. cit.*, p. 52.

Mandate. This was summarized by the Supreme Court of Palestine, on 28 February 1929, in *Palevitch v. Chief Immigration Officer*.[681] The case related to an immigrant Jew from Italy who applied for naturalization in Palestine. It was held:

> Article [7 of the Mandate] is concerned with the enactment of a nationality law in which, so says this Article of the Mandate, there are to be included provisions framed so as to facilitate the acquisition of Palestinian citizenship by Jews who take up their permanent residence in Palestine. This has been done by the passing of the Palestine Citizenship Order, 1925, in which there are embodied, in Art. 7(1), a number of qualifications which are required before the High Commissioner [for Palestine] may grant a certificate of naturalisation.

The 1925 Citizenship Order as a whole (not only the Order's naturalization provisions) constituted the domestic, or the concrete, execution of Article 7 of the Mandate.[682] But the Court's reference to Article 7(1) of the Order (regarding naturalization) and its connection with the said Article 7 of the Mandate, implied that the naturalization of Jews was deemed to be *the* key subject of the Order in the eyes of its drafters, however important other provisions might have been.

From the outset, the naturalization provisions of the Palestinian Citizenship Order were framed to grant Palestinian nationality, in an organized manner, to foreign Jews who would immigrate into Palestine. To this effect, shortly after the enactment of the Order in 1925, the British Government admitted:

> The qualifications for naturalization are simple: two years' residence in Palestine out of the three years preceding application, good character, and the declared intention to settle in Palestine; knowledge of Hebrew is accepted under the literacy qualification. In special cases the High Commissioner is empowered to grant naturalization even if the period of residence has not been within the three years preceding application. Special naturalization offices have already been opened in Jerusalem, Haifa and Tiberias; and an officer is visiting the Jewish agricultural settlements in the north [of Palestine] to receive applications on the spot.[683]

In fact, as it has been demonstrated above,[684] the British-run Government of Palestine had involved Jewish leaders in the drafting process of the Palestinian Citizenship Order of 1925. Officially, the Jewish Agency and the Zionist Organization were in favour of naturalizing Jews in Palestine. The increased number of Jews who applied for naturalization in 1935, for example, was a result of, *inter alia*, "the campaign of the several Jewish representative institutions to encourage

---

681 *Op. cit.*

682 See above Chapter IV, Section 3.

683 Report on the Administration of Palestine 1925, *op. cit.*, p. 74. See also the following reports of the British Government: *Report to the Council of the League of Nations on the Administration of Palestine and Trans-Jordan*, 1930 (hereinafter: 'Report on the Administration of Palestine 1930'), pp. 58–61; *Report to the Council of the League of Nations on the Administration of Palestine and Trans-Jordan*, 1936 (hereinafter: 'Report on the Administration of Palestine 1936'), p. 44; *Report to the Council of the League of Nations on the Administration of Palestine and Trans-Jordan*, 1938 (hereinafter: 'Report on the Administration of Palestine 1938'), p. 89.

684 See above p. 83.

naturalization among members of the Jewish community [of Palestine]".[685] More specifically, in 1936, the British Government reported:

> [T]he [Jewish] General Council (*Vaad Leumi*) conducted an energetic campaign for the naturalisation as Palestinian citizens of Jewish immigrants, who are qualified therefore by residence, and gave much assistance to the Department of Migration in the acceptance of applications for certificates of citizenship under the Palestinian Citizenship Order, 1925.[686]

Yet not all immigrant Jews had individually applied for naturalization. At the end of 1936, the Palestine Royal Commission reported that out of 292,000 Jews qualifying for Palestinian nationality, "about 166,000 had acquired Palestinian citizenship and the remaining 126,000 or about 43 per cent of the qualified population, were not Palestinian citizens".[687] The reason for this, according to the same Commission, was:

> The Jews have not availed themselves readily of the opportunity afforded them of becoming Palestinian citizens and this is accounted for by the fact that their chief interest is in the Jewish community itself and allegiance to Palestine and to the Government [of Palestine] are minor considerations to many of them.[688]

In collaboration with the Zionist Organization and the Jewish Agency, in a wider context, Britain made and employed immigration laws in order to bring Jews into Palestine,[689] supporting their settlement in the country, and ultimately naturalizing them therein.[690] The systematic, publicly declared, collaboration between Britain

---

685 Report on the Administration of Palestine 1935, *op. cit.*, p. 69.

686 Report on the Administration of Palestine 1936, *op. cit.*, p. 44.

687 Royal Commission Report, *op. cit.*, p. 332. As mentioned above (p. 123), the Government of Palestine reported that the total number of persons who had acquired Palestinian citizenship by naturalization during the period from August 1925 to September 1945 was 132,616 individuals. The divergence between the above-quoted figure of 1936 and this one is due, perhaps, to whether the reported numbers included children or wives of the naturalized men and whether the provisionally naturalized persons before August 1925 were included or not.

688 Royal Commission Report, *op. cit.*, p. 332. For the same conclusion, see Permanent Mandates Commission, *Minutes of the Thirteenth Session*, League of Nations, Geneva, 1928, p. 52. According to the Zionist Organization, in 1932, "Of the 174,610 Jews enumerated in the Census, 100,704 declared themselves to be of Palestinian citizenship, while 7,902 had filed applications for such citizenship". Zionist Organization, *Memorandum of the Development of the Jewish National Home submitted to the Secretary General of the League of Nations*, London, April, 1933, p. 4.

689 With regard to the rule of the Jewish Agency in matters of immigration and naturalization, see the following memoranda (all prepared by the Jewish Agency, London, and sent to the League of Nations and entitled as follows: "Memorandum on the Development of the Jewish National Home, [the year] Submitted by the Jewish Agency for Palestine to the Secretary-General of the League of Nations for the Information of the Permanent Mandates Commission"): October 1924, pp. 16–19; June 1928, pp. 3–9; August 1932, pp. 3–12; April 1933, pp. 5–11; April 1936, pp. 3–9.

690 See Immigration Ordinance, 1933 (Laws of Palestine, p. 849). This Ordinance abrogated and consolidated the provisions of the Immigration Ordinances, 1923–1924. See also

and the Zionist/Jewish representatives was recognized in Article 4 of the Palestine Mandate:

> An appropriate Jewish agency shall be recognised as a public body for the purpose of advising and co-operating with the Administration of Palestine in such economic, social and other matters as may affect the establishment of the Jewish national home and the interests of the Jewish population in Palestine.... The Zionist organization...shall be recognised as such agency....

Thus, as the British Government stated in its report to the League of Nations in 1925, while "the regulations under the Immigration Ordinance, 1925, set up a statutory procedure for the introduction of Jewish immigrant labour into Palestine",[691] "the Palestinian Citizenship Order in Council, 1925, facilitates the acquisition of Palestinian nationality by persons settling in the country".[692]

As a declaratory formulation to the pre-existing practice in Palestine, a special naturalization article was added to the Citizenship Order to serve a specific group of Jews who were already residing in the country.[693] Those Jews who were temporarily naturalized in order to participate in the legislative election of 1922,[694] and who had habitually resided in Palestine since then, were finally deemed to be Palestinians in 1925. In this respect, Article 5(1) of the Citizenship Order reads:

> Persons who have made a declaration of their intention to opt for Palestinian citizenship in accordance with Article 2 of the Palestine Legislative Council Election Order, 1922, and have received provisional certificates of Palestinian citizenship...shall...be deemed to be entitled to acquire Palestinian citizenship.[695]

Although this provision did not mention 'Jews', the British Government had confirmed that "Article 5 of the Order facilitates the acquisition of citizenship by Jews who opted therefore under Article 2 of the Palestine Legislative Council Election Order in Council, 1922".[696] Moreover, "special facilities have been granted to Jewish

---

Immigration Ordinance, 1941 (Palestine Gazette, No. 1082, Supplement 1, 6 March 1941, p. 6). According to the Immigration Regulations, which were enacted in accordance with the Immigration Ordinances, it was possible for the 'Palestine Zionist Executive' to request immigration permissions for groups of persons to come to Palestine. See Article 4(1), Article 7(4) and Article 8 of the Immigration Regulations, 1933 (annexed to the Immigration Ordinance, 1933) and Annex 5 thereof (application form to be submitted by the Palestine Zionist Executive for permission to bring immigrants into Palestine). See also Article 2 of the Immigration (Amendment) Rules, 1935 (Palestine Gazette, No. 500, Supplement 2, 28 March 1935, p. 310) and the annexed form thereof (entry visa to Palestine by the Jewish Agency to immigrant Jews).

691 Report on the Administration of Palestine 1925, *op. cit.*, p. 66.

692 *Ibid.*

693 See Feinberg, *op. cit.*, p. 50.

694 See above pp. 66–67.

695 For the procedures to acquire Palestinian nationality under this article, see Palestinian Citizenship Regulations of 1925, Article 3, and Annex 1, Form 1 attached thereof.

696 Report on the Administration of Palestine 1925, *op. cit.*, p. 74. See also *Attorney-General v. Goralschwili and Another, op. cit.* (provisional certificates of special Palestinian nationality).

students resident abroad to obtain citizenship, if qualified, without being required to present themselves in person [at the Immigration Department] at Jerusalem".[697] Article 13 of the Palestinian Citizenship Regulations, 1925,[698] materialized this practice by authorizing British consuls abroad to grant Palestinian nationality to Jewish students.[699]

Consequently, the vast majority of naturalized foreigners in Palestine were Jews, with minor exceptions. In 1931, for example, the British Government told the League of Nations that out of "the 17,477 individuals and families, representing about 27,000 souls, who have acquired the Palestinian citizenship under Articles 5, 7, and 9 of the [Citizenship] Order in Council, nearly 95 per cent are Jews".[700] Another 1946-conducted official survey estimated the naturalization of non-Jews throughout the mandate period to be "approximately 1% of the total".[701] Immigrants arrived in Palestine from some 61 countries;[702] the vast majority came from twenty-five European states.[703] The admission of foreigners into Palestine, including by immigration, will be addressed in greater detail later in this study.[704]

Lastly, an intensified process to naturalize Jewish soldiers serving in the British forces in Palestine had been carried out, especially during and after World War II. This process started on 19 November 1940, when Britain amended the Palestinian Citizenship Order for the purpose of naturalizing foreign persons serving in the British army.[705] This Order was followed by a series of regulations to the same

---

697 Report on the Administration of Palestine 1932, *op. cit.*, p. 43.

698 *Op. cit.*

699 *Cf.* the treatment of Palestinian natives residing abroad, above Chapter V, Section 2.

700 British Government, *Report to the Council of the League of Nations on the Administration of Palestine and Trans-Jordan*, 1931, p. 40. *Cf.* Report on Palestine Administration 1922, *op. cit.*, p. 53.

701 Survey of Palestine, Vol. I, p. 208.

702 Legally, the presence of such a large number of foreigners in Palestine resulted in an ample amount of case law related to the conflict of laws in personal status matters, such as marriage, divorce, maintenance, will, and succession. In 1947, one writer gathered 388 cases decided by Palestinian courts throughout the mandate on such matters (Vitta, *op. cit.*, pp. XV–XXIII). These cases form a rich source of jurisprudence in the field of private international law. As Palestine's legal system was influenced by the Common Law system, such judicial precedents significantly contributed to the law-making in that particular field of law.

703 See Survey of Palestine, Vol. I, pp. 204–205. It seems that the Jewish refugee problem in Europe in the inter-war period (1919–1939) encouraged Jewish immigration into Palestine. See Israel B. Brodie, *The Refugee Problem and Palestine*, The American Economic Commission for Palestine, New York, 1938; John Hope Simpson, *Report on Immigration, Land Settlement and Development*, His Majesty's Stationary Office, London, 1930; Jewish Agency for Palestine, *Palestine: Land Settlement, Urban Development and Immigration*, London, 1930. See also Palestine Royal Commission Report, *op. cit.*, pp. 279–307; British Government, *Report to the Council of the League of Nations on the Administration of Palestine and Trans-Jordan*, 1934 (hereinafter: 'Report on the Administration of Palestine 1934'), pp. 28–45.

704 See below Chapter IX.

705 See Palestinian Citizenship (Amendment) Order of 1940.

effect.[706] Such naturalization continued through the latter stages of the war and thereafter towards the end of the mandate.[707]

This policy coincided with the end of the mandate and with a number of international proposals to solve the Palestine question by establishing two states, Jewish and Arab, in that country. Individuals who were present in Palestine and participated in the military service of the British forces were overwhelmingly Jews.[708] Thus, the apparent purpose of naturalizing Jewish soldiers was to strengthen the army of the projected Jewish state.[709] It was estimated that the number of Jews who participated in the British forces during World War II in Palestine amounted to approximately 27,000 men: seven-thousand regular soldiers and twenty-thousand volunteers.[710] "In addition... there were... 35,000 Civil Defence Workers. There were also about 1,500 Jews from Palestine and the Middle East in the R.A.F. [Royal Air Forces].... In addition... 15,000 were serving as special policemen in Palestine".[711] As a result, it was proposed that "a Jewish Army consisting of 200,000 Palestinian and stateless Jews"[712] to be created.[713] It seems, therefore, that these naturalized soldiers had later become part of the Israel army.

In brief, the naturalization process in Palestine constituted the chosen formula for increasing the number of Jews in the country and legalizing their presence by conferring Palestinian nationality on them. (As already seen, in mid-1925, the number of Jews who were Ottoman subjects and who then became *natural* Palestinian citizens did not exceed 1% out of the total, overwhelmingly Arab, population of Palestine.)[714] For this reason, some writers concluded that the Palestine Mandate, including its nationality article and therefore the entire Citizenship Order of 1925, is internationally invalid. It was said:[715]

---

706 See Palestinian Citizenship (Amendment) Regulations of 12 March 1942; Palestinian Citizenship (Amendment) Regulations of 18 June 1942; Palestinian Citizenship (Amendment) Regulations (No. 2), 1942 of 3 December 1942. For judicial implementation, see *Albert Schutz v. Commissioner for Migration and Statistics, op. cit.* (13 May 1942).

707 See Palestinian Citizenship (Amendment) Regulations, 1944; Palestinian Citizenship (His Majesty's Forces) (Amendment) Regulations of 21 June 1945; Palestinian Citizenship (His Majesty's Forces) (Amendment No. 2) Regulations of 6 September 1945.

708 See, in some detail, Esco Foundation for Palestine, *op. cit.*, Vol. II, pp. 1020–1035.

709 On the Jewish army's proposal starting as early as 1944; see *ibid.*, pp. 1029–1035.

710 See Norman Bentwich, "The Mandated Territories under the Second World War", *The British Year Book of International Law*, 1944, p. 165.

711 Esco Foundation for Palestine, *op. cit.*, Vol. II, p. 1028.

712 *Ibid.*, pp. 1029–1030. Such Jewish army "was to be composed about half of Palestinian Jews... and about half of stateless Jews. There were 100,000 Jews in Palestine and the Middle East among whom were trained and experienced fighters, and another 100,000 [non-Palestinian] Jews... who were anxious to join the Jewish Army" (*ibid.*, p. 1033).

713 Officially, it was in September 1944 that the British Government approved that the Jewish soldiers in Palestine to form part of the British forces therein. See *ibid.*, pp. 1034–1035.

714 See above pp. 93–94.

715 Boustany, *op. cit.*, pp. 19–20.

> 'Jewish People' of the world who on the 24th of July, 1922, when this mandate was confirmed by the Council of the League, were not the 'community formally belonging to the Turkish Empire'[716] and were in no sense a *community of the territory of Palestine*.[717]

Be that as it may, naturalization in Palestine had achieved its objective. Immigrant Jews who became Palestinian citizens by naturalization, among other actors, had succeeded in creating the State of Israel (i.e. the 'Jewish national home') in Palestine by 1948. Upon the establishment of Israel, Jewish Palestinians were converted into Israel citizens and ceased to be Palestinians; foreign Jews who were residing in Palestine became Israel citizens as well.[718] The status of these ex-Palestinians after 1948 is beyond the scope of the present study.[719]

716 This quotation is extracted from Article 22, paragraph 4, of the Covenant of the League of Nations.

717 Emphasis in original. For other reasons, see also Boustany, *op. cit.*, pp. 17–37; Cattan, *op. cit.*, pp. 63–68. *Cf.* Stoyanovsky, *op. cit.*, pp. 61–69 (based his argument on what he called the 'historical connection of the Jewish People with Palestine') and, more generally, Bentwich, *Palestine*, *op. cit.*, pp. 188–205. Whatever the argument might be, the discussion here is concerned with the *practical* effects of naturalization as it was implemented under the British rule. The question of 'Jewish nationality' has been discussed in detail in W.T. Mallison, Jr., "Zionist-Israel Juridical Claims to Constitute the Jewish People Nationality Entity and to Confer Membership in It: Appraisal in Public International Law", *George Washington Law Review*, Vol. 32, 1963–1964, pp. 983–1075.

718 All Jews who were residing permanently in Palestine, both Palestinian citizens and foreign immigrants, acquired Israel citizenship after the establishment of Israel on 15 May 1948. Article 4 of the Israel Law of Return of 6 July 1950 (Laws Concerning Nationality, p. 263) gave every Jew who came to the country as a permanent immigrant the right to obtain an immigration certificate. Article 2(*a*) of the Israel Nationality Law of 1 April 1952 (*op. cit.*), considered every immigrant under the Law of Return of 1950 as an Israel citizen. In particular, Article 2(*b*)(1) of the latter law regarded any immigrant Jew who entered Palestine before the establishment of Israel as an Israel citizen.

719 On Israel nationality, see, for example, Gouldman, *op. cit.*, pp. 17 ff.; Davis, *op. cit.*, pp. 39–65.

VII

EXPATRIATION: LOSS OF NATIONALITY

1. *Overview*

The Palestinian Citizenship Order of 1925, as in many other states,[720] regulated the question of expatriation in four ways. The first was general and related to all Palestinian citizens who acquired another nationality by naturalization. The second concerned naturalized Palestinians. The third and fourth cases of expatriation dealt with married women and minor children, respectively. Most of the expatriation provisions of the Citizenship Order were taken from the British law. This chapter will address these four forms of expatriation.

"Expatriation is the converse of naturalization".[721] And the person who expatriates himself became a foreigner.[722] However, expatriation does not release such person "from any obligation, duty, or liability in respect of any act done before he ceased to be a Palestinian citizen" (Article 17 of the Citizenship Order).[723] As it was drawn in general terms, this provision would apply to all types of expatriation.[724]

---

720 See, in general, John Westlake, "On Naturalisation and Expatriation, or, on Change of Nationality", *The Law Magazine and Law Review*, Vol. 25, 1868, pp. 124–143; Preuss, "International Law and Deprivation of Nationality", *Georgetown Law Journal*, 1934–1935, pp. 250–276; Walter Stein, "Revocation of Citizenship—'Denaturalization'", *Marquette Law Review*, Vol. 28, 1944, pp. 59–74; Aysha Mechbat, *Loss of Nationality: Comparative Study*, Institute of Law and Administration at Algeria University, Algiers, 1987 (Arabic); T. Alexander Aleinikoff, "Theories of Loss of Citizenship", *Immigration & Nationality Law Review*, Vol. I81, 1988, pp. 81–113; Sandifer, *op. cit.*, pp. 261–278; Davies, *op. cit.*, pp. 296 ff.; Weis, *op. cit.*, pp. 119–138; Brownlie, "The Relations of Nationality...", *op. cit.*, pp. 339–344.

721 Piggott, *op. cit.*, p. 135.

722 See Palestinian Citizenship Order of 1925, Articles 11 and 14–16.

723 This article is taken directly from Article 16 of the British Nationality Act, 1914.

724 For a background on this article in British law, see Piggott, *op. cit.*, pp. 152–154.

2. *By any Palestinian: naturalization abroad*

Any Palestinian citizen, whoever natural-born or naturalized, would cease to be a Palestinian citizen if he, by his voluntary action abroad, acquired another nationality. In this regard, Article 15 of the 1925 Citizenship Order reads:

> A Palestinian citizen, who, when in any foreign State and not under disability, by obtaining a certificate of naturalization or by any other voluntary and formal act, becomes naturalized therein shall thenceforth be deemed to have ceased to be a Palestinian citizen.

This article was identical, *mutatis mutandis*, to Article 13 of the British Nationality Act, 1914. It is essential, therefore, to interpret the Palestinian article along the lines of its British counterpart. Three terms of the above-quoted Article require illustration: 'disability', 'foreign State' and 'voluntary and formal act'.

The expression 'not under disability' implied that only a person *sui juris* could divest himself or herself of Palestinian nationality. The categories of persons under disability were already defined by Article 21(4) of the Citizenship Order: "The expression 'disability' means the status of being a married woman or a minor, lunatic or idiot or otherwise legally incompetent". It was impossible, for example, for a married woman to change her nationality by naturalization abroad. If she did so, she would continue nonetheless to be considered as a Palestinian citizen under Article 15 of the Order.[725] Such a woman thereby became a dual national: she continued, on the one hand, to be a Palestinian citizen in the eyes of Palestinian law and, on the other hand, she enjoyed her newly acquired nationality.

As to the second expression ("when in any foreign State"), it appears from the language of Article 15 that the loss of nationality occurred as a result of naturalization *outside* of Palestine. Thus, it was said that a citizen "must be physically present in the foreign state at the time the formal act takes place".[726] It is unclear, however, why the effects of naturalization did not apply if it occurred while the naturalized person was present in Palestine or in a third state.[727] In practice, the result of naturalization in all cases was one; the person became a dual national. Perhaps for this reason some states regarded naturalization as a cause for nationality loss, whenever it occurred.[728]

On the other hand, the meaning of 'foreign state' in Britain did not at first include countries over which Britain had been exercising extraterritorial jurisdiction, such as colonies, protectorates and mandated territories. In other words, the

725 For the same situation in Britain, see Jones, *British Nationality Law and Practice*, *op. cit.*, p. 199; Piggott, *op. cit.*, pp. 138–143.

726 Jones, *British Nationality Law and Practice, op. cit.*, p. 195. See also, Piggott, *op. cit.* p. 136.

727 See Jones, *British Nationality Law and Practice, op. cit.*, p. 195.

728 See, for instance, Austria Federal Law of 30 July 1925 (Collection of Nationality Laws, p. 17), paragraph 10(1); Belgium Law of 15 May 1922, *op. cit.*, Article 18(1); Netherlands Law of 12 December 1892 (Collection of Nationality Laws, p. 440), Article 7(3); Norway Law of 8 August 1924, *op. cit.*, Article 8.

person would not lose his British nationality by naturalization in such countries.[729] Thus, one writer contended in 1929 that Britons who acquired Palestinian nationality by naturalization were able to retain British nationality because "they do not entertain any fresh allegiance, and for this purpose Palestine cannot be regarded as a foreign State in relation to the Mandatory".[730] But by the British administrative practice, such territories were later considered to be foreign states for the purpose of naturalization and, therefore, British citizens naturalized therein were deemed as foreigners in Britain.[731]

In the case of Palestine, this question did not arise as Palestine did not exercise extraterritorial rights in any foreign country. Besides, had this practice been considered valid, it would have explicitly contradicted Article 21(3) of the Citizenship Order, which defined the 'Alien' as a "person who is not a Palestinian citizen" and British citizens were for sure not Palestinians. It follows that all other countries were included in the expression 'foreign state' *vis-à-vis* Palestine. Indeed, in *Jawdat Badawi Sha'ban v. Commissioner for Migration and Statistics*,[732] the Palestine Supreme Court held that the petitioner ceased to be a Palestinian citizen because he had been naturalized in Trans-Jordan.[733]

Lastly, the expression 'voluntary and formal act' excluded the cases of forced naturalization. "The reason or motive underlying the act of acquiring a foreign nationality is not material, but the intention to acquire it must be present".[734] "If, for instance, the name of a child of full age is put on a foreign naturalization certificate by his parents abroad",[735] Article 15 of the Order would not operate to deprive him of his Palestinian nationality, "because it is not a voluntary act on his part".[736] Thus, the involuntary naturalization of a person by the law of another state as a result of residence in that state as well as naturalization of persons *en masse* against their will produced no effect under Article 15 of the Citizenship Order.[737]

There was nothing in the said Order requiring governmental authorization for naturalization abroad. Hence, such authorization was not required, especially because in Britain, since 1870, nationality could be renounced without authorisation.[738] According to this rule, Palestine accepted the principle of nationality change, which had been hitherto prohibited, with the sole exception of special authorization from

729 See Piggott, *op. cit.*, pp. 155–156.
730 Bentwich, "The Mandate for Palestine", *op. cit.*, p. 141.
731 Jones, *British Nationality Law and Practice, op. cit.*, pp. 195–196.
732 *Op. cit.*
733 This example is particularly significant as Trans-Jordan enjoyed special relations with Palestine according to the Palestine Mandate; see above pp. 46–48.
734 Jones, *British Nationality Law and Practice, op. cit.*, p. 196.
735 *Ibid.*
736 *Ibid.*
737 For details on this point in British law, see *ibid.*, pp. 196–199; and Piggott, *op. cit.*, pp. 137–138.
738 Piggott, *op. cit.*, p. 136, pp. 143–144.

the Ottoman government.[739] Still, governmental authorization for the change of nationality continued to be required by other nationality laws at the time, notably in ex-Ottoman states that have a majority of Muslim population, including Albanian,[740] Egypt,[741] Hejaz (Saudi Arabia),[742] Persia (Iran),[743] and Turkey itself.[744]

The principle point of Article 15 was to reduce the number of dual nationality cases to a minimum. This was in conformity with the Convention on Certain Questions relating to the Conflict of Nationality Laws, 1930,[745] whereby every person "should have one nationality only" (preamble). Indeed, the small number of persons who lost their nationality under Article 15 was insignificant: from 1925 to 1945, the nationality of only 205 Palestinian citizens was revoked.[746]

3. *By naturalized citizens: revocation as punishment*

Persons who became Palestinian citizens by naturalization could cease to be Palestinian in the cases spelled out by Article 10(1) of the Citizenship Order:

> Where it appears to the High Commissioner that a certificate of naturalisation granted by him has been obtained by false representation or fraud or by concealment of material circumstances, or that the person to whom the certificate is granted has, since the grant, been for a period of not less than three years ordinarily resident out of Palestine, or has shown himself by act or speech disaffected, or disloyal to the Government of Palestine, the High Commissioner may, subject to the approval of one of His Majesty's Principle Secretaries of State, by order revoke the certificate, and the order of revocation shall have effect from such date as the High Commissioner may direct.

This provision was borrowed, with certain modifications, from Article 7(1) of the British Nationality Act, 1914. It referred to three reasons for, or cases of, nationality revocation; namely fraud, absence, and disloyalty.

In the case of fraud, which constituted a criminal act, and resulted in the revocation of nationality, the person was sometimes subject to another penalty. Such a penalty, which was also applicable to other nationality offences, was prescribed by Article 22 of the Citizenship Order:

> If any person for any of the purposes of this Order knowingly makes any false representation or any statement false in a material particular, he shall, in Palestine, be

739 See above pp. 30–34.
740 Civil Code of 1 April 1929, *op. cit.*, Articles 11 and 12.
741 Decree Law of 27 February 1929, *op. cit.*, Article 12.
742 Law of 24 September 1926, *op. cit.*, Article 6.
743 Law of 7 September 1929 (Collection of Nationality Laws, p. 473), Articles 13(2) and 14.
744 Law of 28 May 1928 (*ibid.*, p. 570), Articles 7 and 8. See also Afghanistan Code of August 1921, *op. cit.*, Article 91.
745 See below Chapter X.
746 Of these, 64 were Jews and 141 Arabs (Statistical Abstract of Palestine 1944–1945, *op. cit.*, p. 47). See also Report on the Administration of Palestine 1935, *op. cit.*, p. 70.

liable on convection in respect of such offence to imprisonment with or without hard labour for any term not exceeding three months.[747]

Residence abroad for three years was considered a sufficient reason for the revocation of Palestinian nationality. This period was a relatively short time by comparison with similar requirements in other states. In Britain, seven years of residence abroad led one to have his or her naturalization status revoked.[748] The reason why Palestinian nationality was revocable following only three years' residence abroad was due to the short period (two years) of residence required for the acquisition of Palestinian citizenship by naturalization.[749] This rule was executed several times, chiefly due to emigration from Palestine. In 1932, for instance, 78 naturalization certificates were annulled for pro longed absence.[750]

Lastly, being 'disloyal to the Government of Palestine' was a vague expression and a rather loose reason by which the Government might revoke the nationalization of its opponents as punishment. In British law there were and continue to be specific criteria for the revocation of naturalization status such as collaborating 'with the enemy', committing certain crimes or continuing to be a national of a country at war with Britain, all of which may be deemed to constitute disloyalty.[751]

Nationality laws of other states tended to revoke nationality if their citizens (natural and naturalized alike) committed acts, which amounted to disloyalty. Such acts included, for example, accepting public office or serving in the military forces in another state, particularly if the person had been requested to cease such activities.[752] The deprivation of nationality might be more widely exercised if the person acted as an agent or carried out other activities, which were deemed to amount to collaboration with the enemy.[753] Thus, while Palestinian law was vague about the revocation of nationality due to acts of disloyalty, it was at least to be commended for limiting such revocations to naturalized citizens.

---

747 This article is a direct application to Article 23 of the British Nationality Act, 1914.

748 See Nationality and Status of Aliens Act, 1914, Article 6(2)(d).

749 See above pp. 116–117.

750 British Government, *Report to the Council of the League of Nations on the Administration of Palestine and Trans-Jordan*, 1932 (hereinafter: 'Report on the Administration of Palestine 1932'), p. 24.

751 See British Nationality Act, 1914, Article 7(2)(a), (b) and (e). See Piggott, *op. cit.*, pp. 154–155; and Jones, *British Nationality Law and Practice, op. cit.*, pp. 200–201.

752 See the following nationality laws: France Law of 10 August 1927, *op. cit.*, Article 9(4); Germany Law of 22 July 1913, *op. cit.*, Article 28; Greece Law of 29 October 1856, *op. cit.*, Article 23(b); Italy Law of 13 June 1912, *op. cit.*, Article 8(3); Netherlands Law of 12 December 1892, *op. cit.*, Article 7(4); Panama Law of 22 August 1916, *op. cit.*, Article 136(2); Poland Law of 20 January 1920, *op. cit.*, Article 11(2); Portugal Civil Code of 1867, *op. cit.*, Article 22(2).

753 France Law of 10 August 1927, *op. cit.*, Article 9(5); Germany Law of 22 July 1913, *op. cit.*, Article 27; Panama Law of 22 August 1916, *op. cit.*, Article 136(4); Romania Law of 23 February 1924, *op. cit.*, Article 41; Turkey Law of 28 May 1928, *op. cit.*, p. 570, Articles 10 and 11; Yugoslavia Law of 21 September 1928, *op. cit.*, Article 33.

In all these cases, the person whose nationality is revoked may have become stateless: having on the one hand lost his foreign nationality when he acquired Palestinian nationality, and, on the other hand, being deprived of his Palestinian nationality. Again, these cases are connected only with naturalized persons; they do not include native Palestinians who acquired nationality by natural change from Ottoman nationality or their descendants. In other words, with the exception of voluntary naturalization abroad, the nationality of natural Palestinians could not be revoked under any circumstance.

4. *By marriage*

As a general rule governing the 1925 Palestinian Citizenship Order, when a man lost his Palestinian nationality by any reason, his wife and minor children would by extension cease to be Palestinian citizens. The loss of nationality in such a case, however, was not automatic. It required a separate governmental decision on a case-by-case basis. This rule was evident in the first phrase of Article 11(1) of the Citizenship Order:

> Where a certificate of naturalization is revoked, the High Commissioner may by order direct that the wife and minor children (or any of them) of the person whose certificate is revoked shall cease to be Palestinian citizens, and any such person shall thereupon become an alien.

This rule implied that if the Government of Palestine did not revoke the nationality of the wife and children of a Palestinian man naturalized abroad, the woman and children would remain Palestinians. Thus, Article 11(1) added that "the nationality of the wife and minor children of the person whose certificate is revoked shall not be affected by the revocation, and they shall remain Palestinian citizens". In particular, the Government could not revoke the nationality of such a woman if she was a natural-born Palestinian. But Palestinian nationality might be revoked if the Government was convinced that the woman was naturalized in the state of her husband's nationality at her own choice (i.e. not *ipso facto* by the foreign law).[754]

If the married woman continued to be a Palestinian citizen, it was possible for her to declare that she did not wish to continue being a Palestinian. In this case, she would have been compelled to make a declaration of alienage within six months after the date of the nationality revocation of her Palestinian husband,[755] "and thereupon she and any minor children of her husband and herself...shall become aliens".[756]

---

754 See Palestinian Citizenship Order of 1925, Article 11(1)(*b*).

755 On the form required for this declaration, see Palestinian Citizenship Regulations of 1925, Article 7 and Annex 1, Form 4 attached thereof.

756 See Article 11(1)(*a*) of the Citizenship Order, 1925.

In all cases, a woman having lost her Palestinian nationality by marrying a foreigner could retain her Palestinian nationality or be exceptionally naturalized as a Palestinian. Such a woman was empowered to retain the status of a Palestinian citizen for the duration of her marriage, even if her husband became a foreigner. This woman was permitted to apply for naturalization in Palestine once she separated (not necessarily divorced) from her foreign husband who had held Palestinian citizenship in the past, if such separation was considered to be permanent. These two cases were recognized in Article 12 of the Citizenship Order:

> (1) ... [W]here a man ceases during the continuance of his marriage to be a Palestinian citizen... it shall be lawful for his wife to make a declaration... that she desires to retain the status of Palestinian citizen and thereupon she shall be deemed to remain a Palestinian citizen.[757]
> (2) Where the wife of an alien who was a Palestinian... is living apart from her husband in such circumstances that the separation may... be presumed to be permanent, the High Commissioner may... grant her a certificate of naturalisation as if the marriage has been dissolved.[758]

These rules constituted exceptions to the general principle that the "wife of a Palestinian citizen shall be deemed to be a Palestinian citizen and the wife of an alien shall be deemed to be an alien".[759]

Another exception to this principle was the death of the husband or the dissolution of the marriage, both of which were not considered as sufficient reasons for the wife to lose her nationality. This rule, as drawn up in Article 13 of the Citizenship Order (which was taken, *mutatis mutandis*, from Article 11 of the British Nationality Act, 1914), stated:

> A woman who, having been a Palestinian citizen has by, or in consequence of, her marriage became an alien, shall not by reason only of the death of her husband, or the dissolution of her marriage, cease to be an alien, and a woman, who, having been an alien has by, or in consequence of, her marriage became a Palestinian citizen, shall not by reason only of the death of her husband or the dissolution of her marriage cease to be a Palestinian citizen.

Thus, a widow or a divorcee who was a Palestinian citizen before her marriage, but became an alien by, or in consequence of, her marriage, could either avail herself of Article 12(1) or become naturalized like any foreigner according to the general terms of naturalization.[760]

---

757 On the procedural aspects which gave effect to this rule, see Palestinian Citizenship Regulations of 1925, Article 8 and Annex 1, Form 5 attached thereof.

758 *Cf.* British Nationality Act, 1914, Article 10, second sentence. For details in Britain, see Jones, *British Nationality Law and Practice, op. cit.*, pp. 185–186.

759 See above pp. 120–121.

760 See Jones, *British Nationality Law and Practice, op. cit.*, pp. 188–189. On the resumption of nationality in Britain, with special reference to married women, see Piggott, *op. cit.*, pp. 159–164.

5. *Declaration of alienage by minors*

The declaration of alienage, by which the persons expresses their desire to abandon their nationality, was recognized in the 1925 Citizenship Order in two instances.[761]

The first relates to children who became Palestinians as a result of the naturalization of their parents. After recognizing the rule that a minor child would acquire Palestinian nationality following the naturalization of his parents, Article 9(1) of the Citizenship Order provided that "any such child may, within twelve months after attaining his majority, make a declaration of alienage and shall thereupon cease to be a Palestinian citizen".[762] The twelve-month period "cannot be extended".[763] Otherwise, the person would have become a dual national.

The second case of the declaration of alienage concerned citizens who were born as Palestinians and had acquired foreign nationality upon their birth or during their minority age for any reason (other than the reason of the first case). Article 16 of the Order stipulates this rule as follows:

> Any person who...has by birth become a Palestinian citizen but who at his birth or during his minority became under the law of any other State a national of that State and is still such a national may, if of full age and not under disability, make a declaration of alienage and on making such declaration shall cease to be a Palestinian citizen.[764]

The object of this rule was to enable persons who acquired foreign citizenship in addition to their Palestinian nationality at birth (e.g. due to the birth in a country where the principle *jus soli* prevailed) or while at a minority age (e.g. as a result of the naturalization of the parents abroad), to elect in favour of a foreign nationality. In order for the person to make the declaration of alienage, he had still to be in the possession of a foreign nationality as he would be otherwise become stateless.[765]

It is true that a citizen could always renounce his Palestinian nationality by acquiring another nationality abroad. But such a citizen could not be naturalized in the country in which he had already acquired its nationality by birth. For this reason, the declaration of alienage was added in order to give such persons the

761 For procedures of the declaration, see Palestinian Citizenship Regulations of 1925, Article 5 and Annex 1, Form 3 attached thereof. This form relates to the first case the declaration only. No form is provided in the Regulations for the second case.

762 The same rule is to be found in Article 5(1) of the British Nationality Act, 1914.

763 Jones, *British Nationality Law and Practice, op. cit.*, p. 166.

764 This rule is inspired by Article 14 of the British Nationality Act, 1914. This British article is more detailed than Article 16 of the Citizenship Order of 1925. Article 14 gave the possibility to renounce nationality for persons who were born in Britain and acquired its nationality by birth although they may never have had any substantial connection with British territory (Jones, *British Nationality Law and Practice, op. cit.*, pp. 202–206). This was not the case in Palestine, in which *jus sanguinis* prevailed, whereby the mere fact of birth therein did not serve as a basis for nationality acquisition.

765 In this meaning, see Jones, *British Nationality Law and Practice, op. cit.*, p. 202.

choice to release themselves from Palestinian nationality.[766] This choice would help such persons to maintain their foreign nationality in countries where dual nationality was strictly forbidden.

In both cases of the declaration of alienage, children of persons who made such a declaration would lose their Palestinian nationality, except if they became stateless (because, for example, the country of their father's new nationality did not confer its nationality on the children of naturalized persons). Article 14(1) of the Citizenship Order advanced this rule as follows:

> Where a person ceases to be a Palestinian citizen, whether by declaration of alienage or otherwise…, every child of that person being a minor shall thereupon cease to be a Palestinian citizen, if such child has already obtained or obtains, on its parent ceasing to be a Palestinian citizen, the nationality of some other country.[767]

Again, any child of such a person "may, within one year after attaining his majority, make a declaration that he wishes to resume the status of a Palestinian citizen, and shall thereupon become a Palestinian".[768]

766 On the historical origin of the declaration of alienage in Britain, see Piggott, *op. cit.*, pp. 146–147.

767 This paragraph added that "where a widow who is a Palestinian citizen marries an alien, any child of hers by her former [Palestinian] husband shall not, by reason only of her marriage, cease to be a Palestinian citizen, whether he is residing outside Palestine or not". This provision covers the children of a Palestinian man in case of their father's death and subsequent marriage of their mother with a foreigner, acquisition by her of his nationality and residing with him abroad. Her Palestinian children may acquire a foreign nationality following her if the law of the state of her naturalization naturalize her children as well. For details, see Jones, *British Nationality Law and Practice*, *op. cit.*, pp. 100, 189–194.

768 Palestinian Citizenship Order of 1925, Article 14(2). This article is the counterpart of Article 12 of the British Nationality Act, 1914. On the procedural aspects of such a declaration, see Palestinian Citizenship Regulations of 1925, Article 9 and Annex 1, Form 6 attached thereof.

VIII

EXTERNAL ASPECTS OF PALESTINIAN NATIONALITY

1. *Recognition of Palestinian nationality by states*[769]

Besides the collective recognition of Palestinian nationality by the League of Nations and its Member States (which had been done, *inter alia*, by Article 7 of the Palestine Mandate), the recognition of the nationality of Palestinian citizens as individuals by other states is significant. It shows the extent to which that nationality was legitimate in principle and effective in practice. Generally, states recognized the existence of a distinct Palestinian nationality and treated its bearers as ordinary citizens of a foreign country. In particular, no state had denied the existence of that nationality.

Nevertheless, certain writers expressed some doubt over the existence of a distinct Palestinian nationality.[770] It has been noted:

> [I]t was arguable that, under the words of the Treaty of Lausanne, the inhabitants of Palestine became nationals of the mandatory state. The point was in fact taken in an extradition case which came before the High Court of Palestine....[771] The Persons were

769 The external aspects of Palestinian nationality, as is the case of other nationalities, are many, and it is not the intention here to discuss them all (see the Introduction of the present study). Moreover, this chapter does not prejudice the relevant external, or international, aspects of nationality within Palestine. All previous chapters contained international elements in one way or another. Determining the nationality of Palestinians in the transitional period (1917–1925) in Palestine according to the British practice, or to the Palestine Mandate and the Treaty of Lausanne, are all international matters. Even studying the substantive provisions of the 1925 Palestinian Citizenship Order relates to international law because it was enacted on behalf of the international community by Britain.

770 Particularly, during the transitional period of Palestinian nationality, December 1917–July 1925; see above Chapter III.

771 *Attorney-General v. Goralschwili and Another, op. cit.* It should be recalled that this case was decided before February 1925, i.e. prior to the enactment of the Palestinian Citizenship Order of 1925; see *supra* note 374.

> wanted by the Italian Government on a charge of fraudulent bankruptcy in Italy, and it was argued that they should not be surrendered because the Anglo-Italian Extradition Treaty (which applies to Palestine) provides that subjects of the Contracting Powers are not to be surrendered, and the accused, who were alleged to be Ottoman subjects resident in Palestine, had become British subjects.[772]

Another jurist repeated this argument in 1947. Based on similar grounds, he said:

> It [Palestinian nationality] emanates from English law and, in a sense, it is a sort of British nationality from the international point of view. The state to which the territory of Palestine has been transferred, as contemplated by Article 30 of the Treaty of Lausanne, is Great Britain; and Palestinian citizens are, within the meaning of that treaty, British nationals. But they are not British subjects under the British nationality legislation of the United Kingdom.[773]

A third writer questioned whether Palestine's inhabitants enjoyed 'full' Palestinian nationality according to international law under the mandate.[774]

These arguments were put forward on two grounds. The first was that the inhabitants of Palestine became British citizens according to the Treaty of Lausanne of 1923. Secondly, the British citizen who acquired Palestinian citizenship by naturalization did not lose his British nationality, whereas naturalization abroad was a reason to lose British nationality according to the British law. Thus, as the argument went, Palestinians were British citizens.

However, the first argument was directly dismissed by repeated cases adjudicated in Palestine and in Britain. Courts in other states had confirmed the distinct existence of Palestinian nationality. Some of these cases will be addressed shortly. As far as the second argument is concerned, one must revert to British legal and administrative practice with regard to the nationalities of British colonies, protectorates and mandated territories.

As there was no statutory text determining the question of naturalization of British subjects in British-controlled territories, some writers concluded that naturalization in such territories did not lead to the loss of British nationality, as this

---

772 Bentwich, "Nationality in Mandate Territories", *op. cit.*, pp. 100–101. A final decision on the merits of this case was never rendered "because the criminal proceedings in Italy were dropped" (*ibid.*, p. 101).

773 Jones, *British Nationality Law and Practice, op. cit.*, p. 280. In his reply to the present argument of Jones, Weis (*op. cit.*, p. 26) accurately concluded: "The conferment of the status of British protected persons on *ressortissants* of Mandated...Territories administrated by the United Kingdom is undoubtedly consistent with international law, but *one can hardly conclude therefrom that they thereby become nationals of the Mandatory*" (emphasis added). Abi-Saab (*op. cit.*, p. 48) explained: "The interpretation of article 30 of the Treaty of Lausanne could have...created a controversy. If interpreted in a vacuum it could be said that 'nationals of the state to which such territory is transferred' meant nationals of the Mandatory. But such an interpretation in addition to straining the text, would be inconsistent with article 22 of the Covenant [of the League of Nations] and with the Mandate instruments...to which it was supposed to give emphasis and sanction".

774 Zimmermann, *op. cit.*, pp. 233–235.

naturalization did not produce a new nationality. British citizens, on the other hand, would have lost their nationality upon naturalization in a foreign country according to Article 13 of the British Nationality Act, 1914. Thus, naturalization in such British-controlled territories, such as Palestine, did not produce, it was thought, a new nationality. However, British administrative practice had subsequently showed that such naturalization was indeed a reason for the loss of British nationality.[775]

In fact, retaining British nationality alongside Palestinian nationality was not possible in Palestine, as a rule. British citizens, as others, were requested to renounce their nationality when they desired to be naturalized as Palestinians. Members of the British forces who applied for naturalization in Palestine, for example, were requested to give up their former passports as part of their application. Yet, as it has been already seen,[776] many naturalized citizens from various nationalities, including Britain's, could in practice retain their former nationality. It should be recalled that Palestinian nationality, unlike nationalities of other British colonies and British mandated-territories,[777] had its own characteristics due to the international status of Palestine at that time.

Moreover, the argument that Palestinian nationality was a British nationality based on the fact that the Palestinian Citizenship Order of 1925 was derived from the British law was manifestly ill-founded. While it is true that Palestinian law was heavily influenced by the British nationality law, this did not mean that Palestinian nationality was interchangeable with British nationality. As it is well known, states tend to copy nationality laws and other legislation of other states as a whole or in part. There are countless examples in this regard.

Probably for this reason, the same jurist who was just quoted above, after introducing the aforementioned argument, added:

> At the same time, although there is no Palestinian state, Palestinian citizenship is a species of distinct nationality, though a very unusual one, deriving its legal validity from the law of the Administration of Palestine.[778]

It is not correct to argue that Palestinian citizenship derived "its legal validity from the law of the Administration of Palestine". Rather, it derived its legal validity from, in the first place, the international law of state succession as embodied in the Treaty of Lausanne (1923)[779] and, in the second place, from the Palestine Mandate (1922).[780] Even the substantive validity of Palestinian nationality, as embodied in the Palestinian Citizenship Order of 1925, was not derived "from the law of the Administration of Palestine"; it was enacted, as has already been seen, in London by the King of Britain in the form of an Order in Council.[781]

775 See above pp. 132–133.
776 See above pp. 119–120.
777 See above pp. 53, 55, 80–81.
778 Jones, *British Nationality Law and Practice, op. cit.*, p. 280.
779 See above Chapter III, Section 4.
780 See above Chapter III, Section 3.
781 See above Chapter IV, Section 1.

Domestic courts had frequently recognized the existence of a 'full', or ordinary, Palestinian nationality. Such examples included the courts of Egypt, United States and Uruguay, in addition to the British and Palestinian judiciary. This practice, by and large, is based on the courts' interpretation of international law as embodied in the nationality rules (Articles 30 to 36) of the Treaty of Lausanne.

As early as 15 December 1925, Palestinian citizens were recognized as foreigners in Egypt. An Egyptian court, in a judgment that summarizes international practice towards the nationality in mandated territories, concluded:[782]

> Ottoman territories placed under a Mandate have the character of regular States, and their inhabitants possess the nationality of these States in accordance with Article 30 of the Treaty of Lausanne. The plaintiff, therefore, has Palestinian nationality, and is a foreign subject in Egypt.[783]

In the United States, Palestinians were considered as ordinary foreigners. In *Klausner v. Levy*,[784] the Court, in recognizing the existence of Palestinian nationality,[785] stated:

> During the mandate Palestine could and did extend citizenship to its inhabitants, grant naturalization to immigrants and issue them passports for travel. Both native and naturalized nationals, at home and abroad, received the protection of the British Government.... Indeed, Britain was authorised to, and did, enter into treaties to gain for them rights and privileges from other nations, including the United States.

Other American courts confirmed this position. In *Lapides v. Clark, Attorney General*,[786] it was held that a naturalized citizen of the United States lost his American nationality if he resided in Palestine for more than five years and had, apparently, acquired Palestinian nationality by naturalization. In *Petition of Ajlouny*, "the petitioner, a native and citizen of Palestine, sought naturalization as a citizen of the United States". It was held that "the petitioner had the right to have his application for citizenship considered by the Court".[787]

In a case before a court in Uruguay, it was decided that the inhabitants of Palestine were not British citizens for the purpose of extradition.[788] It was suggested that "the Treaty of extradition between the British Government and the Uruguayan Government, dated 26 March, 1884, be construed to comprehend mandated territories held by Great Britain...". However, this Latin American Court stated:

---

782 *Saikaly v. Saikaly, op. cit.*

783 See also *N.N. Berouti v. Turkish Government, op. cit.*

784 District Court of Eastern District of Virginia, 10 March 1949 (Annual Digest, 1949, p. 37).

785 *Cf.* Abi-Saab, *op. cit.*, p. 50.

786 United States, Court of Appeals, District of California Circuit, 23 May 1949 (Annual Digest, 1949, p. 194).

787 United States, District Court for the Eastern District of Michigan, 23 April 1948 (Annual Digest, 1948, pp. 226, 693).

788 See The Alta Corte de Justicia de Uruguay, 7 March 1928 (Annual Digest, 1927–1928, p. 47).

> That the said treaty of extradition of 1884 cannot be applied to territories under the mandate mentioned.... As the territories under mandate are not 'one of the parties,' nor colonies or possessions of His Britannic Majesty, we are forced to reach the conclusion that the treaty of 1884 does not embrace the persons residing in those territories over which England exercises no more than a simple mandate.[789]

More importantly, a Palestinian citizen was treated as a foreigner in Britain before the English High Court, *The King v. Ketter*, in 1939.[790] The appellant was born as an Ottoman subject and subsequently became a Palestinian citizen. In 1937, Mr. Ketter travelled to England and overstayed therein, claiming that he was a British citizen and did not need to extend his residence permission. Consequently, he was convicted of an offence by the criminal court. He appealed, insisting that he was not a foreigner but a British citizen. Mr. Ketter based his argument, *inter alia*, on what he considered the invalidity of nationality provisions of the Treaty of Lausanne and Article 7 of the Palestine Mandate. Under Article 30 of the said treaty, he submitted, "Palestine was transferred to Great Britain and every Turkish subject resident in Palestine became *ipso facto* a subject of Great Britain". He added that the 1925 Palestinian Citizenship Order was invalid because it was enacted by Britain, not by the Administration of Palestine as provided in Article 7 of the Mandate.

Both arguments were rejected. The Court held that the provisions of the Treaty of Lausanne made the inhabitants of the territories detached from Turkey citizens of the detached territories, not of the Mandatory. It added that if the argument that the Citizenship Order was invalid according to Article 7 of the Mandate (which was not the case, as the Court noted), the inhabitants of Palestine would have remained Ottoman citizens.[791] The Court ultimately concluded that "nothing has been done in law to make him a subject of Great Britain". And, consequently, that Palestinian citizens were "not within the provisions of the British Nationality and Status of Aliens Act, 1914, because there has been no annexation of Palestine".

This British judgement was in line with British practice in creating a separate Palestinian nationality. From the outset, Britain treated the Palestinians as foreigners on its own territory. In 1929, the League of Nations asked whether residence in Palestine qualifies as residence for the naturalization purpose in Britain.[792] The British Government replied in the negative.[793] It added: "Residence in Palestine was a qualification only for Palestinian naturalisation".

---

789 See also *Attorney-General v. Goralschwili and another, op. cit.*, in which the Supreme Court of Palestine reached the same conclusion.

790 *Op. cit.*

791 Indeed, this practice was in accordance with international law. For example, the Permanent Court of International Justice (in *Mavrommatis Palestine Concessions, op. cit.*, pp. 7, 12–15, 17, 19, 24) did not distinguish between the Government of Palestine and Britain. Both were considered as one entity in relation to Palestine.

792 Mandates Commission Minutes 1929, *op. cit.*, p. 100.

793 *Ibid.*

Accordingly, the position of Palestinian citizens under British law differed from that of British citizens.[794] Palestinians were considered as foreigners for the purpose of the British Aliens Orders.[795] They were unable, as such, to enter Britain without special permission.[796] In the British territory, a Palestinian citizen had no political rights, including voting in parliamentary elections.[797] During World War II, Palestinian citizens in Britain were issued with Certificates of Alien Registration.[798] Finally, the Palestinians were not subject to the obligations of national service.[799]

The Supreme Court of Palestine repeatedly decided that Palestinians were foreigners in Britain. As early as February 1925, in *Attorney General v. Goralschwili and Another*,[800] it held that "subjects of the Mandated territory did not become British subjects". Twenty years later, the same Court, in *Sheinfeld v. Officer Commanding No. 3 Court Martial and Holding Centre*... (16 February 1945),[801] reaffirmed that it was "perfectly true that Palestinians are not British subjects". It did not derogate from this status, as accepted by the League of Nations, the fact that Palestinian citizens were British protected persons.[802]

To sum up, the arguments that the Palestinians were British subjects (citizens or nationals) or that Palestinian nationality was not 'full' citizenship under the mandate are, upon careful investigation, groundless. The relationship between Palestinian and British nationalities did not differ from the relationship between British nationality and the nationality of any other British-controlled territory.

Further evidence of the existence of a distinct Palestinian nationality was the existence, and states' recognition, of Palestinian passports.

2. *Palestinian passports*

As noted earlier,[803] a system of passports was first introduced in Palestine as early as 1920.[804] Recognizing the fact that the passport was inherently connected

794 See also Stoyanovsky, *op. cit.*, p. 278.

795 Mervyn Johns, "Who Are British Protected Persons?", *The British Year Book of International Law*, 1945, p. 128.

796 *Ibid.*

797 *Ibid.*

798 Weis, *op. cit.*, p. 24.

799 *Ibid.*

800 *Op. cit.*

801 *Op. cit.*

802 Permanent Mandates Commission, *Minutes of the Twentieth Session*, League of Nations, Geneva, 1931 (hereinafter: 'Mandates Commission Minutes 1931'), p. 92. For the same conclusion, see Report on the Administration of Palestine 1930, *op. cit.*, p. 37. See also below Chapter VIII, Section 3.

803 See above pp. 54–55.

804 On the passport regime in international law, in general, see Daniel C. Turack, *The Passport in International Law*, D.C. Heath and Company, Massachusetts/Toronto/London, 1972; David W. Williams, "British Passport and the Right to Travel", *International and*

with the nationality, the Government of Palestine enacted the Passport Ordinance on 16 December 1925,[805] a few months after the entering into force of the Palestinian Citizenship Order (1 August 1925). The Passport Ordinance had regulated the rules governing the 'Palestinian passport' in a comprehensive manner. In effect, thereafter, the regular Palestinian passport was first printed in 1926.[806]

In the country, passports had been issued by the Department of Immigration of the Government of Palestine. The Department's headquarters was established in Jerusalem and some branch offices were opened in major districts, such as Jaffa and Haifa. The High Commissioner, who formally signed each passport, was empowered to issue passports in his capacity as Chief Executive of Palestine, on behalf of the British Government.

In its appearance, the passport reflected the relationship between Palestine and Britain in regard to the travel of the Palestinians abroad. The outside cover of the Palestinian passport was marked, in the English language, 'BRITISH PASSPORT', and then followed by 'PALESTINE'. But in both Arabic and Hebrew languages, the word 'PALESTINE' was replaced by 'THE GOVERNMENT OF PALESTINE'.[807] On the internal cover page of the passport, where the High Commissioner put his signature, it was indicated:

Comparative Law Quarterly, Vol. 23, 1974, pp. 642–656; Guy S. Goodwin-Gil, *International Law and the Movement of Persons between States*, Clarendon Press, Oxford, 1978, pp. 24–50; Paul Lansing, "Freedom to Travel: Is the Issuance of a Passport an Individual Right or a Government Prerogative?", *Denver Journal of International Law and Policy*, Vol. 11, 1981, pp. 15–35; Richard Plender, *International Migration Law*, Martinus Nijhoff, Dordrecht/Boston/London, 1988, pp. 95–131; John Torpey, *The Invention of the Passport: Surveillance, Citizenship and the State*, Cambridge University Press, Cambridge, 2000; Weis, *op. cit.*, pp. 219–229.

805 See Passport Ordinance of 1925 (Palestine Gazette, 16 December 1925, p. 1073). The 1925 Ordinance was subsequently amended as passport Ordinances were enacted in 1928, 1932, 1934 and 1938. The most important of these, which has never been repealed, is the Passport Ordinance of 1934 (Palestine Gazette, No. 476, Supplement 1, 9 November 1934, p. 337). In its Annex 2, the latter Ordinance replaced the previous passport Ordinances and consolidated their provisions. Passport Ordinance (Amendment) of 1938 (Palestine Gazette, No. 792, Supplement 1, 30 June 1938, p. 56) is also significant. It, along with the 1934 Ordinance, has never been repealed. On the other hand, procedures to obtain a passport (e.g. the responsible authority of passport's issuance, required documents, application forms and the fees) were regulated by the following instruments: Passport Rules of 1925 (Laws of Palestine, p. 2327); Passport Regulations of 1934 (Palestine Gazette, No. 476, Supplement 1, 9 November 1934, p. 343—annexed to the Passport Ordinance of 1934); Passport Regulations of 1936 (Palestine Gazette, No. 374, Supplement 2, 28 May 1936, p. 501)—this was the main and the most detailed legislation of all passport Regulations); Passport Regulations of 1938 (Palestine Gazette, No. 778, Supplement 2, 28 April 1938, p. 598).

806 Report on the Administration of Palestine 1934, *op. cit.*, p. 62.

807 Without mentioning 'BRITISH PASSPORT' in Arabic or in Hebrew languages.

> By His Majesty's High Commissioner for Palestine
> These are to request and require in the Name of His Majesty all those whom it may concern to allow the bearer to pass freely without let or hindrance and to afford [him/her] every assistance and protection of which [he/she] may stand in need.

In addition, on the first page of the passports, under the heading of 'nationality', the relevant article from the Palestinian Citizenship Order of 1925, according to which Palestinian nationality was obtained, was indicated (e.g. for native Palestinians: Article 1; for naturalized persons: Article 7; for persons naturalized by marriage: Article 12). This, in fact, was similar to the way in which British passports were designed.[808] In recognition of the particular linguistic situation in Palestine and of practical international needs, the contents of Palestinian passports were written in four languages: Arabic, English, Hebrew (the three official languages of Palestine)[809] and French. Palestinian passports were valid for a term of five years or less. They were renewable for a further term or terms of one or more years, provided that the total period of validity was not exceeding ten years.[810]

Moreover, the Government of Palestine had acted on behalf of Britain (or on behalf of governments of British controlled territories—as it will be seen soon) on matters relating to the travel of British citizens and British protected persons residing in Palestine. In *Greenbaum v. Oizerman*,[811] it was reported that: "The applicant submitted her [British] passport issued in her name on April 19, 1941, by the Officer Administrating the Government of Palestine for H.M. High Commissioner in Palestine. On the first page of the said passport is recorded in handwriting 'British subject by marriage, wife of British subject by birth'".[812] Also, the Government of Palestine granted visas to Palestinian citizens and foreign residents who intended to travel to Britain. In 1922, the said Government issued 272 British passports and 11,515 visas to Britain.[813] In 1932, the same Government granted "7,005 passports, visas...on behalf of British, Iraqi, and Sudan Governments".[814]

Palestinians were entitled to request passports from British embassies or consulates abroad. In 1927, for example, 11,900 Palestinian passports were granted, including 767 issued by British consuls abroad.[815] In *Yohannanoff v. Commissioner for Migration and Statistics*,[816] it was indicated that a Palestinian passport was issued from the British consulate in Algiers, Algeria. In Britain (as well as in British domains, colonies and mandated territories), applications for Palestinian

808 See *Greenbaum v. Oizerman, op. cit.*
809 See above p. 118.
810 See Article 4(3) of both Passport Ordinances of 1925 and of 1934.
811 *Op. cit.*
812 Britain provided on a regular basis detailed statistics with regard to passports, travel documents, identity cards and visas related to Palestinians and foreigners residing in Palestine to the League of Nations. See, e.g., Report on the Administration of Palestine 1934, *op. cit.*, p. 61; Report on the Administration of Palestine 1935, *op. cit.*, p. 71.
813 Report on Palestine Administration 1922, *op. cit.*, p. 53.
814 Report on the Administration of Palestine 1932, *op. cit.*, p. 43.
815 British Government, *Report to the Council of the League of Nations on the Administration of Palestine and Trans-Jordan*, 1927, p. 70.
816 *Op. cit.*

passports had to be submitted to the local authorities. Palestinian citizens had to obtain an entry visa to travel to other British controlled territories.[817] This practice had been formulated by Regulation 1 indicated at the last page of the Palestinian passport, which, in part, stated:

> Applications for the issue or renewal of Palestine passports by residents in Palestine should be made on the appropriate form at one of the Offices of the Department of Immigration. Residents abroad should make application to British Diplomatic or Consular Officers and in the case of residents in the United Kingdom, the British Dominions, Colonies and Mandated Territories to the local authorities.

Since its inception, the issuance of Palestinian passports was relatively high. In the last three months of 1926, when the passport started to be regularly printed, the Government of Palestine issued 1,314 Palestinian passports.[818] In the period of 1926 to 1935, some 70,000 Palestinian passports were issued.[819] Travel from and into Palestine was intensive as well. In the year 1932, for instance, it was reported that in addition to travel to Trans-Jordan (which was taking place on a daily basis in simplified procedures),[820] "30,898 residents of Palestine left during the year...and 30,696 returned.... The net balance outwards was 202".[821]

The high demand for passports and the active movement of persons from and into Palestine had been increased under the British rule for a number of reasons. These included the mass foreign, especially Jewish, immigration into, and naturalization in, Palestine;[822] the growth of business and transport relations between Palestine and other states, particularly neighbouring countries and Europe; and the requirement for children over 16 years of age to possess passports.[823] More importantly, Palestine's inhabitants wanted "to be in possession of a Palestinian passport as documentary proof of their legal presence in the country".[824] The latter reason probably arose due to the British policy which favoured the naturalization of immigrant Jews over the return of Arab Palestine-natives to the country.[825]

---

817 Regulation 4 indicated at the last page of the Palestinian passport.

818 British Government, *Report to the Council of the League of Nations on the Administration of Palestine and Trans-Jordan*, 1926, p. 60.

819 Report on the Administration of Palestine 1935, *op. cit.*, p. 71. The total number of the population of Palestine in 1935 was 1,308,112 million (Survey of Palestine, Vol. I, p. 141). This number included women and children under the age of 16 who were included in the passport of their husbands or fathers and did not require separate passports.

820 On the movement between Palestine and Trans-Jordan, see below pp. 161–162.

821 Report on the Administration of Palestine 1932, *op. cit.*, p. 24.

822 In this respect, it may be noted that "the Palestine Committee of the Agency (Palestine Zionist Executive) and the Head Office of the Zionist Organization had been afforded the special opportunity of expressing their views on the draft Passport...Ordinances and Regulations" (Report on the Administration of Palestine 1925, *op. cit.*, p. 67).

823 Report on the Administration of Palestine 1932, *op. cit.*, p. 24.

824 *Ibid.*

825 See above Chapter V, Section 2.B.

A second type of passport called the 'border passport' was regulated in 1934.[826] Issued through a simple procedure, this passport eased the movement of persons between Palestine and its neighbouring countries (especially Trans-Jordan, Lebanon and Syria).[827] No fees were required for the issuance of this passport. Such a passport constituted in effect a sort of border pass. Yet the same rules relating to regular passports were applied to the border passports.[828]

It may be relevant to note that in times of emergency, the Government of Palestine instructed any Palestinian intending to travel abroad to obtain a travel permit, besides possessing the passport or the identity card.[829] Particularly, special permits were developed to travel to Trans-Jordan, Syria and Lebanon.[830]

A form of temporary passport, or travel document, was granted to foreign residents in Palestine as of 1925. This document was known as an 'Emergency Certificate'. It was defined in Article 2 of the Passport Ordinance of 1925 as "a document of identity issued under the authority of the High Commissioner for the purpose of travel outside Palestine". Article 3(1) of the same Ordinance added: "The High Commissioner may issue... emergency certificates to aliens and persons whose national status is not defined".[831] Such a certificate was "available only for the journey or journeys and the period specified thereon. Provided that the period of validity shall not in any case exceed one year from the date of issue".[832] Through this document, foreigners were able to enter Palestine without a visa.[833]

To qualify for such a document, the person had to be either stateless, of doubtful nationality or from a state/territory which had no diplomatic representation in Palestine.[834] These persons, mainly Jewish refugees, were allowed to enter Palestine

---

826 See Passport Ordinance, 1934, Article 2. See Passport Regulations, 1938, Article 2, Form 1 (application for the border pass) and Form 2 (application for the renewal of the border pass) annexed to these Regulations.

827 However, on the movement of persons residing in the border towns located at the Palestinian and Lebanese-Syrian borders, see below p. 162.

828 Passport Regulations, 1934, which fixed passport's fees, was silent with regard to the border passport. One year later, however, special regulations were introduced to issue the border passports free of charge (Palestine Gazette, No. 535, Supplement 2, 5 September 1935, p. 841).

829 Similar travel permits requested by the Israel military authorities from the residents of the West Bank and Gaza Strip after the 1967 occupation.

830 See Defence (Entry and Departure of Palestine) Order, 1942 (Palestine Gazette, No. 1164, Supplement 2, 22 January 1942, p. 229), Article 3 (including travel permit form).

831 See also Articles 2 and 3(*b*) of the Passport Ordinance, 1934.

832 Passport Ordinance of 1925, Article 4(4). See also Passport Ordinance of 1934, Article 4(4). Compare the travel documents that Israel granted to the Arab residents of East Jerusalem after its occupation and annexation of the city in 1967. Israel considered the Arabs of Jerusalem as foreigners who had permanent residence. These residents have the right to travel through an Israel-issued Laissez-passer, valid for one year. See Usama Halabi, *The Legal Status of Jerusalem and its Arab Citizens*, Institute for Palestine Studies, Beirut, 1997 (Arabic), pp. 79–120.

833 Passport Ordinance of 1934, Article 4(5).

834 Instructions to Immigration Officers, Article 60.

on exceptional cases. In this connection, Article 5(1) of the Immigration Ordinance of 1925,[835] stated:

> No person other than a Palestinian citizen shall enter Palestine except by permission of the Chief Immigration Officer; and such permission shall not be granted to any person to whom this Ordinance applies who...(*g*) has not in his possession a valid passport issued to him by or in behalf of the Government of the country of which he is a subject or citizen, or some other document establishing his nationality and identity.... Provided that in special cases the High Commissioner may grant permission to enter Palestine to any person who, either by reason of the fact that he is not recognized as a subject or citizen of any country or otherwise, is *bona fide* unable to obtain such a passport or document, but is, in his opinion, a suitable person for admission into Palestine.[836]

Apparently, this document was issued for humanitarian considerations. In this regard, the British Government declared:

> This form of document was brought into use in Palestine in conformity with the recommendations of the Third General Conference on Communication and Transport adopted by the Assembly of the League of Nations at Geneva on 26th September, 1927,[837] and is granted to stateless persons or to persons of doubtful nationality.[838]

In practice, this travel document was used as an identity document or card for internal use within Palestine.[839] Thus, the same application form was used for both identity cards and emergency travel documents. If the person intended to use the card to travel, he had to mention the countries for which he wished to travel, reasons for travel and the number of trips he expected to make.[840]

Furthermore, the Government of Palestine issued another voluntary identity card in 1938 for Palestinian citizens. In this connection, it was reported that "on 12th October [1938], a system of voluntary identity cards for male persons over 16 years of age was instituted".[841] This identity card was followed on 1 November 1938 by an Order that "issued under the Emergency Regulations prohibiting any male person from travelling by motor car or by train in the rural areas in Palestine without a pass issued by a Military Commander".[842] Thus, it seems that the issuance of these identity cards was motivated mainly by security concerns. Although it was

835 Legislation of Palestine, Vol. I, p. 579.

836 See also Immigration Ordinances of 1933 and of 1941, Article 5(1)(*g*).

837 But, as just mentioned, these documents existed in Palestine before 1925; not only after 1927.

838 Report on the Administration of Palestine 1935, *op. cit.*, p. 72.

839 British Government, *Report to the Council of the League of Nations on the Administration of Palestine and Trans-Jordan*, 1933 (hereinafter: 'Report on the Administration of Palestine 1933'), p. 55.

840 See Passport Regulations of 1936, Article 7, and Form 6 (application for: (a) 'Identity Card', (b) 'Identity Card and Travel'), annexed thereof.

841 Report on the Administration of Palestine 1938, *op. cit.*, p. 21.

842 *Ibid.*

'voluntary', it seems that the identity card had become compulsory in practice; it was strictly required for any motor transport within Palestine.[843]

The authoritarian and imperative character of the passport rules was self-evident. The Government of Palestine enjoyed absolute discretion to refuse issuing or to withdraw any passport or travel document without assigning any reason and without any right for the applicant to appeal these decisions.[844] In such cases, the applicant would be effectively prohibited from leaving the country. Moreover, the penalties related to violations of passport rules were generally strict.[845]

Passports rules discriminated against married women. Such a woman was obliged to be included within her husband's passport.[846] Article 9 and Form 8 of the Passport Regulations, 1936, provided special procedures relating to women in order for her to follow the passport, travel document and identity card of her husband. No similar rules were required to include the husband or children within either the wife's or mother's documents. A woman could not travel alone using her husband's passport. On the last page of the Palestinian passport, under 'Caution', it was indicated: "The wife and/or members of the family included in the passport should not travel on it unaccompanied by the owner". Hence, the wife could travel only accompanied by her husband. Ironically, fathers or guardians were able to request passports for children over the age of 16,[847] but women could not exercise this right (as no rule existed to this effect). This shows another face of the overall discriminatory nature of the nationality rules, as enshrined in the 1925 Citizenship Order, against married women who were considered 'disabled'.[848]

---

843 It is interesting to compare the identity cards issued by the Israel military authorities to the residents of the West Bank and Gaza Strip after the 1967 occupation. In the West Bank, see, for example, Order concerning Identity Cards and Population Registration (West Bank) (No. 297), 8 January 1969 (Proclamations, Orders and Appointments (West Bank), Vol. 19, 1969, p. 609). Article 2 of this military Order made it mandatory for males over the age of 16, but voluntary for women, to acquire identity cards from the military authorities. For similar situation in the Gaza Strip, see, for example, Order concerning Identity Cards (Gaza Strip and North Sinai) (No. 406), 1971, 25 October 1971 (Proclamations, Orders and Appointments (Gaza Strip), No. 31, 1 June 1972, p. 2477).

844 See Passport Ordinance of 1934, Article 3(c). See also *Jawdat Badawi Sha'ban v. Commissioner for Migration and Statistics, op. cit.*

845 These penalties ranged from a term of imprisonment not exceeding one year to fines, or both penalties. See Passport Ordinance of 1925, Articles 6–8; Passport Ordinance of 1934, Articles 5–6.

846 See Passport Regulations of 1936, Article 4, and Form 3 attached thereof (application to add a wife or children to the passport of a husband or a father).

847 Yet all data and documents requested for the passport's application were related to the father only. Again, see Passport Regulations of 1936, Articles 4 and 9, and Forms 3 and 8 attached thereof.

848 See above pp. 121–122. *Cf.* below pp. 187–190.

In the legal system that prevailed in Palestine under the British rule, as in other countries of the Common Law system, the passport alone was not regarded as a definitive proof of nationality.[849] The English High Court held that even if the passport which was in the possession of a Palestinian citizen was termed as a 'British Passport',[850] this would not make him a British citizen.[851] Yet the passport was considered *prima facie* evidence of Palestinian nationality. In order to request a Palestinian passport, for instance, the application "should be supported with evidence that the applicant has acquired Palestinian Citizenship".[852] To this effect, the Government of Palestine instructed its immigration officers with the following:

> As the possession of a Palestinian passport is *prima facie* evidence that the holder is a Palestinian citizen...such passports will not in general be examined.[853]

Under normal conditions, a Palestinian passport enabled its bearer to travel to all countries. In this respect, Regulation 4 of the last page of the Palestinian passport indicated: "This passport is only available for travel to the countries named on page 4". On page 4 of the passport, under the title "COUNTRIES FOR WHICH THIS PASSPORT IS VALID", it was indicated in handwriting: 'all countries'.

Palestinian passports were recognized abroad, including in Britain, as being akin to other ordinary passports. Thus, once abroad and by presenting their passports, Palestinian citizens were treated as British protected persons.[854]

3. *Protection of Palestinian citizens abroad*

In law and practice, the protection of individuals abroad is inherently connected with nationality.[855] It is well-established in international law that it is "the bond

---

849 See, e.g., Borchard, *op. cit.*, pp. 493–514 (with focus on American system); Weis, *op. cit.*, pp. 222–226 (with special reference to British system); Turack, *op. cit.*, pp. 230–232 (in general).

850 It may be recalled here that the Palestinian passport was entitled: '*British* Passport/ Palestine'.

851 *The King v. Ketter, op. cit.* See also *Klausner v. Levy, op. cit.*

852 Instructions to Immigration Officers, Article 58(iii).

853 *Ibid.*, Article 14. See also *Greenbaum v. Oizerman*, District Court of Tel-Aviv, Israel, 25 March 1949 (Annual Digest, 1949, p. 182).

854 Johns, "Who Are British Protected Persons?", *op. cit.*, p. 127; Weis, *op. cit.*, pp. 219–229.

855 See, in general, Everett P. Wheeler, "The Relation of the Citizen Domiciled in a Foreign Country to His Home Government", *The American Journal of International Law*, Vol. 3, 1909, pp. 869–884; Elihu Root, "The Basis of Protection to Citizens Residing Abroad", *ibid.*, Vol. 4, 1910, pp. 517–528; Frederick Sherwood Dunn, *The Protection of Nationals: A Study in the Application of International Law*, the Johns Hopkins Press, Baltimore, 1932; Edwin M. Borchard, "The Protection of Citizens Abroad and Change of Original Nationality", *Yale Law Journal*, Vol. 43, 1933–1934, pp. 359–392; Guy I.F. Leigh, "Nationality and Diplomatic Protection", *The International and Comparative Law*

of nationality between the State and the individual which alone confers upon the State the right of diplomatic protection".[856] But the existence of a special agreement to delegate the protection of citizens to another state is similarly a well-known practice in international law and relations.[857] Throughout the British rule in Palestine, 1917–1948, the protection of Palestinian citizens was exercised in line with these principles, taking into account the special status of Palestine as a mandated territory.[858]

Palestine's inhabitants had been considered as British protected persons since December 1917, when the country fell under British occupation, i.e. before the establishment of a Palestinian nationality.[859] Despite the adoption of the Mandate in 1922 and the enactment of the Palestinian Citizenship Order in 1925, this status had continued without remarkable change until the end of the mandate in 1948. Thus, the examination of the general status of British protected persons and its application to Palestinian citizens under the mandate is of relevance here.

According to general British practice, which had never been codified in a single instrument,[860] the term 'British Protected Person' included those individuals who derived their status from their connection with British colonies, protectorates,[861] and mandated territories.[862] The British Nationality Act, 1914, regulated the nationality of British citizens and not that of British protected persons. The nationality of the latter group was either regulated by domestic legislation issued by the government of its territories, or according to the practice in these territories without having a written nationality law.[863] Although they were considered foreigners in Britain,[864]

Quarterly, Vol. 20, 1971, pp. 453–475; Wilhelm Karl Geck, "Diplomatic Protection and the Extension of Individual Rights Through Treaties", *Law and State*, Vol. 31, 1985, pp. 42–63; Borchard, *The Protection of Citizens Abroad or the Law of International Claims, op. cit.*, particularly pp. 349 ff.; Borchard, "Basic Elements of Diplomatic Protection of Citizens Abroad", *op. cit.*, pp. 497–520; Turack, *op. cit.*, pp. 232–233.

856 *The Panevezys-Saldutiskis Railway (Estonia v. Lithuania)*, Permanent Court of International Justice (Judgement), 28 February 1939 (Permanent Court of International Justice, Series A/B, No. 76, p. 16). This statement of the latter Court was confirmed, as a well-established principle of international law, by the International Court of Justice in *the Nottebohm, op. cit.*, p. 13.

857 *The Nottebohm, ibid.*

858 See Mock, *op. cit.*, pp. 243–253.

859 See above p. 55.

860 This practice, however, was in line with the British Foreign Jurisdiction Act, 1890, *op. cit.*

861 The Palestine Court of Appeal held in 1937 that "in law there is no difference between the status of a Protectorate and that of a Mandated Territory"; *Sheriff Es Shanti v. Attorney General for Palestine, op. cit.*

862 Johns, "Who Are British Protected Persons?", *op. cit.*, p. 123.

863 See Johns, "British Nationality Act, 1948", *op. cit.*

864 Article 27(1) of the British Nationality Act, 1914, defined a 'British subject' as "a person who is a natural-born British subject, or a person to whom a certificate of [British] naturalization has been granted". It added: "The expression 'alien' means a person who is not a British subject".

"All British Protected Persons are, in foreign territory, treated as British nationals[865] and are entitled to the same protection as British subjects".[866] "The common feature of the various groups of British protected persons is that they habitually and permanently enjoy British protection without being British subjects".[867]

As early as June 1919, it was envisaged that the native inhabitants of the territories of mandates B and C (former German possessions) would be "entitled to the diplomatic protection of the Governments exercising authority over those territories", under Article 127 of the Treaty of Versailles with Germany.[868] In 1922, Britain informed the League of Nations that the nationality of the inhabitants of these territories remained unaffected by the mandate; it pointed out:[869]

> [S]uch natives are entitled to diplomatic protection by the Mandatory Power and that under the Foreign Office Consular Instructions natives of territories under British Mandates are already being treated as British-protected persons. The treatment of these natives as British-protected persons does not of course confer upon them British nationality.[870]

Unlike the treaty of Versailles with Germany, no provision regarding diplomatic protection was inserted in the Treaty of Lausanne with Turkey.[871] Yet, along the same lines of the British practice in mandates B and C, the issue of protection was extended to mandate instruments of type A in Iraq,[872] Syria, Lebanon,[873] Palestine and Trans-Jordan. Thus, Article 12 of the Palestine Mandate read:

> The Mandatory Power [i.e. Britain] shall be entrusted with the control of the foreign relations of Palestine and the right to issue exequaturs to consuls appointed by foreign

865 It is to be noted that Jones, in his various studies cited here, used the term 'national' to refer to any British protected person, regardless whether such person was a British 'subject' or not. In this sense, Palestinian citizens are British nationals but not subjects. *Cf.* above Chapter I, Section 1.

866 Johns, "Who Are British Protected Persons?", *op. cit.*, p. 128. It is worth recalling here that both the terms 'subject' and 'citizen' have the same meaning in the present study.

867 Weis, *op. cit.*, p. 21. See also T. Baty, "Protectorates and Mandates", *The British Year Book of International Law*, 1921–1922, pp. 112–113.

868 *Op. cit.*

869 *Nationality of the Inhabitants of B and C Mandated Territories*, Annex 1 ("Memorandum of the British Government"), League of Nations Document No. C.45(a).M.45.1922. VII—League of Nations, *Official Journal*, June 1922, p. 595.

870 This explains why, unlike mandates of types A, there was no reference to the protection of inhabitants abroad in any mandate instrument of types B or C.

871 In Articles 107 and 114 of the draft Treaty of Sèvres of 1920 with Turkey (*op. cit.*), British diplomatic protection was extended to Egyptian and Sudanese citizens, respectively. The Treaty of Sèvres did not extend British protection to citizens of the mandated-territories of Iraq, Syria and Lebanon, Palestine and Trans-Jordan, because it was envisaged that the treaty of peace with Turkey (i.e. the Treaty of Sèvres at the time) was to be read in conjunction with the mandate instruments relating to these territories. *Cf.* above Chapter III, Sections 1 and 3.

872 Mandate for Iraq, *op. cit.*, Article 3.

873 Mandate for Syria and the Lebanon, *op. cit.*, Article 3.

> Powers. He shall also be entitled to afford diplomatic and consular protection to citizens of Palestine when outside its territorial limits.

Again, contrary to Article 127 the Treaty of Versailles with Germany whereby the *inhabitants are entitled* to protection, Article 12 of the Palestine Mandate referred to the *Mandatory* as *entitled* to afford protection. In this regard, one could not but agree with the following conclusion:

> The word 'entitled,' if taken literarily, seems somewhat peculiar, as there can be no doubt that the diplomatic protection of the inhabitants of Palestine... does not constitute a right for the Mandatory but an obligation assumed towards the inhabitants.... [I]n virtue of...Article 127 of the Treaty of Versailles it is 'the native inhabitants of the former German oversea[s] possessions' who are 'entitled to the diplomatic protection...'; and...why in this respect there should be any difference in principle between the above possessions and the territories detached from Turkey.... Such protection involves...the right of active legation, which...can...be exercised only by the Mandatory.[874]

Accordingly, Palestinian citizens were protected abroad (i.e. outside both Palestine and Britain), on the same footing as British citizens and other British protected persons.[875] In a report submitted to the League of Nations in 1930,[876] Britain confirmed this practice:

> His Majesty's Government in practice extend to the inhabitants of territories under British Mandate the same protection as is afforded to other protected persons, which is, generally speaking, the same as that accorded to British subjects.

Palestinian citizens were able to claim the status of British protected persons by, *inter alia*, holding Palestinian passports.[877] Such a claim was indeed invoked in practice and states had recognized the British protection.[878] In this connection, Regulation 3 that appeared on the last page of the Palestinian passport provided:

> Palestinian citizens permanently resident abroad or staying for more than three months in a foreign country are advised to register their names and addresses at the nearest British Consulate. Such registration constitutes the most ready means in emergency or difficulty of enabling all proper assistance or advice to be afforded them. Changes of address or departure from the country of residence should also be notified to the Consulate.

For its part, as a supervisor over the mandatory states, the League of Nations had offered general support to Britain in facilitating the protection of Palestine's inhabitants, like the case in the other mandated territories. In this connection, the

874 Stoyanovsky, *op. cit.*, pp. 276–277.

875 *Cf.* Abi-Saab, *op. cit.*, p. 49 (cited a communication between French and Egyptian governments, "according to which the Syrians and Lebanese would enjoy in Egypt French diplomatic protection, but that the privileges of the Capitulatory system would not be extended to them").

876 Report on the Administration of Palestine 1930, *op. cit.*, p. 37.

877 See above Chapter VIII, Section 2.

878 See, for example, in Egypt, *N.N. Berouti v. Turkish Government, op. cit.*; and, in the United States, *Klausner v. Levy, op. cit.*

Council of the League of Nations, on 9 September 1930, instructed the League's Secretary-General to:

> [A]sk the States Members of the League of Nations to give favourable consideration to any requests that might be made to them by the mandatory Powers with a view to securing to persons belonging to territories under A and B mandates...advantages corresponding to those enjoyed therein by their own nationals.[879]

In summary, under the British rule of 1917–1948, Palestinian citizens abroad enjoyed diplomatic and consular protection conferred on them by Britain. This status was similar to that of British citizens[880] and inhabitants of British controlled-territories, such as those in the mandated, protected and colonized territories.

879 Mandates Commission Minutes 1933, *op. cit.*, p. 97.

880 However, for certain purposes, such as benefiting from special privileges accorded to British citizens by capitulation agreements, Palestinians were not treated abroad as British. See Goadby, *International and Inter-Religious Private Law in Palestine, op. cit.*, pp. 78–79.

IX

ADMISSION OF FOREIGNERS INTO PALESTINE

1. *General*[881]

It is beyond the scope of the present consideration to deal with the overall status of foreigners in Palestine. Nor is this study concerned with all aspects relating to the admission of foreigners into the country. The study will rather address the admission of foreigners in so far as it relates to Palestinian nationality, by looking at the various rules applicable to Palestinian citizens and those applicable to foreigners with regard to their entry into Palestine. This distinction is important because international migration law sets different rules for citizens and foreigners. Such a distinction is based, in turn, on nationality.

A number of legislation governed the admission of foreigners into Palestine. Passport rules regulated departure from the country,[882] while entry into Palestine was governed by immigration legislation.[883] The first Immigration Ordinance was introduced in Palestine by the military administration as early as August 1920.[884] On 1 September 1925, one month after the enforcement of the Palestinian Citizenship

881 See, *inter alia*, Alexis Martini, *L'expulsion des étrangers: étude de droit comparé*, Librairie de la société du recueil, Paris, 1909; Arnold Levandoski, "Citizenship and Deportation", *Notre Dame Lawyer*, Vol. 5, 1929–1930, pp. 81–90; William C. Van Vleck, *The Administrative Control of Aliens: A Study in Administrative Law and Procedure*, Commonwealth Fund, New York, 1932; A. Berriedale Keith, *Memorandum on the Status of Aliens and the Position of British Subjects in the British Empire*, International Institute for International Co-operation, League of Nations, Paris, 1937; Borchard, *op. cit.*, pp. 44–62; Davies, *op. cit.*, pp. 110–159; Weis, *op. cit.*, pp. 49–60; Oppenheim, *op. cit.*, pp. 536–553; Plender, *op. cit.*, pp. 133–157, 459–86; Goodwin-Gil, *op. cit.*, pp. 91 ff; Turack, *op. cit.*, pp. 233–236.

882 See above Chapter VIII, Section 2.

883 'Immigration legislation', for the purpose of this chapter, means the set of immigration ordinances, regulations, instructions and related administrative acts.

884 See above p. 56.

Order, a new Immigration Ordinance was enacted.[885] The latter was subsequently replaced by the Immigration Ordinance of 1933.[886] In light of the then new British policy towards Palestine, which was declared in 1939,[887] the last Immigration Ordinance was adopted in 1941.[888] The procedural aspects for entry into Palestine were organized in detail by the immigration regulations, notably the Regulations of 1933, and other administrative rules and instructions.[889]

The definition of the term 'foreigner' had been the logical result of the recognition of a distinct Palestinian nationality. In virtue of various immigration legislation, a 'foreigner', or 'alien', was regarded as any person who was not a Palestinian citizen under the Citizenship Order of 1925.[890] With regard to admission into Palestine, foreigners of all nationalities were treated, in law, as equals. Broadly speaking, foreigners fell under two classes: travellers and immigrants.[891]

---

885 See Legislation of Palestine, Vol. I, p. 579.

886 *Op. cit.*

887 See the White Paper of 1939, *op. cit.*, p. 10 (limiting the total Jewish immigrants to 75,000 in five years). It may be recalled that the Palestine Royal Commission, which had visited the country in 1936, recommended to the British government, *inter alia*, the restriction of the future Jewish immigration into Palestine. In general, the Government of Palestine's control of immigrates after 1939 was in line with the White Paper's policy. See Survey of Palestine, Vol. I, pp. 165, 175–179.

888 *Op. cit.* While the 1941 Ordinance consolidated the previous ordinances, it imposed stricter penalties against violations of immigration legislation.

889 See Immigration Regulations of 1925 (Legislation of Palestine, Vol. I, p. 334). These Regulations were replaced and elaborated by the Immigration Regulations of 1933 annexed to the Immigration Ordinance of 1933 (Laws of Palestine, p. 860). The latter Regulations were never repealed. They were, however, amended a number of times from 1935 to 1945. These amendments were as follows (the numbers of the reference, dates and page numbers in this note refer to Supplement 2 of the Palestine Gazette): Immigration (Amendment) Regulations of 1935 (No. 500, 28 March 1935, p. 310); Immigration (Amendment) Regulations of 1937 (No. 687, 10 May 1937, p. 527); Immigration (Amendment) Regulations (No. 2) of 1939 (No. 885, 5 May 1939, p. 420); Immigration (Amendment) Regulations (No. 3) of 1939 (No. 912, 24 August 1939, p. 754); Defence (Immigration) Regulations of 1940 (No. 994, 18 March 1940, p. 597); Defence (Immigration) (Amendment) Regulations of 1940 (No. 1030, 11 July 1940, p. 1117); Immigration (Amendment) Regulations of 1943 (No. 1302, 25 November 1943, p. 1345); Immigration Regulations (Amendment) of 1944 (No. 1359, 14 August 1944, p. 1144); Immigration (Amendment) Regulations of 1945 (No. 1457, 24 November 1945, p. 1748). Administrative decisions had given effect to the immigration ordinances and regulations (called instructions and orders), the most significant of which was the legislation called *Instructions to Immigration Officers* (1930), *op. cit.*

890 See Palestinian Citizenship Order of 1925, Article 21(3); Passport Ordinance of 1925, Article 2; Passport Ordinance of 1934, Article 2; Immigration Ordinance of 1925, Article 2; Immigration Ordinance of 1933, Article 2; Immigration Ordinance of 1941, Article 2. *Cf.* the definition of 'foreigner' in Article 59 of the Constitution of Palestine; above pp. 41–42.

891 But see Immigration Ordinances of 1925, of 1933 and of 1941, Article 2; Instructions to Immigration Officers, Articles 21–40. In these articles, other classes of foreigners were mentioned (e.g. travellers, transit travellers, tourists, temporary residents, temporary workers, immigrants, permanent residents and exempted foreigners). Substantively,

2. *Travellers*

Palestinian law, as with the laws of other states, which applied to travellers, comprised legislative and administrative provisions which controlled the movement of foreigners who intended to visit Palestine temporarily. Persons who wished to travel to Palestine were obliged to obtain entry visas, as a general rule, in order to land therein.[892] Also as a rule, the duration of the traveller's visa was limited to a three-month period.[893]

Certain classes of foreigners were exempt from the immigration legislation and could enter Palestine without a visa. These exempted foreigners had to belong to at least one of four groups.

The first group of foreigners who was exempt from immigration legislation, incorporated officials working or linked to the Government of Palestine or the British Government, accredited consuls *de carrière* and any person or class of persons whom the Government of Palestine wished to exempt.[894]

The second group comprised the habitual residents in the territory of Trans-Jordan (who were, chiefly, Trans-Jordanian citizens).[895] To this end, Article 4(2) of the Immigration Ordinance, 1941, stated:

> Persons habitually resident in Trans-Jordan may, unless the High Commissioner shall otherwise direct, enter Palestine direct from Trans-Jordan although they are not in possession of passports or other similar documents.

Thus, Trans-Jordanians were exempt from the possession of travel documents and, therefore, from the acquisition of an entry visa. But that did not change their status as foreigners within Palestine, as the Supreme Court of Palestine decided in *Jawdat Badawi Sha'ban v. Commissioner for Migration.*[896] Exemption from immigration legislation was particularly extended to those Trans-Jordanians who were employed by the Palestine Potash Company, located at the Palestinian-Trans-Jordanian border near the Dead Sea.[897] In April 1939, however, the High Commissioner obliged the Trans-Jordanians to possess passports in order to enter Palestine, further to the power bestowed upon him by the aforementioned provision.[898] Trans-Jordanian citizens continued to retain the right to enter Palestine without visas. This special

---

however, all these were either temporary residents (i.e. travellers) or permanent residents (i.e. immigrants).

892 See Passport Ordinance of 1925, Article 8(1); Immigration Ordinances of 1925, of 1933 and of 1941, Article 5; Immigration Regulations of 1925, Article 2.

893 See Immigration Regulations of 1925, Article 2(2); Immigration Regulations of 1933, Article 2. See also *Attorney General v. Rachel Menkes, op. cit.*

894 See Immigration Ordinances of 1925, of 1933 and of 1941, Article 4(1).

895 See Immigration Ordinances of 1925, of 1933 and of 1941, Article 4(2).

896 *Op. cit.*

897 See Immigration (Exemption of Trans-Jordan Employees of Palestine Potash Ltd.) which was published in the Palestine Gazette, No. 711, Supplement 2, 19 August 1937, p. 754.

898 See Survey of Palestine, Vol. I, pp. 211–212.

treatment of the Trans-Jordanians reflected the peculiar relationship which Trans-Jordan had with Palestine under the Mandate, as well as the British-Trans-Jordanian agreement of 1928 which maintained Trans-Jordan under the supervision of the High Commissioner for Palestine.[899]

Residents of certain Syrian and Lebanese towns lying along the northern borders of Palestine composed the third group that was exempt from Palestinian immigration legislation. As from 1923, Article 10 of the *Bon Voisinage Agreement*,[900] concluded between Britain and France with regard to certain arrangements relating to the Palestinian-Syrian-Lebanese borders provided:

> Facilities shall be given to the inhabitants on each side of the frontier to pass from places in the sub-districts of Acre and Safad [in Palestine] to the Kazas of Tyre, Merjayoun, Hasbeya and Kuneitra [in Syria/Lebanon], and *vice versa*.

The same article, however, required that such persons should hold special border passes; not ordinary passports.[901] Hence, in case "the Lebanese and Syrian holders of these border passes travel beyond the sub-districts in Palestine that lie along the frontier they become illegal immigrants".[902] It seems that the movement across the borders of residents of the aforementioned towns was allowed for humanitarian reasons. This was to facilitate family members located on both sides of the border in maintaining their social and economic connections (as these territories were under the same sovereign, with full freedom of movement, for many centuries before the British and French control of Palestine and Syria after World War I).

The last group of those exempt from the immigration legislation comprised the stateless persons, including refugees, who had failed to produce identity documents. This category comprised foreigners who were unable to obtain passports or travel documents from any state.[903]

Visas had been obtainable both locally and abroad. In Palestine, visas were issued by the Department of Migration of the Government of Palestine.[904] Similar to their mandate to issue Palestinian passports,[905] consular and immigration officers at British embassies and consulates abroad were authorized to grant entry visas

899 See above pp. 46–48.

900 *Op. cit.*

901 See also the same agreement, Article 1 (free passage of trucks and usage of roads), Articles 3 and 8. In addition, see *Bon Voisinage* Agreement of 1926, *op. cit.*, Articles 1 and 10; Notice Relating to Exchange of Notes between the High Commissioner for Palestine and Trans-Jordan and [the High Commissioner for] Syria and Lebanon, Providing for the Exemption of Certain Categories of Travellers from Visa Fees, 1932 (Palestine Gazette, 22 September 1932, p. 635); and Order (issued by the High Commissioner) No. 122 of 1934 (Palestine Gazette, No. 458, Supplement 2, 16 August 1934, p. 1060).

902 See Survey of Palestine, Vol. I, p. 212.

903 See Immigration Ordinances of 1925, of 1933 and of 1941, Article 5(1)(*g*).

904 See Survey of Palestine, Vol. I, p. 165.

905 See above pp. 148–149.

to travellers into Palestine.[906] Visas might be requested directly by the applicant himself or indirectly through a Palestinian citizen, or by a permanent resident of Palestine, on behalf of the applicant.[907] In exceptional cases, visas were obtainable at the entry stations (borders, sea ports or airports) of Palestine.[908]

On exceptional bases, travellers were also allowed to extend their visas or even to apply for the status of 'permanent residents' (i.e. immigrants). Article 2(2) of the Immigration Regulations of 1925, after limiting the duration of the visa to a three-month term, provided that any traveller may apply for permission either: "(*a*) to remain in Palestine for a further period not exceeding nine calendar months or (*b*) to remain permanently in Palestine as an immigrant".[909] However, in 1939 travellers were denied to reside permanently in Palestine.[910] But in 1943, travellers were re-permitted to apply for the status of permanent residents.[911] One year later, it had even become possible to extend visas indefinitely.[912] This change in travel rules reflected the changing British policies towards Palestine, from time to time, in response to the Arab and Jewish conflicting demands relating to immigration, settlement and the naturalization of immigrant Jews in the country.

In practice, however, exceptions in granting permanent residence were widely exercised to the extent that, it can be safely said, the exception became the rule.[913] Such exceptions had started with the beginning of British rule in Palestine. Thus,

---

906 See Passport Ordinance of 1925, Article 5; Immigration Ordinances of 1933 and of 1941, Article 5(1)(*g*); Immigration Regulations of 1925 and of 1933, Article 2; Instructions to Immigration Officers, Article 11(v). In *Barbara Polsky v. Attorney General* (Supreme Court of Palestine sitting as a Court of Civil Appeal, 9 February 1943 (Annotated Law Reports, 1943, Vol. I, p. 303)), it was reported that the appellant obtained a three-month permit to come to Palestine from the British consul in Frankfurt, Germany. In *Ellie Papadimitriou v. 1. Inspector General of Police and Prisons, 2. Officer in Charge of Detention Camp, Sarona* (Supreme Court of Palestine sitting as a High Court of Justice, 3 August 1944 (Annotated Law Reports, 1944, Vol. II, p. 824)), the accused acquired her visa from the British consul in Beirut, Lebanon. In *Attorney General v. Rachel Menkes* (*op. cit.*), the visa was issued by the British consul in Warsaw, Poland. A tourist visa was also issued by the British consul in Venice, Italy (*Attorney General on behalf of the Government of Palestine v. Rebecca Notrica Bouenos*, Supreme Court of Palestine sitting as a Court of Appeal, 30 March 1939—Law Reports of Palestine (Baker), 1939, Vol. 6, p. 162).

907 See Instruction to Immigration Officers, Article 11(v); Immigration Ordinances of 1933 and of 1941, Article 6(2).

908 For example, tourists (especially those who obtained British visas) having arrived to Palestine without a visa, if their entry was permitted, were required to pay additional fees as a fine (Instructions to Immigration Officers, Article 32). However, the visa rules did not specify whether it might be obtained at the entry stations of Palestine.

909 This provision was confirmed by the Immigration Regulations of 1933, Article 2(1).

910 Immigration (Amendment) Regulations of 1939, No. 3.

911 Immigration (Amendment) Regulations of 1943, Article 2.

912 Immigration (Amendment) Regulations of 1944, Article 2.

913 See, for example, Annex 1 of the Immigration Regulations of 1933 (application by traveller for permanent residence); and Annex 7 of the same Regulations (application by traveller for residence not exceeding one year).

in 1925, "1,674 travellers, including 1,251 Jews, were granted permission to remain permanently in Palestine after it had been ascertained that they fell within the categories of settlers defined in the Immigration Ordinance".[914] Similarly, during 1936, "1,817 persons who originally entered as travellers...subsequently received permission to remain permanently".[915] As a result, the number of travellers who were registered as immigrants from 1924 until 1945 totalled 38,325 persons.[916]

A foreigner did not have an absolute right of admission into Palestine.[917] This was the case even if the foreigner had been legally permitted to enter the country and even if he satisfied all the legal criteria for admission.[918] Immigration officers, stationed at the entry points of Palestine, reserved discrete authority to refuse that admission.[919] In these cases, passports of such persons had to be stamped as: "Refused permission to enter Palestine".[920] This signified that such persons were "not desired in Palestine in any circumstances".[921] In 1925, for example, 731 persons, who failed to comply with the immigration legislation, were rejected at the borders and ports of Palestine.[922] As such, entry into Palestine constituted a *privilege* to the foreigner, which might or might not be granted, rather than a *right*.

Immigration officers were authorized to attach any condition before, or even after, allowing the foreigner to enter.[923] In 1933, for instance, all applicants for visas were handed a printed warning on the consequences of illegal stay in Palestine.[924]

Moreover, it was lawful to detain any foreigner who had been denied entry into the country.[925] In such cases, foreigners had to be removed from Palestine to the state of their citizenship or to the place from where they exited, normally via the same transport means by which the foreigner had arrived. And the master or the owner of the means of transport (ship, plane, car) by which the foreigner had arrived was obliged, under criminal responsibility in cases of refusal, to comply with the removal decision at his own cost.[926]

Even after the admission into Palestine, a foreigner might be deported in certain cases. These cases included, *inter alia*, (1) if a Palestinian court convicted the

---

914 Report on the Administration of Palestine 1925, *op. cit.*, p. 70.
915 Jewish Agency Memorandum 1936, *op. cit.*, p. 5.
916 Statistical Abstract of Palestine 1944–1945, *op. cit.*, p. 40.
917 See Immigration Ordinances of 1933 and of 1941, Article 5(2).
918 See Immigration Ordinances of 1925, of 1933 and of 1941, Article 5(1).
919 See Instructions to Immigration Officers, Articles 27–28 and 44–53.
920 *Ibid.*, Article 45.
921 *Ibid.*, Article 44.
922 Report on the Administration of Palestine 1925, *op. cit.*, p. 71.
923 See Immigration Ordinance of 1925, Article 5(2); Immigration Ordinances of 1933 and of 1941, Article 6(1).
924 Report on the Administration of Palestine 1933, *op. cit.*, p. 16.
925 See Immigration Ordinance of 1925, Article 6(2); Immigration Ordinances of 1933 and of 1941, Article 8(2).
926 See Immigration Ordinance of 1925, Article 6(3); and Immigration Ordinances of 1933 and of 1941, Article 8(3), (5).

foreigner of an offence, (2) if such foreigner had been found wandering without visible means of subsistence, or (3) if the Government of Palestine deemed the foreigner's deportation to be conducive to the public good for any reason.[927]

The practice of the Palestinian courts had confirmed the foregoing rules. *Batatian v. Inspector General of Police*,[928] of the High Court of Palestine, 26 May 1942, served as a typical example in this respect. The facts of this case were as follows:

> The petitioner obtained a visa, valid for one year, from His Majesty's Consul in Lebanon. At Ras En-Naqura Frontier Control, an endorsement was made on the petitioner's passport to the effect that he was allowed to remain in Palestine for three months only as from March 26, 1942, the date of his entry. On May 16, the petitioner was apprehended and ordered to leave the country forthwith. The petitioner thereupon petitioned the High Court praying for an order to issue directed to the respondents calling upon them to show cause why he should not be allowed to remain in Palestine, on the grounds that the Frontier Control could not alter the period of one year granted by the Consul; that petitioner could not be deported from the country unless he had overstayed his lawful period of sojourn; that petitioner had an equitable right to stay in Palestine so long as he lawfully remained in the country; and that the Commissioner for Migration arbitrarily refused the application of petitioner's employers.

In rejecting the petitioner's contentions, the Court held:

> The grant of a visa by a Consul to a person to enter Palestine does not give the person to whom the visa was granted a right to stay in the country for any specified period, if the Immigration Authorities so decide. The directions as imposed by the Frontier Authorities are perfectly valid, and in these days the Government has complete powers to expel any foreigner from the country as no one has any inherent rights to remain.[929]

The foregoing discussion shows that Palestinian nationality was evident from the prominent distinction that was constantly drawn, legally and in practice, between Palestinian and foreign citizens in regard to admission into Palestine. The rules relating to the admission of foreigners remained in force until the end of the mandate and they have not been repealed even to the present day. Consequently, these rules should be taken into account in the policy and legislation relating to the admission of foreigners into the future state of Palestine.

---

927 See Immigration Ordinance of 1925, Article 8; and Immigration Ordinances of 1933 and of 1941, Article 10(1).

928 *Op. cit.*

929 For similar conclusions, see *Ellie Papadimitriou v. 1. Inspector General of Police and Prisons* (1944), *op. cit.*, in which the Supreme Court of Palestine upheld the decision of detention, then deportation, of a foreigner as she had stayed in Palestine for a period which exceeded the duration of her visa. See also *Attorney General v. Fishel Abraham Moskovitz*, Supreme Court of Palestine sitting as a Court of Criminal Appeal, 3 June 1938—Law Reports of Palestine (Baker), 1938, p. 345.

3. *Immigrants*

Immigrants constituted the bulk of foreigners who entered Palestine under the British rule, most of whom were Jews.[930] From 1920 until 1945, the total number of persons registered as immigrants and, therefore, permanent residents in the country, was estimated at 401,149. Of these, 367,845 (about 91%) were Jews.[931] Thus, about one-fourth of Palestine's inhabitants, citizens and foreigners, at the end of the mandate period were immigrants.

At the international level, Jewish immigration into Palestine was first legally formulated by the Palestine Mandate in 1922.[932] Article 6 of the Mandate, which was followed by Article 7 regarding the naturalization of Jews in Palestine, stated: "The Administration of Palestine…shall facilitate Jewish immigration".[933] The primary objective of the immigration rules was envisaged, therefore, as to bring immigrants to settle in Palestine.[934] Thus, "the Palestine Committee of the [Jewish] Agency (Palestine Zionist Executive) and the Head Office of the Zionist Organization have been given the special opportunity of expressing their views on the draft…Immigration Ordinances and Regulations".[935] Indeed, the Jewish Agency had submitted detailed comments on these drafts, many of which were taken into account.[936]

Both the Government of Palestine and the Jewish Agency cooperated in bringing immigrants into Palestine.[937] Such cooperation was stipulated in Article 7(4) of the Immigration Regulations of 1925, which was confirmed in the same article of the Immigration Regulations of 1933, *inter alia*, as follows:

---

930 It is beyond this study, as a juridical exercise, to examine Jewish immigration at length. But this immigration is an issue that will be touched upon in so far it relates to Palestinian nationality.

931 Survey of Palestine, Vol. I, p. 185.

932 This was in line with the overall goal of the Mandate, namely to establish a Jewish national home in Palestine. See above Chapter III, Section 3.

933 In this sense, it is important to reiterate that the subsequent article of the Mandate (Article 7) had obliged the Palestine Administration to grant Palestinian citizenship to immigrant Jews.

934 For a detailed legal discussion, see Mock, *op. cit.*, pp. 118–132.

935 Report on the Administration of Palestine 1925, *op. cit.*, p. 67.

936 See, for instance, Jewish Agency Memorandum 1933, *op. cit.*, p. 5.

937 In practice, both the Jewish Agency and the Zionist Organization represented the same entity *vis-à-vis* the Government of Palestine. The two bodies officially represented the Jewish community in Palestine and were recognized by the British-run Government of Palestine. The status of these two bodies was explicitly recognized in Article 4 of the Mandate (this article was fully quoted above pp. 125–126). Under this article, "the Palestine Administration, being closely linked with the Zionist Organization, is obliged…to cooperate with the Jewish Agency" (*Readaptation of the Mavrommatis Jerusalem Concessions* (*Greece v. Great Britain*), Permanent Court of International Justice (Jurisdiction—Dissenting Opinion by M. Coloyanni), 10 October 1927—Permanent Court of International Justice, Sires A, No. 11, 1927, p. 56).

> It shall be lawful for the Palestine Zionist Executive to notify...that there is a reasonable prospect of employing a number of persons...in Palestine and to make application for permission for their entry into Palestine.[938]

The Jewish Agency had declared that, amongst other reasons, it had brought the immigrants for the purpose of engaging them in the labour market of Palestine.[939] Thus, the Immigration Regulations divided immigrants into four categories: A, B, C and D. Categories A and B comprised, respectively, persons who already had and who would have independent financial means (mainly by the possession of, or the ability to possess, a certain amount of money). Category C consisted of persons who had a definite prospect of employment in Palestine. And Category D incorporated dependants of persons from all other categories.[940] For the same purpose, in order to determine the number of workers who were to be admitted into Palestine, "Labour Schedules shall be prepared...after considering any proposals made in that regard by the Palestine Zionist Executive".[941]

With respect to formalities, unlike travellers who were obliged to obtain visas to enter Palestine, immigrants were required to obtain immigration certificates.[942] Similar to the visa, an immigration certificate was issued either by the Government of Palestine or by the British consulates abroad.[943]

---

938 See also Schedule 5 attached to these Regulations (application by the Palestine Zionist Executive to bring immigrants of Category C into Palestine).

939 See, e.g., Report on Palestine Administration 1922, *op. cit.*, p. 52; Bentwich, *Palestine*, *op. cit.*, p. 10; Jewish Agency Memorandum 1936, *op. cit.*, pp. 29–37. See also Arthur Ruppin, *The Agricultural Colonization of the Zionist Organization in Palestine*, Martin Hopkinson and Company Ltd., London, 1926; G. Muenzner, *Jewish Labour Economy in Palestine*, Victor Gollancz Ltd., London, 1945.

940 See Immigration Regulations of 1925, Article 4(2); Immigration Regulations of 1933, Article 4(1). For greater details, see Survey of Palestine, Vol. I, pp. 166–173.

941 Immigration Regulations of 1925 and of 1933, Article 8(1). See also Immigration Regulations of 1925 and of 1933, Articles 7(1–2), 8(3–4), 9 and 14 (additional facilities to bring immigrants to work in Palestine).

942 See the following articles of the Immigration Regulations of 1933: Article 4 (general rules on immigration certificates); Article 5 (immigration certificate, 'Category A'); Article 6 (immigration certificate, 'Category B'); Article 7 (immigration certificate, 'Category C'); Article 9 (additional certificate for urgent workers); Article 10 (immigration certificate, 'Category D'); and Article 11 (immigration certificate for other immigrants). See also Article 14 of the Immigration Regulations of 1933 (certificate of temporarily employment permission); Immigration Regulations of 1925, Articles 4(2) 5, 6, 8, 9, 10, 11 and 14 (all replaced by articles having the same numbers in the 1933 Regulations); Instructions to Immigration Officers, Article 11(vi).

943 See the following annexes to the Immigration Regulations of 1933: Annex 2 (application for immigration certificate and registration of immigrants upon their arrival to Palestine); Annex 3 (immigration certificate form); Annex 4 (application for permission to bring immigrants, Category C); Annex 5 (application by the Palestine Zionist Executive to bring immigrant, Category C); Annex 6 (application by a Palestinian inhabitant to bring in immigrant dependants, Category D).

By obtaining an immigration certificate, a foreigner would *ipso facto* obtain the status of permanent resident in Palestine.[944] Yet this status did not amount, in terms of rights, to the level of a Palestinian citizen. Nor was it equivalent to the status of an ordinary foreigner. Rather, a permanent resident stood in between both; i.e. at a level below the Palestinian citizen and above an ordinary foreigner.

This peculiar status yielded a special set of rights. A permanent resident could exercise, *inter alia*, the right to reside, with his dependants, permanently in Palestine; the right to work; and the right to invite other travellers to Palestine.[945] Yet such a resident, as a foreigner, had no absolute right to return to Palestine after his departure.[946] He was obliged to apply for a return visa before leaving Palestine or alternatively request another return permit from abroad if he desired to come back.[947] He risked being deported from Palestine for the same reasons applicable to ordinary foreigners.[948] And, of course, permanent residents had no political rights, such as participating in legislative election or holding public office.

Above all, immigration, which implies legal residence, was considered as the first step towards satisfying the two-year residence that was required for the acquisition of Palestinian nationality by naturalization under the 1925 Citizenship Order.[949]

Besides the legal travellers and immigrants, thousands of foreigners illegally entered Palestine for the purpose of permanent residence therein. Throughout the British rule in the country, a "considerable movement of illegal immigration occurs across the borders of Palestine".[950]

The British-appointed High Commissioner for Palestine, in a public statement in February 1933, characterized the problem of illegal immigration as follows:

> I am distressed that many immigrants have entered Palestine without the permission of Government. I can assure you that I am anxious to stop in the future this immigration without permits. Palestine has long frontiers and it is obviously not very easy for the Government to stop illegal immigration altogether.[951]

Illegal immigrants comprised two categories. While the first incorporated travellers who entered Palestine legally and then overstayed, the second included persons who entered the country by crossing Palestine's borders or arriving to Palestinian ports without a visa or immigration certificate. In practice, most illegal immigrants belonged to the latter category. Such immigrants were considered 'illegal' or 'prohibited' as their entry or stay in the country was contrary to the immigration legislation (ordinances, regulations and rules) in force in Palestine.

---

944 It should be noted that, according to the overall provisions of immigration rules, the status of 'immigrant' was equivalent to that of 'permanent resident'.
945 See Immigration Ordinance of 1941, Article 6(2).
946 Immigration Ordinance of 1941, Article 5(2).
947 Immigration Regulations of 1933, Article 3.
948 Immigration Ordinance of 1941, Article 10.
949 See above pp. 116–117.
950 See Survey of Palestine, Vol. I, p. 162.
951 Report on the Administration of Palestine 1933, *op. cit.*, p. 15.

Officially, the British-run Government of Palestine had employed various measures to overcome the problem of illegal immigration.[952] Such measures included obliging travellers to deposit a certain amount of money as a guarantee to leave Palestine,[953] inspecting passengers at the ports and borders, employing immigration forces for deployment at land and on sea and constructing frontier fences and roads.[954] The Government also imposed strict penalties against those who failed to comply with the immigration rules. Illegal immigrants were often fined, detained and imprisoned.[955]

Other measures had targeted suspected ships, on which most illegal immigrants arrived at Palestinian ports, especially after the outbreak of World War II.[956] The Emergency Regulations of 1945 brought in further measures to deal with illegal immigration.[957] Such measures included, *inter alia*, the authorization of the security forces to stop vehicles, vessels and aircrafts;[958] the confiscation of those vessels or aircrafts used to import illegal immigrants;[959] the imposition of fines or eight year prison sentences on the owners, agents and masters of any vessel or aircraft convening illegal immigrants,[960] and the arrest of illegal immigrants.[961] In *Basile Vucashinovitch v. Attorney General*,[962] the appellant, the master of a ship, "was convicted of aiding and abetting 919 Jewish immigrants to enter Palestine illegally".

952 *Ibid.*, pp. 214–222.

953 See, *inter alia, David Yochels v. Attorney General*, Supreme Court of Palestine sitting as a Court of Appeal, 16 February 1939 (Supreme Court Judgements, 1939, Vol. I, p. 62); *Attorney General v. Rachel Menkes, op. cit.; Attorney General... v. Rebecca Notrica Bouenos, op. cit.*

954 See Report on the Administration of Palestine 1938, *op. cit.*, pp. 28–29; Survey of Palestine, Vol. I, pp. 114–122.

955 See Immigration Ordinances of 1933 and of 1941, Article 10. A number of acts were considered as immigration offences. These acts include, *inter alia*, the following: the refusal to produce any document in one's possession; illegal return into Palestine or the submission of a false statement regarding applications for a permit or a passport; the tampering with any immigration document; the forgery or use of immigration documents; and overstay in Palestine beyond the permitted period. Persons who committed any of these acts were liable to receive a fine and/or imprisonment of a term not exceeding six months. If the person had been deported but then returned to Palestine, as long as the deportation order remained in force, he was liable to imprisonment for a term not exceeding three years and/or to a fine. Lastly, persons who encouraged the violation of immigration rules were liable for imprisonment for a term not exceeding eight years and/or a greater fine. See Immigration Ordinance of 1941, Article 12.

956 See Immigration Ordinance of 1941, Articles 13–15. See also Defence (Immigration) Regulations of 1940, Articles 3–4.

957 See Defence (Emergency) Regulations of 1945, *op. cit.*

958 *Ibid.*, Article 77.

959 *Ibid.*, Article 103.

960 *Ibid.*, Article 104.

961 *Ibid.*, Article 105.

962 Supreme Court of Palestine sitting a Court of Appeal, 14 August 1939—Supreme Court Judgments, 1939, Vol. I, p. 452.

He was fined, imprisoned for nine months and the ship on which the illegal immigrants were brought, was forfeited to the Government of Palestine.[963]

The deportation of illegal immigrants, in particular, was frequent.[964] In 1935, 1,557 illegal immigrants were detected, sentenced to imprisonment and recommended for deportation. 1,079 of such deportations were carried out in the year. In addition, 1,354 persons were summarily deported to Syria and Egypt.[965] In the period of 1941 to 1945, 12,165 non-Jews and 221 Jews were deported from Palestine.[966] And "during the six months starting from mid-October 1946, approximately 15,000 Jewish illegal immigrants from various European ports were intercepted in Palestinian waters and diverted to camps in Cyprus".[967]

In many cases, Palestinian courts had confirmed the validity of deportation orders against illegal immigrants.[968]

---

963 See also *Attorney General v. Vladimir Nikolaiovitch & 15 Others*, Supreme Court of Palestine sitting as a Court of Civil Appeal, 4 January 1940 (Supreme Court Judgements, 1940, Vol. I, p. 3); *Attorney General v. Alexander Glinsky*, Supreme Court of Palestine sitting as a Court of Criminal Appeal, 26 February 1940 (Law Reports of Palestine (Baker), 1940, Vol. 7, p. 114); *Philippacopoulos and Another v. S.S. Alisa and Others*, Supreme Court of Palestine sitting as a Court of Admiralty, 25 November 1940 (*ibid.*, p. 542); *Attorney General v. Spiros Yanoulatos*, Supreme Court of Palestine sitting as a Court of Criminal Appeal, 23 October 1941 (Supreme Court Judgements, 1941, Vol. II, p. 559); *Ellie Papadimitriou v. 1. Inspector General of Police and Prisons…, op. cit.*; *Attorney General v. Fishel Abraham Moskovitz, op. cit.*

964 See Immigration (Custody Pending Deportation) Order of 1933 (Laws of Palestine, p. 2103); Immigration (Custody Pending Deportation) (Amendment) Order (No. 2) of 1939 (Palestine Gazette, No. 962, Supplement 2, 9 November 1939, p. 1314); Immigration (Deportation Orders) of 1944 (Palestine Gazette, No. 1347, Supplement 2, 20 July 1944, p. 809); Defence (Entry Prohibition) Regulations of 1940, Article 2 (Palestine Gazette, No. 1052, Supplement 2, 18 October 1940, p. 1709); Defence (Entry Prohibition) (Amendment) Regulations of 1940, Article 2 (Palestine Gazette, No. 1062, Supplement 2, 9 December 1940, p. 2017); Instructions to Immigration Officers, Article 54.

965 See Report on the Administration of Palestine 1935, *op. cit.*, p. 13. For similar practice, see Report on the Administration of Palestine 1938, *op. cit.*, pp. 28–29.

966 See Survey of Palestine, Vol. I, pp. 221–222.

967 UN Doc. A/AC. 13/NC/34, 23 June 1947. On the diplomatic procedures of deportation, see Survey of Palestine, Vol. I, pp. 218–220.

968 See, *inter alia*, the following cases: *Attorney General v. Alexander Aharon Reich*, Supreme Court of Palestine sitting as a Court of Appeal, 28 June 1938 (Supreme Court Judgements, Vol. I, p. 422); *Ellie Papadimitriou v. 1. Inspector General of Police and Prisons, 2. Officer in Charge of Detention Camp, Sarona*, Supreme Court of Palestine sitting as a High Court of Justice, 3 August 1944 (Annotated Law Reports, 1944, Vol. II, p. 824); *Yitzhak Funt, a member of the Executive of the Jewish Community Council of Jerusalem, Jerusalem v. 1. The Chief Secretary, Government of Palestine, Government Offices, Jerusalem, 2. The General Officer Commanding, Palestine and Trans-Jordan, Force Headquarters, Jerusalem, 3. The Military Commander, Haifa Area, Force Headquarters, Haifa, 4. The Acting Inspector General of Police and Prisons, Police Headquarters, Jerusalem, 5. The Senior Navel Officer, Levant Area, Navel Headquarters, Haifa, 6. The Officer Commanding the s/s "Ocean Vigour", Haifa Port, Haifa, 7. The Officer Commanding the s/s "Empire Heywood", Haifa Port, Haifa*, Supreme

Certain measures against illegal immigrants were challenged before Palestinian courts. One of the arguments was that the Immigration Ordinance was contrary to Article 6 of the Palestine Mandate, which requested the Administration of Palestine to facilitate the Jewish immigration to the country. Therefore, it was argued that the Ordinance was, essentially, *ultra vires*. In a detailed case before the Palestine Supreme Court sitting as a High Court of Civil Appeal on 11 November 1946 (*Haim Molvan v. Attorney General*),[969] it was concluded:

> It is clear that the provisions of the Immigration Ordinance do not purport to give the Government of Palestine complete legal control over the immigration of Jews or other persons who are not nationals of Palestine. It is also a matter of common knowledge that the Government of Palestine is making use of its powers under the Ordinance in order to prevent illegal Jewish immigration. But this does not enable me to find that the Ordinance is *ultra vires* the Mandate.... The Ordinance does not contain any provisions against the immigration of Jews as such. Its provisions apply with equal stringency against all unlawful immigration.

In the same case, it was reported that a ship was bringing 733 immigrant Jews into Palestine, which was sighted by a British destroyer; none of these immigrants possessed passports, travel documents or visas to enter Palestine. The Government of Palestine confiscated the ship and the owner of the ship appealed the decision until the final stage at the British Privy Council (that constituted the highest judicial body to which decisions of Palestinian courts could be challenged). Both the Supreme Court of Palestine sitting as a High Court of Justice, on 11 November 1945, and the Privy Council, on 2 March 1948, dismissed the appeal.[970]

Shortly before ending its rule in Palestine, Britain tried to solve the question of illegal immigration by diplomatic means. In 1947, the British government called upon European states (from where most Jewish immigrants embarked for Palestine),[971] to prevent transit via their territory, and departure from their ports, of Jews attempting to enter Palestine illegally.[972]

Illegal immigrants used various techniques to remain in Palestine. Such techniques included an immigrant's refusal "to give particulars for identification and have to be detained until travel documents are discovered in one of the countries through which they passed on their way to Palestine. A number of women released

---

Court of Palestine sitting as a High Court of Justice, 29 November 1946 (Annotated Law Reports, 1947, Vol. I, p. 15); *Fatmeh bint Mahmoud As'ad Ammar v. Assistant Inspector General C. I. D. of Jerusalem*, *op. cit.*

969 Annotated Law Reports, 1946, Vol. II, p. 721. Though this passage is a quotation from a separate opinion of Mr. Shaw, a British Puisne Judge of the said Palestinian Court, it was consistent, in regard to validity of the Immigration Ordinance, with the judgment of the Court.

970 Annual Digest, 1948, p. 115.

971 See above p. 127.

972 UN Doc. A/AC.13/NC/34, *op. cit.*

[from prison or detention centre] on bail have quickly contracted marriages with Palestinian nationals and thus evaded deportation".[973]

Yet the Government of Palestine, notably before the outbreak of World War II, showed some flexibility towards illegal immigrants, who constituted *de facto* residents, by regularizing their status in the country. For example, in 1931 "special facilities were granted to persons in the country without permission to regularize their presence, and some six thousand in all were registered [as immigrants]".[974] Additionally "the Palestine Government... granted a number of administrative concessions: it issued three thousand Immigration Certificates in 1933".[975] Thus, in 1933, it was estimated that "the number of these unauthorized [Jewish immigrant] settlers had reached a total of 22,400 in the last two years".[976]

This position was to change after the outbreak of World War II. In December 1939, the British government decided that "no facilities were to be granted to any person of whatever nationality who came from or who had visited German territory since the beginning of the war".[977] Thus, immigration into Palestine became restricted for two reasons. The first, as already noted, was the British policy adopted with the White Paper of 1939, which reflected Palestinian Arab fears of Jewish immigration.[978] The second reason related to the status of enemy nationals of those persons who possessed German nationality, which related, in turn, to security concerns surrounding persons coming from Germany.[979]

Nonetheless, certain exceptions to these rules were accorded on humanitarian grounds to Jewish refugees escaping from Europe. These exceptions, by 31 March 1944, had resulted in the legal immigration of 31,221 persons into Palestine. During the same period, 19,965 illegal immigrants had entered the country.[980]

Consequently, dozens of thousands of illegal immigrants remained in Palestine until the end of the mandate.

Notwithstanding the peculiar objective of the immigration rules enacted under the Palestine Mandate and the general validity of these rules until the present day, the provisions related to Jewish immigration and, in particular, the cooperation with the Jewish Agency, are no longer applicable. While this may seem to be self-evident, two logically connected reasons can be advanced to this effect. First, Jewish immigration was based on the Palestine Mandate; the Mandate lapsed on 14 May 1948. Secondly, the *raison d'être* of the said immigration, namely to

973 Report on the Administration of Palestine 1935, *op. cit.*, p. 13.
974 Report on the Administration of Palestine 1933, *op. cit.*, p. 15.
975 *Ibid.*, p. 16.
976 *Ibid.*, p. 15.
977 See Survey of Palestine, Vol. I, p. 178.
978 See above p. 108; and see *supra* note 887.
979 See, in general, Daphne Trevor, *Under the White Paper: Some Aspects of British Administration in Palestine from 1939 to 1947*, The Jerusalem Press Ltd., Jerusalem, 1948 (reprinted in 1980, Kraus International Publishers, München).
980 Survey of Palestine, Vol. I, p. 180 and pp. 204–205.

contribute to the establishment of the Jewish national home in Palestine, had been achieved upon the creation of that home, i.e. the State of Israel.

4. *Note on the admission of Palestinian citizens*[981]

It is necessary to mark, first of all, that the entry, or return, of Palestinian citizens into Palestine did not constitute an area of concern under the British rule.[982] While entry of Palestinians had not been regulated by any legislation, it was generally understood that such entry of citizens into, and their residence in their own country, was a natural right which should be safeguarded. This understanding was manifested, for example, in the following instruction extended by the Government of Palestine to its immigration officers:

> Apart from holders of British passports endorsed for Palestine, Palestinian passports [i.e. passports held by Palestinian citizens]...no person should be admitted whose passport has not been visaed for Palestine....[983]

This practice was in line with international law. As the admission of nationals has been an element inherent in the very nature of nationality,[984] it is not contested in international law that states are under obligation, *vis-à-vis* other states, to admit to their territory their own citizens.[985] Accordingly, the admission of Palestinian citizens into Palestine was, in principle, guaranteed.

Since the commencement of its rule, however, Britain permitted the deportation of persons from Palestine. The deportation of those convicted of crimes, was regulated by Articles 68–72 of the Palestine Order in Council (Constitution) of 1922. According to Article 68, if an offender was convicted by a court, the High Commissioner might decide that such an offender should spend the term of his imprisonment outside Palestine. Deportation was further regulated by Article 15 of the Emergency Regulation, in 1936.[986] The latter article was reaffirmed by Article

981 In cases relating to the legality of deportation of Palestinians by Israel from the 1967 occupied territories, the arguments and counter-arguments were based mainly on the validity of the 1945 Defence (Emergency) Regulations (*op. cit.*) enacted by the British-run Government of Palestine. No reference has been made in these cases to the context in which the deportation of Palestinians under the British rule had been carried out (see, for instance, references mentioned in *supra* note 57). It is for contemporary issues relating to the Israel occupation polices in the Palestinian territories, such as the legality of inhabitants' deportation, this background note is inserted here.

982 But see the question of return, or acquisition of Palestinian nationality, of Palestinian natives who were residing abroad upon and after the enactment of the Palestinian Citizenship Order in 1925; above Chapter V, Section 2.

983 Instructions to Immigration Officers, Article 11(v).

984 See Weis, *op. cit.*, pp. 49, 55.

985 *Ibid.*, pp. 49–60.

986 Palestine Gazette, No. 584, Supplement 2, 19 April 1936, p. 1.

112 of Defence (Emergency) Regulations in 1945.[987] Neither the Constitution nor the Regulations referred to the nationality (Palestinian or otherwise) of the person who might be deported from Palestine.[988]

In practice, the British-run Government of Palestine had deported Palestinian citizens. In 1937, for example, this Government deported five Palestinians, leaders of Arab communities, to the Island of Mahe, Seychelles. The men were kept in a prison on that Indian Ocean Island, which was under British control.[989]

Courts confirmed the validity of such deportation. In *Batatian v. Inspector General of Police*,[990] 26 May 1942, the Supreme Court of Palestine sitting as a High Court of Justice held that "even Palestinians can be expelled". Likewise, the legality of deportation of a Palestinian citizen to Eritrea, and his detention in that British-controlled territory, was confirmed by the same Court on 18 December 1945 in *Eliezer Zabrovsky v. The General Officer Commanding Palestine and Another*.[991] On 4 December 1946, the British Privy Council sitting in London as a Court of Appeal from the Supreme Court of Palestine decided that this deportation as legal.[992] The Privy Council added:

> The Palestine Court has accepted the legality of the orders of deportation which are clearly within the competence of the Palestine Government. While the deportation order stands and its legality is not overruled its effect is that Eliezer is required to leave and remain thereafter out of Palestine. Such an order [of deportation] is not *ultra vires* of a limited territorial power like Palestine nor are the further or ancillary powers of providing a place to which the deportee may proceed.... The order indeed so long as it remains in force renders it unlawful for Eliezer to seek to enter Palestine.[993]

Nonetheless, a number of issues merit consideration here.

While the deportation of Palestinian citizens *per se* was not permitted, foreigners were susceptible.[994] Deportation was closely connected with imprisonment. The title of Article 68 of the Palestine Constitution speaks of the 'removal of prisoners' rather than 'deportation'. In addition, deportation was intended to be temporary,

987 *Op. cit.*

988 Deportation for the purpose of imprisonment in any British-controlled territory has been regularized by Articles 7–8 of the British Foreign Jurisdiction Act of 1890 (*op. cit.*) which was, as already noted, enforced in Palestine as the case in other British colonies and possessions outside the United Kingdom.

989 See Permanent Mandates Commission, "Petitions: (a) dated September 2nd, 1938, from Dr. H.F. El-Khalidi, and (b) dated September 24th, 1938, from four other Arab deportees in the Seychelles, transmitted on November 18th, 1938, by United Kingdom Government with its observations" (League of Nations, Document No. C.P.M.2128, Geneva, 13 December 1938—un-published).

990 Annual Digest, 1941–1942, p. 293.

991 Annotated Law Reports, 1946, Vol. I, p. 174.

992 Appeal No. 4346, *op. cit.*, p. 282.

993 *Ibid.*, p. 287.

994 See above pp. 170–171.

lasting for such a time as to allow for the improvement of the offender who was "convicted before any Court". In no way was such deportation to be permanent.

Moreover, the deportation should be carried out to a British controlled territory, not to an entirely foreign country. Article 68 defined such territory as "a place in some part of His Majesty's Dominions out of the United Kingdom". Thus, for Britain, deportation was merely a transfer of the deportee from one part of its controlled territories to another. No international deportation, which would violate the sovereignty of other states if it carried out without the consent of the state to which the person would be deported, was involved. This explains why the deportation from Palestine in the two above-mentioned cases was carried out to Seychelles and Eritrea; both were controlled by Britain at the time.

With regard to the "deportation of political offenders", as it is described by Article 69 of the Palestine Constitution,[995] deportation was to be carried out to "a place... to which the person belongs...". Such a place should be located in either "part... of His Majesty's Dominions... or... under the protection of His Majesty" or "in the country out of His Majesty's Dominions to which that person belongs".[996] Hence, deportation rules were chiefly directed against foreigners. In other words, the deportation of Palestinians occurred and was carried out only in exceptional cases. This conclusion was in line with the immigration legislation which only permitted, as already noted, the deportation of those foreigners who had violated or were suspected of having violated the immigration instructions.[997] None of the immigration rules denied Palestinian citizens to enter, or return to, Palestine.

Finally, the Government of Palestine was obliged to report, with justification, each case of deportation to the British Government.[998] That is to say, there was administrative supervision over deportation cases.

Accordingly, rules relating to deportation were to be read in their historical context. They were developed by the British Empire as part of its extraterritorial jurisdiction in its controlled territories out of the United Kingdom. It was not surprising, therefore, that the deportation was processed, as Article 68 of the Constitution put it, "under Article 7 of the [British] Foreign Jurisdiction Act, 1890".[999] This Article opened the possibility for executing any penalty, including imprisonment, ruled by any British court in a foreign country outside the place in which the offence occurred. Hence, the question of deportation in Palestine was part of the overall Britain's policy implemented in those territories that were under its control.

995 Paragraph (1) of this article defined the political offender as "any person [who] is conducting himself so as to be dangerous to peace and good order in Palestine, or is endeavouring to excite enmity between the people of Palestine and the Mandatory, or is intriguing against the authority of the Mandatory in Palestine".

996 Palestine Constitution, Article 69(2).

997 Again, see above pp. 170–171.

998 Royal Instructions of 1922, *op. cit.*, Article 24.

999 *Op. cit.*

Consequently, the *raison d'être* of deportation of Palestinian citizens had lapsed after the end of the mandate and is no longer applicable today. Yet if the deportation provisions were to continue to be valid after the mandate, arguably, the subsequent international legal developments, especially in the filed of human rights and humanitarian law in addition to the law of state responsibility, must be observed.[1000] This question, however, cannot be discussed further here.[1001]

1000 See, e.g., Guy S. Goodwin-Gil, "The Limits of the Power of Expulsion in Public International Law", *The British Yearbook of International Law*, Vol. 47, 1975, pp. 55–156 (on the expulsion of foreigners).

1001 On deportations undertaken by the Israel occupation authorities against inhabitants of the West Bank after 1967 based on the British-enacted legislation during the mandate period and the violation of such deportations to international law, see the references in *supra* note 57.

X

APPLICABILITY OF INTERNATIONAL NATIONALITY INSTRUMENTS TO PALESTINE

1. *The Hague Conference*

The First Conference on the Codification of International Law was convened from 13 March to 13 April 1930 at The Hague, Netherlands.[1002] Under the auspices of the League of Nations, the Conference adopted, *inter alia*, certain rules relating to nationality.[1003] These rules were laid down in a convention and three protocols: the Convention on Certain Questions Relating to the Conflict of Nationality Laws (hereinafter: 'the Convention' or the 'nationality Convention'); Protocol relating to Military Obligations in Certain Cases of Double Nationality;[1004] Protocol

1002 See, *inter alia*, David Hunter Miller, "Nationality and Other Problems Discussed at the Hague", *Foreign Affairs*, Vol. 8, 1929–1930, pp. 632–640; Manley O. Hudson, "The First Conference for the Codification of International Law", *The American Journal of International Law*, Vol. 24, 1930, pp. 447–466; Richard W. Flournoy, Jr., "Nationality Convention, Protocols and Recommendations Adopted by the First Conference on the Codification of International Law", *ibid.*, pp. 467–485; Weis, *op. cit.*, pp. 29–31; Brownlie, "The Relations of Nationality…", *op. cit.*, pp. 299–300. On earlier preparations for the Conference, see Charles Cheney Hyde, "The Nationality Convention adopted by the League of Nations Committee of Experts for the Progressive Codification of International Law", *The American Journal of International Law*, Vol. 20, 1926; and *ibid.*, Special Supplement, 1926, pp. 21–61. See also Harvard Research on Nationality, *op. cit.*, which was prepared in 1929 as part of the preparations for the said Conference.

1003 The Conference comprised delegates of 48 states (members and non-members of the League of Nations). It dealt, in addition to nationality, with another two international law issues: territorial water and responsibility of states for damage caused in their territory to the person or property of foreigners.

1004 Hereinafter, the Protocol relating to Military Obligations in Certain Cases of Double Nationality will be referred to as 'Protocol on Military Obligations'.

relating to a Certain Case of Statelessness;[1005] and Special Protocol Concerning Statelessness. Apart from the last protocol, all these instruments came into force at the international level in 1937.[1006] The same three instruments were extended to Palestine in 1938.

With a view to solving certain difficulties arising from conflicting nationality laws among states,[1007] the Convention and its protocols adopted a limited number of rules. While some of these rules were considered as declarations of already existing international law, others were new. But the adoption of such rules did not necessarily mean that they formed part of international law.[1008] Although the instruments were considered to be defective in various respects, they indeed contained, it was believed, some carefully considered and useful provisions.[1009]

As a general rule codifying existing state's practice,[1010] the Convention left "for each State to determine under its own law who are its nationals".[1011] The Convention also obliged states to recognize the domestic nationality laws of each other.[1012] Yet such recognition was envisaged to be limited to the extent that the internal law "is consistent with international conventions, international custom, and the principle of law generally recognized with regard to nationality".[1013] In other words, the domestic nationality legislation should be consistent with international law in order to generate legitimacy on the international plane. In this regard, it was correctly pointed out:

> While it may be competent for a state to confer rights of citizenship within its territories upon whomsoever it pleases..., it is quite a different matter for it to stretch its hands into the recognized domain of other states and claim as its nationals persons having no connection with it.[1014]

This chapter will examine the validity of the aforementioned nationality instruments with regard to Palestine before 1948. It will start by looking at the applicability of

---

1005 Hereinafter, the Protocol relating to a Certain Case of Statelessness will be referred to as 'Protocol on Statelessness'.

1006 League of Nations, *Official Journal*, Special Supplement, No. 181, Geneva, September 1938 ("Ratification of Agreements and Conventions Concluded under the Auspices of the League of Nations"), pp. 71–74.

1007 See the Convention's preamble.

1008 In this connection, the Convention and the two protocols set forth the following common article: "The inclusion of the abovementioned principles and rules in the Convention [or protocols] shall in no way be deemed to prejudice the question whether they do or do not already form part of international law" (Convention, Article 18(2); Protocol on Military Obligations, Article 4(2); and Protocol on Statelessness, Article 2(2)).

1009 Flournoy, *op. cit.*, p. 485.

1010 *Ibid.*, pp. 469–470.

1011 Article 1. In a complementary provision to this article, the Convention added: "Any question as to whether a person possesses the nationality of a particular State shall be determined in accordance with the law of that State" (Article 2).

1012 The Convention, Article 1.

1013 *Ibid.*

1014 Flournoy, *op. cit.*, p. 469.

these instruments from a procedural point of view according to Britain's practice regarding the extinction of treaties to territories under its control, particularly its mandated territories.[1015] The chapter will then review the substantive significance of these instruments and their application in Palestine as reflected in Palestinian legislation enacted after the adoption of the nationality instruments. It will conclude by examining the validity of these instruments in the West Bank and Gaza Strip after the end of the mandate.

It should be emphasised from the outset that addressing the general validity of the international treaties to Palestine under the British rule is beyond the scope of this study.[1016] But certain aspects relating to this general validity will be touched upon to the extent that they relate to the validity of the nationality instruments.

2. *Procedure*

Britain had acquired general authorization to conclude international conventions on behalf of Palestine. To this effect, Article 19 of the Palestine Mandate states:

> The Mandatory shall adhere on behalf of the Administration of Palestine to any general international conventions already existing, or which may be concluded hereafter with the approval of the League of Nations, respecting the slave traffic, the traffic in arms and ammunition, or the traffic in drugs, or relating to commercial equality, freedom of transit and navigation, aerial navigation and postal, telegraphic and wireless communication or literary, artistic or industrial property.[1017]

More generally, the Mandatory Powers were not given a simple choice to conclude treaties on behalf, and for the benefit, of mandated territories. Indeed, as it has been concluded, an "obligation was imposed on Great Britain and France to extend certain international conventions concluded under the auspices of the League of Nations, mainly humanitarian in character, to the mandated areas".[1018]

At first glance, it may appear that Article 19 authorized Britain to adhere to an exclusive type of conventions on the behalf of Palestine. But a rapid review of

---

1015 With regard to the treaty extension to British colonies, see Stoyanovsky, *op. cit.*, p. 280.

1016 See, in general, *ibid.*, pp. 279–290; Mock, *op. cit.*, pp. 236–243.

1017 Aside from Article 19, another three articles of the Mandate conferred treaty-making power to Britain on behalf of Palestine. Article 10 authorized Britain to extend to Palestine extradition treaties that Britain concluded with other states. Article 12 gave implicit power to conclude treaties on diplomatic and consular matters. Under Article 18, the Mandatory had the power to apply or conclude commercial agreements on behalf of the mandated territory. In addition, Article 20 of the Mandate authorized the Mandatory on behalf of Palestine to cooperate "in the execution of any common policy adopted by the League of Nations for preventing and competing disease…". It was said that "this provision refers to certain international agreements mainly concluded with the assistance of the Health section of the League of Nations" (Stoyanovsky, *op. cit.*, p. 289).

1018 O'Connell, *State Succession…*, *op. cit.*, Vol. II, p. 150. For a similar conclusion in regard to Palestine, see Stoyanovsky, *op. cit.*, p. 290.

British practice in regard to treaty-making in relation to Palestine shows that the conventions enumerated in the aforementioned article were inserted by way of example. Britain extended to Palestine over 120 multilateral and bilateral agreements in various international fields, many of which were not included within the scope of Article 19. The subject-matter of nationality, by its nature, is indeed similar to that found in other types of the treaties set out in the aforesaid article.[1019]

Thus, by 1946, Palestine's accession (which was made by Britain on behalf of Palestine) to various treaties included: forty-three multilateral treaties; forty-three treaties on extradition;[1020] treaties related to trade and navigation with twenty-six states; and twenty-seven other treaties on various issues including reciprocal enforcement of judgements and legal proceedings in civil and commercial matters.[1021] Besides, Palestine was made a party to a number of international labour treaties which were brought to the country either directly by the accession of Britain on behalf of Palestine or through Palestinian legislation which applied specific labour treaty or certain number of treaty's provisions.[1022]

The applicability of various types of treaties to Palestine was recognized by the League of Nations as well as by individual states.[1023] While Palestine alone "could not conclude international conventions, the mandatory Power... concluded them on her behalf, in virtue of Article 19 of the mandate".[1024] The fact that the nationality Convention and its protocols were initiated by the League and prepared under its auspices indicates "the approval of the League of Nations", as required in Article 19 of the Palestine Mandate. Hence, it can be said, the nationality Convention and protocols were merely part of the bulk of treaties which had been extended to Palestine during the period of British rule.

The form by which the League of Nations expressed its consent to the treaties to which Britain had adhered on behalf of Palestine was not specified in the Mandate. The approval of neither the Council nor the Assembly of the League was mentioned. It was perhaps intended that the mere silence (or 'general supervision')[1025] of the League's organs on the concluded treaties was sufficient for that consent. Indeed, "no special approval in each particular case has ever been considered

---

1019 Examples included, among others, the following: Convention relating to the development of hydraulic power affecting more than one State, Geneva, 1923; International Sanitary Convention, Paris, 1926 (Palestine acceded in 1928); International Convention for the Amelioration of the Conditions of the Wounded and Sick in Armies in the Field, Geneva, 1929 (extended to Palestine in 1931).

1020 For details on the extradition treaties between Palestine and other states, see Stoyanovsky, *op. cit.*, pp. 283–288.

1021 See Survey of Palestine, Vol. II, pp. 963–968.

1022 *Ibid.*, pp. 751–756.

1023 See, for example, Report on the Administration of Palestine 1935, *op. cit.*, pp. 308–311; Report on the Administration of Palestine 1939, *op. cit.*, pp. 118–125.

1024 Mandates Commission, *Minutes of the Thirty-Second (Extraordinary) Session, op. cit.*, p. 86.

1025 See Stoyanovsky, *op. cit.*, p. 288 (note 2).

necessary".[1026] By informing the League Council on these treaties through, for example, the annual reports of the Mandatory, it may be then safe to say that the treaties were approved by the League of Nations.[1027] And yet the case of the nationality Convention and its protocols is a peculiar one as these instruments were concluded under the League's umbrella.

Britain itself ratified, and therefore became a party, to the nationality Convention in 1932 and to its protocols in 1934.[1028] Upon the signature of these instruments, it was assumed that the Convention and its protocols would apply to the territories under the mandate of any Contracting Party. In this regard, Article 29 of the Convention reads:

> 1. Any High Contracting Party may, at the time of signature, ratification or accession, declare that, in accepting the present Convention, he does not assume any obligations in respect of all or any of his colonies, protectorates, overseas territories or territories under suzerainty or mandate, or in respect of certain parts of the population of the said territories; and the present Convention shall not apply to any territories or to the parts of their population named in such declaration....
> 3. Any High Contracting Party may, at any time, declare that he desires that the present Convention shall cease to apply to all or any of his colonies, protectorates, overseas territories or territories under suzerainty or mandate, or in respect of certain parts of the population of the said territories, and the Convention shall cease to apply to the territories or to the parts of their population named in such declaration one year after its receipt by the Secretary-General of the League of Nations.
> 4. Any High Contracting Party may make the reservations... in respect of all or any of his colonies, protectorates, overseas territories or territories under suzerainty or mandate, or in respect of certain parts of the population of these territories, at the time of signature, ratification or accession to the Convention or at the time of making a notification under the second paragraph of this Article....

An identical provision was reproduced in Article 15 of the Protocol on Military Obligations and Article 13 of the Protocol on Statelessness.

As Britain did not exclude Palestine (or any of its controlled, mandated or other territories) from the nationality instruments, it follows that these instruments were deemed to be applicable to Palestine in the same way in which they applied to Britain itself. Britain never made any declaration that the Convention and the protocols had ceased to apply to Palestine. Nor had Britain made any reservation

---

1026 *Ibid.*

1027 For further details on this meaning, see Permanent Mandates Commission, *Minutes of the Eighteenth Session*, League of Nations, Geneva, June–July 1930, pp. 14–15.

1028 Britain ratified the Convention on 6 April 1934. See *Procès-verbal of Ten Ratifications or Accessions According to Article 25 of the Convention on Certain Questions Relating to the Conflict of Nationality Laws Signed in the Hague on 12 April 1930* (Palestine Gazette, No. 756, Supplement 2, 3 February 1938, p. 299). It also ratified both the Protocol on Military Obligations on 14 January 1932 (Palestine Gazette, No. 750, Supplement 2, 20 January 1938, p. 101); and the Protocol on Statelessness on the same date (Palestine Gazette, No. 756, Supplement 2, 3 February 1938, p. 279).

on these instruments relating to that mandated territory.[1029] Indeed, at the preamble of the Convention and protocols, Britain was represented as:

> Great Britain, Ireland, Oversees British colonies, British India and all the countries of the British Empire, which are not members of the League of Nations.

Through this process, the Convention and its protocols were extended to Palestine.

On the other hand, the three instruments were published in the Official Gazette of Palestine shortly after entering into force at the international level. The Convention and the Protocol on Statelessness, which both entered into force at the international level on 1 July 1937, were published in the said Gazette on 3 February 1938.[1030] Earlier, the Protocol on the Military Obligations, which came into force on 25 May 1937, was published in the Gazette on 20 January 1938.[1031] This was the second step in the process of extending the Convention and its protocols into Palestine. By comparison, these instruments had gained more weight, in terms of formalities, than other treaties to which Palestine was a party.

It is unclear, however, in which form the nationality instruments were extended into Palestine apart from their publication in the Gazette. Neither the Mandate nor the Palestine Constitution had addressed the form by which Palestine might become a party to treaties. Hence, one should look at the practice of the British and Palestine Governments in regard to treaties in order to draw a conclusion.

As just mentioned, a variety of multilateral and bilateral treaties were extended to Palestine. Only a few of these were gazetted. Rather, various ways were employed to make such treaties public. Generally, however, it seems that a distinction was made between multilateral and bilateral treaties.

Multilateral treaties had been extended to Palestine in particular or as part of general extension to other British controlled territories. The extension was undertaken in two ways. The first took the form of a 'Notice' from the British government to the Government of Palestine informing the latter that Britain made Palestine a party to a certain treaty.[1032] The second way took the form of an 'Order in Council', by the British government, declaring the applicability of a certain treaty to Palestine.[1033]

1029 See League of Nations, *Official Journal*, 1938, *op. cit.*, pp. 71–73.

1030 No. 756, Supplement 2, p. 281 (the Convention), and p. 271 (the Protocol).

1031 No. 750, Supplement 2, p. 93.

1032 Examples of the Notices included: Notice relating to the Accession of Palestine to the International Convention for the Suppression of the Circulation of, and Traffic in, Obscene Publications [of 1921], 1928 (Palestine Gazette, 15 May 1928, p. 68); and Notice relating to the Accession of Palestine to the International Agreement for the Suppression of White Slave Traffic [of] 1904 and the International Convention for the Suppression of the Traffic in Women and Children [of] 1921, 1932 (Palestine Gazette, 24 March 1932, p. 211).

1033 Such Orders in Council included: Carriage by Air [of 1929] (Colonies, Protectorates and Mandated Territories) Order, 1935 (Palestine Gazette, No. 511, Supplement 2, 9 May 1935, p. 609); and Geneva Conventions [wounded and sick in armies in the field of] 1906 and [of] 1929 (Mandated Territories), Order in Council, 1937 (Palestine Gazette, No. 774, Supplement 2, 14 April 1938, p. 549).

These Notices or Orders in Council were then published in the Palestine Gazette without the full publication, usually, of the treaty itself.[1034]

As for bilateral treaties, the full text was usually published in the Palestine Gazette. The extension of these treaties took three forms. The first comprised treaties concluded between Palestine and its neighbouring countries without the direct involvement of Britain. Such treaties were regarded as Palestinian law, either merely by the publication in the Gazette or by enacting and publishing the treaty in the form of an Ordinance signed by the High Commissioner.[1035] The second form of treaty extension was exemplified by those treaties which Britain concluded with Palestine's neighbouring countries. Here, only the full text of the treaty was gazetted without additional legislative form.[1036] Thirdly, there were certain treaties concluded between Britain (not particularly on behalf of Palestine) and other states, which were then enforced in Palestine. Such treaties were extended to Palestine in the same way as the multilateral treaties (i.e. by publishing a Notice or an Order in Council in the Gazette without the treaty's text).[1037]

The foregoing review leads to two tentative conclusions. Firstly, extending treaties to Palestine, especially those reached between Britain and other states, was similar to the extension of British laws to that mandated territory.[1038] Secondly, there was no one fixed form whereby the treaties were extended to Palestine.[1039]

For the purpose of the present study, it is important to note that the nationality Convention and protocols were first acceded to by Britain on behalf of Palestine, and then published, in full, in the Palestine Gazette. Accordingly, the way by which the nationality instruments were extended to Palestine constituted a unique form of extension which was stronger than other forms of extension.

1034 The full text of the treaties mentioned in the previous two notes was not published in the form of Notices or Orders in Council in the Palestine Gazette.

1035 See, for example, Palestine-Syria and Palestine-Lebanon Customs Agreements (Validation) Ordinance, 1940 (Palestine Gazette, No. 1014, Supplement 1, 3 June 1940, p. 73); Iraq Petroleum Companies Agreements Ordinance, 1936 (Palestine Gazette, No. 909, Supplement 1, 10 July 1939, p. 61); and Agreement to Regulate the Service of Judicial Documents between Palestine and Trans-Jordan, 1935 (Palestine Gazette, No. 484, Supplement 2, 3 November 1935, p. 2).

1036 See, *inter alia*, Special Customs Agreement to Facilitate Trade between Palestine and Iraq, 1937 (Palestine Gazette, No. 668, Supplement 2, 20 February 1937, p. 97); Agreement relating to Facilitating Further Commercial Relations between Egypt and Palestine, 1936 (Palestine Gazette, No. 642, Supplement 2, 29 October 1936, p. 1474).

1037 See, e.g., Notice relating to the Extension to Palestine of the Convention between the United Kingdom and Greece Regarding Legal Proceedings in Civil and Commercial Matters [of 1926], 1939 (Palestine Gazette, No. 873, Supplement 2, 23 March 1939, p. 242); Switzerland (Extradition) Order in Council [of 1880 and of 1934], 1935 (Palestine Gazette, No. 580, Supplement 2, 2 April 1936, p. 239).

1038 See, e.g., Colonial Prisoners Removal Act, 1884; Foreign Jurisdiction Act, 1890; Merchant Shipping Act, 1894 (all these Acts indicated in Articles 35–37 of the Palestine Constitution).

1039 All the examples of treaties mentioned in the previous notes had exceptions.

One year after extending the nationality Convention and its protocols to Palestine, an amendment of the Palestinian Citizenship Order, 1925, was introduced on 25 July 1939.[1040] One of the purposes of this amendment was to bring, in concrete terms, domestic nationality rules in line with the international standards as reflected in the nationality Convention and its protocols. In addition to their adoption and publication in the Palestine Gazette, the integration of these instruments in the domestic legislation of Palestine, the third step in the extension process, left no doubt as to their validity in Palestine.

3. *Substance*

The Convention on Certain Questions Relating to the Conflict of Nationality Laws and its protocols addressed a number of substantive issues.[1041] These issues were, generally speaking, either a declaration of existing international law or consistent with existing domestic legislation in Palestine. A few modifications in the Palestinian law were introduced in order to harmonize certain rules of this law with the Convention and the Protocol on Statelessness.[1042] These substantive issues can be enumerated as follows: diplomatic protection of dual nationals;[1043] question of an effective link as a test to determine the nationality of dual nationals; right of dual nationals to renounce their other nationalities; expatriation, or voluntary renunciation of nationality; nationality of married women; nationality of children; and military obligations of dual nationals.[1044]

In its first Article, the Convention codified a rule of international law relating to diplomatic protection of dual nationals. It declared:

> A State may not afford diplomatic protection to one of its nationals against a State whose nationality such person also possesses.[1045]

This article is a logical result of another provision of the same Convention, which considered a dual national to be a citizen "by each of the States whose nationality

1040 *Op. cit.*

1041 Of its thirty-one articles, only the first seventeen articles of the Convention contained substantive provisions. Only the first three articles, of the seventeen-article Protocol on Military Obligations, were substantive. Among the fifteen-article Protocol on Statelessness, only Article 1 embodied a substantive provision. The rest of the articles included procedural provisions (e.g. reservation, accession, entering into force, renunciation).

1042 The Protocol on Military Obligations had merely a nominal effect in Palestine under the British rule, as there was no military obligation on Palestinian citizens which conflicted with other states.

1043 The term 'dual national' here means individuals having two or more nationalities.

1044 Only a brief explanation on the relevance of these issues to Palestine will be provided here. A full consideration of such matters is beyond the scope of this study.

1045 Article 4.

he possesses".[1046] The latter rule, in turn, "is hardly more than recognition of the fact that an individual may have the nationality of two or more states".[1047]

The principle of an effective link between the state and dual nationals, as a criterion by which to determine the applicable law in cases where nationalities conflict in a third state, was also recognized. Such recognition was formulated in Article 5 of the Convention as follows:

> Within a third State, a person having more than one nationality shall be treated as if he had only one.

This article was a mere codification of a well-established principle of international law.[1048] The exclusive validity of one nationality in cases of dual nationals should be determined based on one of two criteria: the first is the nationality of the state in which the person is habitually and principally resident; or, secondly, the nationality of the state with which such person appears to be in fact most closely linked.[1049] Yet adopting these two criteria does not prejudice the possibility of applying the law of the third state itself in which the conflict might arise (in this case, Palestinian law) or any other treaty relating to matters of personal status.[1050] Thus, in cases involving a conflict of laws in personal matters in Palestine, courts may apply one of the following four laws: the Palestinian law; any law referred to by special treaty; the law of the state in which the foreigner in question is habitually and principally resident; or the law of the state in which the foreigner has an effective link. These solutions had illustrated the pre-existing rules in Palestine. As early as 1922, Article 64 of the Palestine Constitution stated, in part, the following:

> Matters of personal status affecting foreigners...shall be decided by the District Courts which shall apply the personal law of the parties concerned.... The personal law shall be the law of the nationality of the foreigner concerned.[1051]

1046 Article 3.

1047 Flournoy, *op. cit.*, p. 470. See also Pierre Klein, "La protection diplomatique des doubles nationaux: reconsidération des fondements de la règle de non-responsabilité", *Revue belge de droit international*, Vol. 21, 1988, pp. 184–216.

1048 The principle of genuine link was applied (although in a comparatively different context) by the International Court of Justice in the *Nottebohm, op. cit.*, pp. 20–26. See also Brownlie, "The Relations of Nationality...", *op. cit.*, pp. 349 ff.

1049 In practice, the facts that indicate this link may vary from one case to the next. These facts include (in addition to the habitual residence), the centre of business, family ties, participation in public life, attachment shown by the person to a certain country and the inculcation of his children. See the *Nottebohm, op. cit.*, p. 22.

1050 In this respect, Article 5 of the Convention made the application by a third state of the aforesaid criteria conditional, by providing: "Without prejudice to the application of its law in matters of personal status and of any conventions in force".

1051 In Palestine, the term 'personal status' referred to the following matters: "marriage or divorce, alimony, maintenance, guardianship, legitimation and adoption of minors, inhibition from dealing with property of persons who are legally incompetent, successions, wills, legacies and the administration of the property of absent persons" (Palestine Constitution, Article 51). For details, see Goadby, "Religious jurisdiction in matters of personal status in Egypt, Cyprus and Palestine", *op. cit.*, pp. 293–320;

The Convention further recognized the right of the dual national to renounce the nationalities that he might have acquired without his voluntary action. To this effect, Article 6 reads:

> Without prejudice to the liberty of a State to accord wider rights to renounce its nationality, a person possessing two nationalities acquired without any voluntary act on his part may renounce one of them with the authorisation of the State whose nationality he desires to surrender. This authorisation may not be refused in the case of a person who has his habitual and principal residence abroad, if the conditions laid down in the law of the State whose nationality he desires to surrender are satisfied.[1052]

This rule already existed in Palestine in two instances. Firstly, if a man ceased to be a Palestinian citizen, his wife was eligible to remain a Palestinian; but, at the same time, such a wife was also permitted to renounce her Palestinian nationality by declaration.[1053] Secondly, any Palestinian citizen who at his birth or during his minority age became a national of another state was authorized, upon reaching eighteen years of age, to surrender his Palestinian citizenship by the declaration of alienage.[1054] Obviously, these provisions resulted from the general logic underlying the Palestinian Citizenship Order of 1925 which permitted the change of nationality (expatriation).[1055] By taking this liberal approach, the Palestinian law, on this point, had accorded wider rights relating to expatriation than those rights adopted by the Convention itself.

As a number of states made the change of nationality subject to governmental authorization,[1056] the Convention touched upon this practice with a view of avoiding, or at least reducing, the cases of statelessness in the world.[1057] Thus, the first paragraph of its Article 7 provides:

> In so far as the law of a State provides for the issue of an expatriation permit, such a permit shall not entail the loss of the nationality of the State which issues it, unless

and Vitta, *op. cit.*, pp. 14–59, 102 ff. On judicial implementation, see, for instance: *Nazmi Bey Badrakhan Pasha v. 1. Yumna, Bint Mikhail Nassar, 2. Badi', Bint Yussef Aboud, 3. Siham Badrakhan Pasha, 4. Yussef Badrakhan Pasha*, Supreme Court of Palestine sitting as a Court of Civil Appeal, 15 July 1943 (Annotated Law Reports, 1943, Vol. II, p. 421); *Gertrud Freyberger v. Otto Friedmann*, Supreme Court of Palestine, 16 July 1943 (Annotated Law Reports, 1943, Vol. I, p. 395); *Della Goldenberg v. Moshe Goldenberg*, Special Tribunal constituted under Article 55 of the Palestine Order in Council, 1922, and Section 9 of the Courts Ordinance, 1940, 7 January 1947 (Annotated Law Reports, 1947, Vol. I, p. 25); *Nadeen Markoff v. Habib George Daoud Homsi, op. cit.*

1052 For a commentary on this article, see Flournoy, *op. cit.*, pp. 471–473.

1053 See above p. 136.

1054 See above Chapter VII, Section 5.

1055 See above Chapter VII.

1056 See above pp. 30–34, 133–134.

1057 For a commentary, see Flournoy, *op. cit.*, pp. 473–477.

> the person to whom it is issued possesses another nationality or unless and until he acquires another nationality.[1058]

This clause had no significance in Palestine as the loss of one's nationality did not require authorization from the Government of Palestine.[1059]

But, following a pre-existing practice in Palestine, the third paragraph of Article 7 of the Convention added:

> The State whose nationality is acquired by a person to whom an expatriation permit has been issued, shall notify such acquisition to the State which has issued the permit.

As already noted, it was the practice of the Government of Palestine to inform the consuls of states, whose citizens acquired Palestinian nationality by naturalization, of their citizens' naturalization in Palestine.[1060] Yet this provision is still useful because it formalized the previous practice which lacked a clear legal basis.

Following a long history of discrimination against married women in terms of nationality almost everywhere in the world, the Convention succeeded in advancing the question of married women's nationality. The Convention's provisions were, indeed, "designed to prevent or remedy cases of hardship resulting to married women through differences between the laws of various countries. In general, they give more freedom of choice to the woman".[1061] However, the Convention was still far from having achieved a full equality between the two sexes on nationality-related matters.

In Palestine, the Convention's provisions relating to married women were entirely transferred into the 1939 amendment of the 1925 Citizenship Order and altered the latter's discriminatory provisions.[1062] Nonetheless, Article 6(1) of the new Order maintained, as a general rule derived from the original 1925 Citizenship Order, that "the wife of a Palestinian citizen shall be deemed to be a Palestinian citizen and the wife of the alien shall be deemed to be an alien". This means that the said amendment considered the new nationality rights for married women as exceptions.

It may be of interest to mention that the Government of Palestine regarded this amendment not as an improvement of a women's status or as an application to the Convention, but, rather, as a tool to avoid the fraudulent naturalization of female immigrants by marriage with Palestinians. As mentioned earlier, many illegal female immigrants employed the technique of marrying Palestinian citizens as an excuse to escape from the immigration rules (especially to avoid deportation after

1058 For details, see Borchard, *Diplomatic Protection of Citizens Abroad or the Law of International Claims, op. cit.*, pp. 674–712.

1059 The second paragraph of Article 7 of the Convention (regarding the termination of expatriation permits) similarly had no influence in Palestine.

1060 See above p. 120.

1061 Flournoy, *op. cit.*, p. 476. For details, see Waltz, *op. cit.*, pp. 99–113.

1062 See above pp. 120–121.

the expiry of their travel visas) in order to remain in Palestine.[1063] Being aware of this technique, the Government of Palestine pointed out:

> In these cases the [female's] applications [for Palestinian nationality by marriage] would be approved if the marriages were held to be genuine, but would be declined if the marriages were held to be fictitious and designed solely to bring a woman into Palestine as a Palestinian citizen who otherwise would not be qualified for admission under the immigration legislation.[1064]

For its part, the Supreme Court of Palestine on 23 July 1941 confirmed the Government's position. It held that the "effect of the 1939 amendment to the Immigration Rules was to make it impossible for a traveller to obtain permission to remain permanently in Palestine".[1065]

Nonetheless, the real value of the new and favourable provisions on the nationality of married women in Palestine could not be undermined.

A foreign woman became no longer subject to automatic dependency on her husband's nationality. Rather, such a woman was given the choice to apply for naturalization in case she desired to become a Palestinian citizen by marriage.[1066] In this connection, it was held:

> There is no doubt that if the Petitioner married a Palestinian citizen prior to 1939 she did acquire Palestinian citizenship by virtue of such marriage. It was only in 1939 that Article 12 of the Palestinian Citizenship Order, 1925, was amended. The position since 1939 is that a woman does not acquire Palestinian citizenship, as of course, by marrying a Palestinian.[1067]

If she so desired, such a woman could be naturalized even if she did not satisfy the naturalization conditions.[1068] Thus, the new amendment gave the married woman the choice whether or not to retain her foreign nationality and, at the same time, made it easy for her to follow the nationality of her Palestinian husband if she so wished.

1063 See above pp. 171–172.

1064 See Survey of Palestine, Vol. I, p. 207. See also Department of Statistics (Government of Palestine), *Statistical Abstract of Palestine*, Government Printer, Jerusalem, 1944–1945, p. 46.

1065 *Dr. Jeanette Sara Benjamin v. Commissioner for Migration & Statistics and Another, op. cit.*

1066 See Palestinian Citizenship Order (Amendment) of 1939, Article 6(2)—marriage to a Palestinian citizen; and Article 6(6)—marriage to a person to be naturalized in Palestine. This rule is an application to Article 10 of the Convention, which reads: "Naturalisation of the husband during marriage shall not involve a change in the nationality of the wife except with her consent".

1067 *Fatmeh bint Mahmoud As'ad Ammar v. Assistant Inspector General C.I.D. of Jerusalem, op. cit.*

1068 Palestinian Citizenship Order (Amendment) of 1939, Article 6(2), second sentence.

On the other hand, a Palestinian woman who married a foreigner was entitled to remain a Palestinian citizen until she acquired her husband's nationality.[1069] This provision was a direct application of Article 8 of the Convention, which states:

> If the national law of the wife causes her to lose her nationality on marriage with a foreigner, this consequence shall be conditional on her acquiring the nationality of the husband.

Yet the Government of Palestine considered the said change as an application of the British nationality law and not as a result of the Convention.[1070]

Similarly, where a man ceased to be a Palestinian citizen during his marriage, his wife was eligible to remain a Palestinian until she acquired her husband's new nationality.[1071] This rule is consistent with Article 9 of the Convention:

> If the national law of the wife causes her to lose her nationality upon a change in the nationality of her husband occurring during marriage, this consequence shall be conditional on her acquiring her husband's new nationality.

This article is more advanced than Article 12(1) of the 1925 Citizenship Order, which gave a woman the right to remain a Palestinian citizen even if her husband ceased to be a Palestinian but obliged her *to declare* her desire to remain a Palestinian. Rather, this new provision presumed that the woman would continue to be a Palestinian citizen (without undertaking the said declaration), until acquiring her husband's new foreign nationality.

Besides, if a woman ceased to be a Palestinian citizen by marriage to a foreigner and, subsequent to this, her husband changed his nationality or their marriage was then dissolved, it became possible for such a woman to recover her Palestinian nationality.[1072] This rule followed Article 11 of the Convention:

> The wife who, under the law of her country, lost her nationality on marriage shall not recover it after the dissolution of the marriage except on her own application and in accordance with the law of that country. If she does recover it, she shall lose the nationality which she acquired by reason of the marriage.

Despite their limited influence,[1073] these rules improved the status of married women in Palestine, as had been the case in those other countries which had adopted the Convention. Indeed, it was envisioned that the Convention would be a starting point towards the realization of full equality between men and women on nationality matters. In this vein, the *Final Act of The Hague First Conference on the*

1069 *Ibid.*, Article 6(3).
1070 See Survey of Palestine, *op. cit.*, p. 207.
1071 Palestinian Citizenship Order (Amendment) of 1939, Article 6(4).
1072 Palestinian Citizenship Order (Amendment) of 1939, Article 6(5), (7).
1073 This is particularly true when one compares the subsequent international evolution with regard to the nationality of married women and women's rights as a whole (see *infra* note 1093).

Codification of International Law[1074] recommended that states study the possibility: (1) to introduce into their law the principle of equality of the sexes in matters of nationality…, (2) and especially to decide that in principle the nationality of the wife shall henceforth not be affected without her consent either by the mere fact of marriage or by any change in the nationality of her husband.[1075]

In so far as the nationality of children was concerned, unlike the nationality of married women, both the Convention and the Protocol on Statelessness had codified the relevant pre-existing rules in Palestine.[1076]

The said Convention and Protocol conferred the nationality of the state of birth to the children born in a territory where the principle *jus sanguinis* prevailed (as was the case in Palestine)[1077] to a stateless or to unknown father or to unknown parents. The Convention laid down this provision in two articles. Article 14 states:

> A child whose parents are both unknown shall have the nationality of the country of birth. If the child's parentage is established, its nationality shall be determined by the rules applicable in cases where the parentage is known. A foundling is, until the contrary is proved, presumed to have been born on the territory of the State in which it was found.

Article 15 of the Convention adds:

> Where the nationality of a State is not acquired automatically by reason of birth on its territory, a child born on the territory of that State of parents having no nationality, or of unknown nationality, may obtain the nationality of the said State. The law of that State shall determine the conditions governing the acquisition of its nationality in such cases.

The Protocol on Statelessness limited such a conferral of nationality to those cases where the child was born to a mother possessing the nationality of that state.[1078] All these cases had been covered under the general terms of Article 3(*c*) of the Citizenship Order of 1925, which considered the person to be a Palestinian citizen (quoted earlier)[1079] as: any person who was "born whether in or out of lawful matrimony within Palestine who does not by his birth or by subsequent legitimisation acquire the nationality of any other State or whose nationality is unknown".

1074 *Supplement to the The American Journal of International Law*, Vol. 24, 1930, p. 183.

1075 However, for well-known reasons, Palestine did not engage in the progressive development of international law in this respect.

1076 For a commentary, see Flournoy, *op. cit.*, pp. 478–479, 481.

1077 See above pp. 109–110.

1078 Article 1 of the Protocol provided: "In a State whose nationality is not conferred by the mere fact of birth in its territory, a person born in its territory of a mother possessing the nationality of that State and of a father without nationality or of unknown nationality shall have the nationality of the said State".

1079 See above pp. 109–110.

Furthermore, according to various articles of the Palestinian Citizenship Order, the naturalization of the parents (especially fathers) includes their children.[1080] This rule was then laid down in Article 13 of the Convention as follows:

> Naturalisation of the parents shall confer on such of their children as, according to its law, are minors the nationality of the State by which the naturalisation is granted. In such cases the law of that State may specify the conditions governing the acquisition of its nationality by the minor children as a result of the naturalisation of the parents. In cases where minor children do not acquire the nationality of their parents as the result of the naturalisation of the latter, they shall retain their existing nationality.

The last sentence of this article was, however, not relevant to Palestine as the naturalization of the father in Palestinian nationality led, in all cases, to the naturalization of his minor children.

The Convention embodied certain provisions concerning children which could not be extended to Palestine. That is because either such provisions were applicable only to *jus soli* states (such as excluding children born to officials of foreign states from the acquisition of nationality of the country in which such children were born),[1081] which is not the case in Palestine whereby *jus sanguinis* applied;[1082] or due to the fact that the Palestinian law did not contain the problems that the Convention intended to resolve in other states where such problems existed.[1083]

Finally, the Protocol relating to Military Obligations in Certain Cases of Dual Nationality could be applied only in inter-state relations.[1084] There was no necessity therefore for this Protocol to be incorporated into domestic (in this case Palestinian) law. The Protocol simply provided that dual nationals might undertake military obligations in one state. These persons should be then exempt from such obligations in other state(s) and could lose the nationality of the latter as a consequence of serving in the military of another state (Article 1). Article 2 stipulates that if the dual national has the right to renounce any nationality upon attaining

---

1080 See Articles 6, 9, 11, 14 and 20. See also above pp. 122–123.

1081 See Article 12 of the Convention. While the first paragraph of this article (concerning the nationality of children born to parents enjoying diplomatic immunity) was a declaratory statement of existing international law, the second (relating to the nationality of children of officials not enjoying diplomatic immunity) posed a new rule requiring states to adopt legislation under which children born to such officials may be divested of their nationality acquired by birth. See Flournoy, *op. cit.*, p. 478.

1082 See above pp. 109–110.

1083 These rules were set forth in Articles 16 and 17 of the Convention. Article 16 (on the loss of nationality due to the recognition of an illegitimate child), was not applicable to Palestine as the Palestinian law did not require the loss of nationality by the mere fact of legitimization. Similarly, Article 17 (on the loss of the child's nationality as a result to his adoption) was not enforced in Palestine. This was due to the fact that the mere adoption of a Palestinian child by foreigners did not cause the loss of the child's Palestinian nationality.

1084 See Article 4 of the Protocol (the High Contracting Parties agreed to apply the Protocol in their relations with each other). See Flournoy, *op. cit.*, pp. 479–481.

his majority, he shall be exempt from undertaking military service in the state in which he renounced its nationality. Article 3 exempted any person who changed his nationality from the military obligations in his former state. These two articles are merely a logical consequence of Article 1.

4. *On-going validity?*

Are the nationality Convention and its protocols still applicable in the West Bank and Gaza Strip today? What will be their impact in the future Palestinian state?

In general, "obligations created by treaty 'run with the land', and bind the territory, so that any State succeeding to possession of the territory continues to be bound by them".[1085] In 1930, the League of Nations adopted the view that "all treaties made by the Mandatory on behalf of the [mandated] territory remain in force until denounced by the new State".[1086] In particular, the United Nations resolution on the Partition of Palestine, 1947,[1087] provided that the two (Arab and Jewish) states which were projected to be established in the post-mandate Palestine "shall be bound by all the international agreements and conventions, both general and special, to which Palestine has become a party".[1088]

The Convention and its protocols were never repealed or renounced by any authority exercising power in the West Bank and Gaza Strip.[1089] It follows that they are also still valid at the international level today.[1090] Moreover, the fact that the Convention and its protocols were part of Palestinian domestic law (which remains unchanged in this regard), provides ongoing validity to these instruments even if, arguably, the instruments themselves, for whatever reason, have been abrogated. While it is true that some provisions within these instruments require the existence

---

1085 Mervyn Johns, "State Succession in the Matter of Treaties", *The British Year Book of International Law*, 1947, p. 362. For details, see O'Connell, *State Succession…*, *op. cit.*, Vol. II, pp. 141–163. *Cf.* Shabtai Rosenne, "Israël et les Traités Internationaux de la Palestine", *Journal du Droit International*, Vol. 77, 1950, pp. 1140–1173.

1086 "General Conditions to be Fulfilled before the Mandate Regime Can be Brought to an End in Respect of A Country Placed under that Regime", League of Nations Document No. C.P.M.1183 (Permanent Mandate Commission, *Minutes of the Twentieth Session, op. cit.*).

1087 See below Chapter XI.

1088 See Chapter 3, Part 2, of the Partition Plan.

1089 The denunciation of these instruments is possible under three articles: Article 28 of the Convention; Article 14 of Protocol on Military Obligations; and Article 12 of Protocol on Statelessness. In general, see O'Connell, *State Succession…*, *op. cit.*, Vol. II, pp. 212–291.

1090 The nationality instruments, as multilateral treaties, have been valid since their enforcement. They were never terminated due to the reasons laid down in the Vienna Convention on the Law of Treaties, 1969, such as the withdrawal (Article 54), or denunciation of nationality (Article 56), impossibility of performance (Article 61) or fundamental change of circumstances (Article 62).

of a state in order to be invoked *vis-à-vis* other states,[1091] most of these provisions could be executed internally as part of Palestinian law.

Although today's Palestine, i.e. the West Bank and Gaza Strip, has not followed the developments relating to nationality at the international level since, at least, 1948, the future state of Palestine must adhere to the nationality obligations established by international law, as embodied in "international custom, and the principle of law generally recognized with regard to nationality".[1092] This includes the duty to amend the existing legislation which contradicts international legal developments. The would-be state of Palestine could, of course, become a party to other treaties concluded in this domain through accession.[1093]

1091 See the following articles of the Convention: Article 18 (application among contacting parties), Article 21 (settlement of disputes among states), Article 27 (revision of the Convention), and Article 28 (denunciation).

1092 See Article 1 of the Convention.

1093 These developments include, *inter alia*, the following instruments: Universal Declaration of Human Rights, 10 December 1948 (UN Doc. A/811, 16 December 1948—in *The American Journal of International Law*, Vol. 43 (supplement), 1949, p. 127), Article 15; Convention relating to the Status of Stateless Persons, New York, 28 September 1954 (UN Treaty Series, Vol. 360, 1960, p. 130); Convention on the Nationality of Married Women, New York, 20 February 1957 (*ibid.*, Vol. 309, 1958, p. 66); Convention on the Reduction of Statelessness, New York, 30 August 1961 (*ibid.*, Vol. 989, 1983, p. 176); International Convention on the Elimination of All Forms of Racial Discrimination, New York, 7 March 1966 (*ibid.*, Vol. 660, 1969, p. 212), Article 5(d)(iii); International Covenant on Civil and Political Rights, New York, 19 December 1966 (*ibid.*, Vol. 999, 1976, p. 172), Article 24(3); Convention on the Elimination of All Forms of Discrimination against Women, New York, 18 December 1979 (*ibid.*, Vol. 1249, 1990, p. 14), Article 9; Convention on the Rights of the Child, New York, 20 November 1989 (*ibid.*, Vol. 1577, 1999, p. 44), Articles 7 and 8. On the nationality and human rights, see, for example, Johannes M.M. Chan, "The Right to a Nationality as a Human Right: The Current Trend Towards Recognition", *Human Rights Law Journal*, Vol. 12, 1991, pp. 1–14; Alina Kaczorowska, "Le Droit à la nationalité est-il un droit fondamental de l'homme?", *Turkish Yearbook of Human Rights*, Vol. 19–20, 1997–1998, pp. 119–136. See also references of *supra* note 17.

XI

PALESTINIAN NATIONALITY IN THE PARTITION PLAN

1. *Law versus reality*

As the United Nations Partition Plan of Palestine, 29 November 1947,[1094] has never been implemented, the intention here is to review the nationality provisions of the Plan as a means to view the position of the international community regarding the future of Palestinian nationality at the end of the mandate. The conformity of the Plan's provisions with international law relating to nationality and state succession will be briefly evaluated in the light of the facts concerning the population in Palestine, Palestinian citizens and foreigners alike, at the time.

At the end of the British rule, the law and facts concerning nationality in Palestine faced a new controversy.[1095] In legal terms, original and naturalized Palestinian citizens (Christians, Jews, Muslims and others) were equal nationals, regardless of their religion. In reality, however, these citizens were divided into two 'Palestinian peoples':[1096]

1094 UN Doc. A/RES/181(II) (A+B). The Plan was adopted by a General Assembly resolution on 29 November 1947. The resolution was adopted with 33 states in favor; 13 states against; and 10 states abstained. It was considered an 'important question', which required a two-thirds majority, in accordance with Article 18(2) of the United Nations Charter.

1095 See, for example, Frank C. Sakran, *Palestine Dilemma, Arab Rights Versus Zionist Aspirations*, Public Affairs Press, Washington D.C., 1948; Arthur Koestler, *Promise and Fulfilment: Palestine 1917–1949*, Macmillan & Co. Ltd., 1949; Esco Foundation for Palestine, *op. cit.*, Vol. I, pp. 493–593.

1096 The term 'Palestinian peoples' was mentioned in Part III, C(b), of the Partition Plan. In addition, the United Nations Committee on Palestine (UNSCOP) which had prepared the said Plan had frequently employed similar expressions such as: 'the two peoples of Palestine', 'Arab and Jewish peoples', 'Arabs and Jews...these two peoples', 'the peoples of Palestine', 'its [Palestine] peoples', 'both peoples [of Palestine]'. See United Nations Special Committee on Palestine, *Report to the General Assembly*, New York, UN Doc. A/364, 3 September 1947 (hereinafter: 'UNSCOP Report'). Similar language was used, *inter alia*, in the policy statement declared by Britain (the White Paper of 1939, *op. cit.*, pp. 8–11).

Arab and Jewish.[1097] In such a situation, Palestinian nationality, as well as the entire future of the country, was arriving at a historical juncture.

According to statistics relied upon by the United Nations,[1098] as of 31 December 1946, the inhabitants (citizens and foreigners) of Palestine were estimated at 1,972,560 persons. These comprised 1,212,840 Arabs (1,067,780 Muslims; 145,060 Christians) and 608,230 Jews.[1099]

Racial and religious criteria had been formally adopted and had divided the 'Palestinian people' into two peoples: Arab and Jewish. The racial criterion of 'Palestinian Arab'[1100] incorporated Arabic-speaking individuals who belonged chiefly to Muslim and Christian religions. These Arabs, as already detailed earlier, were originally Ottoman subjects who became Palestinian citizens through the natural change of nationality on 1 August 1925.[1101] In the meantime, 'Palestinian Jews',[1102]

1097 As to the actual division of the Arab and Jewish communities in Palestine at the end of the mandate, see, for example, Survey of Palestine, Vol. II, pp. 933–962. See also Enzo Sereni and R.E. Ashery, eds., *Jews and Arabs in Palestine: Studies in a National and Colonial Problem*, Hechalutz Press, New York, 1936.

1098 Statistics provided in this chapter are fairly accurate. However, there would be a margin of error because the last census was conducted by the Government of Palestine in 1931. The subsequent estimations of Palestine's inhabitants were based on records of births, deaths, immigration and migration. Likewise, differences of various statistics might appear due to the criteria employed (e.g. time sphere, including or excluding certain category of persons present in Palestine—such as nomadic Bedouins, British forces—or geographical areas). Lastly, certain statistical totals were accounted by the writer based on comparisons among various available statistics.

1099 United Nations, *Report of the Sub-Committee 2 to the Ad Hoc Committee on the Palestinian question* (UN Doc. A/AC.14/32 and Add. 1, 11 November 1947), p. 304. It is to be noted that the said *Ad Hoc* Committee had created two sub-committees to draw up detailed proposals for the General Assembly based on UNSCOP's Report. Sub-Committee 1, which was in charge of drafting a detailed partition plan and discussing, *inter alia*, the nationality question. It formed a working group and appointed a Special Rapporteur on that question. This working group was the final drafter of the nationality text of the Partition Plan. UN Doc. A/AC.14/34 and Corr. 1 and Add. 1, 19 November 1947, p. 244; see also p. 253 (nationality in the Arab and Jewish States), and p. 262 (nationality in Jerusalem).

1100 See, for example, "The Palestinian Arabs", in *Palestine* (a Jewish-run magazine), The Garden City Press, Letchworth, Vol. XI, 4 March 1936, p. 4. As to the judicial application of the division between Palestinian Arabs and Palestinian non-Arabs, the Supreme Court of Palestine, for instance, held that: "It was that Mrs. Albina was for the technical purpose of the Land Transfer Regulations a non-Palestinian Arab although her husband was a Palestinian Arab, consequently the transfer to her of this land...would have been null and void" (*Antoine F. Albina v. 1. Mrs. Agnes, wife of Antoine F. Albina, 2. Bassam Fawzi Ghussein & an. and Bassam Fawzi Ghussein & an. v. 1. Agnes Michal Takountieff (alias Agnes Antoine Francis Albina), 2. Antoine F. Albina*, Supreme Court of Palestine, 6 March 1947—Annotated Law Reports, 1947, Vol. I, p. 234).

1101 See above Chapter V, Section 1.

1102 See above pp. 93–94. This should not be mixed with the non-legal term of 'Jewish nationality' which was commonly used as a synonym for the 'Jewish people'. Such terms meant to include all Jews in the world and not only those Jews who acquired

a religious criterion, incorporated two categories: (1) original Palestinian Jews who were, like the Arabs, Ottoman subjects and afterwards became natural Palestinian citizens;[1103] and (2) Palestinian Jews who became Palestinian citizens by naturalization.[1104] A wholly different group of Jews comprised foreign individuals residing in Palestine. The latter group, in turn, incorporated either legal residents or illegal immigrants.[1105]

Consequently, two *de facto* nationalities had been created. This came about as a result of British policy in Palestine. In a report prepared by the League of Nations in 1945, such British policy had been accurately characterized as follows:

> Since the outset of the mandate, the *classification* of the population of Palestine by *religions* has been recognised as necessary, in view of the fact that the personal status of every inhabitant is dependent on the law of the religious community to which he belongs.... [I]t was also found that a classification by 'race' (or nationality)—i.e., as Arabs, Jews or 'others'—had become a political necessity...the immigration and emigration statistics have been prepared on a racial basis. Of recent years, therefore, the population of Palestine has been classified according to the criteria both of religion and race.[1106]

The foregoing facts arose at the international level, when Britain brought the question of Palestine to the United Nations on 2 April 1947 requesting the organization's intervention.[1107] Thus, on 15 May, the United Nations Special Committee on Palestine (UNSCOP) was formed.[1108] After extensive work, the UNSCOP submitted its report (dated 3 September 1947) to the United Nations General Assembly. The most

---

Palestinian nationality. See Stoyanovsky, *op. cit.*, pp. 60–61; Mallison, *op. cit.*, pp. 983 (footnote), 998–1035, 1050–1069.

1103 The status of this category of Jewish Palestinians is identical with the status of Arab Palestinians; both were Ottoman citizens residing in Palestine. See above Chapter V, Section 1.

1104 See above Chapter VI, Section 2.

1105 See above Section IX, Section 3.

1106 League of Nations, *The Mandate System: Origin—Principles—Application*, Geneva, 1945, p. 78 (emphasis in original). See also the following publications: Department of Migration (Government of Palestine), *The Statistics of Migration and Naturalization*, Government Printer, Jerusalem, 1941, 1942, 1943 (separate annual volumes). Also see a separate publication entitled *Statistical Abstracts of Palestine* prepared by the Department of Statistics of Government of Palestine (Government Printer, Jerusalem), 1936, pp. 27–31; 1937–1938, pp. 34–41; 1939, pp. 31–38; 1940, pp. 31–38; 1941, pp. 31–38; 1942, pp. 19–26; 1943, pp. 12–23; 1944–1945, pp. 36–47. For a combination of the statistics mentioned in this note, see Survey of Palestine, Vol. I, pp. 140–224.

1107 See "Letter dated 2 April 1947 from the United Kingdom delegation to the Acting Secretary-General requesting a special session of the General Assembly on Palestine", UN Doc. A/286, 2 April 1947.

1108 UN Doc. A/RES/106 (S-1), 15 May 1947. See, in general, Jacob Robinson, *Palestine and the United Nations: Prelude to Solution*, Public Affairs Press, Washington, D.C., 1947; Joseph Jermiah Zasloff, *Great Britain and Palestine: A Study of the Problem of Palestine before the United Nations*, Graduate Institute of International Studies, Geneva, 1952 (Ph.D. thesis); Hazem Z. Nuseibeh, *Palestine and the United Nations*, Quartet Books, London/New York, 1982.

important outcome of that Committee's efforts was the proposal to divide Palestine into three entities: Arab State; Jewish State; and to endow a special international status (*corpus separatum*) upon the City of Jerusalem.[1109] With slight modifications, the General Assembly adopted the UNSCOP's proposal by Resolution 181(II) of 29 November 1947, which incorporated a proposed solution entitled 'Plan of Partition with Economic Union'. This Plan is known as 'the Partition Plan'.

Amongst other issues, the Plan addressed the question of the future nationalities in the projected Arab and Jewish States as well as in the City of Jerusalem.

The Partition Plan defined the nationality of the inhabitants of both the Arab State and the Jewish State as follows:[1110]

> Palestinian citizens residing in Palestine outside the City of Jerusalem, as well as Arabs and Jews who, not holding Palestinian citizenship, reside in Palestine outside the City of Jerusalem shall, upon the recognition of independence, become citizens of the State in which they are resident and enjoy full civil and political rights. Persons over the age of eighteen years may opt, within one year from the date of recognition of independence of the State in which they reside, for citizenship of the other State, providing that no Arab residing in the area of the proposed Arab State shall have the right to opt for citizenship in the proposed Jewish State and no Jew residing in the proposed Jewish State shall have the right to opt for citizenship in the proposed Arab State. The exercise of this right of option will be taken to include the wives and children under eighteen years of age of persons so opting.[1111]

1109 UN Doc. A/RES/106 (S-1), 15 May 1947, *op. cit.*, pp. 47–58. Another proposal introduced by the minority members of the UNSCOP, which suggested the establishment of one federal state in Palestine, was not adopted by the General Assembly (*ibid.*, pp. 59–64).

1110 Part I(C), Chapter 3(1).

1111 The original text of the UNSCOP report dealt with the nationalities of the Arab State and the Jewish State as well as the City of Jerusalem in a single paragraph: "Palestinian citizens, as well as Arabs and Jews who, not holding Palestinian citizenship, reside in Palestine, shall, upon the recognition of independence, become citizens of the State in which they are resident; or, if resident in the City of Jerusalem, who sign a notice of intention provided in section B, paragraph 2 above, of the State mentioned in such notice, with full civil and political rights, provided that they do not exercise the option mentioned hereafter. Such persons, if over eighteen years of age, may opt within one year for the citizenship of the other State or declare that they retain the citizenship of any State of which they are citizens…; provided that no person who has signed the notice of intention referred to in section B, paragraph 2 above shall have the right of option" (p. 50). Section B, paragraph 2, stated, in part: "Qualified voters for each State for this [constituent assemblies] election shall be persons over twenty years of age who are: (*a*) Palestinian citizens residing in that State and (*b*) Arabs and Jews residing in the State, although not Palestinian citizens, who, before voting, have signed a notice of intention to become citizens of such State. Arabs and Jews residing in the City of Jerusalem who have signed a notice of intention to become citizens, the Arabs of the Arab State and the Jews of the Jewish State, shall be entitled to vote in the Arab and Jewish States, respectively" (pp. 48–49). Obviously, the final text of the Partition Plan, provided above, is clearer (though substantively identical) than this draft.

With respect to the nationality of the inhabitants of Jerusalem, the Plan provided:[1112]

> All the residents shall become *ipso facto* citizens of the City of Jerusalem unless they opt for citizenship of the State of which they have been citizens or, if Arabs or Jews, have filed a notice of intention to become citizens of the Arab or Jewish State respectively.... The Trusteeship Council shall make arrangements for consular protection of the citizens of the City outside its territory.

2. *Nationality in the post-mandated Palestine: the principle*

The Partition Plan's principle on nationality in the future entities of Palestine was straight-forward. Palestinian citizens, irrespective of their religion, residing in the Arab State, would become citizens of that Arab State (but not Arab citizens). Likewise, Palestinian citizens, also regardless of their religion, residing in the Jewish State would become citizens of that Jewish State (but not Jewish citizens).

This principle was not new. Its content had already been suggested in earlier proposals concerning the Palestine problem. The principle was also consistent (despite the fact that it was embodied in a political document) with international law relating to nationality at the time of territorial succession.

Before reaching its recommended solution, UNSCOP had examined previous proposals to solve Palestine's problem,[1113] including the proposal of the Palestine Partition Commission of 1938,[1114] which also suggested the creation of Arab and Jewish States.[1115] Concerning the inhabitant's nationality, the 1938 proposal stated:

> A Palestinian habitually resident in the Jewish State would automatically cease to be a Palestinian citizen...and would *ipso facto* become a citizen of the Jewish State. Similarly, a Palestinian habitually resident in the Arab State would *ipso facto* become a citizen of that state.[1116]

This proposed solution was the origin of the automatic change from Palestinian nationality to the nationalities of the Arab and Jewish States. However, it should be noted that this proposal, unlike the Partition Plan, was based on two legal criteria. In order to qualify for the nationality of either the Arab State or the Jewish State,

---

1112 Part III(C),(11).

1113 UNSCOP Report, *op. cit.*, pp. 39–41.

1114 See Palestine Partition Commission, *Report Presented by the Secretary of State for Colonies to Parliament by Command of His Majesty*, October 1938, His Majesty Stationary Office, London, 1938. This Commission was also known, following the name of its Chairman, Mr. John Woodhead, as the 'Woodhead Commission'. It was formed pursuant to the Palestine Royal Commission's recommendation of 1937, *op. cit.* On the various proposals to resolve the question of Palestine, see, e.g., Esco Foundation for Palestine, *op. cit.*, Vol. II, pp. 799–955, 1077–1186.

1115 The Partition Commission did not propose a distinct nationality for the inhabitants of Jerusalem, as the city was expected to remain under British mandate.

1116 Palestine Partition Commission, *op. cit.*, p. 155.

the individual should be, firstly, a Palestinian citizen and, secondly, a habitual resident in one of the two projected States.[1117] In other words, foreigners residing in the Arab State or the Jewish State (regardless of whether they were Arabs, Jews or neither) could not automatically become citizens in either State.

The principle of the automatic change from the nationality of the predecessor state to one of the nationalities of the successor states as laid down in the Partition Plan had affirmed an existing rule of international law.[1118] As already illustrated, such a rule had been adopted by various peace treaties which had led to territorial change.[1119] The rule "is believed to express a rule of international law which is generally recognized".[1120] In the absence of an agreement between the concerned parties (the Arabs and Jews of Palestine), the United Nations General Assembly had decided that the inhabitants of the predecessor territory (Palestine) should acquire the nationality of the successor territories. In other words, Palestinians should acquire either: (1) the nationality of the Arab State (but not an 'Arab nationality'—in the sense that the Arab State nationality should not only be given to persons belonging to the Arab race); or (2) the nationality of the Jewish State (but not a 'Jewish nationality'—which means that the Jewish State nationality could be conferred on non-Jews). Thus, the Plan had merely applied an established rule of international law with regard to this point.[1121]

The basis of the automatic change from Palestinian nationality into the nationalities of post-Palestine entities, therefore, is derived from the law of state succession, whatever the legal validity of the Plan itself.[1122] This was not the only case in which the United Nations General Assembly resolutions had embodied rules of international law; indeed, the Assembly had often "adopted resolutions declaring what it finds to be an existing rule of international law".[1123] In other words, the Partition Plan had merely declared the legal rules relating to the future nationalities in the Arab State and the Jewish State; it did not create these nationalities.

1117 See, in general, Herman L. Weisman, *The Future of Palestine: An Examination of the Partition Plan*, Lincoln Printing Company, New York, 1937.

1118 See Harvard Research on Nationality, *op. cit.*, Article 18; ILC Articles on Nationality and State Succession, 1999, *op. cit.*, Article 5 (the two articles were quoted in *supra* note 386). The question of nationality and state succession has been thoroughly examined by many writers and it is sufficient here to apply the relevant rules on the present case. See references in *supra* note 384.

1119 See above pp. 69–70.

1120 Harvard Research on Nationality, *op. cit.*, p. 61.

1121 After recommending the establishment of separate Jewish and Arab nationalities in Palestine, the Palestine Partition Commission (*op. cit.*, p. 156) added that this recommendation was "in accordance with the recognized principles [of international law]".

1122 See above pp. 63–70, 102–103.

1123 F. Blaine Sloan, "The Binding Force of a 'Recommendation' of the General Assembly of the United Nations", *The British Year Book of International Law*, 1948, p. 24; see also pp. 1–33. More generally, see Yuen-il Liang, "The General Assembly and the Progressive Development and Codification of International Law", *The American Journal of International Law*, Vol. 42, 1948, pp. 66–97.

3. *Special provisions*

In addition to the general principle set out above, a number of special provisions concerning the future nationality of Palestine's inhabitants were addressed by the Partition Plan. Some of these provisions related to the inhabitants of the Arab and Jewish States, while others dealt with the nationality in Jerusalem. These special rules constituted significant exceptions to the aforementioned principle.

A. *Inhabitants of the Arab and Jewish states*

The Partition Plan posed two exceptions to the international law rule just introduced.

Firstly, the Plan conferred nationality on those foreigners who were residing in the assigned territories within the Arab State and the Jewish State.[1124] In order to understand the reason of this exception, one should examine who these foreigners in Palestine were.

A considerable number of foreign Jews (about 261,975 persons) were present in Palestine in 1946. This figure included three categories of Jews: (1) legal residents,[1125] (2) illegal immigrants,[1126] and (3) refugees.[1127] On the other hand, the number of foreign Arabs in Palestine stood at about 16,148 persons.[1128] Thus, foreign Arabs in Palestine were a minor group (about 6%) when compared with foreign Jews (about 94%) presented in the country.[1129] Hence, the actual reason for conferring

1124 This provision is consistent with Section B, paragraph 2, of the Plan; quoted in *supra* note 1111.

1125 The number of legal Jewish immigrants who were residing in Palestine but who did not constitute Palestinian citizens were estimated at 192,445 persons. In turn, this figure was a result of the total number of registered Jewish immigrants in the period of 1925–1945, which was 325,061 (See Survey of Palestine, Vol. I, p. 185), minus the total number of persons who acquired Palestinian nationality by naturalization in the same period, which was 132,616 (see above p. 123) who were overwhelmingly Jews.

1126 They were estimated between 50,000 and 60,000 persons (Survey of Palestine, Vol. I, p. 210).

1127 Some 14,530 European refugees, mostly Jews, entered and remained in Palestine during World War II (*ibid.*, p. 223). See also above pp. 169–172.

1128 These were as follows: 2,081 individuals who were brought (under the auspices of the British Army) from Syria and Lebanon as labourers in October 1942; 4000 persons, mostly Egyptians, employed directly by the British Army; 380 persons, mostly Egyptians as well, employed by the British Royal Air Forces; and 9,687 individuals (including 7,000 Syrians and Lebanese, with the remainder being Egyptians and Sudanese), working for contractors engaged in military construction or in other civil employment (*ibid.*, pp. 112–114). Apart from these, in 1940–1945, 12,160 persons (Arab) were deported to Lebanon, Syria, Egypt and Trans-Jordan (*ibid.*, p. 221).

1129 Other foreigners, who were neither Arab nor Jewish, had not been entitled to obtain the nationality of either the Arab or the Jewish States. The Partition Plan did not specify the criteria according to which a person may be considered as 'Arab'. However, one

nationality on foreigners was to regularize the status of foreign Jews by granting them a fresh nationality.[1130]

Unlike the partition proposal of 1938, which limited the granting of nationality status in the future to Palestinian citizens only, the United Nations Plan intended to confer nationality on citizens and foreign Arab and Jewish persons who were *de facto* residing in the two States. In other words, the former proposal was based on a purely legal criterion (i.e. nationality) while the latter took into account not only the legal but also political (i.e. racial and religious) criterion. Granting nationality to foreign residents is an unusual practice in cases of state succession. Most, if not all, peace treaties, which regulated future nationalities in the territories affected by change of sovereignty, had recognized future nationalities only to *citizens* of the predecessor territory, not to *foreign residents*.[1131]

The second exception from the general principle was the recognition of the right of option. This right was given to certain citizens of one state to opt for the nationality of the other state. Thus, any person over eighteen years of age, Arab or Jew, was entitled to opt for the citizenship of the other state if he found himself residing in a state where its majority differed from his race or religion. Namely, an Arab who would find himself in the Jewish State could opt for the nationality of the Arab State; and, similarly, a Jew who would find himself in the Arab State could opt for the nationality of the Jewish State. In this connection, the Plan was based on facts and law.

The right of option corresponded to the fact that Arabs and Jews were deployed in the cities, towns and villages of Palestine in such a way as to make the complete division of land between the two sides impractical. UNSCOP, following the population data provided by Britain, characterized this situation as follows:[1132]

> There is no clear territorial separation of Jews and Arabs by large contiguous areas. Jews constitute more than 40 per cent of the total population in the districts of Jaffa (which includes Tel Aviv), Haifa and Jerusalem. In the northern inland areas...they represent between 25 and 34 per cent of the total population. In the inland northern districts..., Jews form between 10 and 25 per cent of the total population, while in the central districts and the districts south of Jerusalem they constitute not more than 5 per cent of the total.[1133]

The population of the area allocated to the Arab State presumed to include some 725,000 Arabs and 10,000 Jews.[1134] While, on the other hand, it had been assumed that the population of the area assigned to the Jewish State would have

---

may say that fluency in the Arabic language or/and the possession of the nationality of an Arab country might be sufficient criteria in this respect.

1130 *Cf.* the similar proposal of the Palestine Royal Commission, above p. 199.

1131 See above pp. 69–70.

1132 UNSCOP Report, *op. cit.*, p. 13.

1133 See also Survey of Palestine, Vol. I, p. 152.

1134 UNSCOP Report, *op. cit.*, p. 54.

comprised about 498,000 Jews and 407,000 Arabs.[1135] "In addition, there will be in the Jewish State about 90.000 [Arab] Bedouins".[1136] Thus, while a small minority of Jews were expected to reside in the Arab State, the Jewish State would incorporate a large minority of Arabs.

By giving the inhabitants belonging to the minority group in one state the right to opt for the nationality of the other state, the Plan recognized a well-established rule of international law.[1137] As it has been noted previously, the right of option was admitted in many peace treaties.[1138] On this point, the Plan, in one sense, had substituted the absence of a treaty between the Arabs and Jews of Palestine.

Moreover, by recognizing the right of option on an individual basis, the Plan differed from the 1938 Partition Commission, which suggested the exchange of population between the projected Arab and Jewish States in lieu of the option of nationality.[1139] Although the implementation of the right of option would require more complicated procedures than a population exchange, the option took the individual's concerns into account rather than the pure interest of the states.[1140] The admission of the right of option reflected an evolution within international law, particularly in the field of human rights.[1141]

B. *Inhabitants of Jerusalem*

'The City of Jerusalem', as the Plan called Jerusalem and a wide area of its surrounding towns, was envisioned to have a special international status. Thus, the

1135 *Ibid.*

1136 *Ibid.*

1137 See Harvard Research on Nationality, *op. cit.*, Article 18. As discussed above pp. 71–72, the right of option was given to the inhabitants of territories detached from Turkey, including Palestine, according to Articles 31–34 of the Treaty of Lausanne, 1923. See also Article 11 of the ILC Articles on Nationality and State Succession, *op. cit.*

1138 See above pp. 102–103.

1139 See Palestine Partition Commission, *op. cit.*, pp. 52–72. This Commission took as a precedent guiding its plan, the peace Convention concerning the Exchange of Greek and Turkish Populations of 1923 (see above p. 89). This involved the transferal of persons of Orthodox religion residing in Turkey to Greece, and the transferal of Muslim persons living in Greece to Turkey. See also Weisman, *op. cit.*, pp. 29–39.

1140 The Plan included some details relating to the implementation of the right of option: (1) persons who wish to opt should be over eighteen years of age; (2) a one-year period starting from the declaration of independence of the proposed states, was fixed as time limit to exercise the right of option; (3) the inclusion of the wives and children of those persons exercising the right of option; (4) the prohibition of those Arabs residing in the area of the proposed Arab State from opting for the citizenship of the Jewish State and, equally, preventing those Jews residing in the Jewish State from opting for the citizenship of the proposed Arab State. The last provision of the Plan on nationality was not mentioned in the UNSCOP's proposal.

1141 See Brownlie, "The Relations of Nationality…", *op. cit.*, p. 341.

nationality of Jerusalem's inhabitants was similarly drafted in a special manner that had no precedent in the history of international law or relations.

Unlike the Arab and Jewish States,[1142] the Partition Plan conferred with automatic effect Jerusalem's nationality on all residents of the City, regardless of their nationality, race or religion. This can be understood from a clause in the Plan (already quoted), which stated that "*all the residents* shall become...citizens of the City of Jerusalem unless they opt for *citizenship of the State of which they have been citizens*".[1143] Thus, Palestinian citizens as well as foreigners of all nationalities who were residing at the time in Jerusalem were eligible to be Jerusalem's nationals.

By the end of 1944, the settled population in Jerusalem numbered 240,880. Of this number, 140,530 persons were Arabs (96,760 Muslims and 43,770 Christians), 100,200 were Jews (both Palestinian and foreign), and there were 150 others.[1144] The exact number of non-Jews and non-Arab foreigners was unknown. Such foreigners might include British and other government officials, travellers, tourists, illegal immigrants and refugees.

Such a granting of nationality to foreigners was a strange proposal. While the reason for granting nationality to foreign Arabs and Jews in the projected Arab and Jewish States was politically justified,[1145] the reason for conferring Jerusalem's nationality on non-Arab or non-Jewish foreigners was unclear. It is also difficult to say whether such provisions were in conformity with the international law of state succession as no precedent existed in this respect in other parts of the world.

As was the case in the Arab and Jewish States, the Plan admitted the right of option in the City of Jerusalem. The Arab and Jewish residents of Jerusalem were given the right to opt for the nationality of the Arab State or the Jewish State, respectively. The criterion for the exercise of the option had been fixed as to fill a notice expressing an intention to participate in the election of the legislative assembly of either the Arab State or the Jewish State.[1146] In such cases, the person in question would lose his nationality in Jerusalem and become a citizen in either the Arab State or the Jewish State, as the case might be.

Lastly, because it was expected to coordinate the administration of the City of Jerusalem, the United Nations Trusteeship Council was expected to make arrangements for the diplomatic protection to the city's citizens abroad.[1147] In this regard, the inhabitants of Jerusalem differed from the citizens of both the Arab and Jewish States, whose protection was presumed to be the responsibility of their respective governments, as was the case in any independent state.

1142 Whereby the foreigners who were considered eligible for the future nationalities were Arabs and Jews only, not all foreigners.

1143 Emphasis added.

1144 See Survey of Palestine, Vol. I, p. 152. *Cf.* UNSCOP Report, *op. cit.*, p. 54.

1145 As the Arab race and the Jewish religion were the bases for the whole idea of partition.

1146 See Part I, B(9) of the Plan.

1147 See Partition Plan, Part III, A.

4. *Evaluation*

Irrespective of the binding force or validity of the Partition Plan,[1148] the present discussion is concerned only with the Plan's nationality stipulations. Yet, it should be noted that the juridical force of the Partition Plan derived from the validity of the Palestine Mandate. If the Mandate was considered as valid, the plan should be consequently deemed as valid also. In the Mandate of Palestine, as in other mandates, there were two parties, the League of Nations and the Mandatory (Britain). The League of Nations, as the international supervisor over the Mandatory,[1149] had entrusted Britain to administrate Palestine. As a natural successor to the Council of the League of Nations with regard to the mandated territories, the International Court of Justice had concluded on 11 July 1950:

> [T]he General Assembly of the United Nations is legally qualified to exercise the supervisory functions previously exercised by the League of Nations with regard to the administration of the [mandated] Territory.[1150]

As Britain declared its intention to abandon its mandate in April 1947,[1151] the United Nations undertook (or recovered) its responsibility over Palestine. Hence, the General Assembly had the legal capacity to, and it did, divide Palestine into two States.[1152]

1148 See, *inter alia*, Clyde Eagifton, "Palestine and the Constitutional Law of the United Nations", *The American Journal of International Law*, Vol. 42, 1948, pp. 397–399; Pitman B. Potter, "The Palestine Problem Before the United Nations", in *ibid.*, pp. 859–861; Shabtai Rosenne, "Directions for a Middle East Settlement: Some Underlying Legal Problems", *The Middle East Crisis*, Oceana Publications, New York, 1969, pp. 44–67; Henry Cattan, *Le partage de la Palestine du point de vue juridique*, Geneva, 1970; Nathan Feinberg, *On an Arab Jurist's Approach to Zionism and the State of Israel*, Magnes Press, Jerusalem, 1971, pp. 34–43; Yoram Dinstein, "The United Nations and the Arab-Israeli Conflict", in John Norton Moore, ed., *The Arab-Israeli Conflict*, Princeton University Press, New Jersey, 1974, Vol. II, pp. 481–509; Thomas S. Kuttner, "Israel and the West Bank: Aspects of the Law of Belligerent Occupation", *Israel Year Book on Human Rights*, Vol. 7, 1977, pp. 171–172; William Thomas Mallison and Sally V. Mallison, *An International Law Analyses of the Major United Nations Resolutions Concerning the Palestine Question*, United Nations, New York, 1979 (UN Doc. ST/SG/SER.F/4), pp. 10–30; Mahnoush H. Arsanjani, "United Nations Competence in the West Bank and Gaza Strip", *International and Comparative Law Quarterly*, Vol. 31, 1982, pp. 426–450; Julius Stone, "Israel, the United Nations and International Law: Memorandum of Law", in Moore, *op. cit.*, *The Arab-Israeli Conflict, The Difficult Search for Peace, 1973–1988*, Princeton University Press, New Jersey, 1991, Vol. IV, pp. 777–820; Sloan, *op. cit.*, pp. 21–29.

1149 On the League's supervisory power in regard to Palestine, see, for example, Baumkoller, *op. cit.*, pp. 111–142; Pic, *op. cit.*, pp. 40–48.

1150 *International Status of South-West Africa*, *op. cit.*, p. 137.

1151 The termination of the Mandate was also lawful under Article 28 of the Palestine Mandate.

1152 *Cf.* Report of the Sub-Committee 2, *op. cit.*, pp. 276–278. See also Cattan, *Palestine and International Law…*, *op. cit.*, pp. 69–89. This point, however, cannot be discussed further here. Yet the Partition Plan has relevance until the present. This has been

By recognizing the *de facto* presence of foreign Jews in Palestine, the nationality provisions of the Plan recognized the pre-existing facts in Palestine. However, while the provisions admitted certain rules of international law relating to state succession, they generally ignored the domestic nationality law applicable in Palestine (i.e. the Palestinian Citizenship Order of 1925 and its amendments).[1153] Obviously, the Plan attached greater importance to the Arab race and to the Jewish religion (both political criteria) than to the bond of nationality (a legal criterion) as bases for the future nationalities in the projected post-Palestine entities.

Happily, the existence of a distinct Palestinian nationality was not denied in principle.[1154] In the three entities (Arab State, Jewish State, and Jerusalem), Palestinian citizens constituted the majority of the population.

It was envisaged that, amongst other provisions in the Plan, the nationality stipulations should form part of the 'fundamental laws' in both the Arab and Jewish States.[1155] As such, "no law, regulation or official action shall conflict or interfere with these stipulations, nor shall any law, regulation or official action prevail

---

expressed in ample General Assembly resolutions such as: A/RES/186 (S-2), 14 May 1948; A/RES/35/169(A-E), 15 December 1980; A/RES/43/177, 15 December 1988; A/RES/55/55, 1 December 2000; A/RES/56/33, 3 December 2001; A/57/L.44, 20 November 2002; A/RES/57/107, 14 February 2003; A/RES/58/21, 22 January 2004; A/RES/59/31, 31 January 2005; A/RES/60/36, 10 February 2006. And the Plan was also mentioned by the International Court of Justice in its Advisory Opinion, *Legal Consequences of the Construction of a Wall in the Occupied Palestinian Territory*, of 9 July 2004, *op. cit.*, pp. 165, 188.

1153 This might be regarded as part of the overall failure of UNSCOP to take a number of legal matters into account. Such failure was criticized, at length, in the Report of the Sub-Committee 2, *op. cit.*, pp. 272–283. It seems that the Sub-Committee 2 had considered the 'Palestinians' as the bulk of persons who possessed Palestinian nationality, irrespective of race or religion. This was evident from its references to the 'Palestinian people', 'people of Palestine', and 'indigenous population' without mentioning the religion. In denying the residents of Palestine (especially illegal immigrants) to be Palestinian future citizens, the said Sub-Committee proposed that: "The law of naturalization and citizenship [of the one federal State of Palestine—see *infra* note 1154] shall provide, amongst other conditions, that the applicant should be a legal resident of Palestine for a continuous period to be determined by the constituent assembly" (p. 303).

1154 It is to be added here that the minority proposal of UNSCOP, which suggested the creation of a federal state in Palestine instead of the partition, recognized the existence of Palestinian nationality in clearer terms than that of the Partition Plan. It was suggested that "all adult persons who have acquired Palestinian citizenship as well as all Arabs and Jews who, though non-citizens, may be resident in Palestine and who shall have applied for citizenship in Palestine not less than three months before the date of the election [of the constituent assembly], shall be entitled to vote therein" (UNSCOP Report, *op. cit.*, p. 60). Accordingly, it was proposed, "There shall be a single Palestinian nationality and citizenship, which shall be granted to Arabs, Jews and others on the basis of such qualifications and conditions as the constitution and laws of the federal State may determine and equally apply" (*ibid.*).

1155 Partition Plan, Part 1(C) ('General Provisions').

over them".[1156] The Plan should, it was also suggested, be the supreme reference in determining the nationality in the three projected entities. This shows the importance which the international community had attached to the future nationalities in the various territories of the post-mandated Palestine.

Other nationality matters were left, apparently, to be regulated by the internal laws of the said three entities. Alternatively, it may have been accepted that certain nationality matters would subsequently be arranged through subsidiary agreements between the three entities, such as the procedures to exercise the individual right to nationality option.

Unfortunately, the United Nations Partition Plan has never been implemented. Instead, after the end of the mandate on 14 May 1948, a number of *de facto* statuses for Palestinian citizens emerged. Today, some sixty years after the Partition Plan, with the exception of the nationality in those areas of Palestine which became Israel, the question of Palestinian nationality has yet to be resolved.

1156 *Ibid.*

XII

CONCLUSION

By the end of the British rule in Palestine, which lasted from December 1917 to May 1948, Palestinian nationality had become well-established in accordance with both domestic law and international law. Accordingly, the origin of Palestinian nationality in international law lies in this nearly thirty-year period. And, as a result, any legal consideration relating to the future status of the individuals who once held Palestinian nationality should commence from the point upon which the British rule over Palestine had been terminated.

From 1516 to 1917, Palestine had been part of the Ottoman Empire and, therefore, Palestine's inhabitants were Ottoman citizens. Ottoman nationality was first codified by the Nationality Law of 1869. This law turned the Empire's nationality, which was previously based on religion, into a secular relationship between the state and its subjects, or citizens, like the case in other states at the time. By the end of the Empire, Ottoman nationality had become well-established. It was plainly evident who the Ottoman citizens were based on *jus sanguinis* or *jus soli* principles. Naturalized citizens were known. A distinction was made between citizens and foreigners. And change of Ottoman nationality, as a rule, was prohibited. At the international level, Ottoman nationality was recognized by other states, and the Empire's citizens were able to travel abroad using Ottoman passports. Hence, at the eve of the British occupation of Palestine on 9 December 1917, the status of each and every individual present in Palestine in relation to nationality was known.

After the British occupation, nationality in Palestine remained in transition until 1925. During this almost eight-year transitional period, the nationality of Palestine's inhabitants started to emerge. Each neighbouring country of Palestine had developed nationality for its own inhabitants, and it became clear that the inhabitants of Palestine acquired a distinct nationality from that of other ex-Ottoman subjects in Egypt, Lebanon, Syria and Trans-Jordan. At the international level, Palestinian nationality was first created, however *de facto*, upon the withdrawal of Ottoman forces from Palestine. The international community had admitted the existence of Palestinian nationality in Article 7 of the Palestine Mandate, which was adopted by the League of Nations on 24 July 1922. One year later, Turkey and Britain, among other states, signed a treaty of peace in Lausanne; according to the Treaty of Lausanne, the Turks/Ottomans relinquished all of their titles over Palestine. When the Treaty of Lausanne came into force on 6 August 1924, the nominal Ottoman nationality in Palestine came to a permanent end and, at the same moment, Palestinian nationality was established from the international law standpoint. Hence, the day on which the people that is known now as 'Palestinian people', as a legal animal, dates back to the sixth day of August 1924.

At the domestic level (i.e. within Palestine), Palestinian nationality was first regulated by a legislation enacted by Britain, called Palestinian Citizenship Order, on 24 July 1925; it entered into force on 1 August 1925. As a sign of its significance, this legislation was the only 'Order in Council' enacted by Britain, as a Mandatory, among all British mandated-territories and it was placed at the same level of the constitution of Palestine. Substantively, most of the Citizenship Order's provisions were taken from British law, and other provisions from the Treaty of Lausanne. The Order had reformed the 1869 Ottoman Nationality Law.

In its first provision, the Palestinian Citizenship Order of 1925 considered all Ottoman subjects who were habitually resident in Palestine on 1 August 1925 as Palestinian citizens. These inhabitants, numbered 729,873 individuals, formed the first-ever Palestinian citizens from the viewpoint of domestic law. Of these Palestinians, 99% were comprised of Arabs (Muslims, Christians and 'Others') and 1% consisted of Jews. In regard to Ottomans who were born in Palestine but were residing abroad on 1 August 1925 (estimated at about 40,000 in 1936), the British-run Government of Palestine denied them to return to their homes in Palestine. As a result, these native Palestinians had become stateless; on the one hand, they lost their Ottoman nationality by virtue of the Treaty of Lausanne and, on the other hand, they had not acquired Palestinian nationality according to Palestinian law. This group of Palestinian natives, who were largely residing in the Americas and Western Europe, constituted the first generation of Palestinian refugees.

Naturalization in Palestine was precisely designed to confer Palestinian nationality on foreign Jews who immigrated into Palestine throughout the British rule. At the end of this rule, the total number of persons who acquired Palestinian nationality by naturalization was estimated at 132,616; about 99% of them were Jews. This naturalization of Jews had been systematically carried out in coordination between the Zionist Organization and Britain, under the League of Nations' support. In consequence, the number of Palestinian Jews had been significantly increased. Palestinian Jews, as well as foreign and stateless Jews, became Israel citizens after the establishment of the State of Israel in most of Palestine on 15 May 1948.

Palestinian nationality had been evident not only within Palestine but also abroad. In addition to the recognition of Palestinian nationality by the League of Nations and its member states, which is a significant political and legal bases for that nationality, courts in other states recognized the status of Palestinian citizen and treated the Palestinians like other foreigners. Citizens had been travelling abroad using Palestinian passports that constituted a *prima facie* indication by which Palestinian nationality could be proved. As Palestine had not formed a fully independent state, Britain extended its diplomatic protection to the Palestinian citizens similar to citizens of other British-controlled territories, including colonies, protectorates, domains and other mandated territories.

The admission of foreigners into Palestine had a direct influence on Palestinian nationality. Foreigners entered Palestine as travellers or immigrants. Travellers were obliged to acquire an entry visa to land in Palestine with certain exceptions, notably relating to the habitual residents of Trans-Jordan and inhabitants of the border towns in Syria and Lebanon. Many travellers, however, had extended their stay in Palestine and acquired the status of permanent residence or remained in the country illegally. More significantly, immigrants constituted the bulk of foreigners who entered and remained in Palestine under the British rule. Most of these immigrants were Jews. From 1920 until 1945, the total number of persons registered as immigrants in Palestine was estimated at 401,149. Of these, 367,845 individuals (about 91%) were Jews. Thus, about one-forth of Palestine's inhabitants, citizens and foreigners, at the end of the mandate period were immigrants. Immigration constituted the first step towards the acquisition of Palestinian nationality by naturalization after a two-year residence. Britain had systematically (by immigration legislation) collaborated with the Zionist Organization in bringing Jews, especially from Europe, into Palestine and settling them therein. However, almost half of the immigrant Jews had entered or remained in Palestine illegally, i.e. without permission from the Government of Palestine.

As a result of the British and international (i.e. the League of Nations) policies towards Palestine, Palestinian citizens and other inhabitants of the country were turned into two *de facto* nationalities, or peoples: Arabs and Jews. This situation had been recognized when the future of Palestine had to be examined by the United Nations General Assembly (which replaced the Council of the League of Nations with regard to the Mandates System) in its resolution of 29 November 1947, known as the United Nations Partition Plan. In accordance with this Plan, Palestine had to be divided into three political entities: an Arab State, a Jewish State and a special international status (*corpus separatum*) for the City of Jerusalem. It was envisaged, as a rule, that the nationality of the inhabitants of these three entities should be conferred based on the individual's place of residence regardless of the individual's religion or race. But, alas, the Partition Plan was never implemented. Rather, new anomalous *de facto* situations had emerged. These situations were (and still are), for the most part, contrary to international law and need to be settled.

The foregoing shows that Palestinian nationality had become a complete nationality, i.e. like the nationality of any other state, by the end of the British rule. The fact that Palestine had not constituted an independent state does not derogate from that status. Modern history has witnessed many instances in which non-independent states conferred their nationality on their inhabitants. International law had recognized the existence of such nationalities. Nationalities were recognized in protected states such as Egypt and Morocco before their independence from Britain and France, respectively. Countries controlled by the British Empire had distinct nationality based on locally-enacted legislation, including in the British domains (e.g. Canada, New Zealand, South Africa) and British colonies, notably India.[1157] As it has been elaborated previously,[1158] distinct nationalities had been recognized for the inhabitants of mandated-territories of types B and C. In mandates of type A territories, the national character of the inhabitants, including nationality, was beyond question. In the case of Palestine, in addition to being a mandate of type A for which general recognition had been already in place, Palestinian nationality was recognized in the Palestine Mandate instrument itself. The Palestine Mandate was the only mandate instrument, amongst all other mandates, whereby nationality was specifically referred to and admitted. This constituted an additional weight to the legal existence of Palestinian nationality in comparison with the nationality in other non-independent states at the time.

The distinct existence of Palestinian nationality cannot be undermined by the fact that Britain, as the Mandatory Power, had extended its diplomatic protection to Palestinians abroad. It is well-accepted practice in international law and relations that states do afford diplomatic protection to citizens of other states.

Besides, it might be said, in so far as the nationality is concerned, that Palestine formed an independent state. Should Palestine have gained its independence after the end of the mandate, Palestinian nationality would not have differed from the nationality of independent states. It follows that any succeeding state or states of parts of Palestine are under international legal obligation to admit the status of Palestinian citizen as a basis for the future determination of the inhabitants' status.

Yet, as is known, Palestine was divided into three separate entities controlled by different states after 14 May 1948. These areas were: (1) the territory of Palestine that had become the "State of Israel", (2) the territory of Palestine that has been called later the "West Bank", which fell under Jordan's control and subsequently annexed by the Hashemite Kingdom, and (3) the territory of Palestine that has become known as the "Gaza Strip", which was controlled by Egypt and administrated, but not annexed, by that Arab Republic. Since then through the 1967 Israel's military occupation of the West Bank and Gaza Strip (both become known as the 'occupied Palestinian territory') until the present time, the status of the inhabitants who found themselves in the occupied territories has never been settled in international law.

Although Israel might have the right to grant its nationality to whomever it wishes, it could not, according to international law, deny the nationality of the Palestinian Arabs who were residing in the parts of Palestine that had become Israel. In 1950 the Israel Law of Return, which was confirmed by the 1952 Israel Nationality Law, conferred Israel nationality to any Jew who was present in or would immigrate to Israel. This had been done regardless whether the Jew was a Palestinian citizen or not. Most of the non-Jewish Palestinians who remained in

---

1157 For more cases in which the nationality was recognized in non-state entities, see Zimmermann, *op. cit.*, pp. 242 ff.; and Grossman ("Nationality and Non-Recognized States"), *op. cit.*, pp. 853 ff.

1158 See above pp. 61–62.

Israel did not acquire Israeli nationality. This practice was a manifest violation of the international law of state succession by which the successor state should *ipso facto* confer its nationality to the citizens of the predecessor state who were habitually resident in the new territory—this was, however, corrected in 1980 when Israel law granted Israeli nationality to all Arabs residents of the Jewish state. Under international law, Israel had no power to decide that Palestinian nationality had ceased to exist in the entire world after the creation of the Jewish state in Palestine. Israel could, however, decide that Palestinian nationality had ceased to exist in the area under Israel's jurisdiction, but not beyond that area. Yet, this freedom of decision is not without limitation; Israel could not, according to international law, remove the nationality, or the right to recover it, from those Palestinian citizens who were displaced from their places of residence in the territory of Palestine in which Israel was established—i.e. the 1947–1949 war (and afterwards) refugees.

In international law, the key basis for the right of return for any person, refugee or non-refugee, to his or her country is derived from the person's nationality status;[1159] the case of Palestinian refugees is no exception.[1160] In addition to other bases for the right of Palestinian refugees to return, the individual's possession of Palestinian nationality prior to 14 May 1948 constitutes, in international law, the first basis for the right of return. All other bases for the right of return, such as human rights law and refugee law, are derived from the bond of nationality between the refugee and the territory from which he or she resided prior to displacement. Thus, again according to international law, Palestinian citizens who left the area of Palestine that became Israel had the right to return, or the right to recover their Palestinian nationality. It follows that each Palestinian citizen who become refugee has an individual right to acquire Israeli nationality once he (or she) would be allowed to return to the place of his habitual residence from where he had voluntarily left or had been forced to leave before, during or after the 1947–1949 conflict. Descendants of these Palestinian refugees have, and would continue to have, identical status and right.

Negotiations between Israel and the PLO might yield a political solution to the Palestinian refugee problem by, for example, allowing these refugees to return to the Palestinian state that would be established in the West Bank and Gaza Strip.

1159 See above p. 173. It is sufficient to refer to Article 13, paragraph 2, of the Universal Declaration of Human Rights (*op. cit.*): "Everyone has the right…to return to his country"; and Article 12, paragraph 4, of the International Covenant on Civil and Political Rights (*op. cit.*): "No one shall be arbitrarily deprived of the right to enter his own country".

1160 For examples on studies relating to the right of return, see references cited in *supra* notes 58–59 and in notes 64–70. Since its adoption of Resolution 194 (III) of 11 December 1948 (particularly paragraph 11) on the right of Palestinian refugees to return to their homes from which they were displaced in the parts of Palestine in which Israel was established, the United Nations General Assembly has annually reaffirmed that resolution. See, most recently and as a way of example, UN Doc. A/RES/62/104 and UN Doc. A/RES/62/105, both adopted on 17 December 2007.

In international law, however, such a solution would not alter the right of refugees to return to their places of residence inside Israel that they left or were forced to leave. In other words, the right of return based on Palestinian nationality as existed prior to 14 May 1948 can be exercised solely by each individual (and his descendent), who once held Palestinian nationality. Such return would be to the refugee's place of residence inside Israel. The following example illustrates the point. If a refugee who is currently residing in Beirut, Lebanon, and whose place of residence before 1948 was the city of Haifa, now in Israel, returns to the city of Ramallah, now in the West Bank, and gets the nationality of the Palestinian state, one cannot say that this refugee has exercised his or her right of return. This analysis leads to the conclusion that such returnees would acquire Israeli nationality once they returned to Haifa—exactly like those Palestinians, Arabs and Jews, who did not leave Haifa during the 1947–1949 war and had acquired Israeli nationality. The acquisition of Israeli nationality is a right based on the inherent right of Palestinian nationality that cannot be taken away by a unilateral action by one state (i.e. Israel), nor by a political solution, even if such a solution would be approved by the legitimate representative of the Palestinian people, i.e. the PLO. By the same token, the hundreds of thousands refugees presently residing in the occupied Palestinian territories, and whose place of residence had been in a given area of the territory of Palestine that became Israel, would return to nowhere if the solution of the refugee problem were to be exercised within the Palestinian state. Hence, to give another example, a refugee who is residing in the city of Bethlehem, the West Bank, whose place of residence before 1948 was the city of Jaffa, now in Israel, would, in all circumstances, have the right of return to Jaffa. Yet the return to the Palestinian state can be considered as an exercise of the right of return by those individuals who were displaced from the territories that were occupied by Israel in 1967. Thus, as a final example on this hypothesis, a Palestinian refugee residing now in Cairo, Egypt, whose place of habitual residence was Gaza at a given moment from 1917 through the present, could exercise his right of return if he acquires the nationality of the Palestinian state that would be established in the 1967–occupired territories.

The right of refugees to Palestinian nationality has another connected result on the status of these refugees in their states of refuge. There is no reason based on international law for the states that host Palestinian refugees to distinguish between or discriminate between these refugees and other non-Palestinian refugees. This is true despite the exclusion of Palestinian refugees from the scope of the 1951 Convention relating to the Status of Refugees, by Article 1D, and despite the fact that there is another organization, i.e. the United Nations Relief and Works Agency for Palestine Refugees in the Near East (UNRWA), that assists them. Thus, host countries of Palestinians refugees are under international law obligation to treat these refugees on the same footing as other refugees. UNRWA, on the other hand, has an international legal duty to extend its mandate to protection (besides humanitarian assistance) similar to that under the mandate given to the United Nations High Commissioner for Refugees *vis-à-vis* other refugees. Further discussion on this issue, however interesting, is beyond the present purpose.

A paradoxical legal status had emerged concerning Palestinian nationality in the West Bank, including East Jerusalem, in 1948.[1161] Shortly after invading and occupying the area of Palestine that lies to the west of the Jordan River, Jordan decided by an amendment to the Trans-Jordan Nationality Law, enacted on 13 December 1949, to confer its nationality on Palestinian residents in the West Bank. The Jordanian Nationality Law of 1954 had reaffirmed the status of Jordanian citizens on these residents of the West Bank, which was annexed to Jordan in 1950. Here, the conferment of Jordanian nationality had no effect under international law because Jordan had no right whatsoever to annex that part of Palestine. Such conferment produced effects only under the Jordanian law and not in accordance with international law. This position was, however, corrected on 31 July 1988 when Jordan decided to terminate its legal and administrative ties with the West Bank.[1162] Ample case law of the Jordanian Supreme Court has since then confirmed that residents of the West Bank are no longer Jordanian citizens.[1163]

Nationality in the Gaza Strip under the administration of Egypt (1948–1967) had a particular, *de facto*, character. As Egypt had not annexed the Gaza Strip into Egypt's territory, the Strip's inhabitants had retained a form of Palestinian nationality, quite similar to the nationality that existed under the British rule. The Palestinian Citizenship Order of 1925 continued to be in force therein and the Gaza government that was set up by Egypt treated the inhabitants as Palestinian citizens. Although Egypt granted Egyptian travel documents to the Gaza Strip's inhabitants, these inhabitants needed a visa to enter Egypt. Persons could retain and recover Palestinian nationality within the Strip. Naturalization into Palestinian nationality in the Gaza Strip was also possible. For example, a non-Palestinian woman who married a Palestinian man residing in Gaza could acquire permanent residency in the Strip and would be registered as Palestinian citizen, naturalized by marriage. Similar nationality had been given to Palestinian refugees who were residing at the time in other countries and returned to the Gaza Strip. Such persons were obliged to revoke other nationalities that they might have acquired as a condition to get Palestinian nationality. Decisions relating to the acquisition of Palestinian nationality by naturalization or the revocation of that nationality were published in

---

1161 Details can be found in Qafisheh, *Nationality and Domical in Palestine, op. cit.*, pp. 56–60.

1162 See King Hussein's Speech of 31 July 1988, "Termination of Jordan's Ties with the West Bank", reproduced in William B. Quandt, ed., *The Middle East: Ten Years after Camp David*, The Brookings Institution, Washington D.C., 1988, p. 494. See also Emile Sahliyeh, "Jordan and the Palestinians", in *ibid.*, pp. 279–318.

1163 The present writer has collected 95 cases held by the Jordanian Supreme Court of Justice, between 1988 and 2003, with regard to the nationality of the West Bank's inhabitants. All these cases have been published in the *Journal of the Jordanian Bar Association* in Arabic. The essence of these cases is that inhabitants of the West Bank have become Palestinian citizens since the decision of the Jordan King to terminate the legal and administrative ties with the West Bank and that these inhabitants are no longer Jordanians. Such cases and issues relating to the nationality in the West Bank and its relation with Jordan need to be considered in detail in another study.

the *Palestine Gazette*, the official journal of the government of Gaza. It should be noted that this nationality constituted anomalous Palestinian nationality. Its nature depended on the way that states regarded that nationality. In the Gaza Strip, this nationality had full domestic effects similar to that of other nationalities, in the sense that such nationality enabled its holders to enjoy all citizens' rights, such as the participation in parliamentary elections and holding public office as well as residing permanently in the Gaza Strip. In Egypt, Palestinians of Gaza were viewed as foreigners for certain purposes, such as the entry visa to Egypt as well as residency and the enjoyment of the political rights in that country. But these Gaza people were treated on the same footing with Egyptians with regard to certain social rights, like the admission to public schools and access to medical treatment in public heath institutions. While abroad, Palestinians of Gaza were protected by the Egyptian diplomatic and consular missions—similar to that protection under the British rule (Chapter VIII.3 above). Hence, in the Gaza Strip there was a special nationality that can be described as "the Gaza nationality". And this anomalous situation is merely one form of the many anomalous situations resulting from the absence of a Palestine state. Such anomalous status has characterized Palestinian nationality since 1917 until, it is safe to generalize, the present, and the nationality of the Gaza Strip's inhabitants was no exception. Exploring these issues in detail is clearly beyond the scope of this study.[1164]

The occupation by Israel of the rest of Palestine, i.e. the West Bank and Gaza Strip, in 1967 did not alter the previous status of the inhabitants. Although the Israel military occupation has introduced certain procedures relating to the residence and travel of the inhabitants, such as obliging them to hold identity cards and to acquire travel permissions, the inhabitants continued to be treated as before. The occupied territory's inhabitants did not acquire Israel nationality and continued to use Jordanian passports and Egyptian travel documents in the West Bank and Gaza Strip, respectively.

A somewhat different position has been created by Israel in East Jerusalem. Israel, although it purported to annex the city after 1967 and considered it as Israeli territory, did not confer Israeli nationality on the inhabitants of the city. However, this anomalous situation created by the occupation authorities has no legal effects in international law. The annexation of the city has been constantly considered, not least by the International Court of Justice in 2004, as null and void.[1165]

The peace agreement between Israel and the Palestine Liberation Organization, 1993–1995, maintained the *status quo* in relation to Palestinian nationality. Most of the issues relating to sovereignty in the West Bank and Gaza Strip were excluded from the jurisdiction of the interim Palestinian Authority. Certain matters relating to Palestinian nationality emerged after the creation of that Authority, such as the issuance of Palestinian passports and recognizing limited Palestinian control at the crossing borders of the occupied territory. This, however, did not change the

1164 Qafisheh, *Nationality and Domicile in Palestine*, *op. cit.*, pp. 60–62.
1165 *Ibid.*, pp. 73–83.

fundamental status that was effectively created after the end of the British rule in Palestine, which resulted from the absence of a sovereign Palestinian state. That probably explains why the Palestinian Authority has failed to adopt a Palestinian nationality law until the present day—despite an attempt to enact such a law, which was initiated by the Palestinian Ministry of Interior, as early as April 1995.[1166]

Studying Palestinian nationality under British rule offers a profound explanation of the legal position relating to the many issues that resulted from the anomalous situation of Palestinian nationality emerging after the mandate. Most of these issues still have relevance today and might have relevance in the future as well. These issues, *inter alia*, include: Israeli nationality, particularly the acquisition of that nationality through immigration to Israel by any Jew according to the Israeli Law of Return; the status of Palestinian refugees and their right of return; the deportation of Palestinians by Israel outside the occupied territories; the denial of foreigners, especially those belonging to states that have no diplomatic relations with Israel, to enter the occupied territories; the right to family reunification for those Palestinians residing in the occupied territories with their foreign spouses; the status of the inhabitants of East Jerusalem in accordance with Israeli law; the nature of identity cards that being granted by Israel to Palestinians in the occupied territories; travel permits imposed by Israel on the inhabitants of the 1967–occupied territories for the travel abroad, including the prohibition of such travel and the denial of certain inhabitants to return to the said territories; the Israeli law of nationality that was enacted in 2002 to prevent Palestinians from the West Bank and Gaza Strip who marry with Israel nationals to acquire Israeli nationality by naturalization or even to reside with their spouses in Israel; the legal character of Jordanian passports that are still being issued to the inhabitants of the West Bank until now without considering the West Bankers as Jordanian citizens; the status of present Palestinian passport that was regularized under the 1995 Oslo agreement; and, above all, Palestinian nationality within the future state of Palestine.

1166 *Ibid.*, pp. 83–89.

BIBLIOGRAPHY

1. *References cited by title*

Annotated Law Reports	Levanon, M. and Apelbom, A.M. and Kitzinger, H. and Gorali, A., eds., *Annotated Law Reports*, S. Bursi, Tel-Aviv (date will be mentioned upon citation).
Annual Digest	McNair, Arnold D. and Lauterpacht, H., eds., *Annual Digest of Public International Law Cases*, Longmans, London/New York/Toronto (date will be mentioned upon citation).
Collection of Nationality Laws	Flournoy, Richard W., Jr. and Hudson, Manley O., eds., *A Collection of Nationality Laws of Various Countries as Contained in Constitutions, Statutes and Treaties*, Oxford University Press, New York/London/Toronto/Melbourne/Bombay, 1929.
Consolidated Treaty Series	Parry, Clive, ed., *The Consolidated Treaty Series*, Oceana Publications, New York (date will be mentioned upon citation).
Digest of International Law	Moore, John Bassett, ed., *A Digest of International Law*, Government Printing Office, Washington, Vol. III, 1906.
ICJ Reports	International Court of Justice, *Reports of Judgments, Advisory Opinions and Orders* (date will be mentioned upon citation).
Law Reports of Palestine (Baker)	Baker, Henry E., ed., *The Law Reports of Palestine*, Azriel Press, Jerusalem (date will be mentioned upon citation).
Law Reports of Palestine	McDonnell, Mechael, ed., *The Law Reports of Palestine*, Waterlow & Sons, London, 1934.
Laws Concerning Nationality	United Nations, *Laws Concerning Nationality*, New York, 1954.
Laws of Palestine	Drayton, Robert Harry, ed., *The Laws of Palestine in Force on the 31st Day of December 1933*, Waterlow and Sons, London, 1934 (Arabic; available also in English and Hebrew—see footnote 249).
Legislation of Palestine	Bentwich, Norman, ed., *Legislation of Palestine 1918–1925*, Whitehead Morris Limited, Alexandria, 1926.
LN Treaty Series	*League of Nations Treaty Series* (date will be mentioned upon citation).

Completion of Ottoman Laws	Ramadan, Aref, ed., *Completion of Laws: Ottoman Laws Valid in Arab States Detached from the Ottoman Government*, Science Press, Beirut, 1928 (Arabic).
Supreme Court Judgements	Apelbom, Arnold M., ed., *Annotated Supreme Court* [of Palestine] *Judgements*, S. Bursi and P. Kadi, Tel-Aviv/Jerusalem, 1938.
Survey of Palestine	Government of Palestine, *A Survey of Palestine* (Prepared for the information of Anglo-American Committee of Inquiry), Government Printer, Jerusalem, 1946.
UN Treaty Series	*United Nations Treaty Series* (date will be mentioned upon citation).

2. *Treaties*

Regulations Respecting the Laws and Customs of War on Land, 1899 (Annex to Convention with respect to the Laws and Customs of War on Land, The Hague, 1899).

Agreement between Egypt and Turkey for the fixing of an Administrative Line between the Vilayet of Hejaz and the Governorate of Jerusalem and the Sinai Peninsula, Rafah, 1906.

Exchange of Notes between Britain and Turkey relative to the Maintenance of the *Status Quo* in the Sinai Peninsula, Constantinople, 1906.

Regulations Concerning the Laws and Customs of Land Warfare, 1907 (Annex to Convention Regarding the Laws and Customs of Land Warfare, The Hague, 1907).

The Treaty with Austria, St. Germain-en-Laye, 1919.

Treaty with Bulgaria, Neuilly-sur-Seine, 1919.

Treaty with Czechoslovakia, St. Germain-en-Laye, 1919.

Treaty with Germany, Versailles, 1919.

Treaty with Poland, Versailles, 1919.

Treaty with Romania, Paris, 1919.

Treaty with the Serb-Croat-Slovene State, St. Germain-en-Laye, 1919.

Franco-British Convention on Certain Points Connected with the Mandates for Syria and the Lebanon, Palestine and Mesopotamia, Paris, 1920.

Treaty with Hungary, Trianon, 1920.

Treaty of Sèvres, 1920 (draft).

Treaty with Turkey, Lausanne, 1923.

Bon Voisinage Agreement between Syria and Palestine, Jerusalem, 1923.

Convention relating to the development of hydraulic power affecting more than one State, Geneva, 1923.

Anglo-American Convention on Palestine, London, 1925.

Bon Voisinage Agreement to Regulate Certain Administrative Matters in Connection with the Frontier between Palestine and Syria, Jerusalem, 1926.

International Sanitary Convention, Paris, 1926.

Agreement between the United Kingdom and Trans-Jordan, Jerusalem, 1928.

International Convention for the Amelioration of the Conditions of the Wounded and Sick in Armies in the Field, Geneva, 1929.

Convention on Certain Questions Relating to the Conflict of Nationality Laws, The Hague, 1930.

Protocol relating to a Certain Case of Statelessness, The Hague, 1930.

Protocol relating to Military Obligations in Certain Cases of Double Nationality, The Hague, 1930.

Special Protocol Concerning Statelessness, The Hague, 1930.

Agreement to Regulate the Service of Judicial Documents between Palestine and Trans-Jordan, 1935.

Agreement relating to Facilitating Further Commercial Relations between Egypt and Palestine, 1936.
Convention regarding the Abolition of the Capitulations in Egypt, Montreux, 1937.
Special Customs Agreement to Facilitate Trade between Palestine and Iraq, 1937.
Treaty of Alliance between His Majesty in respect of the United Kingdom and His Highness the Amir of Transjordan, London, 1946.
Convention relative to the Protection of Civilian Persons in Time of War, Geneva, 1949.
Convention relating to the Status of Refugees, Geneva, 1951.
Convention relating to the Status of Stateless Persons, New York, 1954.
Convention on the Nationality of Married Women, New York, 1957.
Convention on the Reduction of Statelessness, New York, 1961.
International Convention on the Elimination of All Forms of Racial Discrimination, New York, 1966.
International Covenant on Civil and Political Rights, New York, 1966.
Convention on the Elimination of All Forms of Discrimination against Women, New York, 1979.
Convention on the Rights of the Child, New York, 1989.
Statute of the International Criminal Court, Rome, 1998.

3. *Legislation*

A. *Palestine*

Ottoman Nationality Law, 1869.
Regulations Relative to the Passports Offices in the Empire, 1869 (Ottoman).
Colonial Prisoners Removal Act, 1884 (British, extended to Palestine).
Foreign Jurisdiction Act, 1890 (British, extended to Palestine).
Merchant Shipping Act, 1894 (British, extended to Palestine).
Ottoman Passport Law, 1911.
Ottoman Population Law, 1914.
Imperial *Irade* concerning the Abolition of the Capitulation, 1914 (Ottoman).
Proclamation (issued by the British military in Palestine), 1918.
Palestine Passports Regulations, 1920.
Palestine Mandate, 1922.
Palestine Order-in-Council, 1922.
Palestine Legislative Council Election Order-in-Council, 1922.
Regulations Made under Article 67 of the Palestine Order-in-Council, 1922, concerning the Powers of Consuls in matters of Personal Status of Nationals of their State, 1922.
Royal Instructions, 1922.
Personal Status (Consular Powers) Regulations, 1922.
Order defining Boundaries of Territory to which the Palestine Order-in-Council does not apply, 1922.
Palestine (Amendment) Order-in-Council, 1923.
Succession Ordinance, 1923.
Immigration Ordinances, 1923–1924.
Criminal Procedure (Trial upon Information) Ordinance, 1924.
Treaty of Peace (Turkey) Ordinance, 1925.
Palestinian Citizenship Order, 1925.
Palestinian Citizenship Regulations, 1925.

Passport Ordinance, 1925.
Passport Rules, 1925.
Immigration Regulations, 1925.
Foreign Jurisdiction Rules, 1928.
Passport Ordinance, 1928.
Notice relating to the Accession of Palestine to the International Convention for the Suppression of the Circulation of, and Traffic in, Obscene Publications [of 1921], 1928.
Companies Ordinance, 1929.
Instructions to Immigration Officers and Deputy and Assistant Superintendents of Police, 1930.
Palestinian Citizenship Order (Amendment), 1931.
Passport Ordinance, 1932.
Notice Relating to Exchange of Notes between the High Commissioner for Palestine and Trans-Jordan and [the High Commissioner for] Syria and Lebanon, Providing for the Exemption of Certain Categories of Travellers from Visa Fees, 1932.
Notice relating to the Accession of Palestine to the International Agreement for the Suppression of White Slave Traffic [of] 1904 and the International Convention for the Suppression of the Traffic in Women and Children [of] 1921, 1932.
Immigration Ordinance, 1933.
Immigration Regulations, 1933.
Immigration (Custody Pending Deportation) Order, 1933.
Revised Edition of the Laws Ordinance, 1934.
Landlords and Tenants (Ejection and Rent Restriction) Ordinance, 1934.
Arbitration (Foreign Awards) Ordinance, 1934.
Palestinian Citizenship Regulations (No. 2), 1934.
Palestinian Citizenship Regulations (No. 3), 1934.
Passport Ordinance, 1934.
Passport Regulations, 1934.
Order (issued by the High Commissioner) No. 122, 1934.
Palestinian Citizenship Regulations, 1935.
Immigration (Amendment) Regulations, 1935.
Immigration (Amendment) Rules, 1935.
Medical Parishioners Ordinance, 1935.
Switzerland (Extradition) Order in Council [of 1880 and of 1934], 1935.
Carriage by Air [of 1929] (Colonies, Protectorates and Mandated Territories) Order, 1935.
Palestine (Amendment) Order-in-Council, 1935.
Palestinian Citizenship Regulations, 1936.
Iraq Petroleum Companies Agreements Ordinance, 1936.
Criminal Code Ordinance, 1936.
Bankruptcy Ordinance, 1936.
Passport Regulations, 1936.
Immigration (Amendment) Regulations, 1937.
Immigration (Exemption of Trans-Jordan Employees of Palestine Potash Ltd.), 1937.
Geneva Conventions [wounded and sick in armies in the field of] 1906 and [of] 1929 (Mandated Territories), Order in Council, 1937.
Passport Ordinance, 1938.
Passport Regulations, 1938.
Notice relating to the Extension to Palestine of the Convention between the United Kingdom and Greece Regarding Legal Proceedings in Civil and Commercial Matters [of 1926], 1939.
Palestinian Citizenship Order (Amendment), 1939.
Palestinian Citizenship Regulations, 1939.
Notice relating to Palestinian Citizenship Order, 1939.

Immigration (Amendment) Regulations (No. 2), 1939.
Immigration (Amendment) Regulations (No. 3), 1939.
Immigration (Custody Pending Deportation) (Amendment) Order (No. 2), 1939.
Defence (Immigration) Regulations, 1940.
Defence (Immigration) (Amendment) Regulations, 1940.
Palestine-Syria and Palestine-Lebanon Customs Agreements (Validation) Ordinance, 1940.
Defence (Entry Prohibition) Regulations, 1940.
Palestinian Citizenship Order (Amendment), 1940.
Defence (Entry Prohibition) Regulations, 1940.
Defence (Entry Prohibition) (Amendment) Regulations, 1940.
Immigration Ordinance, 1941.
Palestinian Citizenship Order (Amendment), 1942.
Palestinian Citizenship (Amendment) Regulations, 1942.
Palestinian Citizenship Regulations, 1942.
Palestinian Citizenship (Naturalization of Alien Women) Regulations, 1942.
Palestinian Citizenship (Amendment) Regulations (No. 2), 1942.
Defence (Entry and Departure of Palestine) Order, 1942.
Immigration (Amendment) Regulations, 1943.
Civil Wrongs Ordinance, 1944.
Consolidated Palestinian Citizenship Orders, 1925–1941, 1944.
Palestinian Citizenship (Amendment) Regulations, 1944.
Immigration Regulations (Amendment), 1944.
Immigration (Deportation Orders), 1944.
Immigration (Amendment) Regulations, 1945.
Palestinian Citizenship (His Majesty's Forces) (Amendment) Regulations, 1945.
Palestinian Citizenship (His Majesty's Forces) (Amendment No. 2) Regulations, 1945.
Palestinian Citizenship (Amendment) Regulations, 1947.
Palestinian Citizenship (Amendment No. 2) Regulations, 1947.
Palestine (Revocations) Order in Council (No. 1004), 1948.
Additional Law to the [Trans-Jordan] Nationality Law, 1949 (applied in the West Bank).
Jordan Nationality Law, 1954 (applied in the West Bank).
Companies Law, 1964 (Jordan, applied in the West Bank).
Order concerning Identity Cards and Population Registration (West Bank) (No. 297), 1969 (issued by Israel for the West Bank).
Order concerning Identity Cards (Gaza Strip and North Sinai) (No. 406), 1971 (issued by Israel for the Gaza Strip).
Presidential Decree No. 1, 1994 (Palestinian Authority).

B. *Nationality legislation of various countries*

Afghanistan Code, August 1921.
Argentina Law, 8 October 1869.
Austria Federal Law, 30 July 1925.
Belgium Law, 15 May 1922.
Brazil Legislative Decree, 7 June 1899.
Britain Nationality and Status of Aliens Act, 1914.
Brazil Legislative Decree, 12 November 1902.
China Law, 5 February 1929.
Egypt Decree-Law, 26 May 1926.
Finland Law, 20 February 1920.
France Law, 10 August 1927.
Germany Law, 22 July 1913.

Hejaz Law, 24 September 1926.
Hungary Law, 20 December 1879.
Israel Law of Return, 6 July 1950.
Israel Law, 1 April 1952.
Italy Law, 13 June 1912.
Japan Law, March 1899, as revised on 1 December 1924.
Latvia Law, 2 June 1927.
Lebanon Ordinance, 30 August 1924.
Mexico Law, 28 May 1886.
Netherlands Law, 12 December 1892.
Norway Law, 8 August 1924.
Panama Law, 22 August 1916.
Persia Law, 7 September 1929.
Poland Law, 20 January 1920.
Romania Law, 23 February 1924.
Sweden Law, 23 May 1924.
Syria Ordinance, 30 August 1924.
Trans-Jordan Law, 1 May 1928.
Turkey Law, 28 May 1928.
United States Law, 14 April 1802.
United States Law, 10 February 1855, as amended in revised statutes, 1878.
Yugoslavia Law, 21 September 1928.

C. *Other*

Albania Civil Code, 1 April 1929.
Bolivia Civil Code, 1830.
Brazil Constitution, 1891.
Costa Rica Constitution, 7 December 1871.
Luxemburg Civil Code, 1807.
Luxemburg Constitution, 17 October 1868.
Paraguay Constitution, 25 November 1870.
Portugal Civil Code, 1867.
Spain Civil Law, 1889.

4. *Cases*

Gout and Another v. Cimitian, British Privy Council, 17 November 1921.
Mavrommatis Palestine Concessions (*Greece v. Great Britain*), Permanent Court of International Justice (Objection of the Jurisdiction of the Court), 19 August 1924.
Robinson v. Press and Others, Supreme Court of Palestine sitting as Court of Appeal, 20 February 1925.
Exchange of Greek and Turkish Populations, Permanent Court of International Justice (Advisory Opinion), 21 February 1925.
Saikaly v. Saikaly, 15 December 1925 (Egypt).
Attorney-General v. Goralschwili and Another, Supreme Court of Palestine, 1925.
Nahum Razkovsky v. Leonine Razkovsky and Others, Supreme Court of Palestine sitting as a Court of Appeal, 23 May 1927.
Readaptation of the Mavrommatis Jerusalem Concessions (*Greece v. Great Britain*), Permanent Court of International Justice (Jurisdiction—Dissenting Opinion by M. Coloyanni), 10 October 1927.

Antoine Bey Sabbagh v. Mohamed Pacha Ahmed and Others, Mixed Court of Mansura, Egypt, 15 November 1927.
N.N. Berouti v. Turkish Government, Anglo-Turkish Mixed Tribunals, 14 December 1927.
Kattaneh v. Chief Immigration Officer, Supreme Court of Palestine sitting as a High Court of Justice, 16 December 1927.
Apostolidis v. Turkish Government, 23 May 1928.
Attorney-General v. Abraham Altshuler, Supreme Court of Palestine, May 1928.
The Alta Corte de Justicia de Uruguay, 7 March 1928.
Palevitch v. Chief Immigration Officer, Supreme Court of Palestine sitting as a High Court of Justice, 28 February 1929.
Saad v. Tabet, Civil Tribunal of the Seine, France, 2 July 1930.
'Ata Naser Eddin and Others v. President and Members of the Supreme Moslem Council, Supreme Court of Palestine sitting as a High Court of Justice, 7 May 1932.
Salem Case, United States v. Egypt, 8 June 1932.
Hausdorff v. Director of Immigration, Palestine Court sitting as High Court of Justice, 6 July 1933.
Sheriff Es Shanti v. Attorney General for Palestine, Supreme Court of Palestine sitting as a Court of Appeal, 12 March 1937.
Heirs of the Prince Mohamed Selim v. The Government of Palestine, Palestine Land Court of Jaffa, October and November 1937.
The Palestine Mercantile Bank v. Jecob Freyman and Ritan Belkind, Supreme Court of Palestine sitting as a Court of Appeal, 4 March 1938.
Sara Mandelberg Rogalsky v. Director of Medical Services, Supreme Court of Palestine sitting as a High Court of Justice, 25 March 1938.
Attorney General v. Fishel Abraham Moskovitz, Supreme Court of Palestine sitting as a Court of Criminal Appeal, 3 June 1938.
Attorney General v. Alexander Aharon Reich, Supreme Court of Palestine sitting as a Court of Appeal, 28 June 1938.
Nahas v. Kotia and Another, Supreme Court of Palestine sitting as a Court of Appeal, 31 October 1938.
The King v. Ketter, England, Court of Criminal Appeal, 21 February 1939.
David Yochels v. Attorney General, Supreme Court of Palestine sitting as a Court of Appeal, 16 February 1939.
The Panevezys-Saldutiskis Railway (*Estonia v. Lithuania*), Permanent Court of Internal Justice (Judgement), 28 February 1939.
Attorney General on behalf of the Government of Palestine v. Rebecca Notrica Bouenos, Supreme Court of Palestine sitting as a Court of Appeal, 30 March 1939.
Basile Vucashinovitch v. Attorney General, Supreme Court of Palestine sitting a Court of Appeal, 14 August 1939.
Attorney General v. Vladimir Nikolaiovitch & 15 Others, Supreme Court of Palestine sitting as a Court of Civil Appeal, 4 January 1940.
Pessia Nuchim Leibovna Schwalboim v. Hirsh (Zvi) Schwalboim, Supreme Court of Palestine sitting as a Court of Appeal, 31 January 1940.
Attorney General v. Alexander Glinsky, Supreme Court of Palestine sitting as a Court of Criminal Appeal, 26 February 1940.
Eliyahu Bichovsky v. Nitsa Lambi-Bichovsky, Supreme Court of Palestine sitting as a Court of Appeal, 15 May 1940.
Philippacopoulos and Another v. S.S. Alisa and Others, Supreme Court of Palestine sitting as a Court of Admiralty, 25 November 1940.
Arnold Gronner v. Director, Department of Immigration, Supreme Court of Palestine sitting as a High Court of Justice, 8 April 1941.
Arieh Leopold Zwillinger v. Blanka Schuster, Supreme Court of Palestine sitting as a Court of Civil Appeal, 8 May 1941.

Attorney General v. Spiros Yanoulatos, Supreme Court of Palestine sitting as a Court of Criminal Appeal, 23 October 1941.

Batatian v. Inspector General of Police, Supreme Court of Palestine sitting as a High Court of Justice, 26 May 1942.

Albert Schutz v. Commissioner for Migration and Statistics, Supreme Court of Palestine sitting as a High Court of Justice, 13 May 1942.

Joachim Suchier v. Superintendent of the Detention Camp, Supreme Court of Palestine sitting as a High Court of Justice, 12 June 1942.

Attorney General v. Rachel Menkes, Supreme Court of Palestine sitting as a Court of Civil Appeal, 11 January 1943.

Barbara Polsky v. Attorney General, Supreme Court of Palestine sitting as a Court of Civil Appeal, 9 February 1943.

Nazmi Bey Badrakhan Pasha v. 1. Yumna, Bint Mikhail Nassar, 2. Badi', Bint Yussef Aboud, 3. Siham Badrakhan Pasha, 4. Yussef Badrakhan Pasha, Supreme Court of Palestine sitting as a Court of Civil Appeal, 15 July 1943.

Gertrud Freyberger v. Otto Friedmann, Supreme Court of Palestine, 16 July 1943.

Nabiha Salim Zahwa v. 1. Attorney General, 2. Inspector General of Police and Prisons, Supreme Court of Palestine sitting as a High Court of Justice, 27 March 1944.

Fernand Nandor Weiss v. Assistant Commissioner for Migration, Haifa and others, Supreme Court of Palestine sitting as a High Court of Justice, 30 June 1944.

Ellie Papadimitriou v. 1. Inspector General of Police and Prisons, 2. Officer in Charge of Detention Camp, Sarona, Supreme Court of Palestine sitting as a High Court of Justice, 3 August 1944.

Sheinfeld v. Officer Commanding No. 3 Court Martial and Holding Centre…, Supreme Court of Palestine sitting as a High Court of Justice, 16 February 1945.

Nadeen Markoff v. Habib George Daoud Homsi & 7 ors., all heirs of George Daoud Homsi, Supreme Court of Palestine sitting as a Court of Civil Appeal, 20 April 1945.

Jawdat Badawi Sha'ban v. Commissioner for Migration and Statistics, Supreme Court of Palestine Sitting as a High Court of Justice, 14 December 1945.

Eliezer Zabrovsky v. The General Officer Commanding Palestine and Another, Supreme Court of Palestine sitting as a High Court of Justice, 18 December 1945.

Fatmeh bint Mahmoud As'ad Ammar v. Assistant Inspector General C. I. D. of Jerusalem, Supreme Court of Palestine sitting as a High Court of Justice, 11 April 1946.

Elena Cattan, widow of Issa Ya'coub Cattan v. Saliba Ya'coub Cattan & 4 Others and Mania alias Mary, wife of Elias Ayoub v. Saliba Ya'coub Cattan & 4 Others (two connected cases), Special Tribunal constituted under Article 55 of the Palestine Order in Council, 28 May 1946.

Eliezer Zabrovsky v. The General Officer Commanding Palestine and Another, England, Privy Council sitting as a Court of Appeal from the Supreme Court of Palestine, 4 December 1946.

Della Goldenberg v. Moshe Goldenberg, Special Tribunal constituted under Article 55 of the Palestine Order in Council, 1922, and Section 9 of the Courts Ordinance, 1940, 7 January 1947.

Antoine F. Albina v. 1. Mrs. Agnes, wife of Antoine F. Albina, 2. Bassam Fawzi Ghussein & an. and Bassam Fawzi Ghussein & an. v. 1. Agnes Michal Takountieff (alias Agnes Antoine Francis Albina), 2. Antoine F. Albina, Supreme Court of Palestine, 6 March 1947.

Yitzhak Funt, a member of the Executive of the Jewish Community Council of Jerusalem, Jerusalem v. 1. The Chief Secretary, Government of Palestine, Government Offices, Jerusalem, 2. The General Officer Commanding, Palestine and Trans-Jordan, Force Headquarters, Jerusalem, 3. The Military Commander, Haifa Area, Force Headquarters, Haifa, 4. The Acting Inspector General of Police and Prisons, Police Headquarters, Jerusalem, 5. The Senior Navel Officer, Levant Area, Navel Headquarters, Haifa, 6. The Officer Commanding the s/s "Ocean Vigour", Haifa Port, Haifa, 7. The Officer Commanding the s/s "Empire

Heywood", Haifa Port, Haifa, Supreme Court of Palestine sitting as a High Court of Justice, 29 November 1946.
Yohannanoff v. Commissioner for Migration and Statistics, Palestine Supreme Court sitting as a High Court of Justice, 27 March 1947.
Amine Namika Sultan v. Attorney-General, Supreme Court of Palestine sitting as a Court of Civil Appeal, 31 March 1947.
London Society for Promoting Christianity among the Jews v. Orr and Others, Supreme Court of Palestine sitting as a Court of Civil Appeal, 13 May 1947.
Rozenblatt v. Register of Land, Supreme Court of Palestine sitting as a High Court of Justice, 9 June 1947.
Haim Molvan v. Attorney-General of Palestine, Supreme Court of Palestine sitting as a High Court of Justice (judgement, 11 November 1945) and British Privy Council (appeal, 2 March 1948).
Greenbaum v. Oizerman, Israel, District Court of Tel-Aviv, 25 March 1949.
Petition of Ajlouny, United States, District Court for the Eastern District of Michigan, 23 April 1948.
Lapides v. Clark, Attorney General, United States, Court of Appeals, District of California Circuit, 23 May 1949.
International Status of South-West Africa, International Court of Justice (Advisory Opinion), 11 July 1950.
The *Nottebohm* (*Liechtenstein v. Guatemala*), International Court of Justice (Judgment, Second Phase), 6 April 1955.
Legal Consequences of the Construction of a Wall in the Occupied Palestinian Territory, International Court of Justice (Advisory Opinion), 9 July 2004.

5. *Official documents*

A. *League of Nations*

Mandate over former German possessions in the Pacific Ocean lying north of the Equator, Geneva, 17 December 1920 (Mandatory: Japan).
Mandate over the German possessions in the Pacific Ocean situated South of the Equator, with the exception of German Samoa and Nauru, Geneva, 17 December 1920 (Mandatory: Britain).
Mandate for German Samoa, Geneva, 17 December 1920 (Mandatory: Britain).
Mandate for Nauru, Geneva, 17 December 1920 (Mandatory: Britain).
Mandate for German South-West Africa, Geneva, 17 December 1920 (Mandatory: Britain on behalf of South Africa).
Mandate for Iraq, 23 August 1921 (Mandatory: Britain).
Mandate for Cameroons, London, 22 July 1922 (Mandatory: Britain).
Mandate for Cameroons, London, 22 July 1922 (Mandatory: France).
Mandate for East Africa, London, 22 July 1922 (Mandatory: Belgium).
Mandate for East Africa, London, 22 July 1922 (Mandatory: Britain).
Mandate for Syria and the Lebanon, London, 22 July 1922 (Mandatory: France).
Mandate for Togoland, London, 22 July 1922 (Mandatory: Britain).
Mandate for Togoland, London, 22 July 1922 (Mandatory: France).
League of Nations, *Mandate for Palestine: Questionnaire Intended to Assist the Préparations of the Annual Reports of the Mandatory Powers*, League of Nations Document No. C.553.M.335.1922.VI, 23 August 1922.
Alberto, Marquis, *Report Submitted to the Council on the Question of Nationality of the Inhabitants of B and C Mandated Areas*, June 1922.

Memorandum by Lord Balfour, League of Nations Document No. C.66.M.396.1922.VI, 16 September 1922.

Memorandum read by the Turkish Delegate [to the Lausanne Conference] at the Meeting of December 2, 1922, of the Commission on the Regime of Foreigners.

Nationality of the Inhabitants of B and C Mandated Territories, Annex 1 ("Memorandum of the British Government"), League of Nations Document No. C.45(a).M.45.1922.VII., 1922.

Council of the League of Nations, Resolution [on nationality of the inhabitants of B and C mandated territories], 23 April 1923 (League of Nations, *Official Journal*, June 1923).

Council of the League of Nations, *Minutes of the Sixty Meeting*, 20 April 1923.

"Note by the Secretary-General" (League of Nations, *Official Journal*, October 1923).

Permanent Mandates Commission, *Minutes of the Fifth Session (Extraordinary)*, Geneva, 1924.

Permanent Mandates Commission, *Minutes of the Ninth Session*, League of Nations, Geneva, 1926.

Committee of the Defenders of the Rights of Palestine Arab Emigrants in Palestinian Naturalization, *Memorandum submitted to the High Commissioner for Palestine*, League of Nations Document No. 60395, 29 July 1927.

"Petitions from Certain Turkish Subjects of Palestinian Origin, now living some in Honduras, others in Salvador and others in Mexico, dated April 23rd, June 10th, and September 19th, 1927" (Permanent Mandates Commission, *Minutes of the Twelfth Session*, League of Nations, Geneva, 1927).

Permanent Mandates Commission, "Petition from M.M. Sikaffy and other Arabs living in Honduras and from the 'Sociedad Frateznidad Palestina' of San Salvador: Observations from the British Government", League of Nations Document No. C.P.M. 656, Geneva, 28 October 1927 ('confidential' document).

Permanent Mandates Commission, *Minutes of the Thirteenth Session*, League of Nations, Geneva, 1928.

"Letter from Centro Social Palestino in Mexico to the British Minister of Foreign Affairs", with a cover letter to the League of Nations, 9 September 1929 (un-published—a copy is available in the League archives in Geneva).

Council of the League of Nationas, *Minutes of Twenty-First Meeting*, 1929.

Permanent Mandates Commission, *Minutes of the Fifteenth Session*, League of Nations, Geneva, 1929.

"General Conditions to be Fulfilled before the Mandate Regime Can be Brought to an End in Respect of A Country Placed under that Regime", League of Nations Document No. C.P.M.1183 (1930).

Permanent Mandates Commission, *Minutes of the Eighteenth Session*, League of Nations, Geneva, 1930.

Permanent Mandates Commission, *Minutes of the Twentieth Session*, League of Nations, Geneva, 1931.

Permanent Mandates Commission, *Minutes of the Twenty Third Session*, League of Nations, Geneva, 1933.

Permanent Mandates Commission, *Minutes of the Twenty-Seventh Session*, League of Nations, Geneva, 1935.

Permanent Mandates Commission, *Minutes of the Thirty-Second (Extraordinary) Session Devoted to Palestine*, League of Nations, Geneva, 1937.

Permanent Mandates Commission, "Petitions: (a) dated September 2nd, 1938, from Dr. H.F. El-Khalidi, and (b) dated September 24th, 1938, from four other Arab deportees in the Seychelles, transmitted on November 18th, 1938, by United Kingdom Government with its observations" (League of Nations, Document No. C.P.M.2128, Geneva, 13 December 1938).

League of Nations, *The Mandate System: Origin—Principles—Application*, Geneva, 1945.

B. *Britain*

Historical Section of the Foreign Office, *Syria and Palestine*, H.M. Stationary Office, London, 1920.
Historical Section of the Foreign Office, *Mohammedanism: Turkey in Asia*, H.M. Stationary Office, London, 1920.
Mandate for Palestine: Letter from the Secretary to the Cabinet to the Secretary-General of the League of Nations of July 1, 1922, enclosing a Note in reply to Cardinal Gasparri's letter of May 15, 1922, addressed to the Secretary-General of the League of Nations presented to Parliament by Command of His Majesty, His Majesty Stationary Office, London, 1922.
British Policy in Palestine: Correspondence with the Palestine Arab Delegation and the Zionist Organization, His Majesty's Stationary Office, London, 1922 (reprinted in 1929).
Report on Palestine Administration 1922, His Majesty Stationary Office, London, 1923.
Lausanne Conference on Near Eastern Affairs, 1922–1923: Records of the Proceedings and Draft Terms of Peace, His Majesty's Stationary Office, London, 1923.
First Annual Report to the League of Nations on the Palestine Administration, Colonial Office, London, June 1924.
Report on the Administration under Mandate of Palestine and Transjordan, 1924.
Report of the High Commissioner on the Administration of Palestine, 1920–1925, His Majesty's Stationary Office, London, 1925.
Report to the Council of the League of Nations on the Administration of Palestine and Trans-Jordan, 1926.
Report to the Council of the League of Nations on the Administration of Palestine and Trans-Jordan, 1927.
Report to the Council of the League of Nations on the Administration of Palestine and Trans-Jordan, 1928.
Report to the Council of the League of Nations on the Administration of Palestine and Trans-Jordan, 1930.
Report to the Council of the League of Nations on the Administration of Palestine and Trans-Jordan, 1931.
Report to the Council of the League of Nations on the Administration of Palestine and Trans-Jordan, 1932.
Report to the Council of the League of Nations on the Administration of Palestine and Trans-Jordan, 1933.
Report to the Council of the League of Nations on the Administration of Palestine and Trans-Jordan, 1934.
Report to the Council of the League of Nations on the Administration of Palestine and Trans-Jordan, 1935.
Report to the Council of the League of Nations on the Administration of Palestine and Trans-Jordan, 1936.
Palestine Royal Commission, *Report presented by the Secretary of State for the Colonies by Command of His Britannic Majesty*, His Majesty Stationary Office, London, 1937.
Report to the Council of the League of Nations on the Administration of Palestine and Trans-Jordan, 1937.
Report to the Council of the League of Nations on the Administration of Palestine and Trans-Jordan, 1938.
Palestine Partition Commission, *Report Presented by the Secretary of State for Colonies to Parliament by Command of His Majesty*, October 1938, His Majesty Stationary Office, London, 1938.
Statement of Policy Presented by the Secretary of State for the Colonies to Parliament by Command of His Majesty, 1 May 1939, His Majesty's Stationery Office, London, 1939.
Statutory Instruments Other Than Those of a Local, Personal or Temporary Character for the Year 1948, His Majesty Stationary Office, London, 1949.

C. *British-run Government of Palestine*

Samuel, Herbert, *An Interim Report on the Civil Administration of Palestine, 1 July 1920–30 July 1921*, League of Nations, Geneva, 1921.
Department of Statistics, *Statistical Abstracts of Palestine*, Government Printer, Jerusalem, 1936.
Department of Statistics, *Statistical Abstracts of Palestine*, Government Printer, Jerusalem, 1937–1938.
Department of Statistics, *Statistical Abstracts of Palestine*, Government Printer, Jerusalem, 1939.
Department of Statistics, *Statistical Abstracts of Palestine*, Government Printer, Jerusalem, 1940.
Department of Statistics, *Statistical Abstracts of Palestine*, Government Printer, Jerusalem, 1941.
Department of Migration, *The Statistics of Migration and Naturalization*, Government Printer, Jerusalem, 1941.
Department of Migration, *The Statistics of Migration and Naturalization*, Government Printer, Jerusalem, 1942.
Department of Statistics, *Statistical Abstracts of Palestine*, Government Printer, Jerusalem, 1942.
Department of Statistics, *Statistical Abstracts of Palestine*, Government Printer, Jerusalem, 1943.
Department of Migration, *The Statistics of Migration and Naturalization*, Government Printer, Jerusalem, 1943.
Department of Statistics, *Statistical Abstracts of Palestine*, Government Printer, Jerusalem, 1944–1945.

D. *United Nations*

"Letter dated 2 April 1947 from the United Kingdom delegation to the Acting Secretary-General requesting a special session of the General Assembly on Palestine", UN Doc. A/286, 2 April 1947.
UN Doc. A/RES/106 (S-1), 15 May 1947.
UN Doc. A/AC. 13/NC/34, 23 June 1947.
United Nations Special Committee on Palestine, *Report to the General Assembly*, New York, UN Doc. A/364, 3 September 1947.
Report of the Sub-Committee 2 to the Ad Hoc Committee on the Palestinian question (UN Doc. A/AC.14/32 and Add. 1, 11 November 1947).
UN Doc. A/AC.14/34 and Corr. 1 and Add. 1, 19 November 1947.
UN Doc. A/RES/181(II) (A+B), 29 November 1947 ('Plan of Partition with Economic Union'—United Nations Partition Plan on Palestine).
UN Doc. A/RES/186 (S-2), 14 May 1948.
Universal Declaration of Human Rights, 10 December 1948.
United Nations General Assembly Resolution 194 (III), 11 December 1948.
Mallison, William Thomas and Mallison, Sally V., *An International Law Analyses of the Major United Nations Resolutions Concerning the Palestine Question*, United Nations, New York, 1979 (UN Doc. ST/SG/SER.F/4).
UN Doc. A/RES/35/169(A-E), 15 December 1980.
UN Doc. A/RES/43/177, 15 December 1988.
UN Doc. A/RES/55/55, 1 December 2000.
International Law Commission, *Draft Articles on Nationality of Natural Persons in Relation to the Succession of States*, 1999; endorsed by the United Nations General Assembly, Resolution 55/153, 30 January 2001.

UN Doc. A/RES/56/33, 3 December 2001.
UN Doc. A/57/L.44, 20 November 2002.
UN Doc. A/RES/57/107, 14 February 2003.
UN Doc. A/RES/58/21, 22 January 2004.
UN Doc. A/RES/59/31, 31 January 2005.
UN Doc. A/RES/60/36, 10 February 2006.
UN Doc. A/RES/62/104, 17 December 2007.
UN Doc. A/RES/62/105, 17 December 2007.

E. *Other*

Jewish Agency, *Memorandum on the Development of the Jewish National Home, 1924, Submitted by the Jewish Agency for Palestine to the Secretary-General of the League of Nations for the Information of the Permanent Mandates Commission*, London, October 1924.

Department of State (United States), *Mandate for Palestine*, Government Printing Office, Washington, 1927.

Jewish Agency, *Memorandum on the Development of the Jewish National Home, 1928, Submitted by the Jewish Agency for Palestine to the Secretary-General of the League of Nations for the Information of the Permanent Mandates Commission*, London, June 1928.

"Final Act of The Hague First Conference on the Codification of International Law" (The Hague, 1930), *Supplement to the The American Journal of International Law*, Vol. 24, 1930.

Jewish Agency for Palestine, *Palestine: Land Settlement, Urban Development and Immigration*, London, 1930.

Jewish Agency, *Memorandum on the Development of the Jewish National Home, 1932, Submitted by the Jewish Agency for Palestine to the Secretary-General of the League of Nations for the Information of the Permanent Mandates Commission*, London, August 1932.

Zionist Organization, *Memorandum of the Development of the Jewish National Home submitted to the Secretary General of the League of Nations*, London, April 1933.

Jewish Agency, *Memorandum on the Development of the Jewish National Home, 1933, Submitted by the Jewish Agency for Palestine to the Secretary-General of the League of Nations for the Information of the Permanent Mandates Commission*, London, April 1933.

Jewish Agency, *Memorandum on the Development of the Jewish National Home, 1936, Submitted by the Jewish Agency for Palestine to the Secretary-General of the League of Nations for the Information of the Permanent Mandates Commission*, London, April 1936.

6. *Books*

Alfariq, Mahmoud H., *The Egyptian Constitutional Law and the Development of the Egyptian State*, The Great Commercial Printer, Cairo, 1924 (Arabic).

Alhalawani, Majid, *Private International Law*, Literature and Science Press, Damascus, 1965 (Arabic).

Aljader, Adel, *Impact of the British Mandate Laws in Establishing the Jewish National Home in Palestine*, Center of Palestine Studies, Baghdad University, Baghdad (Arabic—undated).

Alwakil, Shams Eddin, *Nationality and Status of Foreigners*, Munshaat Al-Maaref, Alexandria, 1966 (Arabic).

Al-Zohayli, Mohammad, *History of the Judiciary in Islam*, Dar Al-Fikr, Beirut/Damascus, 1995 (Arabic).

Andrews, Fannie Fern, *The Holy Land under Mandate*, The Riverside Press, Borton/New York, 1931.

Arminjon, Pierre, *Etrangers et protégés dans l'Empire ottoman*, Librairie Marescq Ainé, Paris, 1903.

Aruri, Naseer, ed., *Palestinian Refugees: The Right of Return*, Pluto Press, London/Sterling/Virginia, 2001.

Barbour, Nevill, *Nisi Dominus: A Survey of the Palestine Controversy*, George G. Harrap, London, 1946.

Baron, Xavier, *Les Palestiniens: genèse d'une nation*, Seuil, Paris, 2003.

Baumkoller, Abraham, *Le mandat sur la Palestine*, Librairie Arthur Rousseau, Paris, 1931.

Benoit, Auguste, *Etude sur les capitulations entre l'Empire ottoman et la France*, Librairie nouvelle de droit et de jurisprudence, Paris, 1890.

Bentwich, Norman, *England in Palestine*, the Mayflower Press, London, 1932.

Bentwich, Norman, *Palestine*, Ernest Benn, London, 1934.

Bentwich, Norman, *The Mandates System*, Longmans, Green and Co., London/New York/Toronto, 1930.

Borchard, Edwin M., *The Protection of Citizens Abroad or the Law of International Claims*, the Banks Law Publishing, New York, 1919.

Bouchard, Mathieu, *L'Exode Palestinien: construction d'une représentation occidentale du conflit israélo-arabe*, L'Harmattan, Paris, 2003.

Boustany, W.F., *The Palestine Mandate: Invalid and Impracticable*, American Press, Beirut, 1936.

Brodie, Israel B., *The Refugee Problem and Palestine*, The American Economic Commission for Palestine, New York, 1938.

Brownlie, Ian, *Principles of Public International Law*, Clarendon Press, Oxford, 1977.

Buehrig, Edward H., *The UN and the Palestinian Refugees: A Study in Nonterritorial Administration*, Indiana University Press, Bloomington/London, 1971.

Cattan, Henry, *Le partage de la Palestine du point de vue juridique*, Geneva, 1970.

Cattan, Henry, *Palestine and International Law: The Legal Aspects of the Arab-Israeli Conflict*, Longman, London/New York, 1976.

Cuinet, Vital, *Syrie, Liban et Palestine, géographie administrative: statistique, descriptive et raisonnée*, Ernest Leroux, Paris, 1896.

Darweish, Marwan and Rigby, Andrew, *Palestinians in Israel: Nationality and Citizenship*, Department of Peace Studies, University of Bradford, Bradford, 1995.

Davies, William Evan, *The English Law Relating to Aliens*, Stevens and Sons, London, 1931.

Davis, Uri, *Citizenship and the State: A Comparative Study of Citizenship Legislation in Israel, Jordan, Palestine, Syria and Lebanon*, Garnet Publisher and Ithaca Press, London, 1997.

Dawwas, Amin Raja, *Conflict of Laws in Palestine*, Dar Al-Shorok, Amman/Ramallah, 2001 (Arabic).

Dinh, Nguyen Quoc, Daillier, Patrick and Pellet, Alain, *Droit international public*, LGDJ, Paris, 1992.

Donner, Ruth, *The Regulation of Nationality in International Law*, Transnational Publishers, New York, 1994.

Dunn, Frederick Sherwood, *The Protection of Nationals: A Study in the Application of International Law*, the Johns Hopkins Press, Baltimore, 1932.

Engelhardt, Ed, *La Turquie et le Tanzimat, ou histoire des réformes dans l'Empire Ottoman depuis 1826 jusqu'a nos jours*, Libraires du Conseil d'Etat, Paris, 1884.

Erskine, Steuart, *Palestine of the Arabs*, George G. Harrap & Co. Ltd., London/Bombay/Sydney, 1935.

Esco Foundation for Palestine, Inc., *Palestine: A Study of Jewish, Arab, and British Politics*, Yale University Press, New Haven/London/Oxford, 1947.

Farsoun, Samih K. and Zacharia, Christina E., *Palestine and the Palestinians*, Westview Press, Colorado, 1997.
Feinberg, Nathan, *On an Arab Jurist's Approach to Zionism and the State of Israel*, Magnes Press, Jerusalem, 1971.
Feinberg, Nathan, *Some Problems of the Palestine Mandate*, Tel-Aviv, 1936.
Ficheleff, Samuel, *Le statut international de la Palestine orientale (la Transjordanie)*, Librairie Lipschutz, Paris, 1932.
Garnett, Lucy M., *Turkey of the Ottomans*, Sir Isaac Pitman & Sons Ltd., London, 1911.
Ghali, Paul, *Les nationalités détachées de l'Empire ottoman à la suite de la guerre*, Les Editions Domat-Montchrestien, Paris, 1934.
Goadby, Frederec, *Introduction to the Study of Law: A Handbook for the use of Law Students in Egypt and Palestine*, William Clowes and Sones Limited, London/Beccles, 1921.
Goadby, Frederic, *International and Inter-Religious Private Law in Palestine*, Hamadpis Press, Jerusalem, 1926.
Goodwin-Gil, Guy S., *International Law and the Movement of Persons between States*, Clarendon Press, Oxford, 1978.
Goodwin-Gill, Guy S., *The Refugees in International Law*, Clarendon Press, Oxford, 1996.
Gouldman, M.D., *Israel Nationality Law*, Institute for Legislative Research and Comparative Law, the Hebrew University, Jerusalem, 1970.
Grant, Elihu, *The People of Palestine*, J.B. Lippincott Company, Philadelphia and London, 1921.
Halabi, Usama, *The Legal Status of Jerusalem and its Arab Citizens*, Institute for Palestine Studies, Beirut, 1997 (Arabic).
Hall, Rodney Bruce, *National Collective Identity: Social Constructs and International Systems*, Columbia University Press, New York, 1999.
Hankey, *The Supreme Control at the Paris Peace Conference 1919*, George Allen and Unwin Ltd., London, 1963.
Harb, Mohammad, *The Ottomans in History and Civilization*, Al-Qalam House, Damascus, 1999 (Arabic).
Hathaway, James C., *The Law of Refugee Status*, Butterworths, Toronto/Vancouver, 1991.
Helmreich, Paul C., *From Paris to Sèvres: The Partition of the Ottoman Empire at the Peace Conference of 1919–1920*, Ohio State University Press, Columbus, 1974.
Herbert, Sydney, *Nationality and its Problems*, Methuen & Co., London, 1920.
Hertz, Frederick, *Nationality in History and Politics: A Psychology and Sociology of National Sentiment and Nationalism*, Routledge & Kegan Paul Ltd., London, 1951.
Hokayem, Antoine and Bittar, Marie Claude, *L'Empire Ottoman: les Arabes et les grandes puissances, 1914–1920*, Les editions universitaires du Liban, Beyrouth, 1981.
Holbraad, Carsten, *Internationalism and Nationalism in European Political Thought*, Palgrave Macmillan, New York, 2003.
Hooper, C.A., *The Civil Law of Palestine and Trans-Jordan*, Jerusalem, 1936.
Huntington, Ellsworth, *Palestine and its Transformation*, Houghton Mifflin Company, Boston/ New York, 1911.
Hyamson, Albert M., *Palestine: The Rebirth of an Ancient People*, Sidgwick & Jackson, London, 1917.
Hyamson, Albert M., *Palestine under Mandate, 1920–1948*, Methuem & Co., London, 1950.
Ingrams, Doreen, *Palestine Papers, 1917–1922: Seeds of Conflict*, Cox & Wyman, London, 1972.
Jamal Eldeen, Salah Eldeen, *The Legal System of Nationality in the Islamic State*, Dar Alfikr Aljamie, Alexandria, 2004 (Arabic).
Johannet, René, *Le principe des nationalités*, Nouvelle librairie nationale, Paris, 1918.
Jones, J. Mervyn, *British Nationality Law and Practice*, Oxford University Press, Oxford, 1947.

Joseph, Bernard, *Nationality: Its Nature and Problems*, George Allen & Unwin Ltd., London, 1929.
Josling, J.F., *Naturalisation and other Methods of Acquiring British Nationality*, the Solicitors' Law Stationary Society, Ltd., London, 1949.
Karsh, Efraim and Karsh, Inari, *Empire of the Sand: The Struggle for Mastery in the Middle East, 1789–1923*, Harvard University Press, Cambridge/Massachusetts/London, 1999.
Kayyali, *Palestine: A Modern History*, Billing and Sons, London, 1979.
Keith, A. Berriedale, *Memorandum on the Status of Aliens and the Position of British Subjects in the British Empire*, International Institute for International Co-operation, League of Nations, Paris, 1937.
Khadduri, Majid and Liebesny, Herbert, eds., *Law in the Middle East*, The Middle East Institute, Washington, D.C., 1955.
Khalidi, Rashid, *Palestinian Identity: The Construction of Modern National Consciousness*, Colombia University Press, New York, 1997.
Khela, Mahmoud K., *Palestine and the British Mandate, 1922–1939*, Institute for Palestine Studies, Beirut, 1974 (Arabic).
Kimmerling, Baruch and Migdal, Joel S., *Palestinians: The Making of A People*, Harvard University Press, Harvard/Cambridge/Massachusetts, 1994.
Koestler, Arthur, *Promise and Fulfilment: Palestine 1917–1949*, Macmillan & Co. Ltd., 1949.
Kourula, Pirkko, *Broadening the Edges: Refugee Definition and International Protection Revised*, Martinus Nijhoff, The Hague/Boston/London, 1997.
Landa, M.J., *Palestine as It Is*, Edward Goldston Ltd., London, 1932.
Lesch, Ann M. and Lustick, Ian S., *Exile and Return: Predicaments of Palestinians and Jews*, University of Pennsylvania Press, Philadelphia, 2005.
Liebich, André, ed., *Citizenship East and West*, K. Paul International, London/New York, 1995.
Malanczuk, Peter, *Akehurst's Modern Introduction to International Law*, Poutledge, London/New York, 1997.
Mandelstam, André, *Le sort de l'Empire Ottoman*, Librairie Payot, Lausanne/Paris, 1917.
Manna, Haytham, *Citizenship in Arab Islamic History*, Cairo Institute for Human Rights, Cairo (undated).
Marston, F.S., *The Peace Conference of 1919: Organization and Procedure*, Oxford University Press, London/New York/Toronto, 1944.
Martini, Alexis, *L'expulsion des étrangers: étude de droit comparé*, Librairie de la société du recueil, Paris, 1909.
McCrackan, W.D., *The New Palestine*, Jonathan Cape, London, 1922.
McDonnell, Mechael, *The Law Reports of Palestine*, Waterlow & Sons, London, 1934.
Mechbat, Aysha, *Loss of Nationality: Comparative Study*, Institute of Law and Administration at Algeria University, Algiers, 1987 (Arabic).
Milhem, Feras, *The Origins and Evolution of the Palestinian Sources of Law*, Vrije Universiteit Brussel, Faculty of Law, 2004 (un-published).
Miller, William, *The Ottoman Empire and its Successors, 1801–1922*, University Press, Cambridge, 1923.
Mock, Maurice, *Le mandat britannique en Palestine*, Editions Albert Mechelinck, Paris, 1932.
Molony, William O'Sullivan, *Nationality and the Peace Treaties*, George Allen & Unwin Ltd., London, 1934.
Morris, Benny, *The Birth of the Palestinian Refugee Problem, 1947–1949*, Cambridge University Press, Cambridge, 1989, 2004.
Muenzner, G., *Jewish Labour Economy in Palestine*, Victor Gollancz Ltd., London, 1945.
Musallam, Adnan A., *Folded Pages from Local Palestinian History in the 20th Century*, WIAM/Palestinian Resolution Center, Bethlehem, 2002 (Arabic).

Novik, Paltiel, *La situation de la Palestine en droit international*, Jouve & Editeurs, Paris, 1927.

Nuseibeh, Hazem Z., *Palestine and the United Nations*, Quartet Books, London/New York, 1982.

Oakesmith, John, *Race and Nationality: An Inquiry into the Origin and Growth of Patriotism*, Frederick A. Stokes Company, New York, 1919.

O'Connell, D.P., *State Succession in Municipal Law and International Law*, Cambridge University Press, London, 1967.

Oppenheim, L., *International Law*, Longmans, London/New York/Toronto, 5th ed. (by H. Lauterpacht), 1937.

Parry, Clive, *British Nationality, including Citizenship of the United Kingdom and Colonies and the Status of Aliens*, Stevens & Sons Limited, London, 1951.

Pecora, Vincent P., ed., *Nations and Identities: Classic Readings*, Blackwell Publishers, Malden/Oxford, 2001.

Perrin, Georges J., *Droit international public: sources sujets, caractéristiques*, Schulthess Polygraphischer Verlag, Zurich, 1999.

Peters, Joan, *From Time Immemorial: The Origins of Arab-Jewish Conflict over Palestine*, Harper & Row, New York, 1984.

Pic, Paul, *Syrie et Palestine: mandats français et anglais dans le Proche-Orient*, Librairie Ancienne Edouard Champion, Paris, 1924.

Piggott, Francis, *Nationality including Naturalization and English Law on the High Seas and beyond the Realm*, William Clowes and Sons, London, 1907.

Pillsbury, W.B., *The Psychology of Nationality and Internationalism*, D. Appleton and Company, New York/London, 1919.

Pinon, René, *L'Europe et l'Empire Ottoman: les aspects actuels de la question d'orient*, Librairie académique, Paris, 1917.

Plender, Richard, *International Migration Law*, Martinus Nijhoff, Dordrecht/Boston/London, 1988.

Pollock, Frederick, ed., *The Law Reports of the Incorporated Council of Law Reporting* (House of Lords, Judicial Committee of the Privy Council and Peerage Cases), W. Speaight & Sons, London, 1922.

Porath, Y., *The Emerging of the Palestinian-Arab National Movement: 1918–1929*, Frank Cass, London, 1974.

Qafisheh, Mutaz, *Nationality and Domicile in Palestine*, International Studies Institute, Birzeit University, Birzeit, 2000 (Arabic).

Qafisheh, Mutaz, *Palestinian Nationality: Nationality of Individuals and Nationality of Companies*, Institute of Law, Birzeit University, Birzeit, 2001 (Arabic).

Rappoport, Angelo S., *Histoire de la Palestine des origines jusqu'a nos jours*, Payot, Paris, 1932.

Rausas, G. Pélissié du, *Régime des capitulations dans l'Empire ottoman*, Arthur Rousseau, Paris, 1910.

Robinson, Jacob, *Palestine and the United Nations: Prelude to Solution*, Public Affairs Press, Washington, D.C., 1947.

Rogan, Eugene L., *Frontiers of the State in the Late Ottoman Empire, Transjordan, 1850–1921*, Cambridge University Press, Cambridge, 1999.

Ruppin, Arthur, *The Agricultural Colonization of the Zionist Organization in Palestine*, Martin Hopkinson and Company Ltd., London, 1926.

Saba, Jean S., *L'Islam et la nationalité*, Librairie de jurisprudence ancienne et moderne, Paris, 1931.

Safwat, Ahmad, *Legislative and Judicial System in Palestine*, Aletimad Press, Egypt, 1918 (Arabic).

Sakran, Frank C., *Palestine Dilemma, Arab Rights Versus Zionist Aspirations*, Public Affairs Press, Washington D.C., 1948.

Scholch, Alexander, *Palestine in Transformation 1856–1882: Studies in Social, Economic and Political Development*, Institute for Palestine Studies, Washington, D.C., 1993.
Schulze, Hegen, *States, Nations and Nationalism from the Middle Ages to the Present*, Blackwell Publishers, Cambridge/Oxford, 1996.
Segev, Tom, *One Palestine Complete: Jews and Arabs under the British Mandate*, Little, Brown and Co., London, 2001.
Sereni, Enzo and Ashery, R.E., eds., *Jews and Arabs in Palestine: Studies in a National and Colonial Problem*, Hechalutz Press, New York, 1936.
Shafer, Boyd C., *Le Nationalisme: Mythe et Réalité*, Payot, Paris, 1964.
Shaw, Malcolm N., *International Law*, Grotius Publications Limited, Cambridge, 1991.
Shepherd, Naomi, *Ploughing Sand: British Rule in Palestine, 1917–1948*, John Murray, London, 1999.
Sidebotham, Herbert, *England and Palestine, Essays towards the Restoration of the Jewish State*, Constable and Company Ltd., 1918.
Sidebotham, Herbert, *Great Britain and Palestine*, Macmillan and Co., London, 1937.
Simpson, John Hope, *Report on Immigration, Land Settlement and Development*, His Majesty's Stationary Office, London, 1930.
Smith, Charles D., *Palestine and the Arab Israeli Conflict*, St. Martin's Press, New York, 1992.
Spensky, Martine, *Citoyenneté(s): perspectives internationales*, Presses Universitaires Blaise Pascal, Clermont-Ferrand, 2003.
Stoyanovsky, J., *The Mandate for Palestine: A Contribution to the Theory and Practice of International Mandates*, Longmans, Green and Co., London/New York/Toronto, 1928.
Takkenberg, Lex, *The Status of Palestinian Refugees in International Law*, Clarendon Press, Oxford, 1998.
Torpey, John, *The Invention of the Passport: Surveillance, Citizenship and the State*, Cambridge University Press, Cambridge, 2000.
Toye, Patricia, ed., *Palestine Boundaries 1833–1947*, University of Durham, Durham, 1989.
Trevor, Daphne, *Under the White Paper: Some Aspects of British Administration in Palestine from 1939 to 1947*, The Jerusalem Press Ltd., Jerusalem, 1948.
Turack, Daniel C., *The Passport in International Law*, D.C. Heath and Company, Massachusetts/Toronto/London, 1972.
Van Vleck, William C., *The Administrative Control of Aliens: A Study in Administrative Law and Procedure*, Commonwealth Fund, New York, 1932.
Vanlande, René, *Le chambardement oriental, Turquie—Liban—Syrie—Palestine—Transjordanie—Irak*, J. Peyronnet & Cie, Paris, 1932.
Varouxakis, Georgios, *Mill on Nationality*, Routledge, London/New York, 2002.
Verhoeven, Joe, *Droit international public*, Larcier, Bruxelles, 2000.
Verney, Noël and Dambmann, George, *Les puissances étrangères dans le levant en Syrie et en Palestine*, Librairie Guillaumin, Paris, 1900.
Vitta, Edoardo, *The Conflict of Laws in Matters of Personal Status in Palestine*, S. Bursi Ltd., Tel-Aviv, 1947.
Waltz, Waldo Emerson, *The Nationality of Married Women: A Study of Domestic Policies and International Legislation*, The University of Illinois Press, 1937.
Wasserstein, Bernard, *The British in Palestine: The Mandatory Government and the Arab-Jewish Conflict, 1917–1929*, Royal Historical Society, London, 1978.
Weil, Patrick and Hansen, Randall, eds., *Nationalité et Citoyenneté en Europe*, Editions la Découverte, Paris, 1999.
Weis, P., *Nationality and Statelessness in International Law*, Stevens & Sons Limited, London, 1956.
Weisman, Herman L., *The Future of Palestine: An Examination of the Partition Plan*, Lincoln Printing Company, New York, 1937.
Winsch, Gert, *Le régime Anglais en Palestine*, M. Müller & fils, Berlin, 1939.

Wise, Stephen S. and De Haas, Jacob, *The Great Betrayal*, Stratford Press, New York, 1930.
Zasloff, Joseph Jermiah, *Great Britain and Palestine: A Study of the Problem of Palestine before the United Nations*, Graduate Institute of International Studies, Geneva, 1952.
Zeedan, Adulkarim, *The Status of Themiyyeen* [non-Muslim citizens] *and Mustamineen* [foreigners] *in the Islamic State*, Alresala Foundation, Cairo, 1988 (Arabic).
Ziff, William B., *The Rape of Palestine*, Argus Books Inc., New York, 1946.

7. *Articles*

Abi-Saab, George M., "Nationality and Diplomatic Protection in Mandated and Trust Territories", *Harvard International Law Club Bulletin*, Vol. 3, 1961–1962.
Akram, Susan M., "Reinterpreting Palestinian Refugee Rights under International Law", in Aruri, Naseer, ed., *Palestinian Refugees: The Right of Return*, Pluto Press, London/Sterling/Virginia, 2001.
Akzin, Benjamin, "The Palestine Mandate in Practice", *Iowa Law Review*, Vol. 25, 1939–1940.
Al-Azhari, Mohammad K., "The Palestinian Concept of Self-Determination between the End of the Ottoman Rule and the British Mandate", *Journal of Arab Affairs*, No. 40, December 1984 (Arabic).
Aleinikoff, T. Alexander, "Theories of Loss of Citizenship", *Immigration & Nationality Law Review*, Vol. 181, 1988.
Anaya, S. James, "The Capacity of International Law to Advance Ethnic or Nationality Rights Claims", *Human Rights Quarterly*, Vol. 13, 1991.
Arias, Harmodio, "Nationality and Naturalisation in Latin America from the Point of View of International Law", *Journal of the Society of Comparative Legislation*, Vol. 11, 1910–1911.
Arminjon, P., "De la nationalité dans l'Empire ottoman spécialement en Egypte", *Revue générale de droit international public*, Vol. VIII, 1901.
Arsanjani, Mahnoush H., "United Nations Competence in the West Bank and Gaza Strip", *International and Comparative Law Quarterly*, Vol. 31, 1982.
Batchelor, Carol A., "Statelessness and the Problem of Resolving Nationality Status", *International Journal of Refugee Law*, Vol. 10, 1998.
Baty, T., "Protectorates and Mandates", *The British Year Book of International Law*, 1921–1922.
Bentwich, Norman, "Le système des mandates", in *Recueil des course*, Académie de droit international (The Hague), 1929–IV, Librairie Hachette, Paris, Vol. 29, 1930.
Bentwich, Norman, "Mandated Territories: Palestine and Mesopotamia (Iraq)", *The British Year Book of International Law*, 1921–1922.
Bentwich, Norman, "Nationality in Mandated Territories Detached from Turkey", *The British Year Book of International Law*, 1926.
Bentwich, Norman, "Palestine Nationality and the Mandate", *Journal of Comparative Legislation and International Law*, Vol. 21, 1939.
Bentwich, Norman, "State Succession and Act of State in the Palestine Courts", *The British Year Book of International Law*, 1946.
Bentwich, Norman, "The End of Capitulation System", *The British Year Book of International Law*, 1933.
Bentwich, Norman, "The Mandate for Palestine", *The British Year Book of International Law*, 1929.
Bentwich, Norman, "The Mandate for Trans-Jordan", *The British Year Book of International Law*, 1929.
Bentwich, Norman, "The Mandated Territories under the Second World War", *The British Year Book of International Law*, 1944.

Benvenisti, Eyal and Zamir, Eyal, "Private Claims to Property Rights in the Future Israeli-Palestinian Settlement", *The American Journal of International Law*, Vol. 89, 1995.

Bhabha, Jacqueline, "'Get Back to Where You Once Belonged': Identity, Citizenship and Exclusion in Europe", *Human Rights Quarterly*, Vol. 20, 1998.

Bicknell, Beroe, "The Nationality of Married Women", *Problems of Peace and War*, Vol. 20, 1935.

Blackman, Jeffrey L., "State Succession and Statelessness: The Emerging Right to an Effective Nationality under International Law", *Michigan Journal of International Law*, Vol. 19, 1998.

Bonacquist, Harold F., Jr. and Mittleman, Philip A., "The Evaluation of Good Moral Character in Naturalization Proceedings", *Albany Law Review*, Vol. 38, 1973–1974.

Borchard, Edwin M., "Basic Elements of Diplomatic Protection of Citizens Abroad", *The American Journal of International Law*, Vol. 7, 1913.

Borchard, Edwin M., "The Mavrommatis Concessions Cases", *The American Journal of International Law*, Vol. 19, 1925.

Borchard, Edwin M., "The Protection of Citizens Abroad and Change of Original Nationality", *Yale Law Journal*, Vol. 43, 1933–1934.

Bosniak, Linda, "Citizenship and Work", *North Carolina Journal of International Law and Commercial Regulation*, Vol. 27, 2001–2002.

Bosniak, Linda, "Multiple Nationality and the Postnational Transformation of Citizenship", *Virginia Journal of International Law*, Vol. 42, 2002.

Brown, Bartram S., "Nationality and Internationality in International Humanitarian Law", *Stanford Journal of International Law*, Vol. 34, 1998.

Brown, Philip Marshal, "British Justice in Palestine", *The American Journal of International Law*, Vol. 12, 1918.

Brownlie, Ian, "The Application of Contemporary Standards of International Law to Cases Involving Separation of Husband and Wife as a Consequence of Administrative Action by the Israeli Authorities in the Occupied Territories", *The Palestine Yearbook of International Law*, Vol. 6, 1990–1991.

Brownlie, Ian, "The Relations of Nationality in Public International Law", *The British Year Book of International Law*, 1963.

Budlender, Geoff, "On Citizenship and Residence Rights: Taking Words Seriously", *South African Journal on Human Rights*, Vol. 5, 1989.

Cabler, Cleveland, "The Citizenship of Corporations", *American Law Review*, Vol. 56, 1922.

Chan, Johannes M.M., "The Right to a Nationality as a Human Right: The Current Trend Towards Recognition", *Human Rights Law Journal*, Vol. 12, 1991.

Collins, George D., "Citizenship by Birth", *American Law Review*, Vol. 29, 1895.

Crane, Lucius F., "The Nationality of Married Women", *Journal of Comparative Legislation and International Law*, Vol. 7, 1925.

Crozier, Blanche, "The Changing Basis of Women's Nationality", *Boston University Law Review*, Vol. 14, 1934.

Dajani, Mohammed S., *The Palestinian Authority and Citizenship in the Palestinian Territories*, Al-Quds University, Jerusalem, 1997 (un-published).

Daly, Lawrence F., "Diversity of Citizenship as Applied to Corporations", *The Marquette Law Review*, Vol. 17, 1932–1933.

De Hart, Edward Louis, "The English Law of Nationality and Naturalisation", *Journal of the Society of Comparative Legislation*, Vol. 2, 1900.

Deen-Racsmany, Zsuzsanna, "The Nationality of the Offender and the Jurisdiction of the International Criminal Court", *The American Journal of International Law*, Vol. 95, 2001.

Dinstein, Yoram, "The Israel Supreme Court and the Law of Belligerent Occupation: Deportations", *Israel Yearbook on Human Rights*, Vol. 23, 1993.

Dinstein, Yoram, "The Israel Supreme Court and the Law of Belligerent Occupation: Reunification of Families", *Israel Yearbook on Human Rights*, Vol. 18, 1988.

Dinstein, Yoram, "The United Nations and the Arab-Israeli Conflict", in Moore, John Norton, ed., *The Arab-Israeli Conflict*, Princeton University Press, New Jersey, 1974.
Eagifton, Clyde, "Palestine and the Constitutional Law of the United Nations", *The American Journal of International Law*, Vol. 42, 1948.
Economides, Constantin P., "Les effets de la succession d'Etats sur la nationalité des personnes physiques", *Revue Générale de Droit International Public*, Vol. 103, 1999.
Edwards, Percy L., "Should Women Be Admitted to Full Citizenship?" *The Green Bag: An Entertaining Magazine for Lawyers* (Boston), Vol. 7, 1895.
Elliott, William Grafton, Jr., "Some Constitutional Aspects of Corporate Citizenship", *Georgetown Law Journal*, Vol. 16, 1927–1928.
Esahak, George M., "Diversity Jurisdiction: The Dilemma of Dual Citizenship and Alien Corporations", *Northwestern University Law Review*, Vol. 77, 1982–1983.
Estapa, Jaume Saura, *Criteria for the Establishment of the Palestinian Citizenship within the Framework of a Palestinian Sovereign State*, Universitat de Barcelona, Barcelona, 1997 (un-published).
FitzGerald, Gerald F., "Nationality and Registration of Aircraft Operated by International Operating Agencies and Article 77 of the Convention on International Civil Aviation, 1944", *The Canadian Yearbook of International Law*, Vol. 5, 1967.
Flournoy, Richard W., "The New British Imperial Law of Nationality", *The American Journal of International Law*, Vol. 9, 1915.
Flournoy, Richard W., Jr., "Dual Nationality and Election", *Yale Law Journal*, Vol. 30, 1920–1921.
Flournoy, Richard W., Jr., "International Problems in Respect to Nationality by Birth", *Proceedings of the American Society of International Law*, Vol. 20, 1926.
Flournoy, Richard W., Jr., "Nationality Convention, Protocols and Recommendations Adopted by the First Conference on the Codification of International Law", *The American Journal of International Law*, Vol. 24, 1930.
Forbath, William E., "Civil Rights and Economic Citizenship: Notes on the Past and Future of the Civil Rights and Labor Movements", *University of Pennsylvania Journal of Labor and Employment Law*, Vol. 2, 1999–2000.
Fraser, C. Fred, "Transfer of Sovereignty and Non-Recognition as Affecting Nationality", *Alberta Law Quarterly*, Vol. 4, 1940–1942.
Fraser, R.S., "Nationality and Allegiance", *International Law Notes*, Vol. 4, 1919.
Gabrielle, Buckley, M., "Immigration and Nationality", *The International Lawyer*, Vol. 32, 1998.
Gazdik, J.G., "Nationality of Aircraft and Nationality of Airlines as Means of Control in International Air Transportation", *The Journal of Air Law and Commerce*, Vol. 25, 1958.
Geck, Wilhelm Karl, "Diplomatic Protection and the Extension of Individual Rights Through Treaties", *Law and State*, Vol. 31, 1985.
Gertler, Z. Joseph, "Nationality of Airlines: A Hidden Force in the International Air Regulation, Equation", *Journal of Air Law and Commerce*, Vol. 48, 1982–1983.
Gettys, C. Luella, "The Effects of Change of Sovereignty on Nationality", *The American Journal of International Law*, Vol. 21, 1992.
Goodwin-Gil, Guy S., "The Limits of the Power of Expulsion in Public International Law", *The British Yearbook of International Law*, Vol. 47, 1975.
Gordon, Leland J., "The Turkish American Controversy over Nationality", *The American Journal of International Law*, Vol. 25, 1931.
Gottlieb, Gidon, "Nations without States", *Foreign Affairs*, Vol. 73, 1994.
Griffin, William L., "The Right to a Single Nationality", *Temple Law Quarterly*, Vol. 40, 1966–1967.
Grossman, Andrew, "Nationality and the Unrecognized State", *The International and Comparative Law Quarterly*, Vol. 50, 2001.
Hackworth, Green H., "Naturalization and Loss of Nationality", *Proceedings of the American Society of International Law*, Vol. 19, 1925.

Hales, James C., "Some Legal Aspects of the Mandate System: Sovereignty—Nationality—Termination and Transfer", *Problems of Peace and War*, Vol. 23, 1937.
Hanna, John, "Nationality and War Claims", *Columbia Law Review*, Vol. 45, 1945.
Harnden, Ron, "Corporations: Corporate Citizenship—Principal Place of Business", *Washburn Law Journal*, Vol. 11, 1971–1972.
Harrison, Gladys, "The Nationality of Married Women", *New York University Law Quarterly Review*, Vol. 9, 1931–1932.
Harvard Law School, "Research on International Law", *The American Journal of International Law*, Vol. 23, Special Number, 1929.
Hazard, Henry B., "International Problems in Respect to Nationality by Naturalization and of Married Women", *Proceedings of the American Society of International Law*, Vol. 20, 1926.
Hedges, Job E., "Citizenship and the Constitution in Time of War", *The Constitutional Review*, Vol. 1, 1917.
Hendry, John O., "Duties and Obligations of Citizenship", *Royal Law Journal*, Vol. 6, 1924–1925.
Hill, Cyril D., "Citizenship of Married Women", *The American Journal of International Law*, Vol. 18, 1924.
Hiltermann, Joost R., "Israel's Deportation Policy in the Occupied West Bank and Gaza", *The Palestine Yearbook of International Law*, Vol. 3, 1986.
Hudson, Manley O., "The First Conference for the Codification of International Law", *The American Journal of International Law*, Vol. 24, 1930.
Hurewitz, J.C., "Introduction: boundaries of mandated Palestine", in Toye, Patricia, ed., *Palestine Boundaries 1833–1947*, University of Durham, Durham, 1989.
Hyde, Charles Cheney, "The Nationality Convention adopted by the League of Nations Committee of Experts for the Progressive Codification of International Law", *The American Journal of International Law*, Vol. 20, 1926.
Ide, Henry C., "Citizenship by Birth—Another View", *American Law Review*, Vol. 30, 1896.
Janoski, Thomas and Gran, Brian, "Political Citizenship", in Engin N. Isin and Turner, Bryn S., eds., *Handbook of Citizenship Studies*, SAGE, London/Thousand Oaks/New Delhi, 2002.
Jones, Mervyn, "British Nationality Act, 1948", *The British Year Book of International Law*, 1948.
Johns, Mervyn, "State Succession in the Matter of Treaties", *The British Year Book of International Law*, 1947.
Johns, Mervyn, "Who Are British Protected Persons?", *The British Year Book of International Law*, 1945.
Kaczorowska, Alina, "Le Droit à la nationalité est-il un droit fondamental de l'homme?", *Turkish Yearbook of Human Rights*, Vol. 19–20, 1997–1998.
Karpat, Kemal H., "The Ottoman Emigration to America, 1860–1914", *International Journal of Middle East Studies*, Vol. 17, 1985.
Kassim, Anis F., "The Palestinians: From Hyphenated to Integrated Citizenship", in Butenschon, Nils A. and Davis, Uri and Hassassian, Manuel, eds., *Citizenship and the State in the Middle East: Approaches and Applications*, Syracuse University Press, 2000.
Kattan, Victor, "The Nationality of Denationalized Palestinians", *Nordic Journal of International Law*, Vol. 74, 2005.
Kelke, W.H. Hastings, "Nationality and the Common Law", *The Law Magazine and Review & Quarterly Review of Jurisprudence and Quarterly Digest of All Reported Cases*, Vol. 8, 1882–1883.
Kingsley, Robert, "Nationality of Aircraft", *The Journal of Air Law*, Vol. 3, 1932.
Kleen, Richard, "De l'application du jus soli en matière de nationalité", *Revue générale de droit international public*, Vol. III, 1896.

Klein, Pierre, "La protection diplomatique des doubles nationaux: reconsidération des fondements de la règle de non-responsabilité", *Revue belge de droit international*, Vol. 21, 1988.
Kronstein, Heinrich, "The Nationality of International Enterprises", *Colombia Law Review*, Vol. 52, 1952.
Kuttner, Thomas S., "Israel and the West Bank: Aspects of the Law of Belligerent Occupation", *Israel Year Book on Human Rights*, Vol. 7, 1977.
Lampué, P., "De la nationalité des habitants des pays à mandat de la Société des Nations", *Journal du droit international*, Vol. 52, 1925.
Lansing, Paul, "Freedom to Travel: Is the Issuance of a Passport an Individual Right or a Government Prerogative?", *Denver Journal of International Law and Policy*, Vol. 11, 1981.
Lapidoth, Ruth, "The Right of Return in International Law, with Special Reference to the Palestinian Refugees", *Israel Yearbook on Human Rights*, Vol. 16, 1986.
Lawand, Kathleen, "The Right to Return of Palestinian Refugees in International Law", *International Journal of Refugee Law*, Vol. 8, 1996.
Leigh, Guy I.F., "Nationality and Diplomatic Protection", *The International and Comparative Law Quarterly*, Vol. 20, 1971.
Lesch, A.W. Ann Mosely, *Arab Politics in Palestine: The Frustration of a National Movement*, Cornell University Press, London, 1979.
Levandoski, Arnold, "Citizenship and Deportation", *Notre Dame Lawyer*, Vol. 5, 1929–1930.
Liang, Yuen-il, "The General Assembly and the Progressive Development and Codification of International Law", *The American Journal of International Law*, Vol. 42, 1948.
Llewellyn-Jones, F., "The Nationality of Married Women", *Problems of Peace and War*, Vol. 15, 1930.
Macmillan, Chrystal, "Nationality of Married Women: Present Tendencies", *Journal of Comparative Legislation and International Law*, Vol. 7, 1925.
Mann, F.A., "The Effect of Changes of Sovereignty upon Nationality", *The Modern Law Review*, Vol. 5, 1941–1942.
Manton, Martin T., "Extradition of Nationals", *Temple Law Quarterly*, Vol. 12, 1935–1936.
Marshall, Thomas R., "The Privileges, Duties and Obligations of Citizenship", *Boston University Law Review*, Vol. 4, 1924.
Maugham, C., "Some Cases of Double Nationality", *The Juridical Review*, Vol. 4, 1892.
McDougal, Myres S. and Burke, William T. and Vlasic, Ivan A., "The Maintenance of Public Order at Sea and the Nationality of Ships", *The American Journal of International Law*, Vol. 54, 1960.
McDougal, Myres S. and Lasswell, Harold D. and Chen, Lung-chu, "Nationality and Human Rights: The Protection of the Individual in External Arenas", *Yale Law Journal*, Vol. 83, 1973–1974.
McGovney, D.O., "French Nationality Laws Imposing Nationality at Birth", *The American Journal of International Law*, Vol. 5, 1911.
McNair, Arnold D., "British Nationality and Alien Status in Time of War", *The Law Quarterly Review*, Vol. 35, 1919.
Miller, David Hunter, "Nationality and Other Problems Discussed at the Hague", *Foreign Affairs*, Vol. 8, 1929–1930.
Mills, Mark Carter, "The Mandatory System", *The American Journal of International Law*, Vol. 17, 1923.
Monahan, Charles O., "Nationality of Minors", *Boston University Law Review*, Vol. 14, 1934.
Morse, Alexander Porter, "Citizenship by Naturalization", *American Law Register*, Vol. 18, 1879.
O'Connell, D.P., "Nationality in C Class Mandates", *The British Year Book of International Law*, Vol. 31, 1954.

Onuma, Yasuaki, "Nationality and Territorial Change: In Search of the State of the Law", *The Yale Journal of World Public Order*, Vol. 8, 1981–1982.
Orfield, Lester B., "Legal Effects of Dual Nationality", *The George Washington Law Review*, Vol. 17, 1948–1949.
Persichetti, Albert S., "Good Moral Character as a Requirement for Naturalization", *Temple Law Quarterly*, Vol. 22, 1948–1949.
Picaudou, Nadine, "Identité-mémoire et construction nationale palestinienne", in Picaudou, Nadine, ed., *La Palestine en transition: crise du projet national et construction de l'Etat*, institut national des langues et civilisations orientales, Paris, 2001.
Pingrey, D.H., "Citizenship and Rights There-under", *The Central Law Journal*, Vol. 24, 1887.
Plachta, Michael, "(Non-)Extradition of Nationals: A Neverending Story", *Emory International Law Review*, Vol. 13, 1999.
Poche, Maurice, "Social Citizenship: Grounds of Social Change", in Isin, Engin N. and Turner, Bryn S., eds., *Handbook of Citizenship Studies*, SAGE, London/Thousand Oaks/ New Delhi, 2002.
Potter, Pitman B., "The Palestine Problem Before the United Nations", *The American Journal of International Law*, Vol. 42, 1948.
Preuss, "International Law and Deprivation of Nationality", *Georgetown Law Journal*, 1934–1935.
Qafisheh, Mutaz, "La nationalite palestinienne selon les principes du droit local et du droit international", in Picaudou, Nadine, ed., *La Palestine en transition: crise du projet national et construction de l'Etat*, institut national des langues et civilisations orientales, Paris, 2001.
Quigley, John, "Mass Displacement and the Individual Right of Return", *The British Year Book of International Law*, 1997.
Randall, H.J., "Nationality and Naturalization: A Study in the Relativity of Law", *The Law Quarterly Review*, Vol. 40, 1924.
Radley, Kurt René, "The Palestinian Refugees: The Right to Return in International Law, *The American Journal of International Law*, Vol. 72, 1978.
Redslob, Robert, "Le principe des nationalités", in *Recueil des cours*, Académie de droit international (The Hague), 1931–III, Librairie du Recueil Sirey, Paris, Vol. 37, 1932.
Redslob, Robert, "The Problem of Nationalities", *Problems of Peace and War*, Vol. 17, 1932.
Rezek, Jose Francisco, "Le Droit international de nationalité", in *Recueil des cours: Collected Courses of the Hague Academy of International Law*, Marrtinus Nijhoff, Dordrecht/ Boston/London, Vol. 203, 1987–III.
Root, Elihu, "The Basis of Protection to Citizens Residing Abroad", *The American Journal of International Law*, Vol. 4, 1910.
Rosenne, Shabtai, "Directions for a Middle East Settlement: Some Underlying Legal Problems", *The Middle East Crisis*, Oceana Publications, New York, 1969.
Rosenne, Shabtai, "Israël et les Traités Internationaux de la Palestine", *Journal du Droit International*, Vol. 77, 1950.
Salim, Walid, "Citizenship in Palestine: Problems of Concept and Framework", *Palestinian Politics*, No. 14, 1997.
Salmond, John W., "Citizenship and Allegiance", *The Law Quarterly Review*, Vol. 17, 1901.
Sandifer, Durward V., "A Comparative Study of Laws Relating to Nationality at Birth and to Loss of Nationality", *The American Journal of International Law*, Vol. 29, 1935.
Scott, James Brown, "Nationality: *Jus Soli* or *Jus Sanguinis*", *The American Journal of International Law*, Vol. 24, 1930.
Shiblak, Abbas, "Residency Status and Civil Rights of Palestinian Refugees in Arab Countries", *Journal of Palestine Studies*, Vol. 25, No. 3, 1996.
Sloan, F. Blaine, "The Binding Force of a 'Recommendation' of the General Assembly of the United Nations", *The British Year Book of International Law*, 1948.

Smith, Willis, "Citizenship and the Bill of Rights in War Time", *Insurance Counsel Journal*, Vol. 9, 1942.
Spiro, Peter J., "Dual Nationality and the Meaning of Citizenship", *Immigration and Nationality Law Review*, Vol. 18, 1997.
Stein, Walter, "Revocation of Citizenship—'Denaturalization'", *Marquette Law Review*, Vol. 28, 1944.
Steinfeld, Robert J., "Subjectship, Citizenship, and the Long History of Immigration Regulation", *Law and History Review*, Vol. 19, 2001.
Stone, Julius, "Israel, the United Nations and International Law: Memorandum of Law", in Moore, John Norton, ed., *The Arab-Israeli Conflict, The Difficult Search for Peace, 1973–1988*, Princeton University Press, New Jersey, 1991.
Strasser, Mark, "The Privileges of National Citizenship: On Saenz, Same-Sex Couples, and the Right to Travel", *Rutgers Law Review*, Vol. 52, 1999–2000.
Stratton, Lisa C., "The Right to Have Rights: Gender Discrimination in Nationality Laws", *Minnesota Law Review*, Vol. 77, 1992–1993.
Tache, Simon W., "The Nationality of Ships: The Definitional Controversy and Enforcement of Genuine Link", *International Lawyer*, Vol. 16, 1982.
Tadmor, Yoav, "The Palestinian Refugees of 1948: The Right to Compensation and Return", *Temple International & Comparative Law Journal*, Vol. 8, 1994.
Thayer, Lucius Ellsworth, "The Capitulations of the Ottoman Empire and the Question of their Abrogation as it affects the United States", *The American Journal of International Law*, Vol. 17, 1923.
Travers, Maurice, "La nationalité des sociétés commerciales", in *Recueil des cours*, Académie de droit international (The Hague), 1930–III, Librairie du Recueil Sirey, Paris, Vol. 33, 1931.
Van Pittius and Gey, E.F.W., "Dominion Nationality", *Journal of Comparative Legislation and International Law*, Vol. 13, 1931.
Walton, Frederick Perker, "Egyptian Law: Sources and Judicial Organization", in Balogh, Elemér, ed., *Les sources du droit positif... Egypte—Palestine—Chine—Japon*, Hermann Sack Verlag, Birlin, 1929.
Wan, Albert K., "Israel's Conflicted Existence as a Jewish Democratic State: Striking the Proper Balance under the Citizenship and Entry into Israel Law", *Brooklyn Journal of International Law*, Vol. 29, 2003–2004.
Warsoff, Louis A., "Citizenship in the State of Israel—A Comment", *New York University Law Review*, Vol. 33, 1958.
Watson, Geoffrey R., "Offenders Abroad: The Case for Nationality-Based Criminal Jurisdiction", *Yale Journal of International Law*, Vol. 17, 1992.
Westlake, John, "On Naturalisation and Expatriation, or, on Change of Nationality", *The Law Magazine and Law Review*, Vol. 25, 1868.
Wheeler, Everett P., "The Relation of the Citizen Domiciled in a Foreign Country to His Home Government", *The American Journal of International Law*, Vol. 3, 1909.
Wilkinson, W.E., "British Nationality", *International Law Notes*, Vol. 2, 1917.
Williams, David W., "British Passport and the Right to Travel", *International and Comparative Law Quarterly*, Vol. 23, 1974.
Willoughby, W.W., "Citizenship and Allegiance in Constitutional and International Law", *The American Journal of International Law*, Vol. 1, 1907.
Woodiwiss, Anthony, "Economic Citizenship: Variations and the Threat of Globalization", in Isin, Engin N. and Turner, Bryn S., eds., *Handbook of Citizenship Studies*, SAGE, London/Thousand Oaks/New Delhi, 2002.
Worsfold, W. Basil, *Palestine of the Mandate*, T. Fisher Unwin Ltd., London, 1925.
Wright, Quincy, "Status of the Inhabitants of Mandated Territory", *The American Journal of International Law*, Vol. 18, 1924.
Young, E. Hilton, "Nationality of a Juristic Person", *Harvard Law Review*, Vol. 22, 1908–1909.

Zilbershats, Yaffa, "Reconsidering the Concept of Citizenship", *Texas International Law Journal*, Vol. 36, 2001.

Zimmermann, Andreas, "The Nationality of the Inhabitants of the Palestinian Autonomous Territories", in Shapira, Amos and Tabory, Mala, eds., *New Political Entities in Public and Private International Law with Special Reference to the Palestinian Entity*, Kluwer Law International, The Hague/Boston/London, 1999.

INDEX

GRADUATE INSTITUTE OF INTERNATIONAL AND DEVELOPMENT STUDIES

1. V. Gowlland-Debbas, H. Hadj-Sahraoui, M. Garcia Rubio: *United Nations Sanctions and International Law*. 2001 (ISBN 90 411 1603 6)
2. V. Gowlland-Debbas, V. Chetail: *Switzerland and the International Protection of Refugees/ La Suisse et la protection internationale des refugiés*. 2002 (ISBN 90 411 1743 1)
3. S. Sadat Akhavi: *Methods of Resolving Conflicts between Treaties*. 2003 (ISBN 90 411 2031 9)
4. V. Gowlland-Debbas: *National Implementation of United Nations Sanctions*. A Comparative Study. 2004 (ISBN 90 04 14090 5)
5. V.-Y. Ghebali, A. Lambert: *The OSCE Code of Conduct on Politico-Military Aspects of Security*. Anatomy and Implementation. 2005 (ISBN 90 04 14292 4)
6. P. Dumberry: *State Succession to International Responsibility*. 2007 (ISBN 90 04 15882 0)
7. M. Qafisheh: *The International Law Foundations of Palestinian Nationality*. A Legal Examination of Nationality in Palestine under Britain's Rule. 2008 (ISBN 978 90 04 16984 5)
8. E. Yahyaoui Krivenko: *Women, Islam and International Law*. Within the Context of the Convention on the Elimination of All Forms of Discrimination Against Women. 2008 (ISBN 978 90 04 17144 2)

MARTINUS NIJHOFF PUBLISHERS – LEIDEN • BOSTON

www.ingramcontent.com/pod-product-compliance
Lightning Source LLC
LaVergne TN
LVHW080847300926
849162LV00003B/360
* 9 7 8 9 0 0 4 1 6 9 8 4 5 *